Essentials of Hospitality Administration

Harold E. Lane
Director of Hotel and Food Administration
Boston University

Mark van Hartesvelt
Director of Marketing
Harrah's Marina Hotel Casino

Reston Publishing Company, Inc.
A Prentice-Hall Company
Reston, Virginia

Library of Congress Cataloging in Publication Data

Lane, Harold E.
    Essentials of hospitality administration.

    Bibliography: p.
    Includes index.
        1. Hotel management.   2. Motel management.
    3. Restaurant management.   I. van Hartesvelt, Mark.
    II. Title.
    TX911.3.M27L36   1983   647'.94   82-15140
    ISBN 0-8359-1771-1

Cover photo: View from the Empress Restaurant, Hyatt Regency
Cambridge, by Gorchev & Gorchev

© 1983 by Reston Publishing Company, Inc.
A Prentice-Hall Company
Reston, Virginia 22090

10   9   8   7   6   5   4   3   2

Printed in the United States of America

To our families:

Jan   Connie
Scott   Hank
          Nancy
          Steve

Contents

Acknowledgments

We have enjoyed writing *Essentials of Hospitality Administration*. This book is the product of the ideas and efforts of many people—faculty colleagues, students, our families and co-workers. We are especially pleased to acknowledge the assistance of Irwin Price, Dean, Metropolitan College, Boston University; Donald I. Smith, Director, School of Hotel, Restaurant, & Institutional Management, Michigan State University; David Ley, James Madison University; Michael Kasavana, Michigan State University; Ray Schmidgall, Michigan State University; Ronald Cichy, University of Denver; W. Earl Sasser, Harvard Business School; Charles Penkowski, Pannell, Kerr, Forster and Company; Peter Gibson, Holiday Inns, Inc.; Paul Martin, Michigan State University; John van Hartesvelt, Brock Hotels; and James Doyle, former graduate assistant in the Graduate School of Business Administration, Michigan State University. Beth Gardner did a tremendous job in typing the manuscript during the final "countdown" stages. We thank her very much. We would also like to thank Reston Publishing Co. for its help.

Finally, our special appreciation to our families. They have endured our obsession with the preparation of this book during times that have been unreasonably long, and have provided support and encouragement above and beyond the call of duty.

Preface

Essentials of Hospitality Administration is a comprehensive, student-oriented introduction to the advanced study of administration in hospitality organizations. The book has been designed so that it can be used in smaller colleges—except at the freshman level—where several courses in hotel and restaurant management may be offered, or in larger business schools offering a full range of management courses relevant to this discipline.

We see this book as a core text with readings, cases, and visiting lecturers as possible supplements. In upper level courses, including those offering specialized expertise, this book may be required before the student moves on to such specific areas as hospitality marketing, managerial accounting and finance, franchising, food and beverage management and the like.

While we have written this book primarily for the student of hospitality administration, we believe the book can also prove useful to the practicing manager who wants to learn more about the special nature of problems and problem solving in his or her role as a management professional.

We believe that *Essentials of Hospitality Administration* differs from other works in two distinctive ways. First, this book centers upon what we believe to be the student's need for a challenging, current, and broadly based assessment of the current state of the art in the administration of hospitality industries. The overall approach is one in which the major areas of contemporary concern unfold in an integrated fashion. We begin with an industry overview encompassing the demographic, economic and lifestyle changes destined to affect the operating environment. Then we discuss the kinds of activities the successful manager actually performs. Finally, in an effort to suggest some sense of the direction in which hospitality industries are heading, we critically assess the methods and goals of strategic planning as practiced by those companies that lead the field.

A Frontier Approach   We place major emphasis throughout the book upon what is happening at the hospitality frontiers; this knowledge will help students and practicing managers alike to chart with care their future courses of action. Thus, this book not only analyzes why what is happening *happens*; it also points out the vast opportunities that lie within the grasp of those whose perception of them is most acute.

The Hospitality Industry: Markets, Economics, and Growth Potential

When you finish this chapter, you should understand:

1. The projected growth in the leisure-time industry during the 1980s, the factors contributing to this growth, and examples of how the hospitality industry will benefit from the growth

2. The impact of changing travel patterns and changing modes of travel on the hospitality industry

3. The different needs and travel patterns of each of the three principal market segments within the hotel industry; which of the subsegments are compatible with each other; and what product, service, and price strategies are necessary with each

4. The importance of demographic and lifestyle trends on the hospitality industry; specific trends that will impact the industry

5. The four stages of the retail life cycle—including the pitfalls of each stage and suggested strategies to avoid these pitfalls

The hospitality industry is typically associated with the management of hotels, motels, clubs, restaurants, fast-food establishments, and institutional catering organizations (i.e., companies that prepare food for hospitals, schools, and colleges). It is from some version of this definition that most hospitality management texts depart in their description of how managers function, the tools required, and how the management skills in the hospitality industry differ from those used in manufacturing industries.

To truly understand the hospitality industry not only in terms of its history and evolution, but most importantly, where it is most likely to be headed in the future, it is necessary to understand the forces that drive the industry. By this we mean that it is important to not only understand how managers manage hotels and restaurants but also to understand why they exist. Who are the customers? Are they the same customers as those who patronized hospitality establishments in years past? Who will be the customers in the future? What, in fact, is the future potential for this industry?

It is from this objective that this book was written. What is the hospitality industry really all about, and what opportunities and threats does it pose for both the student considering a career and the operator or corporate executive who has already made the decision to invest in it? What management tools will be required to keep pace with the changing environment? How should a hospitality student today prepare to be a manager or executive tomorrow?

This chapter focuses on the size and nature of the hospitality industry. We also discuss some of the trends that are occurring which will change the character of the industry. This information is presented with two goals in mind:

1. To provide the student with an overview of the exciting hospitality industry and give reasons why it will provide exciting career opportunities and challenges in the future

2. To develop several concepts and tools that will be helpful in understanding the principles outlined in this book and other texts about the hospitality industry.

Size and Nature of the Hospitality Industry

The hospitality industry is a legitimate industry unto itself. However, it is also an important segment and/or beneficiary of at least two other large industries. These include:

1. The leisure-time industry

2. The travel industry

Each of these industries will be briefly examined as an integral part of the hospitality industry to provide insight into the nature of the customer, the service, and the future.

The Leisure-Time Industry

The leisure-time industry is an extremely complex and changing industry. Leisure includes any activity undertaken during free, unoccupied time. This includes, for example, rest, sports, reading, television, and travel. Today, unoccupied time for most Americans amounts to more than one-third of their entire lifetime and is exceeded only by the amount of time necessary for eating and sleeping. The remaining time is spent working. However, as the number of hours spent working declines, even more time is available for leisure time. The average number of hours

Americans are working decreased 6.8 percent to 38.1 hours between 1948 and 1975. The Bureau of Labor Statistics estimates that the average workweek will decline further to 37.0 hours per week by 1985. In addition, at least three other trends should further increase the amount of time available for leisure activities:

1. The four-day workweek. During the 1970's, there were a number of studies and efforts begun to alter the workweek from 5 days to 4 days in certain industries. This would involve working 10 hours a day instead of 8. While there has been some success in this effort, the 4-day workweek has not become as widespread as anticipated and probably will not for some time to come.

2. Flextime. Flextime refers to a growing trend allowing employees, within given time limits, to work their eight hours any time. For example, a computer programmer who normally works between 9:00 a.m. and 5:00 p.m. might work from 7:00 a.m. to 3:00 p.m. with no lunch.

3. Job sharing. Job sharing is a new trend which is gaining increasing acceptance in non-hospitality businesses. This idea essentially involves a position being filled by two people rather than one, each working a portion of the workweek. For example, in the manufacturing sector, a line employee may work three of the five shifts in a week, allowing another employee to work the other two shifts.

What do these changes in the work leisure mix have to do with the hospitality industry? First, there are a number of factors indicating that leisure spending will increase over the next decade:

○ Discretionary income for the average American family is increasing due to the rising number of two-income families and the reduction in the birth rate.

○ The demographic makeup of the American population is changing (these changes will be discussed in some detail later in this chapter).

○ Lifestyles are changing with more emphasis on activity and enjoyment.

The impact of the growing leisure market on the hospitality industry is substantial. Frequently, the use of hospitality industry services is the direct focus of leisure activities. Examples of this include a family using their leisure time to visit a restaurant for dinner or a couple going to a resort hotel for an "escape weekend."

The hospitality industry can also be an indirect beneficiary of the growing leisure market. When a family takes an annual two-week vacation, staying in motor hotels and eating in restaurants during travel time, the industry receives income even though these activities were not the primary purpose of the trip. The important point is that the longer term growth for leisure time pursuits is quite positive for the hospitality industry. As the manager of a hospitality-oriented business, whether it be a hotel, restaurant, theme park or cruise line, the reason for the customers' purchasing the services you offer must always be kept in mind. This will give insights into the product, pricing and amenity levels necessary to satisfy their needs. We will discuss this in further detail later in this chapter.

The Travel Industry

The travel industry probably relates the closest with the lodging industry, although the demand for meals away from home generated from people traveling away from home is quite significant. Pleasure travel is growing because of the growth in disposable income and some of the lifestyle changes described later in this chapter. Business travel is growing because of a number of factors. For example, the increasing need for communication within organizations (both corporations and associations) has fueled a significant increase in the number of meetings for the purpose of communicating and training in recent years.

Currently, the travel industry is in the midst of an evolution that has caused fundamental changes in the lodging industry, and this evolution will continue into the next several decades. A brief review of the evolution of travel in the twentieth century will provide insight into these changes.

During the early 1900s, the majority of hotels were located in metropolitan areas, typically proximate to rail stations. Why? Because the primary mode of transportation was by rail. Even during the 1940s, when the automobile was being used by an increasing number of Americans, hotels remained in the urban areas because business and industry were still located there.

It was not until the late 1940s and 1950s, when the U.S. highway system was being developed, that hotels left the city and the second phase of the evolution began. Kemmons Wilson, the founder of the Holiday Inn motel chain, is credited with this phase. The motel is a much scaled-down hotel typically located on an interstate highway servicing the traveling businessperson and the vacationing family. Motels flourished through the 1950s and 1960s as more people used the developing national interstate highway system. While this was taking place, occupancies in the major downtown hotels declined, forcing many to close. The declining viability of the urban hotels was due to many reasons including corporate and family flight to the suburbs, rising crime rates in urban areas, and the increasing use of the automobile as the primary mode of transportation.

During the 1970s, airline travel began to become increasingly important. Large regional airports such as those constructed in Chicago and Dallas/Ft. Worth were developed in suburban areas to service the increased traffic. This increase in airline travel had two significant effects on the lodging industry:

1. Airport locations became increasingly important and profitable. Occupancies at airport properties exceeded those of center-city locations throughout the last half of the 1970's.

2. The increased speed of travel afforded to more and more businesspeople caused a decrease in the average length of stay in lodging facilities. Businesspeople were able to fly into and out of a city in one day for a meeting or business appointment, often obviating the need for overnight accommodations.

The move to airport locations also caused a change in the lodging product. Properties became larger, offering more amenities with increased amounts of meeting space. Fly-in meetings at airport hotels became common occurrences, and in an effort to promote weekend occupancy, hotels began to market escape weekends to the higher-income families. By 1980, hotels built in airport locations enjoyed higher occupancies than any other type in the domestic United States.

U.S. lodging industry: comparison of occupancy by location type, 1980

Location type	1980 occupancy
Center city	67.0%
Suburban	68.7%
Highway	71.6%
Resort	72.1%
Airport	74.3%

Source: *U.S. Lodging Industry 1981*, Laventhol & Horwath, Philadelphia, Pa., p. 37.

How will each of the different location types fare in the 1980s? We will examine this next in this chapter. However, the increasing importance of the airlines as a mode of travel will remain with us throughout the remainder of the century. And as airline travel continues to account for a larger share of total travel, the placement of lodging establishments will continue to change.

In summary, then, the travel industry is undergoing an evolution. The hospitality industry, as an integral component of the travel industry, has been affected by this evolution. The hospitality industry manager of today and tomorrow must be aware of these changes. He (and she) must also be able to assess their impact on his specific business and adjust his operating strategies accordingly.*

The Mix of Business

One of the impacts of a dynamic industry is in the segmentation of customers. In the lodging industry, the different segmentation is referred to as the *mix of business.* On a nationwide basis, four principal segments are tracked—namely, the commercial traveler, tourists and vacationers, group and convention attendees, and government officials.

*The authors realize that both women and men are involved in hospitality management. The use of the masculine pronoun throughout this text is done merely to avoid awkwardness.

The following table shows the mix of business for the U.S. lodging industry in 1980 by location type.

U.S. lodging industry: Mix of business by location type, 1980
(percent)

Market segment	City Center	Airport	Suburban	Highway	Resort
Government Officials	6.1	3.2	2.0	2.9	.3
Business-persons	46.6	70.3	77.3	59.1	7.2
Tourists	18.3	9.6	10.9	23.2	66.3
Conference Participants	22.0	13.5	8.6	9.7	22.4
Other	7.0	3.4	1.2	5.1	3.8
Total	100.0	100.0	100.0	100.0	100.0

It is important to notice that each location type serves a different mix of business. For example, the center city hotel is less dependent upon the traveling business person and much more dependent upon the group and convention market (conference participants) than is the hotel located in a suburban area.

Tourists contribute substantially to resort locations but also to highway and center city hotels. However, as we discussed earlier, the tourist staying at a highway motel is generally traveling to another destination by automobile and is merely spending the night. He will undoubtedly travel on in the morning. On the other hand, the tourist staying at a resort hotel has most likely chosen the hotel as the destination. To demonstrate this fact, the following table illustrates the average length of stay in hotels by location type in 1980.

U.S. lodging industry: average stay
(days)

Center city	2.8
Airport	1.8
Suburban	1.7
Highway	1.1
Resort	3.2

Source: *U.S. Lodging Industry, 1981* Laventhol & Horwath, Philadelphia, Pa. p. 38.

The method of arrival is also important to the manager of a lodging establishment. It provides insight into the placement of properties and the service levels that should be provided. For example, as increasing numbers of travelers utilize the airlines as their primary mode of transportation, this tells the developer that the property should be placed in a market with a viable airport that has adequately planned for increasing traffic. It tells the manager of a property in which a large portion of his or her demand arrives by air that free airport transportation to and from the hotel is probably important to guests. In addition, since many airline guests may not have access to an automobile, in-house entertainment outlets and transportation to night spots and commercial centers may have to be provided.

On the local market level, the mix of business can provide insight into profit potential, required service levels, and room-rate strategies. To understand these issues in more depth, each of the three principal market segments will now be examined in further detail.

Commercial Travelers

The commercial traveler has been the mainstay of the lodging industry throughout the century. This segment includes persons who are on a business trip and require overnight accommodations while they are away from home. This means that the primary purpose of their trip is to transact business, not to utilize the hotel's facilities. We will see later that this is increasingly not the case for the group- and pleasure-travel segments.

Within the commercial-travel segment, there are at least three subsegments. These are important because they have different service and facility needs.

Per diem traveler. The first subsegment is the per diem traveler. This person is generally on the road for as many as four nights each week, generally Monday through Thursday. He or she is on an assigned expenditure limit of room and food, indicating some price sensitivity. The per diem traveler will often seek those hotels and motels with room rate discounts for the frequent traveler.

Historically, the primary mode of transportation for per diem travelers was the automobile. These were the persons that filled lodging rooms along the highways and in commercial markets during the weekdays year round.

What about the property and service levels required by this segment? A clean room with a working space to complete the day's paperwork and correspondence. A restaurant with moderate prices serving a fast breakfast and dinner. A pricing structure that falls within the traveler's per diem limit.

While this list is not meant to be exhaustive, it will provide some important insights and comparison points regarding the type of product, level of service, and pricing structure the smart manager will provide when a significant portion of his demand is derived from this type of business traveler.

Executive traveler. The second subsegment of the commercial business market is the executive traveler. This person is generally traveling to a larger city, travels by air, and stays for a shorter period of time than the per diem traveler. His business is usually conducted during the weekdays.

The executive traveler is generally much less price-conscious than the per diem traveler. In addition, while it remains true that his or her hotel is generally not the primary destination of the trip, it is more frequently used during business transactions as a meeting place and for entertainment. Since the executive traveler is not as price-conscious, he or she is willing to pay more but expects higher levels of service in all areas. This might include, for example, larger work areas in the guest rooms, better restaurant and lounge facilities in case clients are to be entertained, and more expensive appointments to reflect the higher price the executive is paying for his room.

Many of the larger downtown hotels are now providing executive floors which include secretarial services, high-amenity work areas, and current periodicals in an attempt to capture a larger portion of this travel segment. The hotel will typically charge extra dollars on the room rate for a room on the executive floors.

Business traveler with spouse. The last segment of business travel we will discuss is the businessperson traveling with his or her spouse. This segment has been relatively small, but has exhibited significant growth in recent years. While the makeup of this segment varies, it includes business travelers who fly their spouses to their location rather than returning home for the weekend. This tactic is becoming increasingly common as household incomes rise and travel becomes a more significant focus of Americans.

What can we imply about this travel segment's location, product, and service needs? From earlier discussions we might suggest that the location should generally be in a destination market. This means that the location should offer or be proximate to entertainment areas such as shopping facilities, restaurants, nightclubs, recreational outlets, and sightseeing spots. In addition, the hotel may have to provide higher levels of service such as live entertainment in the lounge, recreational facilities, and higher class dining facilities.

It is difficult to generalize about pricing for this travel segment. If the hotel is the primary focus of activity, the lodger may be willing to pay more than if the hotel is primarily used for sleeping. Either way, this segment is important because it is likely to exhibit growth in the future, and it provides demand during the weekends. The significance of this last point can be illustrated in the following example.

An example—One measure of a property's success is its occupancy level. Hotel occupancy is calculated by dividing the number of rooms occupied by the number of rooms available times 100 to get rid of decimal points. For example, if a 250-room hotel fills 175 rooms on any given night, its occupancy is 70 percent.

$$\text{Occupancy} = \frac{\text{Rooms occupied}}{\text{Rooms available}}$$

$$= \frac{175}{250} = 70\%$$

Suppose that a 250-room hotel serves strictly the commercial traveler, excluding the businessperson traveling with his or her spouse. In addition, assume that the hotel is filled four nights a week (Monday-through Thursday), 52 weeks each year by primarily commercial travelers. What is the hotel's maximum occupancy potential?

$$\text{Occupancy} = \frac{250 \times 4 \times 52}{250 \times 7 \times 52} \times 100$$

$$= 57.1\%$$

Depending upon the property's financing and rate structure, this is generally not a high enough occupancy to allow a new hotel to break even. In other words, if the hotel wants to make money, it will have to find some source of demand to fill it during the weekends. The commercial traveler with a spouse is one such source.

The Tourist and Vacation Traveler

As we have seen, the tourist and vacation traveler, referred to hereafter as the pleasure traveler, is expected to exhibit growth in the future. There are several additional reasons why this segment is important to the individual hotel:

1. This segment generally travels during the summer and on weekends. This is important because these travel patterns are generally different from the commercial- and the group- and convention-market segments. Therefore, the pleasure traveler requires room-nights during periods when the hotel sees a softening in demand.

2. The pleasure traveler generally pays a higher room rate than the commercial and group segments. This is due to the pricing structure of most hotels and motels; a higher rate is charged for two or more people in one room. As we shall illustrate in Chapter 9 on Rooms Management, the incremental cost of placing additional people in the same room is insignificant. Therefore, the pleasure traveler represents a more profitable market segment than either the commercial or group segments from a "rooms" point of view.

Family-vacation segment. Within the pleasure-travel market segment, there are at least two subsegments. The first is the family-vacation market. This segment generally consists of children and parents taking their annual two-week vacation. The vacation is typically taken during the summer months when the children are out of school. Historically, the primary mode of transportation was the automobile, and while this is still the case, air travel may be used to an increasing extent in the future.

From some of the trends presented earlier and from your observations about your own family vacation, we can make some generalizations about the family vacationer's habits and needs. Remember, we are assuming that there are children on the trip and that it is at least one week in duration. We must also assume that overnight accommodations are not provided by friends and relatives. This last assumption eliminates a relatively significant portion of this market segment, since many vacations are spent at home or with relatives. However, owing to the increasing focus on travel and experience, our assumptions should become increasingly valid in the future.

The family vacation is generally activity-oriented. This means that the family is looking for sights or activities that are entertaining. Because of the children, these activities will involve places like museums, amusement parks, historic sights, and beaches. Most family vacations are informal and flexible. Members of the family are often wearing shorts and/or bathing suits and generally prefer not to change into more formal attire to pursue a particular activity such as eating.

The hotel(s) or motel(s) used during the vacation are generally a necessity rather than a focal point. This implies that this market segment is price-sensitive—i.e., families would prefer to spend budgeted funds pursuing entertainment activities rather than on higher room rates and food and beverage costs. Typically, very little time is spent at the inn.

How do these characteristics translate into the facility and service aspects that a property should consider? Since the family will be spending a minimum amount of time in the room, the furnishings do not need to be elaborate. There should be a working television for entertainment during the time that is spent in the room. Owing to the informality of the trip, it is often best if the room can be reached without the need to pass through a lavish lobby.

The facility should provide some basic amenities. These include a swimming pool which is typically heavily patronized by the family; a gameroom; vending areas for soft drinks, ice, and candy; and rollaway beds. If a significant portion of the property's demand comes from the family traveler, consideration should be given to enclosing the pool for year-round use.

Food and beverage areas should be informal and inexpensive, such as are available in a coffee shop. In dining rooms, consideration should be given to providing children's menus. Cocktail lounges will generally not be patronized frequently by this segment because of the presence of children.

If the above describes some of the product and services needs of family-vacation travelers, can we infer any characteristics of a property which this market would prefer to avoid? Probably regimentation of any type, such as limited pool hours or inflexible package arrangements; and most likely any sort of formality such as dress codes or the necessity to pass through a lavish lobby to reach the rooms or entertainment outlets; also convention-oriented properties inundated with groups. As we shall see shortly, not all market segments are compatible. This means that a property must be able to select which travelers it will target its marketing to and then understand the consequences of this decision on other travelers. We will discuss the identification of market segments in more detail in Chapter 7.

Vacation without children. The second subsegment of the pleasure-travel market is comprised of those vacationers who travel without children. These may appear to be the same travelers as those in the family-vacation subsegment, minus children. However, we are going to place some special demographic parameters around this subsegment to draw a clear differentiation.

This segment is typically comprised of two workers with an annual household income in excess of $25,000. The household is generally comprised of two professional people, typically with some college training in the 25- to 49-year-old age category.

The vacation we intend to discuss is somewhat shorter in duration than the family vacation, such as a long weekend. While people in this category do take extended vacations, the characteristics are quite similar, with only a few modifications.

Some general descriptions of this type of traveler might include the following points:

1. The trips are generally shorter in duration and are therefore taken within a relatively small radius of home unless the mode of travel is by air.

2. The vacation is usually relaxed, with an "escape" or "getaway" theme. However, while the theme is relaxed, it is not necessarily informal

3. The trip is generally meant to be memorable. It is not activity-oriented; therefore, the hotel's facilities or immediate surroundings will be the focal point for the trip. This would imply that dinner, theater and/or shopping areas should be convenient.

Unlike the situation for family vacations, when a hotel is used for the long weekend, it is generally the destination. Therefore, this market is not as price-sensitive.

Service is key to understanding and providing for this segment. Since these vacationers are willing to pay more for a transient room, they are more demanding for services. Similarly, the facility should have a higher-quality level of amenities than those demanded by the family vacationer. Rooms should be smartly appointed. Turndown service at night and fresh flowers are often appreciated, depending upon the price paid for the room.

Since the hotel is often the destination, the restaurant should be more than a coffee shop. If the vacation is for an extended period of time, multiple food outlets are important to provide some variety. Lounges should have some form of entertainment.

Historically, most hotel professionals would have associated the facility and service needs described above with a resort. However, during the 1970s, many suburban, downtown, and airport hotels began to package "escape weekends." Such packages typically included a room, breakfast and dinner, and a cocktail for one price. This was used to build weekend occupancy and was quite successful in many areas.

The Group and Convention Market

The group and convention market segments are the last source of demand we will discuss in this chapter. Nationally, they comprise 22 percent of hotel demand, but this fluctuates significantly on a property-by-property and market-by-market basis, more so than any other market segment except perhaps within resorts. Group and convention travelers are generally more profitable to a hotel or motel than the commercial or pleasure travelers for the following reasons:

1. A group meeting will require a "block" of rooms—that is, a given number of rooms will be reserved for the duration of the meeting or convention. Commercial and pleasure travelers typically book one room at a time.

2. The convention attendee is more likely to patronize the property's non-room revenue outlets. These include meeting rooms, food and beverage outlets (often through catering operations), and equipment rental. Room service is also heavily patronized by this segment.

3. Profit margins are often enhanced through the use of guarantees. Typically, a hotel will require a large group to reserve a minimum number of guaranteed rooms and meals in advance. If the number of rooms and meals actually used is less than the guarantee, the guaranteed number is still billed, increasing the hotel's profit margins.

While the group segment is generally able to negoitate a lower room rate depending upon the number of rooms blocked, in terms of total revenue the hotel is often better off with this market segment.

Convention market. The group and conventions market can be divided into at least two subsegments. The first classification is the convention market. This segment is generally comprised of a large number of delegates patronizing a convention center or a hotel with a large amount of exhibit space. The convention often involves the use of multiple hotel facilities, and for larger conventions may involve all of the hotel rooms within a city.

Convention delegates generally have little choice in the selection of their hotel. The selection process is handled for them by the meeting planner or executive secretary of their association. The purpose of the trip is to visit exhibits in the case of trade shows or to attend meetings and workshops in the case of association meetings and conventions. Delegates often spend a relatively large amount of money during their visit and are therefore actively solicited by cities to increase sales in retail stores and local restaurants. In addition to cities and convention bureaus within cities soliciting the convention segment, large hotels also have marketing and staff funds employed to sell large groups on the merits of their facilities and services. Many cities have constructed civic and convention halls in their downtown areas in the hopes that the resulting conventions will arrest urban decay and help revitalize retail and restaurant sales. As we shall see in Chapter 7 on Feasibility Studies, these attempts have met with mixed success.

Conference market. The second subsegment within the group and convention market is the conference market. This segment is comprised of meetings and training seminars for corporate, trade, and association executives for the purpose of communication, planning, and/or training. The size of the typical conference is significantly smaller than the convention segment, as shown in the following table:

Executive conferences, sources of meeting, and typical size and duration

Source	Percent of total	Typical size*	Typical duration*
Business organizations	57.8	25	3 days
Nonprofit trade and professional associations	16.5	60	3 days
Educational institutions	9.3	50	3 days
Government	8.0	40	3 days
Professional seminar organizations	4.9	20	3 days
Other	3.5	50	3 days
	100.0		

*Mode

Source: "The Executive Conference Center: A Statistical Profile," Laventhol & Horwath, 1977, p. 10.

The impetus behind the growth of this market segment stems from a growing dissatisfaction on the part of training directors from major national companies regarding the existing facilities and services offered by the typical hotel. These problems range from inadequate seating, lighting, and audiovisual equipment to a complete lack of interest in their needs. The principal reasons for this are that the typical executive conference meeting is small in size and extremely demanding on services, equipment, and amenities; most hotels have not been equipped to service the needs of the conference segment. Owing to these problems, some companies were forced to build their own on-site facilities and enter the lodging business, a venture that most did not relish.

Today, executive conferences are recognized as a small but growing segment within the lodging industry. The facility and service needs of this segment include facilities with audiovisual equipment, comfortable chairs and adequate lighting in the meeting rooms, soundproof walls between meeting rooms, and tasteful restaurant and lounge facilities. Recreational needs vary depending on the length of stay and the level of management attending the conference. Many conference centers provide recreational facilities. The amount of recreational amenities is generally determined during the initial feasibility study.

The level of service necessary to successfully penetrate the conference market varies somewhat, but it should include the following elements:

1. A degree of solitude from commercial and tourist traffic. The environment should be conducive to work and learning and free from external distractions.

2. A reliable message service that promptly and accurately relays messages to meeting attendees.

3. Easy and quick check-in and check-out service at the front desk.

4. A meeting coordinator or service staff person specifically assigned to each meeting to insure that all requests and needs are attended to.

While it would be considered good business to provide the last three of these services to *any* of the market segments patronizing a hotel, they are essential service elements of the executive conference market.

Summary The following table summarizes some of the common facility and service needs of each travel segment discussed above. While the list is not meant to be exhaustive, it does illustrate that each particular segment does have specific needs which do not necessarily overlap with those of other segments. In some instances, the needs of some travelers may be the same characteristics which other travelers attempt to avoid.

Facility and service needs of each traveler

Facilities	Commercial			Pleasure		Group	
	Per diem	Exec.	Bus. w/ spouse	Fam. Vac.	Esc.	Conv.	Conf.
Coffee shop	x			x			
Restaurant		x	x		x	x	
Lounge			x		x	x	
Working space within room	x	x					x
Recreational facilities				x	x		x
Meeting space						x	x
Gift shop						x	x
Services							
Quick check-in and out	x	x				x	x
Message service	x	x				x	x
Live entertainment		x	x		x	x	
Bellhop		x				x	
Price	x			x			

Throughout this chapter, we have described the hospitality industry as a component of other service industries. We have shown that changes within these other industries, particularly the travel industry, have produced changes in the hospitality industry. This was illustrated with the lodging industry but holds equally true for other elements of the hospitality industry.

Changing Market for Hospitality Services

In addition, we have introduced the concept of dividing the different types of customers into segments. In the lodging industry, for example, customers can be segmented by purpose of trip (business, tourist, or group) as well as by price and amenity level. This same type of segmentation can be made for the restaurant industry. For example, a businessperson who is entertaining a client for dinner generally has different product, price, and service expectations than a family with children taking a break from home cooking.

In the remainder of this chapter we will examine some of the trends that are occurring outside the hospitality industry that will have an impact on the future dynamics of the industry. Then we will focus on some of the forces that are coming into play within the industry. When combined, the trends from without and within the hospitality industry portend strong growth potential and rapid evolution which hold exciting job opportunities for those pursuing the hospitality industry as a career.

Demographic Trends

Demographics refer to characteristics which describe a population. These characteristics include such factors as age, income, marital status, size of household, and race. Why is it important to track demographic trends? Because people who fall within defined demographic categories are predictable in terms of their most likely consumption habits. For example, the most frequent users of overnight accommodations are people between the ages of 25 and 49 who have family incomes in excess of $25,000 per year. Interestingly, these demographics also describe people who are the most likely to purchase new homes and leisure- and recreation-related products such as skis or pleasure boats. The point is that demographics provide an excellent means to identify who the most common users of particular products or services are and to track the long-term potential of each product's market.

The demographic trends that relate to the hospitality industry look quite good for the remainder of this century. One reason is the aging of the United States population. While the birth rate in the U.S. is declining, the growth in the 25-to-49-year-old group will increase dramatically as the post–World War II baby boom population ages.

Total fertility rate: Average number of children per woman of childbearing age

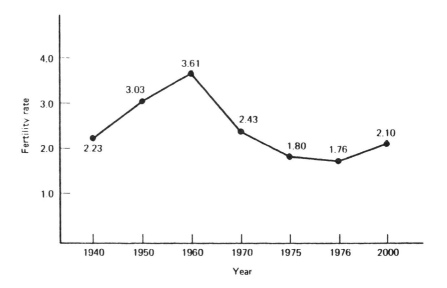

Part of the demographic profile of the U.S., then, is a population growth of between 0.7 and 1.0 percent per year for the remainder of the century but a significant increase in the age groups with earning capacity and a propensity to spend.

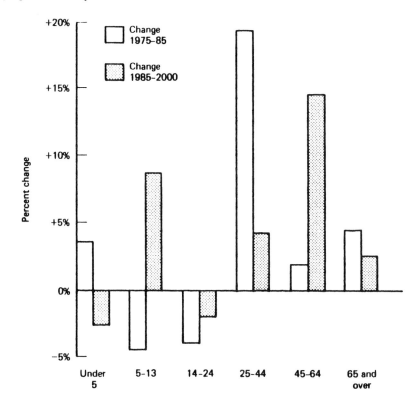

+20%

□ Change 1975–85

▨ Change 1985–2000

+15%

+10%

+5%

0%

−5%

Percent change

Under 5   5–13   14–24   25–44   45–64   65 and over

Source: *Business Week,* February 20, 1978, p. 66.

Much of the projected increase in spending ability over the next ten years is due to the significant increase in two-worker families. Along with the decline in the birth rate has come a significant increase in the number of adult women in the workforce. This second income has not only enhanced family income but has led to a higher incidence of eating away from home, escape weekends to nearby destination areas for relaxation, and an increase in travel in general.

Lifestyles

Together with the changes that are expected to occur in demographics, there are basic changes taking place in the values, attitudes, and lifestyles of a large number of Americans. These attitudes and values are referred to by demographers as *cohort factors* and are important in understanding and predicting the lifestyles a generation group is likely to pursue throughout its life. For example, the young adult today, aged 25 to 34, is beginning to discard ownership of assets such as luxury automobiles and homes as indicators of status. In place of these assets, experiences such as travel to foreign countries and vacations in major resort areas are becoming substitutes in discretionary spending. While it is beyond the scope of this text to investigate these changes in detail, they are sufficiently important to warrant our taking a brief look at some of the trends that are likely to be more visible as time goes on among the future consumers of hospitality services.

A growing trend among today's young adults is the pursuit of self-improvement and self-gratification. College students are enrolling in courses that are career-oriented and will provide jobs; enrollment in business courses and engineering is significantly up. The focus is on career and enjoyment. Marketeers often refer to this group as the "me" generation.

While the trend is toward career-oriented education, there is a definite decrease in workaholism. The future rewards brought by working late and on weekends seem less important than the immediate rewards of pursuing leisure-time activities.

Another emerging lifestyle trend is the growing movement toward outdoor recreation and exercise. An increasing number of people are discovering backpacking, sailing, jogging, and other physically active sports. The impact of this trend is exhibited by the attention marketing executives have given to it in their product introduction and advertising. In the hotel industry, new, larger properties are beginning to include jogging tracks, tennis courts, and racketball courts in their amenity packages.

Impact on the 1980s

How will the changing demographic trends and lifestyles affect the hospitality market throughout the 1980s? The growth potential for the travel and leisure-time industry is very strong. This means that the hospitality industry will also exhibit strong growth. However, the market segments for the industry are likely to become better defined.

Kenneth Roman, Jr., president of Ogilvie & Mather, the leading travel advertising agency in the United States, provides some insight into these market segments. He divides the travel market in the 1980s into four basic segments:

1. *The Younger Haves.* People in this segment tend to be affluent and well educated. They are cautious and sensible. They also represent the "me" generation. They represent those embracing the simple life. They represent a large portion of the growing leisure-time and travel markets.

2. *The Younger Have-Nots.* People in this segment represent an underclassed, disenfranchised, and disillusioned market segment. Their propensity to spend dollars for leisure and travel activities is much lower than that of the more affluent *haves* because they have less discretionary income.

3. *The Older Haves.* This market is characterized by people who are affluent and free-spending. Their children are generally grown, leaving more time and money for travel. Their focus is on the pursuit of intangibles such as travel rather than on accumulating assets.

4. *The Older Have-Nots.* This market segment, unfortunately, is the poorest in terms of income of the four segments. Their potential in terms of the hospitality industry is quite limited because their income is dedicated to essentials such as food and housing.

Thus, the hospitality and travel market during the 1980s is concentrated on the *haves.* The lifestyle for both groups is focused on self. Their travel and leisure activities will not be concentrated in an annual vacation. These activities will become necessary and frequent events. The *haves* will look for quality and for value. They will probably prefer more independent, self-oriented travel and recreational activities. This may mean, for example, package vacations, weekend packages, and fly–drive vacations to cut costs and still provide the freedom the *haves* want.

More attention will be given to the cost of the individual components of travel. With prices escalating quickly, they may "trade down" from the luxury hotel to the first-class hotel to save money. These savings can then be spent on a better dinner, theater tickets, or shopping.

The implications of this scenerio for the hospitality industry are significant. The market for services in the 1980s and beyond will be dramatically different than in the past. It will be larger and more affluent, but more discriminating. The product, pricing, and service strategies of managers must change with this evolution if they are to continue to succeed.

Internal Industry Trends

Within the hospitality industry there are a number of internal trends occurring that are likely to continue throughout the 1980s and beyond. The impact of these trends and the need for unit-level and corporate management to respond to them is critical.

Throughout the remainder of this text, we will present some of the concepts and tools that will be demanded of hospitality managers throughout the 1980s and beyond. Before continuing to Chapter 2, however, we want to present the concept of the *retail life cycle.* As we will illustrate in the next section, the solutions to many of the problems that increasingly face segments of the hospitality industry become more apparent when the problems are viewed from this perspective. In addition, some of the strategies that hospitality organizations as well as individual units have executed were specifically designed to address identifiable problems associated with each of the stages within the retail life cycle.

The Retail Life Cycle

For several decades, executives have put forth theories about the evolution of concepts and organizations. Each theory sought to explain patterns of growth and viability in nearly every organization, whether it

was manufacturing or retailing. The apparent unavoidable pattern is one
of introduction of the product or service followed by rapid growth followed by maturity and ultimately decline.

Earlier theories focused upon changing cost structures and gross
margin relationships. For example, we discussed the changing
demographic trends that are producing a more affluent consumer. One
explanation points out that many retail concepts begin with lower-cost
items and facilities. However, lured by the higher profit margins
associated with higher-cost items combined with the changing
demographics, managers increase the quality of the products, the
facilities, and the services. This produces higher costs.

One problem with this strategy is that if everyone follows it, competition tends to concentrate in the higher-quality merchandise level,
marketing to a smaller segment of the market. This, in turn, creates a
price umbrella that allows new competitors to enter the market with
lower prices, amied at the broader mass of the consumer market.

A second earlier theory concerned managerial evolution. This
theory pointed out that as companies progressed through their growth
cycles, the original entrepreneurial founders were no longer capable of
managing complex organizations. The new generation of more
sophisticated management turned its focus to image and quality rather
than cost control. This placed upward pressure on costs and profit
margins, generally driving the concept up-scale.

More recently, the concept of the retail life cycle[2] has gained acceptance. The retail life cycle is an inevitable evolutionary process which,
while it cannot be reversed, can be managed to sustain profit margins
and minimize decline.

According to the theory, there are four identifiable stages in the life
cycle:

1. Innovation
2. Accelerated development
3. Maturity
4. Decline

Innovation. The first stage in the cycle is generally the most exciting. It
is characterized by an idea about product, service, pricing, or placement
in the market. It is generally entrepreneurial and may include a combination of the above characteristics.

An example—In the early 1950s, Kemmons Wilson developed an
idea for a new lodging product—the motel. It would be built to service the
family market with comfortable air-conditioned rooms, a restaurant,
swimming pool, and free ice (product).

The new motel would be placed near the highways so that it would
be easily accessible to the traveler who required overnight lodging accommodations (location). It would charge a lower rate, and all services

would be included in this rate except food and beverage (price). The motel was to be named Holiday Inn.

If an idea is successful, sales generally increase rapidly owing to increasing customer patronage (as opposed to price increases). However, costs are generally high because of high start-up costs, inefficient control systems, and the lack of economies of scale.

Accelerated development. During this second stage of the cycle, both sales and profits grow rapidly. Control systems are more defined and effective. The concept is refined to get rid of the "rough edges."

It is during this stage that the new product may undergo geographical expansion. If so, it is typically comparatively rapid. Expansion brings the problems of finding investment capital, maintaining quality control, and keeping up with the growth.

If it is decided to expand rapidly, the founder often turns to franchising. This offers the advantage of expanding the product quickly using new investors' money. It also preempts competitors from entering the market as rapidly as they might otherwise.

During the accelerated development stage, management develops the confidence that the concept has regional or national appeal. The founder is no longer able to handle all of the management demands of the organization. Expertise in finance and operations is hired, and these managerial functions are generally delegated.

It is during the accelerated development stage that several potential threats to continued viability can occur. Expenses can get out of control. This results from the organization's need for higher staffing and administration levels. Cost increases can outpace sales increases significantly, depressing earnings. This phenomenon is often referred to as the "Bermuda Triangle of Management." The organization is too small to absorb a high administrative overhead expense, but too large not to provide the centralized staff to service the growing organization.

A second potential threat during this stage is a loss in quality control. This can occur for several reasons. For example,

○ The organization is unable to provide competent operational management fast enough to keep up with growth. As we shall illustrate continually throughout this text, success in the hospitality industry ultimately depends upon expert delivery of a service. This requires strong management at all levels.

○ If the organization is expanding by the franchising vehicle, management as well as product quality control can be lost. If good inspection and quality control systems are not in place, quality can deteriorate rapidly.

If an organization or unit is able to survive the accelerated growth stage, the end of the period is characterized by stabilized market share and profitability.

Maturity. The maturity period of the retail life cycle is a significant turning point for the organization. Market share is steady or declining. Sales may fall off. Profits often drop. These problems can be the result of a number of factors:

1. The concept may have lost its earlier appeal and uniqueness. Most of the primary demand has been tapped and competitors are well entrenched in the marketplace.

2. The market is frequently overbuilt owing to the rapid expansion not only of the original concept but of competition. Additionally, competitors may have refined the concept, "chipping away" at different pieces of the market segments.

3. If the founder of the organization is still in control, he generally is experiencing problems managing the complexity of the organization. It is at this stage that the second generation of management takes control of the organization, putting "caretaker" expertise in place rather than the earlier rapid-expansion orientation.

4. If the company has expanded through franchising, the franchisor often begins to experience problems with franchisees. Franchisees begin to attribute profits to their own management rather than the original concept (franchisor). They may resent paying the royalty fees, which are often increasing at this stage to sustain earnings.

If strategies are not put into place to revitalize the company during this stage, the maturity period will ultimately result in a severe reduction in profitability and the onset of the final stage in the life cycle.

Decline. The final stage, decline, is often avoided or greatly postponed by modification of the original concept. However, if this is not accomplished, major losses in market share can occur, resulting in a loss in investor confidence and ultimate fatality of the concept or company.

The hospitality industry is full of examples of concepts and companies that are entering different stages of the retail life cycle as well as concepts/companies that ultimately died during the fourth stage.

For example, earlier in this chapter we discussed the evolution of the hotel industry by location type. The downtown hotel locations experienced all four stages. Today, many downtown areas house large hotels that were once focal points of the city but today are either closed or operate as nontransient facilities.

The fast-food industry provides another example. As the fast-food chains face the maturity stage, the concepts were modified with more menu items, more meal periods (specifically, breakfast) and upgraded decor packages. This strategy was implemented to revitalize sagging profits owing to market saturation and product saturation.

The hospitality industry is currently faced with a multitude of opportunities and challenges. On the one hand, it is in the midst of unprecedented growth as its customers become more affluent and more willing to spend their income for leisure-time activities and travel. This can only mean career opportunities will continue to grow for those willing to pursue them. **Summary**

On the other hand, the industry is undergoing an evolution due to a more sophisticated and demanding customer whose consumption patterns and characteristics are changing. In addition, the competitive environment is becoming much more sophisticated. This means increased challenges for the hospitality manager of the future.

We believe that these factors add up to exciting opportunities in all areas of the industry.

1. Excerpted from a speech before the New York Chapter of the Travel Research Assocation on March 31, 1980. **Notes**

2. For a more thorough discussion, refer to William R. Davidson, Albert D. Bates, and Stephen J. Bass, "The Retail Life Cycle," *Harvard Business Review* (November–December 1976).

General References

Professor D. Daryl Wyckoff, "Managing the Chain Restaurant Life Cycle," transcripts of a speech before the Chain Operators Exchange Conference, International Foodservice Manufacturers Association, March 3, 1980.

Hospitality Management: Basic Concepts and Theory

When you finish this chapter, you should understand:

1. What the principal schools of management thought are called
2. The significance of the work activity school
3. Why a manager is needed
4. The ten roles of a manager
5. The relevance of managerial roles to the hospitality industry as indicated by Ley's research
6. The three important role behaviors that need to be addressed in your pursuit of a career in hospitality management

As we saw in the preceding chapter, the hospitality industry is growing rapidly because of (1) increasing levels of *disposable income* (i.e. that portion of an individual's income which remains after payment of personal taxes to the government) and (2) because of the aging patterns of our population.

This means that the number of food service workers will almost double from 1972 to 1985 to handle an anticipated gross revenue of some $70 billion (compared to $40 billion in 1972).[1]

There is little doubt that the increasing demand for hospitality managers will continue undiminished even as the industry adopts more sophisticated technology scenarios. Powers expects an "exploding need for food service managers."[2] Professional training centers for employees of managerial caliber—similar to those already established by Hilton International Hotels in Montreal and by Sheraton Hotels in Philadelphia—represent significant strides toward insuring a continuous reservoir of executive people for promotion to hotel positions of increasing responsibility. Moreover, the expansion of hotel, restaurant, and institutional management courses in both two-year and four-year colleges is providing all segments of the hospitality industry with an attractive source of candidates for appointment to a variety of management training programs.

Nevertheless, today's opportunities in hospitality management far outrun the supply of trained candidates—as campus recruiters from a growing number of lodging and food service industries will testify.

Clearly, there's a place in hospitality management for you.

But to most of you reading this book, the idea of just what *management* is all about may not be quite so clear. To be sure, otherwise well-informed persons frequently shrug off the question: What's involved in being the boss? with another question equally simplistic: Isn't it easier than doing the work yourself?

Most of us, when we were children, wondered what our fathers did at the office. To some of us who know that dad was "the boss," it seemed that all he ever did was to sit in his office, sign some letters, answer the telephone, and talk to people. Could this be what managers do?

The confusion over what managers do does not result from ignorance or lack of sophistication. Before 1973, when Professor Henry Mintzberg of McGill University published his pioneer study of managerial work,[3] there were few people who could give a clear-cut answer to the question: "What are the activities that a manager actually performs?"

For more than half a century before, the answer to this question had always evoked Henri Fayol's classic dictum that managers plan, organize, direct, and control—an observation based upon his lifetime of experience solely as a coal-mining engineer in France. Even if one persisted with "Yes, but what do managers *really* do?" you were not much better off than one observer was when he tried to find out what the company president did:

Observer: Mr. R. we have discussed briefly this organization and the way it operates. Will you now please tell me what you do.

Executive: What I do?

Observer: Yes.

Executive: That's not easy.

Observer: Go ahead, tell me anyway.

Executive: As president, I am naturally responsible for many things.

Observer Yes, I realize that. But just what do you *do*?

Executive: Well, I must see that things go all right.

Observer:	Can you give me an example?
Executive:	I must see that our financial position is sound.
Observer:	But just what do you do about it?
Executive:	Now, that is hard to say.
Observer:	Let's take another tack. What did you do yesterday?[4]

And if your search for a more precise answer were to take you through the more recent textbooks on management, you would probably discover that many contemporary scholars are still quite unable, if not unwilling, to cut the Fayol umbilical cord. Thus, Stoner's recent definition is typical:

> Management is the process of planning, organizing, leading, and controlling the efforts of organization members...[5]

As more than one hospitality manager has been heard to say: "I guess I do some of those management things that textbooks describe, but the descriptions are totally lifeless and my job isn't."

Other management scholars—notably Mintzberg of the Faculty of Management at McGill, and Ley of James Madison University—believe that whatever may be the merits of Fayolism as an abstract theory, the facts of management practice today suggest quite a different picture.

Consider these examples: A restaurant manager is called and told that a group of dissatisfied cooks is threatening to resign en masse unless the chef is fired. He advises the caller to tell the group to "shape up or ship out." Is he planning, organizing, directing, or controlling? How about when the manager of a nonunion motor inn rejects a written demand from some of his employees seeking formal recognition of their collective bargaining rights? Or when the manager of a new, inner-city thousand-room hotel is facing the question of hiring more minorities, more women, or more disadvantaged people and receives a computer printout from his MIS (management information system) director showing an acute downside risk to profits if such a policy is to be faithfully pursued?

In point of fact, the classic definition of management functions really does not address the basic question. What *do* managers do? All it does at best is to suggest some vague—and not very useful—objective that managers may have in mind when they are at work.

Before going on to consider the implications of all this for your own career both as a student and as a management practitioner in the world of hospitality enterprises, it is necessary to acquire some perspective of the recent literature about the manager's job.

Most scholars recognize at least eight schools of thought in this area:

1. *The classical school*—The father of this school is Henri Fayol, who in 1916 introduced the idea that to manage is to plan, organize, direct, and control.

2. *The great man school*—The "great man" literature concentrates on the crises, personal anecdotes, philosophies, and concerns of business tycoons like Henry Ford, Alfred P. Sloan, Cornelius Vanderbilt, Conrad Hilton, E. M. Statler, Ray Kroc, and others who have made their mark in the business world...but we are left with little or no information about the actual details of their managerial work.

3. *The entrepreneurship school*—This school emphasizes one component of the manager's job—namely, innovation. It fails, however, to tell us *how* an entrepreneur innovates.

4. *The decision theory school*—Decision-making, according to this school, is of two types: programmed and unprogrammed. A programmed decision is one that can be laid out in advance, step by step. For example, deciding upon how many customer-contact calls a hotel marketing representative will make in an eight-hour day is a programmed decision. An unprogrammed decision is one that you can't adequately plan for in advance. A multinational corporation's surprise announcement that the building across the street from your hotel will be the site of a new John Portman skyscraper hotel requires unprogrammed decisions. In other words, you have to fit your decision to the situation, relying heavily upon judgment, intuition, and imagination.

5. *The leader effectiveness school*—The study of leader effectiveness focuses upon the idea that no one style of managing is best; that, depending upon the situation, effectiveness may be related to the reward structure, the power of the manager's job, the nature of the work he or she supervises, the organizational climate, and his or her personality and skills.

6. *The leader power school*—The right to hire and fire, to promote, to raise salaries, to control or manipulate one's managerial environment are all characteristics of leadership that concerns itself with power and influence.

7. *The leader behavior school*—This approach emphasizes what behavior is essential to leadership and generally revolves around the idea that effective leadership requires task-oriented behavior and/or people-oriented behavior.

8. *The work-activity school*—This is the school of thought in which the work activities of managers are analyzed systematically, and which has yielded important findings about managerial work content. In the hospitality industry these findings by Dr. David Ley have reinforced the findings of earlier work-activity studies in other industries by Henry Mintzberg.

In none of these schools—except in the latter—do we get a very clear picture of just who a manager is or what he or she does. And more often than not, whenever concern for what a manager *does* is shown, it usually reflects a manufacturing bias in contrast to a hospitality industry bias.

As Ley is careful to point out, "virtually no research has been undertaken to study managerial behavior which corresponds to effective performance in the service industries and particularly in the hospitality industry. Yet, in a labor-intensive industry...it would seem important...to identify effective managerial job behavior through examination of what the manager did on the job..."[6]

On balance, therefore, if you are to be responsible for *managing* a hospitality establishment when you graduate, the chances are that you will need to know what a manager does and why he or she is needed.

But first, *who is a manager?*

Who Is a Manager?

The words "manager" and "management" are slippery, to say the least. There is no exact counterpart in German, French, Spanish, Italian, or Russian for the word "manager," and even in the United States its meaning is elusive. According to Webster's unabridged dictionary, a manager is "one who manages"; in the *Dictionary of Management* the manager is identified as "a person who has been appointed to carry out a job of management."[7]

Clearly, the person *in charge* of a hotel, restaurant, or institutional facility, or of any one of its respective departments, is the *manager*. This would include also the person in charge of a whole chain operation. Thus, a manager may be identified as the president, vice president, marketing director, chief engineer, comptroller, food and beverage director, head housekeeper, head bartender, or numerous other titles (such as banquet manager, convention manager, purchasing manager) to which the word *manage* is attached.

We conclude, therefore, that being in charge of an organization or of one or more of its subsidiary units is the principal characteristic that serves to distinguish a manager from a nonmanager.

Why is a Manager Needed?

Although most of us take it for granted that whenever a group of people come together to do a job—whether it be in a bar, a fast-food restaurant, a hotel, or in a General Motors plant—someone must be in charge. But rarely do any of us ever stop to ask why this is so. What purpose, then, does a manager serve?

On this point Dean Wrapp of the University of Chicago Graduate School of Business has written persuasively:

> My definition of a good manager is a simple one: under competitive industry conditions, he is able to move his organization significantly toward the goals he has set, whether measured by higher return on investment, product improvement, development of management talent, faster growth in sales and earnings, or some other standard. Bear in mind that this definition does not refer to the administrator whose principal role is to maintain the status quo in a company or in a department. Keeping the wheels turning in a direction already set is a relatively simple task, compared to that of directing the introduction of a continuing flow of changes and innovations, and preventing the organization from flying apart under pressure.[8]

Mintzberg's research, which we have mentioned earlier, helps us to gain a new perspective on what managers actually do by taking a closer look at their various roles, a concept derived from the field of dramatic art. "When on the stage, actors adopt organized patterns of behavior identifiable with the characters they are playing. Similarly, when an individual becomes a manager, he adopts certain patterns of behavior simply because he is in the position of a manager."[9]

In reaching his conclusions about managerial roles, Mintzberg and his associates studied the work activities of five chief executives, all of whom were affiliated with organizations other than hotels and restaurants. Each was observed for a period of one workweek, and in each case the focus was on the *job* (not the person), on the *similarities* in managers' work (not the differences), and on the basic *content* of the work (not its peripheral characteristics). Mintzberg found that the key to understanding what managers actually do was in being able to classify the *purpose* of each activity. In other words, managerial activities, when analyzed by purpose, yielded three major role categories: *interpersonal roles, informational roles,* and *decisional roles.* These are shown in Figure 2-1. As you look at this diagram you will notice that formal authority gives rise to three interpersonal roles, which in turn give rise to three informational roles; and both of these role sets enable a manager to play the four decisional roles—in all, a total of ten roles. Such roles, with due allowance for varying degrees of emphasis in individual cases, would appear to be descriptive of what managers *do.*

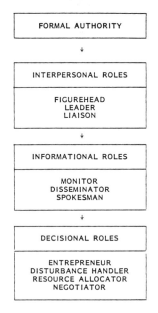

Source: Jay W. Lorsch, James P. Baughman, James Reece, and Henry Mintzberg, *Understanding Management* (New York: Harper & Row, Publishers, 1978), p. 220.

Figure 2-1 The manager's roles

As we commence our consideration of these managerial roles, it is important to remenber that before 1967 no one apparently had ever studied the work activities of hotel managers, nor of any other managerial group within the reach of the hospitality industry.

The first such study took place in England. It was done in 1967 by Philip Nailon, Senior Lecturer of The Department of Hotel and Catering Management, University of Surrey. It showed in detail how in three different hotels, operated by one company (1) managers were more heavily involved with the people from the external environment than they were with their own hotel employees; and (2) managers were engaged in a continuous monitoring of their respective units through fleeting contacts and frequent movement about the establishment.[10]

A second, more rigorous, study was done in this country a decade later by Dr. David Ley of James Madison University.[11] Carefully classifying the work activities of innkeepers at seven comparable inns of an international hotel chain, Ley found that their managerial activities were very much like the ten distinctive work roles shown above in Figure 2–1. Also, he found some significant relationships between activities performed and the caliber of their managerial effectiveness as it was perceived by top management of the hotel chain.

What, then, do managers do?

We began to answer this question earlier when we discussed why a manager is needed. More current research by scholars of the *work-activities school* of management thought leans toward the concept of studying the manager's work roles to attempt to understand what he or she does. This perspective has given rise to a set of ten theoretical roles, each one of which we will examine in the sections following.

Interpersonal Roles

As a consequence of the formal authority inherent in his or her position, the manager engages in interpersonal relationships. That is to say, he attends ceremonial dinners, gives instructions to his subordinates, acknowledges requests that come to him as the highest-ranking figure in the organization, and attends to all those activities that link directly to his status and authority as manager. Hence, the activities which we call interpersonal are best described by the following managerial roles:

1. *Figurehead*—As the in-charge person, the manager symbolizes the company and hence is obliged to perform certain ceremonial duties. Thus, the hotel manager greets the arriving President of the United States and escorts him to his room. The McDonald's manager is on hand to greet the Cub Scout leader and his troop on the occasion of their visit to a McDonald's restaurant. Attending a subordinate's wedding, presiding at retirement parties, taking VIP customers to lunch are all part of the figurehead role.

Other examples of this role include such activities as being available to outsiders (guests, public officials, representatives of the press, etc.) who want to talk to the person in charge; signing letters and official documents (such as the liquor license application); and participating in trade association and public service work (i.e., as an appointee to city, state, or federal regulatory or advisory boards).

2. *Leader*—As the leader, the manager aims to integrate the needs of employees with the goals of the company through such activities as hiring employees, training them, appraising their performance, rewarding them, encouraging them, promoting and/or dismissing them. Although the precise ingredients of leadership have thus far defied most research efforts designed to isolate them, there is little doubt that, in addition to the foregoing activities, a leader exercises his or her authority to make certain that subordinates accomplish important tasks.

3. *Liaison*—In order to establish a network of contacts by which he or she informs himself about his or her environment, a manager frequently spends as much time with people outside the scope of the organizational chain of command as with employees. While such activities are sometimes seen as "ego trips," more often than not such status contacts serve a variety of organizational purposes. For example, the manager joins the most prominent country club to meet the people who are most likely to patronize his establishment; becomes an officer of professional and charitable societies to maintain business contacts; cultivates a network of relationships growing out of his or her graduation from a business school or from a school of hotel, restaurant, and institutional management; acknowledges favors to the industry by writing thank-you letters to legislators representing the district; widens his or her circle of acquaintances among tax consultants, corporate lawyers, and governmental lobbyists, who provide specialized advice; and, in general, fosters and maintains an external linkage system by which he or she can continuously receive information from sources outside the immediate chain of command.

Informational Roles

The manager is also the focal point in his or her organization for both internal and external information. There are three roles in which such information is usually gathered and disseminated.

1. *Monitor*—As monitor, the manager relies heavily upon verbal means of communication (i.e., telephone calls and face-to-face meetings, scheduled and unscheduled) to keep information current and in a hands-on tangible form devoid of any sterile abstractions. Surprisingly, it is *not* the formal MIS which tells a manager what he or she wants to know *now*. Rather, it is his own central intelligence system which is maintained through constant verbal contacts with both insiders and outsiders. As Lorsch and his associates discovered in their studies, "the manager does not leave the telephone or the meeting to go back to work...these contacts *are* his work."[12]

2. *Disseminator*—Being in possession of "privileged" information that his or her employees need but would otherwise not have access to, the manager is able to transmit it to them. In one good illustration of this, the sales manager of a large motor inn attended a meeting of the board of directors of the local convention bureau. There he learned of the prospects of a convention of biochemists being persuaded by a competitor hotel chain to choose that particular city as the site for its annual convention. Upon his return to his own firm, he immediately called a meeting of all four sales representatives, told them about the competitor's efforts to obtain the biochemists' convention, and initiated strategic plans to lure that piece of business away from the competing hotel.

Thus, the sales manager was able to get the information by virtue of his status as a director of the convention bureau and his liaison role with fellow board members. In his role as monitor, he was able to pick up the privileged information about the biochemists' convention; and, as disseminator, he was in a position to share his new information with the sales representatives who were his subordinates.

3. *Spokesperson*—Just as a manager passes information along to employees, so also must he pass some of it along to people outside his unit or outside the company.

The sales manager in the above example will undoubtedly tell the general manager what he has learned about the biochemists' convention in the hope that that person, too, may be in a position to suggest strategy for beating out their competitor. Or a kitchen steward in charge of the ware-washing section of a large restaurant suggests a product modification to a detergent supplier or to a ware-washing machine manufacturer.

To the president of a company, the role of spokesperson means being willing to address the Society of Security Analysts and to answer their questions about the firm's future plans and its anticipated earnings In addition, it may mean assuring consumer groups that recent price rises are not "ripoffs" but are the normal result of inflationary factors in the nation's economy. And if Congress decides to investigate unusual payments abroad by companies engaged in foreign trade, the president must be prepared to explain in detail his or her firm's extraordinary allowances for "sales expense" incurred by any overseas representatives.

Decisional Roles

So far, we have seen the manager gathering and distributing to other people information that he or she has taken pains to obtain. But neither interpersonal nor information roles are ends in themselves. What every manager must ultimately do is to take action..."and a prerequisite to action is decision-making—the determination of what actions are to be taken."[13]

1. *Enterpreneur*—In this role the manager is constantly on the lookout for new ideas to improve his or her operation. This means

authorizing exploratory projects to see if promising opportunities are feasible. And if they are, the manager must see them through to completion.

Perhaps there is a chance to initiate an attractive breakfast menu in a fast-food restaurant which hitherto has catered only to the luncheon and dinner trade. Or perhaps a key marketing person has recently resigned from a competitor hotel chain and would bring valuable sales contacts into the manager's hotel. Or perhaps, in view of the growing population of "senior citizens," the menu of a high-priced, luxury-type restaurant chain can be restructured so as to focus on "Mr. and Mrs. Middle America," with emphasis on food items having the most appeal to the "Geritol set."

2. *Disturbance-Handler*—In the role of disturbance handler, the manager responds to situations beyond his or her control. Because these situations are often too severe to be ignored, they are frequently characterized as being managerial "pressure cookers." High-pressure disturbances include things like strikes, suicides, fires, armed holdups, embezzlement of company funds by a trusted employee, antitrust lawsuits by the Department of Justice, loss of the federal tax exemption now enjoyed by live-in hotel managers under the Treasury Department's Convenience of the Employer rule, and the like.

These, and similar high-pressure disturbances, occupy much of every manager's time not simply because "poor managers ignore situations until they reach crisis proportions but also because good managers cannot possibly anticipate all the consequences of actions taken by their company."[14]

3. *Resource-Allocator*—A third decisional role a manager performs is that of resource-allocator. In this role the manager is responsible for deciding how workforce resources will be deployed, where the firm's financial resources will be distributed, how to schedule his or her own time day by day, and what decisions already recommended by subordinates should be authorized.

4. *Negotiator*—The fourth and final role is that of negotiator. Mintzberg's studies of managerial work at all levels suggest that managers spend much of their time in negotiations. The restaurant manager is required to negotiate with the state liquor control board over threatened revocation of a liquor license because of allegations that minors have been served liquor in his or her restaurant. Or the labor union in a hotel refuses to negotiate a strike issue with anyone else other than the general manager. Or the chef has to negotiate with the local Board of Health about the question of sanitation standards in his walk-in refrigerators. Or the bar-lounge manager negotiates with the state fire marshall about the crowds a certain rock band have attracted to his establishment, much to the displeasure of his across-the-street competitor who has complained that fire regulations are being violated.

In Leonard Sayles' view, "sophisticated managers place great stress on negotiations as a way of life."

In point of fact, managers do spend a great deal of their time as negotiators because only they "have the nerve center information that important negotiations require."[15]

What are we to make of these role classifications in view of the fact that Mintzberg's research was confined to a consulting firm, a hospital, a public school system, and two manufacturing firms?* Are these roles applicable to managers in the hospitality industry?

Indeed they are.

A recent study by Dr. David Ley focuses upon these work roles as they are performed by hotel managers.[16]

The Ley Study

Before we begin our discussion of the hotel managers' roles, however, we should note how Ley's research was conducted. He used what is known as the *structured observation* method. This means that he personally observed each manager as that person performed his or her work as an innkeeper. Further, it means that he categorized each observed event in a number of ways (for example, duration, activity, function, content, location, interaction). In addition, he coded each observed activity by number so as to show separately the explanation and purpose of that activity. Figure 2–2 illustrates the *structured observation record* containing the categories used; while Figure 2–3 illustrates the *structured observation analysis sheet* containing the explanation of each activity.

For his purposes, Dr. Levy also adopted a rigorous sampling procedure which he has described as follows:

1. Selection of an organization (Holiday Inns, Inc.) with a large number of independently functioning unit managers employed by the company at the same hierarchical level. These were innkeepers of company-owned properties only, since innkeepers in franchised properties have varying responsibilities to different ownership consortiums.

2. The properties selected were roadside properties in urban or suburban locations in a large metropolitan area (see Figure 2–4). The clientele therefore consisted of approximately the same mix of businessmen and families on one-night stay.

3. The properties chosen each had between 140 and 170 guest rooms, dining room, cocktail bar, banquet facilities, and swimming pool.

4. In order to ensure that each innkeeper was familiar with the operational procedures of the property, a limitation was imposed that only innkeepers who had held the position of innkeeper at that property for at least six months were to be chosen. This also meant that personnel

---

*Mintzberg's study was completed as a doctoral dissertation at MIT Sloan School of Management in 1968.

Hotel __5__ Date __August 9__ Day of observation __One__ Page __One__

Activity Number	1	2	3	4	5	6	7	8	9	10	11	12	13	14	15
Start Time	9:33	9:35	9:38	9:44	9:58	10:03	10:10	10:12	10:22	10:35	10:40	10:42	10:45	10:46	10:53
Finish Time	9:34	9:37	9:43	9:57	10:02	10:08	10:11	10:21	10:34	10:37	10:42	10:44	10:47	10:52	10:54
Activity															
Corres. In															
Corres. Out															
Reading												x			
Tel. In															x
Tel. Out			x			x	x			x	x			x	
Talking (1)	x	x		x	x										
Interviewing															
Discussion (2+)								x	x				x		
Supervision															
Entertainment															
Personal															
Prod. – ment.															
Prod. – man.															
Inspection															
Function															
Restaurant					x										
Kitchen								x	x				x		
Banq./Conf.															
Accommod.										x	x				
H'keeping															
Bars															
Purchasing						x	x							x	x
Engineering		x													
Personnel	x														
Accounting			x									x			
Maintenance															
Other															
Content															
Technical		x				x	x	x	x	x			x	x	x
Marketing															
Accounting			x												
Finance											x	x			
Personnel	x														
Pub. Rel.				x	x										
Location															
Office	x	x	x	x	x	x	x			x	x	x	x	x	x
Front Office															
Guest Floors															
Restaurant															
Kitchen								x	x						
Bars															
Other															
Interaction															
Corp. H. O.												x			
Reg. H. O.															
Dist. H. O.			x												
Colleague				x		x									
Supplier							x			x				x	x
Cust.															
Poten. Cust.															
Subord./Food	x							x	x				x		
Subord./Accomm.		x									x				
Subord./Staff					x										
Other															

Figure 2–2   Structured observation record

36

Act. no.	Explanation and purpose of activity
1	Innkeeper gives information and notes to F & Bev Director to read prior to latter's exit interview with district director. Does not want F & Bev director to be caught "cold" in interview.
2	Assigns duties to maintenance engineer. Concerns phone installations in dining room and manager's personal phone to improve service and communications.
3	Call to district food and bev director to correct weekly financial statement submitted. Percentages given instead of dollar amounts.
4	Completion of preliminary data form for researcher.
5	Secretary requested to respond to customer dissatisfaction. No charge to be made to customer.
6	Call to Innkeeper in Holiday Inn in neighboring town requesting loan of various supplies, after secretary informs of shortages. To be put on linen delivery truck.
7	Calling local supplier to replenish supplies.
8	Reviewed painting done in kitchen by F & Bev director over weekend. Informed of difficulties and improvements made.
9	Discussion with F & Bev director on mistaken ordering of 50 gallon drum of cleaning fluid. Should have been one gallon. Greatly exceeds budget. Decision made to keep 50 gallon drum.
10	Call to IBM about order of Holidex paper supplies (supplier not reached).
11	Call to F. O. Cashier to ensure that outstanding guest bills over $50 be paid in cash. Ascertains that cashier knows to do this on a regular basis.
12	Reviewing and signing reports to be sent to corporate head office (Memphis).
13	Discussion with F & Bev director on need for new Coke machine. Ideas on advantages on pre and post mix systems. Old machine cannot be replaced (outdated model—15 yrs. old).
14	Further attempt to call IBM supplier of Holidex paper (supplier not reached).
15	Call returned from IBM. Order placed.

Figure 2–3 Structured observation analysis sheet

Figure 2–4 Typical 150–175 room Holiday Inn

attitudes and training were partially a reflection of the innkeeper's ability as a manager.[17]

Hotel Managerial Activities

In addition to personal observation of the work activities of seven innkeepers over a six-week period, Ley clarified his findings by using after the fact a Management Activity Questionnaire, as shown in Figure 2-5, to relate actual work content to the ten Mintzberg roles. After each item on this questionnaire were two scales—not shown in Figure 2-5. One scale asked the manager to show how much time was spent doing the activity; on the other, the manager indicated how important he or she considered the activity. A "0" indicated that the manager had spent no time doing an activity or that it had no importance to him or her. Higher numbers indicated the relative amount of time the manager spent in each activity or its relative importance. Thus, for example, in the activity *Answering requests for information:*

```
       Time  0  1  2  3  4  5  6
 Importance  0  1  2  3  4  5  6
```

The manager answering this question showed that in his job he spent very little time in answering requests for information, but that he believed it to be a relatively important part of his job.

Interpersonal Roles

Figurehead

1. Participating in public service work.

2. Making yourself available to "outsiders" (such as clients, the public) who want to go to "the man in charge."

3. Attending social functions as a representative of your Inn.

4. Signing documents as a representative of your Inn.

5. Answering letters or inquiries on behalf of your Inn.

6. Being available to answer questions by any guest or employee most days and evenings.

Figure 2-5   Hotel management activity check list[18]

7. Evaluating the quality of subordinate job performance.

8. Attending to staffing needs in your Inn (such as hiring, firing, promotion, giving salary increases).

9. Using your authority to insure that your subordinates accomplish important tasks.

10. Encouraging or criticizing subordinates' actions .

11. Delegating as much of daily routine work as possible to subordinates (secretary, department heads).

12. Encouraging and praising employees for work well done.

Liaison

13. Attending social functions which allow you to keep up your contacts.

14. Attending conferences or meetings to maintain your contacts.

15. Joining boards, organizations, clubs, etc., which might provide useful, work-related contacts.

16. Developing new contacts by answering requests for information.

17. Developing personal relationships with people outside your Inn who feed you work or services (e.g., purchasing, suppliers, inspectors, etc.).

18. Developing contacts with important people outside of your Inn.

Figure 2–5 Continued

Informational Roles

Monitor

19. Keeping informed on various events and "gossip of the trade."

20. Keeping up with market changes and trends.

21. Gathering information about trends outside your organization.

22. Gathering information about clients, competitors, associates, etc.

23. Touring the property.

24. Learning about new ideas originating outside of your organization.

Disseminator

25. Keeping employees of your Inn informed of relevant information.

26. Transmitting ideas from your outside contacts to appropriate insiders.

27. Holding meetings to disseminate information to employees of your Inn.

28. Deciding what information responsibilities to delegate to others.

29. Providing guidance to your subordinates on the basis of your understanding of the organization.

30. Forwarding important information to your subordinates.

Figure 2–5 Continued

Spokesman

31. Keeping important people outside of your Inn informed about your unit's activities.

32. Handling "public relations" activities for your own Inn.

33. Presiding at meetings as a representative of your Inn.

34. Serving as an expert to people outside of your Inn.

35. Informing others of your Inn's future plans.

36. Keeping the public informed about your Inn's activities and plans.

Decisional Roles

Entrepreneur

37. Designing projects for organizational improvement.

38. Initiating controlled change in your Inn.

39. Exploiting opportunities to expand or grow as an Inn.

40. Maintaining supervision over changes in your Inn.

41. Solving problems by instituting needed changes in your Inn.

42. Deciding the priorities of internal improvement projects.

Disturbance Handler

43. Responding to unforeseen events.

44. Resolving conflicts between subordinates.

Figure 2-5 Continued

45. Handling employee grievances.

46. Dealing with conflicts between your Inn and other Inns or hotels.

47. Taking immediate action in response to a crisis (e.g., equipment breakdown; sudden scheduling conflicts; an irate client, etc.).

48. Helping department heads resolve emergency problem situations (shortages of manpower or supplies during a busy period, for example).

Resource Allocator

49. Programming work (what is to be done, when and how).

50. Distributing budgeted resources.

51. Making decisions about time parameters for upcoming programs.

52. Deciding which programs to provide resources (manpower, materials, dollars for).

53. Allocating manpower to specific jobs or tasks.

54. Allocating equipment or materials.

Negotiator

55. Writing out contract implementation procedures.

56. Negotiating with outside groups for needed materials, support, commitments, etc.

57. Negotiating contracts.

Figure 2–5 Continued

Obviously, not every minute spent at work could be classified by the researcher as part of a manager's work activity. For example, since all innkeepers lived in, all but one were married, and four had children, it was not uncommon for them to be interrupted at work for such personal activities as taking the children to school, or taking the dog to the veterinarian. Then, too, there were allowances for time out for "small talk" with subordinates about last night's television show or yesterday's performance of the local basketball team.

Nonetheless, while complete and undistorted focus upon significant managerial roles exclusively is an ideal rather than a possibility, Ley's unique study of lodging managers is instructive, for it suggests that in developing your own career strategy toward management positions in the hospitality industry, you had better come to grips with a number of important *role behaviors*. There are at least three that deserve your close attention.

The Leader Role

Few sophisticated practioners in the field of management would deny that leadership is the most widely recognized of all managerial roles. Innkeepers are no exception. All of them regard their leadership role to be more important than any other. Yet, contrary to the conventional wisdom, Ley finds that while leadership embraces those management activities identified elsewhere in this chapter (Figure 2-5), it also does something more. It tends to reflect the character and spirit of a hotel or restaurant organization. To paraphrase the eminent Peter Drucker, if an organization is great in spirit, it's because the spirit of its people in top positions is great. Invariably, when an organization decays, it does so from the top down. In the words of an ancient proverb, "Trees die from the top." Though there are almost as many definitions of leadership as there are people who have attempted to define it, the subjective nature of any definition can scarcely be denied. What is unmistakable, however, is the conviction that however it is defined, we all know it when we see it. Thus, the idea of the leader's role in management—implying as it does the ability to influence others to follow your lead *voluntarily*—is an important one for you to take into account.

The Monitor Role

Many activities performed by the manager of a hospitality enterprise inevitably have their roots in the mix of roles involving the gathering, sorting, and distribution of information. Ley's study confirms the fact that hotel managers spend more time on their *monitor* role—and its associated disseminator and spokesperson roles—than on any other of their work roles. On the average, it amounts to slightly more than 25 percent. This simply means that receiving and communicating information are very important aspects of a manager's job. As a *monitor*, you are constantly on the lookout for information that can be used to the advantage of your hotel or restaurant operation. Through your system of continuous personal contacts both inside and outside your organization, you become and remain the best-informed member of your group. Thus, you are able to transmit to your subordinates important infomation that would otherwise be inaccessible to them as well as to keep your superiors well informed about what is going on. For example, you are monitoring when you discuss with a department head the limitations to be borne in mind in an upcoming interview with a food and beverage candidate who wishes to commute 50 miles from home each day. Or when you are checking with suppliers the costs of installing cable television service in your establishment. Or when your review of the regular linen inventory being sent to the home office discloses a serious omission, requiring that you ask the housekeeper to take a new inventory so as to include the omitted items. Or whenever you make an inspection tour of your property for the purpose of discovering repair and maintenance needs—including the ever-present need to maintain a high level of employee morale. All these as well as others which are shown in Figure 2-2 earlier in this chapter reflect the importance of your *monitor* role.

The Entrepreneur Role

Ley's study confirms the fact that in the hospitality industry—as in other industries—managers view their role of *entrepreneur* as a major criterion for discriminating between effective and ineffective management. Thus, a manager who encourages the exploration of new ideas for menu content and design is being entrepreneurial, as is the manager who institutes an energy conservation contest with prompt cash payoffs to employee winners while at the same time seriously undertaking a feasibility study of the applications of solar energy to his operation. And so is the manager who institutes a Scanlon Plan (see Chapter 3), or the one who operates his establishment on the principle of a continuing feasibility study (see Chapter 10). When a manager is creative, innovative, and a generator of profit-growth through such ventures, he or she is an effective, *entrepreneurial* manager.

A caveat   In conclusion, we must add a caveat. Despite the importance that attaches to the roles here addressed, it would be a mistake to overlook a bundle of factors or variables bearing upon the different roles in which a manager engages. The results of both Mintzberg's and Ley's research strongly indicate that your job as a manager at any particular point in time is influenced by four situational variables:

1. The hotel, restaurant, fast-food organization itself, and its industry requirements

2. The level of your managerial job in the organization and the function it supervises (such as food preparation, accounting, engineering and maintenance, marketing, etc.)

3. The impact of your own personality and management style within the job itself

4. Variations in your job that are attributable to seasonal factors (such as summer resort business) or temporary emergencies (such as failure of any waiters or waitresses to show up for work at Sunday morning breakfast)

Given the pressures of a managerial job, the degree to which you are aware of your own strengths and weaknesses, and the inevitable difficulties and dilemmas inherent in today's hospitality business, an understanding of these variables enables you to prepare effectively for a career in management.

What, then, does this suggest to those of you who may still be attending school? It suggests a number of things. First, you ought to be, if you aren't already, working part-time in the hospitality industry. Experience gained *before* graduation will help materially to widen the job placement opportunities you will have upon graduation. Moreover, you can get to know yourself, your own job, and that of your boss as thoroughly as possible. How does the manager in the place where you work really collect and disseminate his or her information? How do you perceive the boss' leadership? Is it a model that persuades you to follow *voluntarily*? How does your company manage—if it does—to maintain its entrepreneurial stance year after year?

Experience gained now in hospitality administration can, by broadening your perspectives, importantly supplement what you learn in the classroom and help greatly in the development of your managerial career.

As we proceed in the next chapter to look further down the road of competitive survival in the world of hospitality, we urge you to become *aware*—aware of the tools you will be using as a manager, and aware of the problems and opportunities you will be facing.

Summary

This chapter discusses basic concepts and theories as they apply to hospitality management. We belive it is worthwhile for you to learn about these because there is more emphasis today upon what a manager *does*—as interpreted by adherents of the *work-activity* school of management thought.

Mintzberg's research suggests that managers play a complex of ten interpersonal, informational, and decisional roles. This is not to say that all managers give equal attention to each role. As Ley's remarkable study of hotel managers discloses, certain roles—such as *leader, monitor,* and *entrepreneur*—are given significantly greater attention in the hospitality industry. Ley's work is particularly interesting not only because of its real-life definition of management but also because it calls attention to the fact that managers operate in a constantly changing environment as *doers*, coping with events and situations that are often turbulent and unpredictable.

The authors believe that if you want to be more effective in developing your managerial career, it is important that you start *now* to supplement your classroom learning with part-time experiences that will challenge your role-playing abilities in the hospitality industry.

Questions for Discussion

1. Explain in your own words how the idea of what managers do has evolved from Fayol's traditional concept to the theories of Mintzberg; of Ley.

2. Why are the factors relating to disposable income and the aging patterns of the population of consequence to the hospitality industry?

3. What do you understand the meaning of the work-activity school of management to be?

4. On the basis of your own experience in the hospitality industry, do you agree with Ley's assessment that the roles of leader, monitor, and entrepreneur assume greater prominence than other roles do in this industry? Why, or why not?

5. What are Mintzberg's ten managerial roles? Give examples of them from your experience.

6. If hotel and restaurant industry recruiters who come to campus ask you what your strengths and weaknesses are, based upon the hospitality industry experiences you've had thus far, how would you answer them?

Key Terms

- CLASSICAL SCHOOL
- DECISION THEORY SCHOOL
- DECISIONAL ROLES
- ENTREPRENEUR
- ENTREPRENEURSHIP SCHOOL
- GREAT MAN SCHOOL
- INFORMATIONAL ROLES
- INTERPERSONAL ROLES
- LEADER
- LEADER BEHAVIOR SCHOOL
- LEADER EFFECTIVENESS SCHOOL
- LEADER POWER SCHOOL
- MANAGER
- MONITOR
- STRUCTURED OBSERVATION METHOD
- WORK-ACTIVITY SCHOOL

46

Jim applied for a summer job as a front office cashier in the prestigious Plaza Hotel. He knew his salary would be low, but this was the only job he could find in the big midwestern city where he had just completed his junior year in a well-known hotel and restaurant school.

The hotel manager accepted Jim's application and agreed to train him as front-office cashier on Saturday mornings for four weeks, paying him the prevailing minimum wage during this training period.

Jim adapted quickly and the hotel manager believed that he was ready to take the cashier's window by himself after his first two weeks of steady employment.

Three other men had been trained for the same work and the hotel manager was counting on them to help as relief cashiers during the busy summer season while the regular cashiers were on vacation. A schedule was made for the relief cashiers' assignments during the regular cashiers' vacation periods.

Ross, one of the other three trained by the hotel, had not shown counting skill sufficient to handle a cashier's window. The manager kept him two weeks and then released him, because someone was found who could do the counting work satisfactorily and who would work at a lower salary than Ross received.

Jim learned after his first two weeks as a cashier that he could get a job paying twice as much, doing office work for a big construction company. The $200 per week he could make in this job with the construction people would go a long way toward paying his tuition at college for senior year; if he continued at his present rate of pay at the hotel, he would be unable to pay all his bills at school next year.

On the other hand, the hotel would be unable to train another person in time to take his position and if he left, it would leave the hotel short a cashier for the summer. The vacation schedule for the regular personnel, who had already made arrangements for their vacations, would have to be changed.

Jim, of course, had no written contract with the hotel. He considered that they had given Ross a bad deal in releasing him and that they therefore could worry about the front-office cashier problem after he was gone. What he needed most that summer was the money.

Jim gave the hotel a week's notice and took the construction company job.

The hotel manager accused Jim of having no sense of moral responsibility. He figured that the hotel's acceptance of Jim for summer work meant that he would stay on for the entire season. His pay would not have been increased to match the construction company offer because that would have shown partiality and caused dissent among all the other cashiers.

Case Questions

1. What would you have done if you had been in Jim's position? Why? What if you had been the Plaza manager?

2. Which of the managerial roles we have been discussing in this chapter would have been effective in coping with this situation? Explain.

3. What were the alternative solutions here, from the point of view of the hotel management? From Jim's point of view?

4. What do you think the Plaza Hotel management should do now to prevent situations like this from arising in the future?

A Case Study: The Scoop on Steve's Ice Cream*

On the bulletin board in the back of Steve's Ice Cream there is a copy of a letter that owner Steve Herrell sent recently to a customer who complained of bad service and demanded two free sundaes. It notes that copies have been sent to the To-Whom-It-May-Concern Manager, the Easter-Egg-Hunt Manager, the Hot-Fudge Manager, among others.

"Of course you can have two new sundaes," the letter reads, "at twice the usual price"; and it signs off with "Long live the chocolate chip!"

The point being that, unlike other businesses, Steve's is not run on the philosophy that "The customer is always right." It isn't a mammoth bureaucratic operation that bends over backwards to seek out business, keep it, and rake in money.

This self-conscious uniqueness is evident everywhere at Steve's: in the hand-lettered menu; in the rows of framed newspaper clippings about the place that line the wall where endless hordes of people wait for sundaes and mix-ins; in the way Steve leans on the ends of the counter, talking to customers or putting message-bearing hearts on top of their ice cream (if it happens to be Valentine's Day).

But it is even more evident behind the counter and the homemade whipped cream, where the huge bulletin board is covered not only with letters such as the one to the disgruntled customer, open invitations to parties, notices about counterfeit money and Board of Health Inspections, but with the agenda for the next workers' meeting and the minutes from the last one.

That agenda now includes rather minor policy matters, such as maximum number of hours a worker should work per week, or how often to wash the aprons. But it has included items such as wages, prices and store hour changes and whether to invest in a new air conditioner.

Workers' meetings arose partly from a crisis that broke last spring, just about the time I started working at Steve's. Some of the workers felt the store was becoming too much of a business, too much of a success—it was becoming less a homey, comfortable place to work, and Steve was becoming less a fellow worker and more and more a manager and owner. Their suggestion was to turn it into a workers' cooperative.

I remember sitting bewildered through a meeting less like a business discussion than a consciousness-raising session. The details of the cooperative plan were discussed. Then Steve began to read from a

---

*Reproduced by permission from the *Harvard Crimson* of February 26, 1975.

journal he had kept in the days when he was a taxi driver dreaming about opening an ice cream store.

He told the story, now Steve's lore, of how no one would give him credit or rent him space, how he did everything on a shoestring and by himself, and how the place had grown unexpectedly from a tiny operation into an instant success—a business with 25 workers. And how, with so much of himself invested in it, he refused huge sums of money every day from people who wanted to buy the store or the name and start franchises of the business for him.

It was a stirring story, one that brought out one's deeply ingrained but long-forgotten faith in the American ethic of individual enterprise. Even if surplus value and capitalist exploitation were a reality at Steve's, as some of our fellow-workers were telling us, how could we take Steve's hard-won success and identity away from him?

"I can feel you pulling the wool over our eyes," one worker accused Steve. Yet in the end, with bad feelings all around the room, we voted to try a middle course whereby we would hold regular workers' meetings and at the same time leave Steve in ultimate control, all the while retaining the option of taking up again at some later point the issue of a workers' cooperative and profit-sharing.

We haven't done so yet, and although we did set up an official grievance committee, the main role of the workers' meeting is to advise Steve and foster a sense of cooperation and teamwork. And, of togetherness: that has always been a big theme.

Above and beyond the consideration that happy servers working well together create a pleasant atmosphere, it's important to Steve that the place means as much to the people who work there as it does to him. He wants working there to be an emotional commitment, and not just another job.

Emotional commitments have their disadvantages, however, for everybody involved. It was the people who had been devoting their life to the store, working well over 40 hours a week, who precipitated the crisis last spring. And it was that intensity of involvement that caused another upset this past fall, more bitter and painful than the last.

In a moment of panic when costs rose and profits fell, Steve—not being very experienced in business—decided to cut our unusually high wages.

There was an immediate uproar, and talk of a strike. But what became clear in that somber, three-hour-long meeting we had—the first one ever without Steve—was that the real hurt was not the wage cut but the fact that Steve had just decided to do it, without consulting anyone. We felt betrayed. We had always been one big happy family; all of a sudden Steve was asserting his authority over us as our employer.

If we felt betrayed, Steve must have as well when we reacted not as supporters—members of the family—but as employees threatening to close the place down.

Still, however happy and together our family might be, however many potluck suppers and in-jokes we all had together, nobody could get around the reality that he was signing our checks every week. When that became the issue, as it was bound to, eventually (and probably will again), everybody got hurt.

In the end, we did work it out together, avoiding a wage cut by raising prices. Things settled back down to normal, with Steve apologizing to this day for precipitating the crisis. He was right when he wrote the complaining customer that Steve's Ice Cream was not your everyday enterprise, despite the all-too-American success story behind it. The priorities of the place are off: Steve apologizes to the workers and lets the obnoxious customers have it. Which makes it a special place to work. Long live the chocolate chip!

Case Questions

1. What managerial roles do you perceive to have been influential here? Explain.

2. If you were Steve, what view would you have taken in managing Steve's Ice Cream? Why?

Notes

1. Thomas F. Powers, "Food Service in 1985," *Cornell Hotel & Restaurant Administration Quarterly,* May 1976, pp. 48–51. A less optimistic view is expressed by Donald I. Trott in "Exploding the Myth: The Truth about Food Service Growth," *Cornell Hotel & Restaurant Administration Quarterly,* February 1978, pp. 11–17. He argues that all the current demographics (i. e., teenagers, percentage of women in the workforce, real income, the shift to microwave cookery at home, etc.) suggest a much slower growth scenario than is warranted by most extrapolative analyses of the food service industry's future.

2. Ibid., p. 51.

3. Henry Mintzberg, *The Nature of Managerial Work* (New York: Harper & Row, 1973); see also Henry Mintzberg, "The Manager's Job: Folklore and Fact," *Harvard Business Review,* July–August 1975, pp. 49–61.

4. From C. L. Shartle, *Executive Performance and Leadership* (Englewood Cliffs, N.J.: Prentice-Hall, 1956), p. 82.

5. James A. F. Stoner, *Management* (Englewood Cliffs, N.J.: Prentice-Hall, 1978), p. 7.

6. David A. Ley, *An Empirical Examination of Selected Work Activity Correlates of Managerial Effectiveness in the Hotel Industry Using a Structured Observation Approach* (unpublished Ph.D. dissertation, Michigan State University, 1978), p. 6

7. Derek French and Heather Saward, *Dictionary of Management* (New York: International Publications Service, 1975).

8. H. Edward Wrapp, "Good Managers Don't Make Policy Decisions," *Harvard Business Review on Management* (New York: Harper & Row, 1975), p. 18.

9. Jay W. Lorsch, James P. Baughman, James Reece, and Henry Mintzberg, *Understanding Management* (New York: Harper & Row, 1978), p. 219.

10. Philip Nailon, *A Study of Management Activity in Units of a Hotel Group* (unpublished Master's thesis, University of London, 1967).

11. Ley, *An Empirical Examination of Selected Work Activity.*

12. Lorsch, Baughman, Reed & Mintzberg, op. cit. p. 24.

13. *Ibid.,* p. 245.

14. *Ibid.,* p. 257.

15. *Ibid.,* p. 262.

16. Ley, *op. cit.*

17. *Ibid., op. cit.,* pp. 62–63.

18. *Ibid.,* pp. 78–80.

Behavioral Concepts

When you finish this chapter, you should understand:

1. What is meant by "quality of work life"

2. The participative management plan know as MDP

3. The advantages and disadvantages of the Scanlon Plan

4. The eight criteria for a successful QWL program

5. The concept of organizational climate

6. The importance of the performance dimensions and development dimensions as shown on a Climate Profile Chart

It's a little startling sometimes to realize that a decade ago—in 1972—the term *quality of work life* literally hadn't been invented yet. Yet just eight years later—literally in the blink of an eye as history tells time—the term and its acronym, QWL, had become an accepted and sought after staple in Amercian industrial life.

By mid-1980, the Chairman of the Board of the New York Stock Exchange, in a major speech on corporate governance to a couple of hundred leaders of American industry, would say that a management style encouraging employee involvement and participating has become an accepted responsibility of U.S. managerial leadership. . . .

Today . . . perhaps 50,000 companies and several million managers and employees are partially or deeply involved in some kind of worker-involvement scheme, under a bewildering maze of aliases, like Ford's EI (Employee Involvement), GE's BQ2L (Bring Quality to Life), Westinghouse's QC (Quality Circles), and dozens of other terms suggesting the same basic thrust: giving employees a greater voice in making the decisions that affect their daily life at work.

A remarkable transformation in the American way of working (is) clearly underway—and growing exponentially.

Ted Mills, Chairman of the Board
American Center for Quality of Work Life
Excerpts from "Why Quality of Work Life"

$\mathbf{A}$s anyone knows who has ever worked in a hotel, restaurant, or fast-food establishment, bosses are fond of saying things like "Our greatest asset is people," or "It takes happy employees to make happy customers." But paradoxically, the very people whose skillful performance can assure the successful operation of any hospitality organization are too often seen simply as costs to be controlled, problems to be handled, or interchangeable parts to be moved around. Indeed, there is little in the ancient ritual of employer–employee relationships to contradict the old adage "If they can be hired, they can be fired"—a fact of corporate life to which even Ford Motor Company presidents have been painfully exposed on the occasion of their disagreement with Henry Ford II.[1] Whatever their roots may be, such management attitudes are paternalistic at best and autocratic at worst (see the cartoon on p. 56).

Cliches and shibboleths aside, the focus of this chapter is not necessarily on the boss' right to hire and fire, nor upon those other relationships that have been traditionally viewed as functions of the personnel department. These, we believe, are already covered in a wide variety of contemporary texts and professional journals. For those of you wishing to widen your grasp of such functions in hotels and restaurants, the following resources are particularly instructive:

○ American Hotel and Motel Association, *Federal Wage and Hour Standards for the Hotel-Motel and Restaurant Industries* (Washington, D.C.: 1979. A looseleaf, ring-binder service that is periodically updated.)

○ George Koziara and Karen Koziara, *The Negro in the Hotel Industry* (Philadelphia: Wharton School of Finance and Commerce, Industrial Research Unit, University of Pennsylvania, 1973).

○ Sylvia Riggs, "Careers in Slow Motion: What's Holding Women Back," *Institutions,* June 1, 1977.

○ Arch Stokes, *The Equal Opportunity Handbook for Hotels, Restaurants, and Institutions* (Boston: CBI Publishing Co., Inc., 1979).

○ U.S. Department of Health, Education & Welfare, Public Health Service, Center for Disease Control, *Health and Safety Guide for Hotels* and *Motels* (Cincinnati, Ohio: National Institute for Occupational Safety and Health, Division of Technical Services, August 1975).

Instead, our emphasis here will be upon the opportunities for improving the quality of work life for people in the hospitality industry. To paraphrase former Vice President Rockefeller, the critical questions we must address—if we are to enhance the quality of American life—are:

How can work in hospitality industries be organized so the individual can enjoy a greater sense of participation, creativity, and dignity?

How can we tap more fully the reservoir and intelligence of Americans, the most highly educated people in history, to improve the productivity of our hotels and restaurants?[2]

Good as the traditional approaches of personnel management—or "human resources management"—may have been in the past, they are not good enough now. In the modern context of concern for healthier, more satisfied, and more productive employees as well as for more efficient, adaptive, and profitable organizations, yesterday's model is becoming less and less pertinent. And while tomorrow's model has not yet become crystal clear, we can recognize the broad outlines of what Senator Charles H. Percy, in a mid-1973 speech entitled "The Quality of Work Phenomenon," called "an idea whose time has come." This chapter, therefore, will investigate why the quality of life at work is so important and how substantial gains from an improved quality of work life might be achieved.

When Douglas McGregor, nearly two decades ago, introduced his Theory X–Theory Y concept to the business world, he accompanied it with a favorite anecdote about a newly appointed textile-mill manager. In making the rounds of the mill during his first day on the job, he walked directly over to the union steward, who had been conversing with some weave-room employees, and asked: "Are you Jankowski?" The steward replied that he was, whereupon the new manager responded: "I'm the new manager here. When I run a textile mill, I *run* it. Do you understand?" The steward nodded his head and then, turning to his fellow workers, waved his hand in the direction of the machinery they were operating. Instantly, every machine halted. With his eyes fastened upon the new manager, Jankowski answered: "O.K. ... it's all yours. Go ahead and *run* it."

President Kennedy, who was equally adept at sensing great issues, may have had McGregor—then teaching at MIT—in mind during a conversation with Andre Malraux one Sunday in May 1962. They had been discussing the persistence of mythology in modern times:

"In the nineteenth century," Malraux said, "the ostensible issue within the European states was the monarchy vs. the republic. But the real issue was capitalism vs. the proletariat. In the twentieth century, the ostensible issue is capitalism vs. the proletariat. But the world has moved on. What is the real issue now?"

"The real issue today," Kennedy replied, "is the management of industrial society ..."[3]

Today, a generation later, this concern remains deeply imbedded in our national life as we seek energetically to address the twin tasks of making America safe for the employed as well as for the employers.

"I thought we were reducing the staff by attrition."

Source: *New Yorker,* July 17, 1978, p. 21. Drawing by Ed Fisher; © 1978, The New
Yorker Magazine, Inc.

The challenge requires something more, however, than the
"cosmetic exercises practiced today in tens of thousands of companies
seeking to spur worker motivation through various cheering packages of
discussion groups, training films, and so on."[4] More fundamentally, in

the words of Peter Drucker, "we know that we will have to go beyond personnel management ... We will have to learn to look at people as
resource and opportunity rather than as problem, cost, and threat."[5] This
new emphasis upon people as resource and opportunity has given rise
most recently to innovations in work organizations focusing their attention upon the sources of satisfaction for people at work—an area of concern and activity encompassed by the phrase "quality of work life."

What Does Quality of Work Life Mean?

Improving the quality of work life QWL means giving workers the
chance to participate meaningfully with management in making decisions affecting their jobs. It means that workers are *decision-
makers*—instead of decision-takers. It means that the company
realistically accepts you as an adult in the workplace just as it accepts
you as an adult in society at large; and that the democratic values you
cherish at home, at school, and in the community are in large measure
transferable to the place where you work. As a consequence, there
evolves a solid climate of mutual respect between you and your
employer. You, the employee, gain the benefit of increased job satisfaction; while the company, at the same time, gains the benefits of reduced
absenteeism and of improved quality of its product and service.

Management tradition and practice change slowly, however.
Therefore, it is not unusual to find some companies unwilling to sur-
render their otherwise unihibited prerogatives in the treatment of
employees to the notion of participation until they are on the brink of
financial disaster. This was the case for the Hotel St. Jorgen in Malmo,
Sweden, which we discuss next in the first of several sections describing
several employee participation plans.

In the years 1971 and 1972, the operations of the food and beverage
department of the Hotel St. Jorgen included a 100-seat full-service
restaurant, a 270-seat cafeteria that was converted into a tavern in the
evening, a 130-seat pizzeria, and the traditional hotel room service. At
that time, however, the hotel industry generally was experiencing ever-
increasing costs in food and beverage operations as well as union-backed
demands in Sweden for a greater decision-sharing role for its employees.
And, too, keen competition from restaurants unaffiliated with hotels
prevented any serious effort to raise prices. As a result, the Hotel St.
Jorgen was showing total losses in excess of $300,000.

Employee
Participation
Plan: Hotel
St. Jorgen

This was the situation faced by Ingvar Gustafson when he was appointed general manager of the 282-room Hotel St. Jorgen in 1972.

The hotel company (known as RESO, Scandinavia's largest travel
organization) embraces a chain of 13 city hotels, 10 holiday camps, 2
holiday resorts in Italy, and 700 chalets and apartments.

As ably narrated by Professor Donal A. Dermody in *The Cornell
Hotel and Restaurant Administration Quarterly*,[6] the remarkable success
of employee decision sharing in turning a $170,000 food and beverage

58

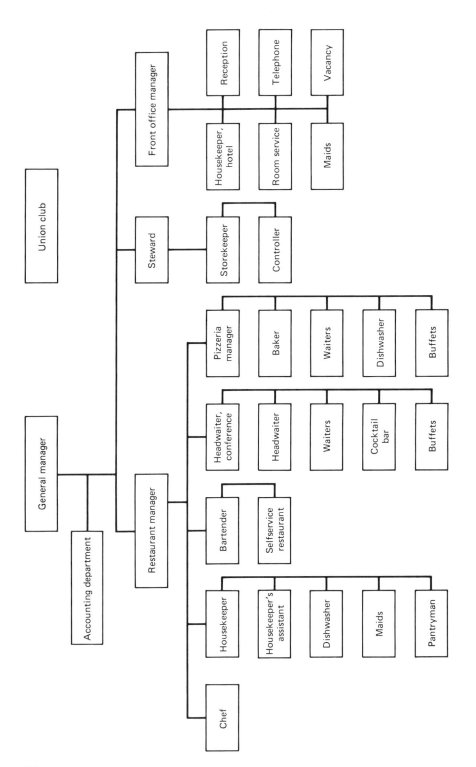

Source: *The Cornell Hotel and Restaurant Quarterly,* May 1976, p. 72

Figure 3–1. Hotel St. Jorgen's organization before June 1, 1972

loss (1972) into a $200,000 profit a year later is explainable only in terms of the participative management principles to which Gustafson had earlier been exposed while attending Cornell.

How did the general manager go about introducing these principles? He galvanized the entire hotel staff of 167 people into improving the quality of their work life through a cooperative program known as MDP—an acronym for Management, Decision-sharing, and Profitability. Briefly, this program entailed the following steps.

1. *Establishment of the decision-sharing concept*—Under Gustafson's leadership as the general manager, it was agreed to delegate all decision making to employees who formed autonomous groups within each department in order to plan and carry out changes aimed at restoring food and beverage operations to profitability. Thus, instead of the traditional chain-of-command organization that had existed previously (as shown in Figure 3–1), the hotel reorganized itself into three operational groupings.

2. *Management Committee*—The first group, known as the Management Committee (Figure 3–2), met in a monthly budget meeting, focusing primarily upon suggestions for profit improvement which were then forwarded to the appropriate autonomous groups for detailed analysis and action.

3. *Establishing Autonomous Department Groups*—The Autonomous Department Groups (see Figure 3–3) included *every* employee and the union representatives. They too met monthly, reviewed current as well as anticipated operating figures, and, after a

The Management Committee's organizational plan under the new MDP-model, with the budget meeting as the central forum. Representatives from all autonomous department groups participate at the monthly budget meetings.

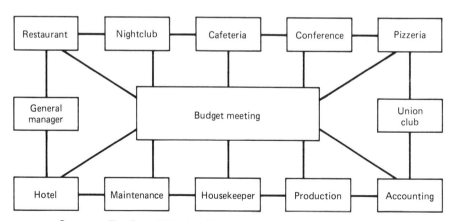

Source: *The Cornell Hotel and Restaurant Quarterly* May 1976, p. 73.
Figure 3–2. Hotel St. Jorgen's organization after June 1972

thorough problem-solving discussion, reached final decisions on any operational changes needed.

4. *Establishing a Purchasing, Stocking, and Controlling Group*—A third group, Purchasing, Stocking, and Controling (see Figure 3–4), surprisingly abandoned the traditional, centralized purchasing system in favor of direct purchases by individual department heads, each of whom was authorized to have his own storage facilities. Outside consultants were engaged to assist in the changeover to assure a continuous delivery flow as well as adequate controls.

Results of the MDP Program

This whole reorganization of the Hotel St. Jorgens took less than two months in 1972, and almost immediately there were valuable employee suggestions on how guests could be better served, as well as on how productivity could be improved and operational costs reduced.

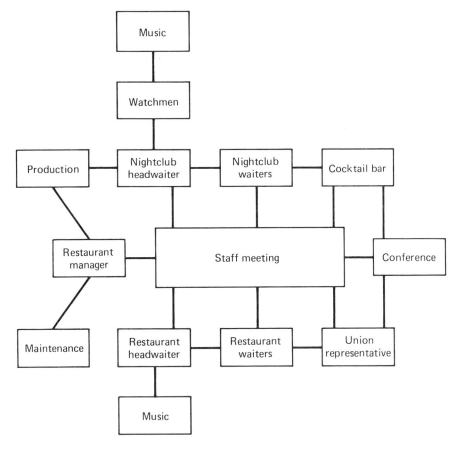

Source: The Cornell Hotel and Restaurant Quarterly, May 1976, p. 73

Figure 3–3. Autonomous Department Groups formed by MDP program.

In terms of food and beverage sales per employee, the productivity results, as indicated below, were remarkable:

Year	Food and beverage sales per employee
1972	$14,000
1973	21,000
1974	28,000

Not surprisingly, a 1974 marketing study of the hotel guests disclosed that two-thirds patronized the hotel food and beverage facilities, and that

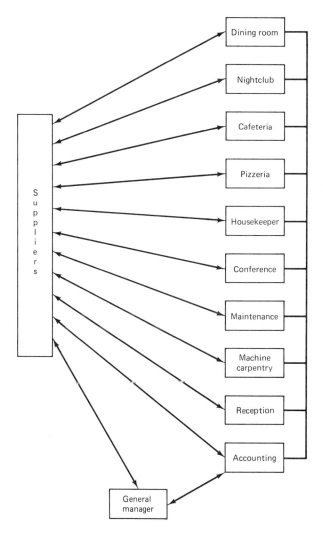

Source: *The Cornell Hotel and Restaurant Quarterly* May 1976, p. 74.

Figure 3–4.   MDP Organization for Purchasing, Stocking, and Controlling after **June 1, 1972**

the vast majority were happy with the menus, quality, service, and decor.
By 1976, the RESO chain was engaged in extending these principles of employee decision sharing to all its other hotels.[7]

**Employee
Participation
Plan: Two
Paris Hotels**

A *New York Times* news dispatch from Paris late in 1975 described
another form of employee participation as having been introduced at the
George V and Plaza Athénée Hotels:

> Participation in commercial and industrial management has long
> been encouraged by the Government, but few hotels ... have accepted
> the practice, and none to the extent that it has been established at the
> George V and the Plaza. Many hotel owners ... fear that participation
> would force them to let the government look at their books, which
> could increase their taxes.
>
> The workers' participation has reached the higher echelons of the
> management of the two hotels, which have been owned since 1969 by
> the London-based Trust Houses Forte Corporation ... The change in
> labor–management relations did not come about altruistically. The
> new balance of power in the halls of luxury seems to be providing
> more money for both owners and workers. The workers have been
> getting 20% of the hotels' profits at the end of each year and the
> hotels, according to the owners, have continued to make money while
> other deluxe competitors have been losing it.
>
> The owners have also permitted the workers' committees to sit in at
> board meetings but not to vote at them, to make their own audit of the
> owners' bookkeeping and to approve the appointment of the top
> management staff, including Paul Bougneaux, the former shop
> steward and porter who led the red-flag-waving hotel workers on the
> streets outside the Plaza in 1968 and is now manager.
>
> In the last year the workers' committee has originated a number of
> changes ... including relocating the Regence Restaurant so that it has
> a view of the garden, the building of several new guest rooms in a va-
> cant space underneath the roof, and the agreement by the chamber-
> maids to water windowbox petunias without extra pay.[8]

Sir Charles Forte, Deputy Chairman and Chief Executive of Trust
Houses Forte, has confirmed that the operation of the worker participation plan at his company's two Paris hotels is indeed highly successful.
He stresses that while "the participation in connection to the staff *is
minimal:* [Forte's emphasis], they enjoy good wages and of course are
also paid by the service charges levied on our clients and on gratuities
which in both hotels are generous. We have no such scheme in operation
in any of our hotels elsewhere worldwide."[9]

A fascinating account of participatory management at the Paris
Plaza Athénée hotel appeared recently in the Spring 1982, issue of
Business and Society Review. In essence, the article points out that the
participative system took root under a 1967 law pressed through parlia-

ment by General Charles de Gaulle. That law provided that all French companies with more than 50 employees must give workers a voice in management along with a modest share of the profits. The subsequent success of this system at the Plaza is attributed to Paul Bougneaux, mentioned in the *Times* article above and general manager for a period of ten years ending in 1979.

Asked for the secret of his success in increasing occupancy from 70 percent to over 85 percent in a 210-room hotel, which averaged $175 per night for a double room, Bougneaux explained:

> People must be happy in their work; they must understand the business well; they must be encouraged to participate, to make the work better; and they must share in the results ... When we started trusting people to work, we didn't need so many to check ... We put people first at the Plaza—not profit, never. The first objective was people. And then profit came.[10]

In the years since World War II, an increasing number of employers in the United States have recognized the need to promote the meaningful involvement of workers in the decision-making process. They have been experimenting with various forms of quality of work-life programs, two of which assume special promise for hospitality administration. They are the Scanlon Plan and the General Motors union–management program to improve the quality of work life.[11]

Quality of Work Life in the United States

The Background

The Scanlon Plan had its origin in the Depression years. Joseph Scanlon, a cost accountant by training, had become a union organizer for the steelworkers in a mill which faced bankruptcy. In desperation, the mill owner sought Scanlon's advice on how to avert what seemed to be inevitable disaster, both for the company and its employees. At Scanlon's suggestion, they both visited the Pittsburgh headquarters of Clinton Golden, then the regional director responsible for Scanlon's local union.

The Scanlon Plan

Golden observed that in his view workers always had ideas on how to improve operations, if only a way could be found to enlist their support. Upon his return to the mill, Scanlon satisfied himself as well as the owner during worker interviews that indeed they did have many useful ideas for improving the plant operations. As a consequence, the steel mill was saved from bankruptcy, and thus was born a concept of employee participation that was destined to endure and to be widely implemented as the Scanlon Plan.

If, today, the Quality of Work Life movement means "giving employees a greater voice in work decisions that affect them," it can scarcely be denied that the idea is rooted in the plan which Joseph Scanlon inaugurated a half-century ago.

The Plan

The Scanion Plan for *total* organizational development is one that challenges us to admit that all of the possibilities for meaningful innovation in our hospitality establishments have not yet been exhausted.

For example, what hotelman or restauranteur would not be happy:

○ To pay monthly bonuses in those months when profits are increased through reduced labor costs

○ To see employee productivity rates double while sales quadruple, and at the same time to be able to reduce prices

○ To see the absenteeism rate drop from 5 percent to a very low 1½ percent

○ To see turnover rate never exceed 5 percent

Or what hotel employee would not take pride in a company that:

○ Paid bonuses averaging more than 10 percent of pay for each of the past five years

○ Permitted its employees to organize into work teams that:
  —Set their own breaks
  —Established their own production standards
  —Eliminated timeclocks and put all employees on salary
  —Handled all hiring and discipline, with the latter sometimes taking the unusual form of sending the offending employee home for a day with pay, while his peers pick up the slack for that day
  —Controlled layoffs and unemployment by finding new jobs for displaced employees

The Scanlon Plan at Donnelly Mirrors

These spectacular accomplishments, and more, have actually taken place at Donnelly Mirrors (Holland, Michigan), a company that produces over 90 percent of all the mirrors in U.S. automobiles. Not surprisingly, international interest in Donnelly's method of operation, based upon the familiar Scanlon Plan (familiar, that is, to many outside the hospitality industry), has resulted in so many requests for information on how the plan works that Donnelly now offers for a fee a two-day workshop in which supervisory and nonsupervisory employees tell the remarkable story of increased productivity.

How did the company come to achieve such spectacular results? According to the president, John Fenlon Donnelly, it wasn't easy. Addressing the Annual Conference of the Society of Personnel Administration, he gave the following explanation:

> About 20 years ago a customer, Herman Miller Furniture Company, installed the Scanlon Plan. I heard about it from one of our truck drivers who delivered mirrors there. The plan sounded like it was the answer to our problems of low productivity, poor quality, misdirected

shipments, and complex incentives. Everyone was to be involved in a single, simply calculated monthly productivity bonus ...

Our simple Scanlon Plan involved us in an ongoing experiment in trying to improve productivity by involving people in their total job. The Plan told us that people were the key to productivity, and that the company had to organize itself to enable people to exert their powers ... To make the Scanlon Plan work, to get genuine involvement of people, we had to make a choice between theories X and Y. This meant "did we trust people or not?" Trusting people was not to be something one did once in a while. It had to become a consistent part of the policy and practice of the company. Over the years we saw that people responded to the degree that we trusted them—trusted them with information, with responsibilities, with opportunities to decide.

A corollary of this experience was the discovery that managers can really manage and that THE ULTIMATE WEAPON OF MANAGEMENT IS NOT AUTHORITY, BUT TRUST ...[12]

What Is the Scanlon Plan?

In a nutshell, the Scanlon Plan creates an atmosphere in which managers and workers have an opportunity to lose their illusions about each other. Employees feel free to make suggestions, to criticize, to ask questions about problems that used to be considered "none of their business." Management, for its part, comes to see the value in sharing all of the company operating information with its employees and in benefiting from suggestions that reveal managerial weakness.

Agreed, there are some organizations that find it difficult, if not impossible, to share information, skills, and ideas which hitherto have been considered confidential. Others find it equally difficult to accept the proposition that executives, including corporate officers, may need to change their behavior, when in fact tradition suggests that it is exclusively the employees' behavior that needs changing.

How the Scanlon Plan Works

The mechanism that promotes the widest possible employee participation is a so-called "open suggestion system" and its associated committee structure. There are two kinds of committees.

Production Committee The departmental *production committee* is composed of one management representative and one or more elected nonsupervisory employees. This committee encourages employees to identify problems that interfere with increasing productivity. It meets every two to four weeks to receive and act upon suggestions for reducing costs or increasing output. The committee can put suggestions into effect immediately, reject suggestions with an appropriate explanation to the suggestor, hold suggestions pending further information or clarification, or forward suggestions to the screening committee.

Screening committee   This group is composed of major company executives and an equal or greater number of elected nonsupervisory representatives. It meets once a month just prior to the time of bonus payments (bonuses are given monthly). It acts on suggestions referred by the production committees, generally when large expenditures are required. It also assumes responsibility for taking action on all suggestions that are not put into effect by production committees, and further oversees the preparation of financial data supporting—or not supporting—the monthly bonuses due under the plan.

In the process of determining the feasibility of suggestions for productivity improvement, committee members necessarily energize the company communication network so that everyone shares the same information about production, productivity improvement, change, financial position, and bonuses.

As the participation system succeeds in generating suggestions and the company's performance improves, it follows that the participants are entitled to an *equity,* a fair share of the resultant rewards. Accordingly, the equity has two features: (1) a ratio, and (2) a bonus plan.

The ratio.   The ratio is usually the total payroll cost divided by total sales value of production, within a time frame that does not work to the disadvantage of either the employees or the company. This ratio becomes the standard by which payroll savings are measured. Suggestions to eliminate waste, to reduce the number of operations, to realign employee work groups, to introduce technological work changes, to discontinue a vice president's position recently vacated through retirement, etc.—all reduce employee costs and yield savings that are put into a bonus pool.

The bonus pool.   The bonus pool is distributed according to three requirements:

1. The company and the employees must receive fair shares of the pool.

2. A portion of the pool must be set aside each month to build a "rainy-day" reserve—i.e., for months when bonus "deficits" are incurred.

3. Each member of the company must receive a fair share of the pool.

The company may take from zero to 50 percent of the pool, while the employees' share ranges from 100 to 50 percent. Some companies take nothing from the pool in the belief that they already profit from more productive operations, a greater receptivity to change, and generally enhanced employee relations.

Calculation of Bonus in a Hotel Operation

The following illustration shows the calculation and distribution of a typical Scanlon Plan bonus pool, based upon a split of 20 percent for the company and 80 percent for the employees:

Methods of calculating a Scanlon Plan bonus, as applied to a hotel

1. Assume that in a twelve-month base period (i.e., one that reflects typical hotel operations) the payroll cost per dollar of sales was 40¢. This establishes a productivity norm or ratio of 40 percent against which to measure hotel performance each month.

2. Assume that in the month of June, sales amounted to $100,000
   (This is referred to under the Scanlon Plan as the *sales value of production.*)

3. If performance had been no better in June than the average for the twelve-month base period, the hotel payroll would have amounted to ..... $ 40,000

4. If, however, the actual payroll for the month of June figured out to...................... $ 30,000

5. This would mean improvement over the norm of $ 10,000
   his/her pay for the period (Item #9 divided by Item #4)................................

6. Set aside 20 percent of the bonus pool as a share to the company .... $ 2,000

7. Set aside 80 percent of the bonus pool as the share to the employees .... $ 8,000

8. Set aside 25 percent of the employees' share to cover future deficits (i.e., failures to achieve a bonus in any given month) .... $ 2,000

9. Pool for immediate distribution to employees .. $ 6,000

10. Bonus for each employee as a percentage of his/her pay for the period (Item #9 divided by Item #4) 20%

The June pay record for a typical employee would be reflected as follows:

Name	Monthly pay for June	Bonus %	Bonus $	Total pay
G. Jones	$600	40%	$120	$720

In a time like the last quarter of the twentieth century, when the pressures of higher payroll costs and productivity shortfalls have all but exhausted the traditional attempts of the hospitality industry to cope with them, the Scanlon Plan experience in other industries can no longer be ignored. While its details may vary from one company to another and its applicability to the hospitality industry has yet to be thoroughly tested, its spirit of total involvement and participation for everyone presents a compelling illustration of one way in which the quality of work life is continuously improving.[13]

GM Union–
Management
Program

In a January 1979 Quality of Work Life Conference sponsored by Wayne State University, General Motors Corporation President E.M. Estes and UAW Vice President Irving Bluestone praised the QWL concept as a tremendously exciting experiment in deciding how the workplace will be managed and how the worker can have a more effective voice in being master of the job rather than subservient to it.

> "We still have a lot to learn about working together toward our common objectives," said GM President Estes ... "It's easy to forget that most industrial traditions and practices were developed over 200 years ago.[14]

In one program at a GM assembly plant in Tarrytown, New York, workers were given training—on company time—in problem-solving techniques. They then participated in sessions aimed at resolving product quality problems in the plant. The result was a rather startling improvement in job satisfaction, quality of product, reduced absenteeism, labor turnover, and in constructive—instead of adversarial—relationships between management and workers.

When 40 senior corporate officers (including two presidents) of General Motors, Xerox, Weyerhauser, and Nabisco met in November 1977, for a two-day QWL conference, it was the experience of General Motors that engendered the most attention and praise. The program had been growing continuously since its inception in 1969 as a joint cooperative project with the University of Michigan. As of 1977, General Motors had a professional QWL staff of 21 people at headquarters, along with an additional staff of 140 trained QWL specialists dispersed throughout the GM organization (this included some 13,000 GM dealer networks). How had all this come about in such a relatively short time? General Motors contended that *real and lasting improvements* had come only through building *mutual trust* through joint union–management programs.

One way GM had built trust was by doing whatever it said it would do.

Another way that it asked union leaders what *they* would do in a problem situation. And GM counseled: "When you ask for their advice, you had better listen carefully. You don't have to agree with them, but you had better respect their opinions."

Still another way is the annual General Motors QWL conference. Once a year at company expense, GM brings together everyone who is working on QWL projects and lets them swap ideas and experiences.

In short, QWL is seen as a *process* and a way of management at General Motors. Speaking at a conference held on April 23, 1981, at the Northeast Labor Management Center, Delmar D. "Dutch" Landen, Director of Organizational Development for GM concluded:

> You have to look at QWL as a process where people like you and me create and nurture organizational principles and their corresponding

processes that will simultaneously meet human and social requirements ...

"Therefore, what you will see happen is that people will be coming together to work on a problem of their own choosing, and if you watch that process, you will see quality improve, attitudes improve, grievances go down, and absenteeism reduced because the process is the solution ... that is what the hell QWL is all about. That is why you must define QWL as a process."

From proceedings of The Fourth Ecology of Work Conference, Baltimore, November 4-6, 1981, under co-sponsorship of the NTL Institute and the OD Network; with permission (Volume IV, No. 7, August 1981 news letter, Northeast Labor Management Center, Belmont, MA).

Basic Criteria of QWL Program

In order for this and all other joint union–management cooperative programs to succeed in improving the quality of work life, United Auto Workers Vice President Irving Bluestone insists that two steps are required: First, there must be a relationship of *trust* between the union and management in day-to-day handling of each others' problems; second, experience with all types of QWL programs indicates that they must meet *eight basic criteria,* as follows:

1. The programs should be voluntary. Workers must have the free opportunity to decide whether to participate in the program or not. To order compulsion is to invite resistance and failure.

2. Workers should be assured that their participation in decision making will not erode their job security or that of fellow workers; that they will not be subject to "speed-up" by reason of it; and that the program will not violate workers' rights under the collective bargaining agreement.

3. Workers should experience genuinely that they are not simply adjuncts to the tool, but that their inclination to creativity, innovation and inventiveness plays a significant role in the production (or service) process.

4. Job functions should be engineered to fit individual workers; the current system is designed to make workers fit the job on the theory that this is a more efficient production system and that in any event economic gain is workers' only reason for working. This theory is wrong on both counts.

5. Workers should be assured the widest possible latitude of self-management, responsibility, and the opportunity to use their own "brain power." Gimmickry and manipulation of workers must not be employed.

6. The changes in job content, the added responsibility and involvement in decision making, should be accompanied by an effective reward system.

7. Workers should be able to foresee opportunities for growth in their work and for promotion.

8. Workers' roles in the business should enable them to relate to the product being produced, or the services being rendered, and to its meaning in society; in a broader sense, it should enable them as well to relate constructively to their role in society.[15]

Organizational Climate

In many ways the term, *"quality of work life"* seems to suggest that a solid *climate* of mutual respect and understanding is needed to pave the way for new approaches to old problems. Although each experiment in worker decision making is revealing in itself (as we have already seen), the thread that connects each of them—whether in a hotel or a factory—is what is commonly called the *climate* of the organization.

The simplest and most useful way to grasp the significance of the climate where we work is through the metaphor of the daily weather report. To this end, researchers Litwin and Wilson have pointed out some similarities to physical climate:

> More than two-thirds of the American population watch or listen to the daily weather report. We organize much of our lives around the next day's forecast. Each year, thousands of Americans move to other states, hoping to find the ideal geographic location. Clearly, we are interested in climate.
>
> Why? The climate in a specific location determines what activities are possible and what behavior is reasonable. A "good" climate provides conditions where we feel comfortable and can do what we want or need to do. Good and bad climates are relative—for example, a weatherman says that he cannot tell callers if the weather is "good" or "bad" until he finds out what activities they were planning. The effect of climate on our lifestyle and on our relations with each other is apparent to anyone who has traveled to New England during the winter or Texas during the summer!
>
> Just as we receive clues about activities and behavior from the physical climate ... we receive clues about what to say, how hard to and how to act from the climate of the organization ... When people refer to an organization as "a fun place to work," "tightly knit," or "a big bureaucracy," they are ... giving us clues about that organization's climate. Although organizational climate might appear to be an intangible quality, it does have a very real effect on the people ... in the organization ... climate dramatically affects not only the people but the performance and growth of the organization as a whole.[16]

Definition How climate affects performance and why it is important are questions that we shall seek to answer presently. First, however, we must turn our attention to what we mean by the term "organizational climate." According to Litwin and Wilson, it is best defined as:

> A set of *measurable properties* of the work environment based on the *collective perceptions* of the people who live and work in the environment, and *demonstrated to influence* their *motivation and behavior.*[17]

As you recall the experiences which you have had working in a particular hotel or restaurant, you can probably describe some characteristics of the organizational climate that colored those experiences and, indeed, affected your performance on the job.

For example, one of the authors of this text was engaged not long ago by an internationally known consulting firm to do a management study of the food and beverage operations of two major hotels. For the sake of convenience, these hotels will be referred to as Hotel X and Hotel Y. Both belonged to the same hotel company. Both were located in a large metropolitan area serving similar markets. Both were unionized. And each one had more than 700 rooms.

Hotel X

Hotel X ran under the classical decision-making school—i.e., there were many written manuals with a wide distribution. Decisionmaking was left to the respective department heads; however, it was very predictable because of the training, indoctrination, and policies all prospective managers received.

The areas of control and management information systems were quite extensive. There was an established food and beverage control department which computed daily food costs, beverage costs, and labor costs by revenue center. These numbers were compared to potential figures on a to-date basis. In addition, the control department checked bar stocks in the bars at least once per week, performed yield tests on food products, was in charge of the month-end inventories, and did commodity breakdown analysis on food and beverage purchases as well as sales. The end-of-the-month food and beverage controllers' report was usually in excess of 20 pages, complete with a profit-and-loss statement through all prime costs, with an editorial on excessive costs or changes from previous months' performances and a list of "additional" accomplishments by the department during the previous month.

A formal purchasing department did fairly technical market research on quantity products, including a limited amount of commodities (futures) research to predict pricing trends. All non–food and liquor-related items required an authorized purchase order and had to be purchased through the purchasing agent.

The management of each department was heavily oriented toward the decision-making school. For example, the restaurant manager was required to complete a weekly schedule for all service personnel. To aid in this process, he had a weekly forecast of expected number of covers (i.e., persons served) by dining room and meal period given to him by the food and beverage director each week before he made his schedule. He also had a staffing guide which told him exactly how many people to schedule in each job classification for any given number of forecased customers.

The management and employee relationships were in most cases peer-level relationships. Managers very rarely socialized with subordinates, and most department managers were addressed by their "sir" names.

Hotel Y

The management style, control and information system, peer relationships, and departmentalization of Hotel Y was in almost complete contrast to that of Hotel X. The hotel had one operations manual (in addition to the corporate employee manual) which was twelve pages long and had no distribution. The only copy was in the general manager's office.

There was no food and beverage control department and consequently very little distribution of written information. Cost information such as food costs, liquor costs, and labor costs was generated on a monthly basis. Managers were calculating certain costs and maintaining certain information, but in most cases it was by choice, because it aided in the management of their own particular department and had almost no distribution.

There was no formal purchasing department. The executive chef and storeroom manager purchased all food-stuffs, the beverage manager purchased the liquor, the housekeeper purchased the guest supplies, and so on.

Comparison The manager of each department in Hotel Y was laden with responsibility and authority. There was a marked contrast in the scheduling of personnel in Hotel X by the restaurant manager as compared to that in Hotel Y. In Hotel Y, the restaurant manager received a weekly forecast of room occupancy, banquets, and any banquet or group that did not have a scheduled food function. The manager then had to take this information, determine how many people would enter the restaurant during any given meal period as opposed to one of the three or four other restaurants within the hotel, and then determine how many employees to schedule. (Any staffing guides were generated by the department head for his or her own use.)

A manager in Hotel Y was evaluated by the results he or she produced, and success or failure was very much a part of an individual's own ability. In Hotel X, however, emphasis was placed in large part on adherence to policy and predictability. Certainly in both hotels, both results and policy were important, but the emphasis was markedly different.

Social relationships in Hotel Y often transcended management levels. Most department managers were on a first-name basis and often saw each other socially.

—Question: Would you prefer to work at Hotel X or Hotel Y? Why?

Which system was best? When most people are asked the question, Which hotel do you think was the most consistently profitable, Hotel X or Hotel Y? they usually guess wrong. It was Hotel Y that invariably turned in the best "bottom-line" performance.

On the other hand, when college students are asked the question, Which one of the hotels would you like to go to work for immediately after graduation? they generally opt for Hotel X because of the "security blanket" effect of elaborate reports and controls.

Clearly, not every worker is amenable to participation in a *Theory Y* workplace. Some people do prefer an autocratic climate in which to work, even though it may mean that jobs are more robotized, monotonous, and uncreative. Equally, others prefer a climate that provides them with opportunity to utilize their innate talents to create and to innovate. Traditionally in the hospitality industry, these issues have been ignored. But the time may be coming—if indeed it is not already here—when employees will no longer accept lack of concern for inflexibility in the workplace or lack of concern for management's climate of indifference to workers feelings of being underutilized.

Brighton Fish Pier Restaurants

An illustration of a chainwide climate, primarily negative in character, may be seen in the following excerpts from questionnaires sent to employees of the "Brighton Fish Pier" restaurants and quoted in Wyckoff and Sasser's book *The Chain-Restaurant Industry:*

San Francisco: Unit Built in 1970 "No concern shown for employees as individuals."

"They have fired or transferred all the people who really cared about people."

"I can't really complain about the pay or benefits, it's a good job."

"They have brought in some tough managers to 'clean up' the operation ... they are just going to make it worse."

"People are punished if they step out of line ... they get the bad assignments."

Memphis: Unit Built in 1974 "They keep sending in new managers. Some are better than others. The current one just wants to make himself look good."

"Managers are not really competent ... they make some dumb moves to try to look like heroes."

"They are not interested in us as individuals."

"This is a good job ... just wish this manager would move to another restaurant."

Boston: Unit Built in 1975 "We are too controlled by headquarters ... we can't make a move without their permission."

"Company has really lost touch with the people ... this questionnair is a good example of insensitivity. Why don't you come and ask me these questions in person?"

"Really appreciate the opportunity to express my opinions. I hope you read this and do something to help."

"The company sets standards ... that's what they get—standard performance. They are missing out on the imagination we all have."

"My manager spends all his time filling out forms in his office. When he comes out he dumps on us!"

"The manager wants us to sell, sell, sell ... I think I'm a waiter, not a salesman."

"This has been a really good job for me. I appreciate the chance to make some real money while I've been going to school. I hope Pier does well."

Jacksonville: Unit Built in 1976 "Had some troubles after start-up. The present manager really knows how to help people."

"This place is really starting to click ... I am too."

"Business is picking up ... so is the tip pool. We are really selling well. The more business we have, the better the tips!"

Denver: Unit Built in 1974 "I am very sensitive to how my manager treats me. The present manager knows how to keep my spirits up. It shows in how I handle my customers."

"This manager spends more time on the floor talking to customers."

Phoenix: Unit Built in 1975 "They say the customer is always right ... but don't let them catch you acting that way. Really, they mean Pier is always right."

"They push us for performance all the time. I think it turns off the customer. Is this what they really want?"

"I have worked in several Pier restaurants. Some managers are much better than others. This one is a good technical manager, she just forgets about people at times."

"The managers really seem to be under pressure."

"I know we have one of the best margins in the Pier group ... so what!"

Oxnard: Unit Built in 1971 "This place is amazing. We are always doing something new. I've worked here two years. I think I would like to get a shot at management."

"Tom (the manager) is a creative guy. He knows how to help people. Thanks for the questionnaire, but don't change anything."[18]

Interestingly enough, based upon extensive research upon the relationship between organizational *climate* and "bottom-line" performance—in banks, airlines, and restaurants—Litwin finds that there is, in fact, an *organizational climate system* (as represented in Figure 3–5). Most importantly, within that system is a *profile* (center of Figure 3–5) which is composed of six dimensions—clarity, commitment, standards, responsibility, recognition, and teamwork—graphically portrayed in Figure 3–6. In the next section we will discuss these dimensions in detail.

Performance Dimensions

Clarity

This dimension can be defined as the individual's sense of understanding an organization's goals and policies and of being clear about his or her job; the feeling that things are organized and run smoothly as opposed to being confused.

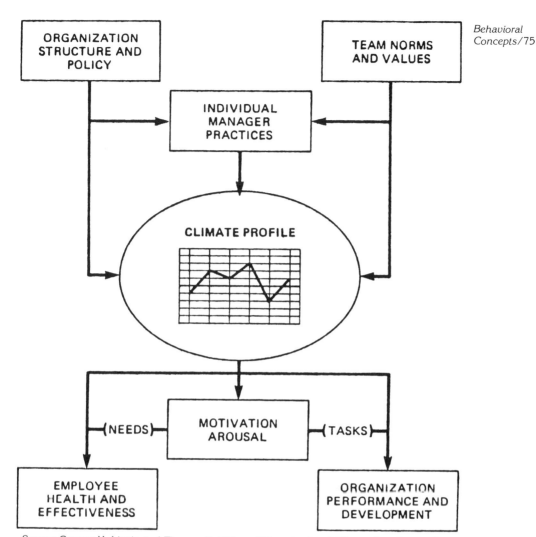

Source: George H. Litwin and Thomas B. Wilson, "Organizational Climate Is a System," Inforum, Summer 1978

Figure 3–5 Organizational Climate System

Understanding what is expected is a strong clue to clarity. *For example:* Under the heading, "You and the Hotel Guest," housekeeping employees of the Hawaii Hotel and Restaurant Industry learn what is expected of their personal appearance and grooming from these clear-cut instructions, which are received during regular training sessions conducted under the joint auspices of the industry and union:

Your grooming is important to three persons:
1. Your grooming is important to YOUR Employer because:
    Your appearance represents the hotel;
    Your appearance shows whether you care about the way things look.

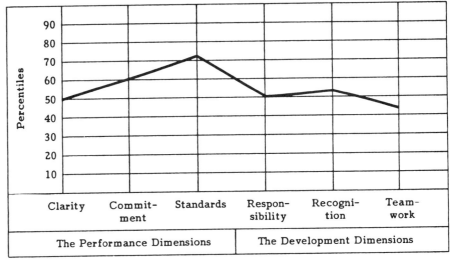

Source: Litwin and Wilson

Figure 3–6 Sample Climate Profile Chart

2. Your grooming is important to THE TOURIST because:

Your appearance will suggest the standards you have for the cleanliness and comfort of his accommodations.

Your appearance helps him understand what the people of Hawaii are like.

3. Your grooming is important to YOURSELF because:

You feel more self-confident when you know you're looking your best.

When you're well-groomed you are more likely to have a sense of pride in your work.[19]

Another clue is evidence of planned organized activity. *For example:* General managers of hotels operated by the Hyatt Corporation are judged to have engaged regularly in planned organized activities if they successfully carry out the following instructions:

A. Get in your office before your department heads.

B. Organize your administrative day.

C. Read your correspondence.
   1. Disseminate it properly.
   2. Schedule answers return and follow up.
   3. Check authenticity.
   4. Answer your superior's inquiries promptly.

D. Attend the meeting of the day (sales, forecast, department heads, food and beverage, credit, and so forth).

E. See your department heads daily—10 minutes scheduled session.
   1. Executive assistant—front

    2. Food & beverage manager

    3. Sales manager

F. Inspect hotel at least five times a day for:
    1. Cleanliness
    2. Repairs and maintenance
    3. Service
    4. Courtesy
    5. General
    6. Bar and dining room
    7. Signs and promotional material

G. Talk daily with your auditor about:
    1. Daily report—meaning
    2. Food and beverage report
    3. Forecast
    4. Repairs and maintenance
    5. Payroll
    6. Accounts receivable
    7. Cash position

H. Check guest areas for personal touch:
    1. Dining room
    2. Bar
    3. Lobby
    4. Front door
    5. Reception, reservations
    6. Credit

I. Take adequate afternoon rest.
    1. Ready for evening
    2. Entertain:
        a) Local Government officials
        b) House V.I.P. (including commercial account)

J. Participate in civic affairs.

K. Check advertising and public relations.

L. Talk to sales manager and discuss call reports.

M. Talk to Personnel Director about:
    1. Training
    2. Control
    3. Sickness reports

N. Spend 30 minutes for new ideas.
    1. Turning dead areas into paying space

O. Make sure your wife and children are reasonably happy.

P. Check your clothes and appearance.

Q. Make sure your hotel entertainment is first class and producing results.

R. Have you developed any new executives for the organization?
    1. Why not?
    2. Start today.
    3. How (training)?

S. Write a sales letter:
    1. Local
    2. Area
    3. International
T. Have you checked your utility cost?
    1. Engineer's reports
    2. Personal observation
U. Have you sent another Hyatt House any business?
V. Have you closed the door to your office?
W. Have you been pleasant and yet efficient?
X. Have you thought about your company advancement?
Y. Have you listened to a problem and offered solutions?
Z. Have you gone to bed early ... enough?

If you haven't, you aren't cutting the mustard![20]

A further clue to clarity is smooth information flow. *For example:* Hospitality establishments provide information to members in a variety of ways, including via computers, oral reports and instructions, memos, policy statements, reward and punishment systems, sales forecasts, and work schedules. An information flow that transfers meaning and understanding from an information *source* to an information *receiver* in a situational context that allows for good receiver-to-sender feedback is the result of a smooth communication process. And few would deny that effective communication is the lifeblood of any organization.

Commitment

This dimension involves the feeling of continuing commitment to goal achievement related to acceptance and realism of goals, involvement in goal setting, and continuing evaluation of performance against goals. Commitment involves

○ Regular goal setting and review meetings
○ Goals that can be considered meaningful and realistic
○ Personal commitment to achievement of goals

Examples of commitment to goal achievement abound in the hotel and restaurant field. A successful housekeeper in a southern hotel has achieved lower turnover rates by paying a bonus for each month that a maid or houseman is neither absent nor tardy. A chain restaurant system gives its employees merit points for continuous service, punctuality, and attendance. These merit points can be exchanged for a wide variety of well-known products at wholesale prices. On the other hand, the general managers of one major hotel chain are known to be evaluated for salary increases and/or promotions primarily on the basis of their long hours of work—as perceived by their superiors.

In a widely-publicized address before the American Marketing

Association, the former president of the Plaza Hotel in New York told of instituting an "Executive Sales Call" program at the hotel in order to make sales goals more meaningful:

> About forty of our top and middle management executives, ones who traditionally don't ever see a prospect, are assigned days on which they make outside calls with our regular salesmen. People like our Personnel Director, our Executive Housekeeper, our Purchasing Director, and our General Manager are on the street making calls. Our prospects seem to like it. Our salesmen love it. And our non-sales "salesmen" are getting an education about what's going on in the real world—the one outside the hotel.[21]

Moreover, in its endeavor to build commitment to such realistic goals, the Plaza borrowed from its Fifth Avenue neighboring retailers the concept of a "bridal consultant" to replace the job of the traditional banquet manager:

> Banquet Managers sell wedding dinners. Bridal Consultants sell strawberries—everything from the bridal shower, the pictures, the ceremony, the reception, the wedding night, to the honeymoon to the first anniversary.[22]

Standards

This performance dimension has to do with the emphasis that management puts on setting high standards of performance; it involves a feeling of

- ○ Pressure to improve one's performance
- ○ Pride in doing a good job
- ○ Tough, challenging goals set by management

For example: A recent Harvard Business School case study of the Imperial Hotel (Albany, New York) found the manager, William Fontano, to be a person who insists on high standards of performance:

> While Mr. Fontano praises excellence in performance he does not accept complacency. He refers to his staff as his "high-salaried employees—presumably to remind them to maintain compatibility between payroll and productivity.
>
> He is highly conscious of the "service" capacity of his operation and believes there is no room for temperamental personalities in hotel work. (He carefully schedules a team of even-tempered personalities for high-abuse periods such as the night shift at the desk.) ...[23]

At the same hotel a waitress reported her feeling of pride in doing her job this way:

> I have worked at union hotels, but this place is really great. I love it here ... I like to help new girls learn their jobs. ... We are a happy group. People often come in early because they like their jobs. We

often have coffee together. Our managers are just great. Mr. Fontano, our manager, is the man we go to when we think we are not getting a square deal from the others. ... This is why I like Mr. Fontano. He knows the way things should be done.[24]

Development
Dimensions

Responsibility

Responsibility is the feeling of personal obligation regarding one's work. In the workplace it involves a sense of autonomy stemming from real delegation, with encouragement for individual initiative. One who has a good feeling of responsibility has

  ○ Sense of independence—a feeling that individual judgment is trusted

  ○ The expectation that individual problem-solving is possible

  ○ The ability to take increased responsibility

For example: A low sense of responsibility will be created in a hotel sales department in which the sales manager insists on not only reviewing with each sales person how to "pitch" each client he or she is to visit that day, but who frequently, during joint sales calls, steps in to close the order rather than letting the salesperson do it.

On the other hand, consider the encouragement a Dobbs House regional manager experienced following an employee's promotion to vice president and general manager:

> How did Jerry gain our confidence and get control? Well, it was a very gradual thing. ... He was here a whole year before he really did. First of all, he understands people. He's beautiful at understanding the needs of each person who works for him. He was able very quickly to determine which people could do things and how well they could do them. He knew what everyone could do and got them working on those things. And he did it in a manner that forced us to take responsibility. For example, if I would ask a question, "How come I can't pay a manager more or fix an air conditioner?" he would say, "Well, why don't you? Why do you ask me what you can do?" Very gradually he put in everybody's minds that the real reason that things were not getting done was because no one had the initiative to do them. Everybody was waiting for someone else to tell them what to do.[25]

Recognition

The dimension of recognition in the organizational climate assumes that people are more likely to be acknowledged and rewarded for doing good work, than criticized for poor performance. In such a climate

  ○ Rewards and recognition outweigh threats and criticism

  ○ A promotion system exists which helps the best person rise to the top

○ Rewards are related to excellence of performance

For example: Recognition will be low in a restaurant chain when the chairman's brother-in-law, known for his alcoholism and general incompetence, is named president in preference to others who have demonstrated an outstanding track record as chain restaurant executives.

Conversely, it will be high among the lower-level members of another restaurant chain where neither nepotism nor seniority governs promotions—where instead, promotions are regarded as fair, are based on merit, and are promptly announced and explained so that all may understand the appropriateness of such moves.

Teamwork

Teamwork involves a feeling of belonging; it is present in an organization characterized by cohesion, mutual warmth and support, trust, and pride. In such a climate there is evidence of

○ Mutual warmth and support
○ People trusting and respecting each other
○ Feelings of personal loyalty and of belonging to the organization

For example: Teamwork will be apparent in a hotel or restaurant operating under a Scanlon Plan wherein management and employees trust and respect each other, and back each other up when the going gets tough. It will also be good in a hotel or restaurant in which there is a rule that the dishwasher can go home as soon as he finishes his work, and get paid for a full day—but his work isn't considered finished until all the other dishwashers are through also. Experience indicates that this policy in some cases provides extraordinary incentive to cooperation—especially on days before holidays when there is an extra incentive to work fast. The reward is directly related to the team's excellence of performance.

Feedback from Climate Profile results Based upon a decade of research experience in measuring organizational climate on the basis of these six foregoing dimensions, Litwin and his associates have established national norm tables from which they interpret and tabulate responses to the results of a Climate Analysis. The result is a Climate Profile, shown in Figure 3–6 as a graphic representation of organization climate scores.

When used as a feedback device to help managers identify and improve climate conditions necessary for sustained high performance, the graphic profile is most persuasive.

Figure 3–7 illustrates a graphic survey that was completed for an international airline. Included in the survey were the sales and airport services units, the data-processing operation, corporate accounting, industrial engineering, reservations, cargo marketing, ramp, and dining and

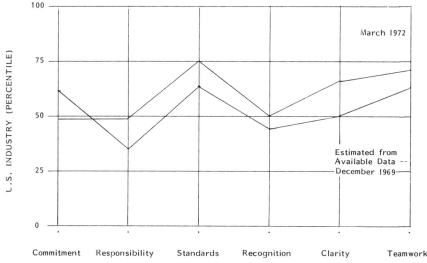

Figure 3-7 Overall Organizational Climate

commissary services. The figure shows that organizational climate improved in the period from December 1969, when the initial survey was made, to March 1972, when a follow-up climate study was completed by the airline's own industrial relations staff.

Summary   In this chapter we have looked at people in the workplace in terms of resource and opportunity rather than as tools to be manipulated, costs to be minimized, and threats to be overcome. This new emphasis upon workers as decision-makers, not as decision-takers, has given rise to an area of corporate activity and concern encompassed by the phrase "quality of work life."

We have seen that the QWL concept appears in many guises—as participative management in one Scandinavian and two French hotels; as the Scanlon Plan in a number of industrial firms in the United States; and as formal QWL programs in a number of America's largest corporations.

With its continuing emphasis upon the necessity for a *climate* of mutual respect and understanding, QWL has also come to embrace the concept of *organizational climate*. Research has demonstrated that the climate of the workplace has an important effect upon the people who work in an organization; and that by changing the climate, both individual and organizational performance can be improved.

Questions
for
Discussion
1. You are the general manager for a 300-room hotel, the owner of which insists that payroll costs, now running at 42 percent of gross revenue, are entirely too high. What QWL means would you use to obtain the results the owner wants? Explain.

2. Why do you think that the hospitality industry in the United States may find it difficult to follow the lead of other major industries in establishing QWL programs?

3. What is a Scanlon Plan?

4. Define the six dimensions that are reflected in a Climate Profile. Discuss these dimensions in terms of your own experience in a hotel or restaurant organization in which you have worked.

5. In your opinion, is the QWL concept just another passing fad—a soft, "do-gooder" approach to working? Or is it a potentially permanent, contemporary method that can provide viable, sound, operational improvements in hospitality industries? Explain.

Key Terms

○ BONUS POOL
○ CLARITY
○ CLIMATE PROFILE
○ COMMITMENT
○ DECISION SHARING
○ DEVELOPMENT DIMENSIONS
○ EMPLOYEE PARTICIPATION
○ ORGANIZATIONAL CLIMATE
○ PERFORMANCE DIMENSIONS
○ PRODUCTION COMMITTEE
○ QUALITY OF WORK LIFE
○ RATIO
○ RECOGNITION
○ RESPONSIBILITY
○ SCANLON PLAN
○ SCREENING COMMITTEE
○ STANDARDS
○ TEAMWORK

A Case Study: Dishing It Out at Ho-Jo's*

In 1925, the late Howard Johnson decided to sell a different kind of ice cream—made from the true vanilla bean instead of synthetic vanilla—in a drugstore in Wollaston, Massachusetts; it was this ice cream that was ultimately expanded into the Twenty-eight Famous Flavors.

In 1972, the total sales of the Howard Johnson Company came to $324,219,000. The net income, or profit, was $19,879,000. In less than fifty years of existence the Company, which is now directed by Howard Johnson, Jr. and worth $175,674,000, has expanded to include 871 Howard Johnson restaurants strategically located on most major highways in forty states, twenty-nine Red Coach Grills, and ten Ground Round sandwich places. The Company also licenses 438 motor lodges, processes and distributes frozen and packaged foods,

*By Nancy Perry, reprinted by permission from *The Progressive,* 409 East Main St., Madison, Wisconsin 53703. © 1973, The Progressive, Inc.

and licenses a line of soft drink beverages in six flavors. It has fulfilled the American Dream.

How did Howard Johnson do it?

What he did was franchise the complete format of the organization, the franchise buyers providing the money that would market the product, and the name, of Howard Johnson. Then, between 1950 and 1960, Johnson bought back most of the franchises; he claimed the franchise holders failed to maintain the Howard Johnson standard. Now, there are 572 restaurants operated by the Company and 229 run by licensees. The Massachusetts Turnpike, where I worked off and on under the orange roof for five years, is one of the highways whose food concessions the Company controls by monopoly. Generally these monopolies are secured by public bidding.

With the restaurants on the road, the Burger Brain devised a scheme to get his travelers in and out fast: pre-cooked, pre-portioned, frozen foods. They could make a fast stop and he could make a fast fortune. No more talent needed to cook, only the ability to warm up food. In this way, the minimum wage could be paid, and when the cook has had it, he can be replaced in a matter of hours. Even machines cannot be replaced so easily.

It was great for the Company, but not for the customer. Jacob Rosenthal, director of the Culinary Institute of America, sees "little hope for the toll road, politically franchised eating and watering holes because there is no incentive to do better." Yet the travelers—particularly the summer tourist—are lured by the orange glow on the horizon, a signal that the Host of the Highways is waiting to welcome them with the Flavor of America. The tourist may not know what he's doing, why he didn't stay home, why he worked so hard all year to spend his vacation in a waiting line of ice-cream-dripping kids, but there's one thing he does know—Howard Johnson. I know Howard Johnson too, but from the other side of the counter.

My early recollections as a Howard Johnson waitress are a whirl of tired feet, white clad and running, while the left half of my body slanted toward the formation of a right angle under the weight of dishes and garbage balanced on my left arm. This load I would transport, at a fast sprint, to the Adamation machine (Ho-Jo terminology for the dishwasher).

A trainee was required to survive a three-day slave period under the eye of an experienced waitress. During this time, the trainee would do all the work for the waitress, who would dart swiftly to the table to pocket the tip after the customer had left and then retire for a cigarette while the trainee bussed the table. Three days of high speed indoctrination into the system. If you didn't cry during this period, you never would. If you didn't quit, you had made it. You were officially a Ho-Jo girl with your own order book and a number to replace your name.

To be a Ho-Jo manager involves giving up all identity as a person—you become the invisible, intangible, impenetrable Company, whose job consists of maintaining the Ho-Jo image: neatly set tables, clean ash trays, an underliner for every bowl. Parsley for all food; the customers never eat it, but it makes the food look attractive. The dining room has to be kept spotless. The waitress must be standing and smiling. The music is soft. A quiet comfortable atmosphere to relax and contemplate the shiny menu with its colorful Ho-Jo classics after a hectic day of traveling. At least until it gets busy. Then you get the bodies in and get them out.

No matter how busy it was or how much a waitress wanted to dash quickly into the kitchen for that second cup of coffee for a customer (it was free, but coffee pots are not allowed in the dining room under the assumption that it encourages a second cup) no one dares make the trip without stopping first to bus a table. The day manager, with those hard glittering eyes behind the party glasses, makes sure every table is cleaned the minute a customer stands up. Bus boys are an unheard of expense in the Ho-Jo budget.

I mean, what are waitresses for? They scrub, they stock supplies, they sweep, they wash windows, they water plants, they wipe silverware and wash walls and mirrors and tables and booths and remove the drooled out cookie spit from high chairs, they separate the tiny sprigs of parsley, they cut lemons, they vacuum (the porter was let go to save money), they make up table settings, they load the dishwasher, they serve food and smile at incessant complaints, they run, they cry, they quit.

For all this Ho-Jo paid me the huge sum of $1.11 [1973] an hour. However, a busy summer's day grosses a waitress as much as $20 in tips. I have made $30 a day. But even this amount of money is not enough to prevent a rapid turnover of employes. In winter, minus the rush periods, tips fall as low as $5 a day.

The management is extremely strict about food portions. The hot food comes pre-portioned (pre-cooked, too, but a ladle of hot gravy is as good as an oven and much quicker). The waitress must prepare the appetizers, salads, garnishes, and desserts. Only three potato chips per sandwich are allowed. The salad includes one small scoop of dressing dribbled over one slice of tomato, one slice of onion, and some wilted greens expertly fluffed up to fill the bowl. Each lemon must be carefully cut into sixteen slices, and the customer who is still laughing when he informs you that you must have forgotten the banana in his banana split is not alone. Although the menu advertised a banana split for ninety-five cents, I never saw a banana in that restaurant in five years.

Naive about Ho-Jo policies at first, I once used the alleged big scoop when making an ice cream float. When "spoken to" about my extreme behavior, I committed the Unpardonable Sin. I tossed the root beer coated, foaming vanilla ice cream into the garbage bucket. Within a matter of minutes, the manager was behind me, and I was diving into the garbage bucket to retrieve what I had innocently believed to be unsalvageable. It was returned to the ice cream bin to await an order from an unsuspecting customer.

The dress code is meant to sustain the Ho-Jo symbol. At the beginning of her employment, the waitress is issued one uniform—a baggy nondescript housedress bunched at the waist with an apron and hanging below the knee. She is also granted one sidetowel. If a towel is lost, a waitress pays ten cents to replace it. White shoes and hairnets the waitress must furnish for herself. Every night the dress, the apron, and the sidetowel must be washed, ironed, starched, and repaired if necessary, and the shoes polished. All this must be done by the waitress.

The Massachusetts Housekeeping Occupations Administrative Regulations state that "the term uniform includes all special wearing apparel whatsoever which is worn by the employe as a condition of employment. Uniforms which employes may be required to wear shall be furnished by the employer. The employer shall launder, clean, and maintain such uniforms without cost to the employe." Ho-Jo got around this triviality by paying the waitress to repair and launder her own uniforms. Checking a back pay stub, I discovered I had been allotted $1.24 to cover the week's expenses.

Learning to be frugal (referred to by the help as "cheap") is the password to Ho-Jo success. The cooks are all hired under the condition that since starting pay is so generous (roughly $3.50 an hour) there will be no overtime pay. One cook I knew worked from four p.m. Tuesday until six a.m. Wednesday every week, and I remember instances of the management's calling him in at eleven a.m. Tuesday to work straight through to Wednesday morning because they needed the help. (They always needed the help.)

One time I worked eight days in a row without a day off. Another time I worked twenty hours straight. There was no overtime pay, except for Christmas. It wasn't like chattel slavery or prison, except for its being unloved. It wasn't humane, but one could always quit. Most girls do. During the month of July last summer, the Ho-Jo restaurant where I worked hired and lost approximately *seventy* waitresses.

A few years ago, on Easter, a blizzard immobilized the Massachusetts Turnpike. Those stuck walked miles to the only place of warmth and food: the Host of the Highways. All the managers left except one. He stationed himself by the door to wave the customers to the back of the waiting line. That was all he did. In a few hours he left, exhausted.

That left four waitresses, one cook, every booth full of sleeping bodies, and a waiting line in which weary travelers stood three hours to get a cup of coffee. Those stranded were patient and sympathetic. "Take your time, we've got all night." We developed that spirit of cooperation that any sort of crisis seems to bring out in people. The line was moving slowly, though, and the cook decided we would be able to feed more people if we served only toast, English Muffins, and cold sandwiches. The line began to move.

At eight a.m. Party Glasses arrived to survey the scene. The sparkling dining room was a clutter of sleeping bodies, dirty cups, discarded food, and uncontrolled confusion. What had happened to the tidy Ho-Jo image? That was her concern. She was Company and she was furious. Those people had to be cleared out and the dining room cleaned for the next shift. That was our thanks for the work we had done all night. When she learned we had stopped serving eggs and hamburgers, she was appalled—did we realize what that decision had cost Howard Johnson's?

Rest was never a reward for devoted service. When a lull occurred during the frantic eight-and-one-half-hour day, you were allowed to collapse for thirty minutes in the Back Room. If it got busy during your break, you were bustled back early.

The Back Room had an interesting history during the five years I observed its metamorphoses. The first phase included sitting on a Ho-Jo Cola supply can and watching the mass of flies over-populating the fly paper dangling down over the center of the garbage and ash covered table.

Later—after a visit from an official looking person rumored to be from the Board of Health—the table was moved into another room where the walls were painted a horrendous shade of ladies-room-pink, but at least supplied with a few chairs. This room was located away from any source of fresh air during the summer heat. In the winter, the single heater available was kept in the office. One day last winter the temperature in the Back Room dropped to thirty-four degrees. It had felt that cold every day, but I don't think anyone had bothered to read the thermometer before.

You ate your meal in the Back Room. For fifty cents a waitress could order anything on the menu under two dollars (as long as you could order and eat it in a half hour). Of course, there were a few exceptions. Excluded from the waitresses' choices were onion rings, salad, chocolate milk, any dessert except ice cream (smallest size), a large anything, onions on your hot dog, or cones with your ice cream.

The decor of the Back Room walls consisted of posted appeals to employes. I remember one which sobbed: "It costs us at Howard Johnson's 15.6 cents to serve a cup of coffee." (Included in this estimate were replacement of cups, maintenance of facilities, electricity, heat, salaries, and ingredients, with the exact tenth of a per cent of cost listed beside each item.) "Yet the Company only charges twenty cents for this same cup of coffee, making just 4.4 cents profit per cup. Would the waitresses please suggest dessert or we'll all *starve.*"

In one average day in the dining room, working with five other waitresses, I alone sold fifty-two cups of coffee. At 4.4 cents profit per cup, that's $2.28 in one day. Or $830 in one year. One waitress, one shift, in the dining room. (Most of the coffee sold is at the counter, where there is a faster turnover.)

And Howard Johnson can't afford to give me a cone with my ice cream?

Some customers insist on ordering their meats cooked to specification. When two steaks arrive at a table, one ordered medium and one rare, only the cook and the waitress know that there is no difference. The customer sees the shiny plastic toothpick stuck in one of the steaks. When the waitress holds it up and asks, "Who has the rare?" he is satisfied.

The worst aspect of the job was trying to avoid the customer's eyes as I slid the check on the table and mumbled, "Thank you." The waitresses always received the brunt of the complaints—the glares, the infuriation, the demands that couldn't be met. Yet we had been trained that the customer was always right, so we listened. Little did

Howard Johnson realize how right the customer usually was.

"But I ordered the quarter pounder with potato chips."

"That's it."

"Three potato chips?"

"Regulation. We have to pay if we serve more."

"There's some sort of scum in my coffee."

"It's the cream."

"Does it always do that?"

"Most of the time."

"There's a dead fly in the bottom of the fruit cup I just ate."

"I didn't see that one. Sorry."

"Can I still get breakfast?"

"We serve it all day."

"Can I see a menu?"

"No. Customers are only allowed to look at the menu that is being used now."

"That's ridiculous."

"Yes, sir."

So why do they come in such droves? And keep coming?

The Company's freeway monopoly makes it the most convenient place to stop; its name, the safest. Clean and comfortable with a little bit of class thrown in as a side order. The customer knows what to expect. He might complain when he gets it, but the security in knowing is more reassuring than venturing off the highway into unknown cuisine. Who knows what horrors await you there? At least the Ho-Jo menu is standard throughout the country.

Only the old and the romantic still extol the ice cream parlor of the past. All that remains now to recall that past is the orange roof and the Twenty-eight Famous Flavors. (There were never twenty-eight in stock. In the winter, there were perhaps sixteen.) The clean, bright Ho-Jo image; never the fear that you might have to gulp down your dinner in some greasy, low class establishment. Poor man's prices with the privileges of plush living: cushioned booths, deep carpets, soft music, a soft lamp on each table, the colorful menu. Poor man's candlelight dining.

If you're in a hurry, who tastes the food?

$324,219,000 at the drop of a name.

Smile. "Thank you. Come again."

Case Questions

1. What are the unusual features of this case?

2. What would you say is "going on" in this case?

3. What would you have done had you been in Nancy Perry's position?

4. Which of the QWL concepts we have been discussing in this chapter would be effective in coping with the Ho-Jo's situation as described?

5. If you were the newly appointed manager of this Ho-Jo's, how would you go about securing the involvement, commitment, trust, and cooperation of *all* the people in the workplace?

A Case Study: A Hamburger and Fries for Joe*

Can one use a Scanlon Plan in a fast-food restaurant that generates $100,000 in annual sales? I ask this because it seems to me that the larger the potential productivity bonus, the greater the chance the plan will be effective. (How motivated would an employee be if he never received a bonus? I don't think the plan would last too long if this happened.) $100,000 annual sales would be considered low volume for most franchised fast-food restaurants. I would think that if the potential payoff was sufficiently large in this size operation, it would certainly be large enough in an operation with a higher sales volume. So let us set up a sample Scanlon Plan for a hypothetical independent fast-food restaurant and a hypothetical chain of fast-food restaurants in Lansing and see how large of a productivity bonus a low-volume store would be able to pay out. After the plan is set up we can then calculate the bonus payment. In setting this plan up we will use the following step-by-step approach ...

Step 1—To determine what ratios to total sales we will use as norms, I suggest we use the average ratios for the Lansing area restaurants of the chain. After some study the standard controllable cost ratios for the Lansing area were calculated to be the following:

	Lansing average %	National average %
Food cost	38.81	37.00
Payroll*	15.51	14.00
Payroll taxes*	1.24	1.05
Other payroll*	.11	--
Supplies (paper)	6.01	5.00
Supplies (office)	.04	.03
Uniforms and laundry	1.00	.75
Total controllable		
Cost percentage	62.72	57.83
	16.86	15.05

*Total payroll cost

We will assume that the productivity norm is 16.86 percent of sales.
Step 2—Assume that the sharing ratio agreed to is 75–25.
Step 3—Assume it is done.
Step 4—It is decided that the reserve fund is 25%.
Steps 5–8—Assume they are carried out.
Three additional assumptions would be that the restaurant's

*Excerpted from unpublished term paper prepared in 1972 by Gary M. Shingler, an MBA candidate at Michigan State University.

operating calendar consists of 13 four-week periods and that the sales for the current period are $7,700 and the area's productivity norm matched the national productivity norm this period. How much of a bonus would be given out? The calculations for the independent restaurant are as follows:

Calculation of bonus

	Low sales volume	High sales volume
A. Total sales	$ 7,700	$ 8,700
B. Target payroll (16.86) (total sales)	1,298	1,467
C. Actual payroll Low vol. = (15.05) (total sales) High vol. = (13.32) (total sales)	1,159	1,159
D. Improvements over norm Bonus pool	139	308
E. Reserve (.25) (improvements over norm)	35	77
F. Amount to be immediately distributed	104	231
G. Company's share (.25) (amount to be distributed)	26	58
I. Employee's share (.75) (amount to be distributed)	78	173
J. Employee's share as % of total payroll	6.7%	14.9%

A 6.7 per cent (J) bonus does not sound that exciting, but for an employee at the $1.70 per hour rate,* it would mean that he earned the equivalent of $1.8139 per hour for the period. Also, keep in mind that there are at least two possibilities for the bonus to be larger. The first concerns the reserve that is set up to "protect" the restaurant from those periods in which total payroll might be above the prescribed norm. If there is any money left in this reserve at the end of the year it is distributed among the employees. If there are no periods that have a negative "D" (improvement over norm) then the total bonus for the period could be considered to be the original "I" (employee's share) plus the "E" (reserve) for that month. The second possibility is having a higher sales volume with no increase in total payroll. Since I calculated our original "standard controllable cost ratios" from some old financial statements of mine, I know that with the total man-hours used to calculate the period payroll costs (644 man-hours) sales could have gone up $1,000 to $1,300 before I would have had to add addi-

Authors' note: It should be borne in mind that the wage scale as stated in this case reflects actual wages being paid in the Lansing area in 1972. Even though today's wage scales—and presumably today's restaurant sales—are much higher, one would expect the ratios to be substantially the same.

tional employees to the schedule. This would lower the actual payroll percentage while raising the total dollar target payroll giving a higher "B".

Table 1 demonstrates the difference in bonus payment range that the two possibilities would give.

Table 1. Possible range in bonus

| | Low volume | | High volume | |
	% of payroll	Cents/ hr.	% of payroll	Cents/ hr.
I	6.7	11.39	14.9	25.33
I+E	9.7	16.49	21.6	36.72

One can see from Table 1 that the bonus percentage could really range from 6.7 per cent of total payroll to 21.6 per cent. This looks impressive, but what do these percentages mean in total dollars of bonus per month for an employee whose standard wage is $1.70 per hour? Table 2 demonstrates this. (Note that calculations were done for part-time employees, working 64 and 100 hours per month [16 and 25 hours per week] and a full-time employee working 160 hours a month (40 hours per week).

Table 2. Period amount of dollar bonus

| Share Amount | Hours worked per 4-week period | | |
	64	100	160
Low volume			
I	$7.29	$11.39	$18.22
I+E	$10.55	$16.49	$26.38
High volume			
I	$16.21	$25.33	$40.52
I+E	$23.50	$36.72	$58.75

From Table 2 one can see that the bonus for an employee who averages 16 hours a week could range from $7.29 to $23.50 for the period and the full-time employee's bonus could range from $18.22 to $58.75. I would think that these amounts are large enough to be a positive motivation. The question now is how much these employee bonuses would differ in a chain restaurant that had one manager sharing in the bonus with the employees. ("I" and "I + E" are assumed to remain the same.)

If the employee bonus differs, it will only differ because their percentage of the "amount to be immediately distributed" will be smaller. How much less this percentage is depends upon what percentage bonus the manager gets. I think the fairest method for determining this is to calculate what percentage of "total payroll" the management payroll is and give the manager that percentage of the bonus.

This writer assumes that the manager is on salary for $10,000 per year. So:

	Dollars	% of total payroll
Total management payroll (including taxes)	$11,240	40%
Total employee payroll	16,860	60
Total payroll	$28,100	100%

The chain restaurant's calculation of bonus would be as follows:

Calculation of bonus

	Low sales volume	High sales volume
A. Total sales	$7,700	$8,700
B. Target payroll (16.86) (total sales)	1,298	1,467
C. Actual payroll Low vol. = (15.05) (total sales) High vol. = (13.32) (total sales)	1,159	1,159
D. Improvements over norm	139	308
Bonus pool		
E. Reserve (.25) (improvements over norm)	35	77
F. Amount to be immediately distributed	104	231
G. Company's share (.25) (amount to be distributed)	26	58
H. Manager's share (.40) (.75) (amount to be distributed)	31.20	69.20
I. Employee's share (.60) (.75) (amount to be distributed)	46.80	103.80
J. Employee's share as % of total payroll	4.03%	8.95%

Table 3 illustrates the employees' share in dollars.

Table 3. Employees' share of bonus

	Low-volume share Employees	High-volume share Employees
I	$46.80	$103.80
I + E	$67.80	$150.00

Table 4 illustrates the possible range of that bonus.

Table 4. Range of employee bonus

| | Low volume | | High volume | |
	% of Payroll	Cents/ hr.	% of Payroll	Cents/ hr.
I	4.03	6.85	8.95	15.21
I+E	5.84	9.92	12.94	21.99

Table 5 illustrates those ranges in dollars per period for part-time and full-time employees with a standard wage rate of $1.70 an hour.

Table 5. Employee bonus per period

| Share Amount | Hours worked per 4-week period | | |
	64	100	160
	Low volume		
I	$ 4.38	$ 6.85	$10.96
I+E	$ 6.34	$ 9.92	$15.87
	High volume		
I	$ 9.73	$15.21	$24.33
I+E	$14.07	$21.99	$35.18

One can readily see that employee bonuses are considerably (40 percent) lower in dollars per month per individual employee for the chain restaurant. One might even feel that it is *too* low.

Conclusion

This writer feels that a Scanlon Plan could produce bonuses large enough to motivate employees in both an independent and a chain restaurant. Granted, the base percent bonuses (J) of 6.7 percent and 4.03 percent, respectively, are not very impressive, but that is precisely why I think a Scanlon Plan would be the most effective form of motivation our industry has ever seen. Any knowledgeable employee, and organizations with Scanlon Plans tend to have an abundance of knowledgeable employees after a short time, can readily see that the ways to make big bonuses are to keep payroll low (so that none of the reserve is used), and to increase sales. Most organizations have known this for years but they have never given their employees a chance to realize it. A Scanlon Plan gives the employee that chance on one hand and asks him to do something about it on the other. Don't believe, for even a minute, that if an employee could make more money by increasing sales he wouldn't be telling everyone he saw to come and eat at the restaurant. I can envision the job classification of "grill man" becoming obsolete and being replaced by the classification "public relations expert."

I have been in the restaurant business for six years and have gotten excellent performance from employees who just didn't give a good damn about decreasing costs and increasing sales (why should they have?). Can you imagine what kind of performance they would have given if they had?

To reiterate, I think a Scanlon Plan would be the most effective form of motivation our industry has ever experienced. Employees desire to get involved. They need to get involved. They will get involved ... if we only let them!

Case Questions

1. Do you think that a Scanlon Plan would be as effective in a fast-food restaurant today as the author of this case suggests it could have been in 1972? Why, or why not?

2. Do you think it should make any difference in the motivational impact of a Scanlon Plan as to whether the restaurant sales volume is low or high? Give reasons for your answer.

3. Have you ever worked in a restaurant in which you are quite sure a Scanlon Plan would not be practicable? Explain.

4. In your opinion, are fast-food restaurants more suitable than table-service, luxury style restaurants for employee participation plans? Explain.

Notes

1. See front-page article, "Power Play: Henry Ford Threatened to Quit if Board Failed to Back Him on Iacocca," *Wall Street Journal,* July 17, 1978.

2. Paraphrased from the Foreword by Nelson Rockefeller to *Improving Life at Work: Behavioral Science Approaches to Organizational Change,* ed. J. Richard Hackman and J. Lloyd Suttle (Santa Monica, Calif.: Goodyear, 1977).

3. From Arthur M. Schlesinger, Jr., *A Thousand Days: John F. Kennedy in the White House* (Boston: Houghton Mifflin, 1965), p. 592.

4. Ted Mills, "Human Resources—Why the New Concern?", *Harvard Business Review,* March–April 1975, p. 124.

5. Peter F. Drucker, *Management: Tasks, Responsibilities, Practices* (New York: Harper & Row, 1974), p. 30.

6. Donal A. Dermody, "RESO's Management System," *The Cornell Hotel and Restaurant Administration Quarterly,* May 1976, pp. 70–75.

7. Ibid., p. 75

8. "Workers at Two Paris Luxury Hotels Join Smoothly in the Management," *New York Times,* November 30, 1975.

9. Letter from Sir Charles Forte to Harold E. Lane, dated December 29, 1977.

10. Barry Nelson, "Participatory Management at a Paris Hotel," *Business and Society Review,* Spring 1982, pp. 31–32.

11. For an in-depth discussion of the Scanlon Plan, consult the following sources: Brian Moore and Timothy Ross, *The Scanlon Way to Improved Productivity* (New York: Wiley & Sons, 1978); Carl Frost, John H. Wakeley, and Robert A. Ruh, *The Scanlon Plan for Organizational Development: Identity, Participation, and Equity* (East Lansing: Michigan State University Press, 1974); Harold E. Lane, "The Scanlon Plan: A Key to Productivity and Payroll Costs," *The Cornell Hotel and Restaurant Administration Quarterly,* May 1976, pp. 76–80. For an excellent discussion of the quality of work life concept, consult Ted Mills, *Quality of Work Life: What's In a Name?* (Washington, D.C.: American Center for the Quality of Work Life, 1978). This publication is copyrighted by The General Motors Corporation.

12. J. F. Donnelly, "Increasing Productivity by Involving People in Their Jobs, *The Personnel Administrator,* September–October 1971, pp. 8–13. Reprinted with permission of the American Society for Personnel Administration.

13. Harold E. Lane, "The Scanlon Plan: A Key to Productivity and Payroll Costs," *The Cornell H. & R. A. Quarterly,* May 1976, pp. 76–80.

14. *Detroit Free Press,* January 27, 1979, "Decision-Making Workers Are Wave of the Future," a news report by Barry Rohan.

15. Based on Irving Bluestone, "Thoughts on Collective Bargaining Developments," a January 1978 monograph prepared for the Work in America Institute, Inc., Scarsdale, New York.

16. George H. Litwin and Thomas B. Wilson, "Organizational Climate Is a System," *Inforum,* a professional journal of the Forum Corporation, Boston, Mass., Summer 1978, pp. 2–8. Much of this material on climate has been drawn from Litwin's studies, including those published by the Forum Corporation. The authors are deeply indebted to Dr. Litwin, formerly of the Harvard Business School faculty and now President of the Human Resources Institute, Boston, for his critical reading of this section.

17. Ibid., p. 3.

18. D. Daryl Wyckoff and W. Earl Sasser, *The Chain-Restaurant Industry* (Lexington, Mass.: Lexington Books, D. C. Heath and Co., 1978), p. 61. Copyright 1978, D. C. Heath & Co. Reprinted by permission of the publisher.

19. "Housekeeping Services," a training manual (Honolulu: Hawaii Hotel and Restaurant Industry Employment and Training Trust, 1974), pp. 36–37.

20. Hyatt Corporation *Management Training Manual,* c. 1973, Hyatt Corporation, Vol. II, pp. 488–490.

21. James Lavenson, "Think Strawberries, Everybody Sells," *Introduction to Hotel and Restaurant Management,* ed. Robert A. Brymer (Dubuque, Ia.: Kendall-Hunt, 1977), pp. 256–62.

22. Ibid.

23. W. Earl Sasser, R. Paul Olsen, and D. Daryl Wyckoff, *Management of Service Operations* (Boston: Allyn & Bacon, 1978), p. 493.

24. Ibid., pp. 482–484.

25. Wyckoff and Sasser, *The Chain-Restaurant Industry,* p. 180.

Labor Relations
in the Hospitality Industry

When you finish this chapter you should understand:

1. The major developments in the growth of the union movement in England and the United States

2. What the functions of a labor union are and the reasons why people join a union

3. The principal functions of a local union

4. The major federal laws that have had a significant effect upon labor–management relations

5. What is meant by the bargaining process

6. What is meant by tradeoffs, strategy, and tactics that are involved in the negotiation of an agreement

> In movements like the organizing drives of the thirties, we just worked like hell. How many times in the wee hours of the morning in some god-forsaken flea-bag hotel did I gaze at the yellowed, peeling wallpaper and wonder what the hell I was doing here. I was a true believer, addressing my co-workers as Sister and Brother in a crusade for the brotherhood of man...
>
> I saw that kind of belief and commitment again in the civil rights movement of the sixties, which motivated people to work with no regard to pay, hours, or working conditions. It seems reasonable to conclude that when people believe, they become highly motivated.
>
> Robert Shrank,
> in *Ten Thousand Working Days,*
> M.I.T. Press, Cambridge, 1979, p. 111.

As the preceding chapter of this book makes clear, there are many alternative approaches available for bringing about improvements in the quality of work life, none of which are more promising than those undertaken jointly, albeit uneasily, by leaders of management and labor. But, like Banquo's ghost, the power of employees to bargain collectively with their employer to protect themselves from arbitrary or unfair treatment has haunted both industry and government with unsettling regularity from ancient times down to the present day. The persistence of this troublesome specter through the centuries, therefore, makes it imperative that we understand something of the historical background for the emergence of today's labor–management relationships in the hospitality industry.

Early
Development
of Labor
Unions

To many of us, the word "labor" suggests a variety of meanings. To the hotel or restaurant owner, "labor" refers to a major cost item in the service delivery system of the business. To a newspaper editor, "labor" means either a union of employees about to go on strike somewhere or an important bloc of voters who work for wages and at whom political campaigns are aimed. To the economist, "labor" is regarded as a commodity for which there is a demand and of which there is a supply...resulting in what is called the *labor market.* For our purposes, however, the newspaper editor who is equating labor with *unions* or *organized labor* is correctly identifying those employee associations which are formed to improved wages and working conditions.

Concerted actions of workers in the form of strikes or slowdowns were not unknown, however, even as early as the fourteenth century. In England, at that time, workers who combined as a group to improve their conditions of employment were repeatedly prosecuted in the courts for engaging in a criminal conspiracy. And not until the middle of the nineteenth century did the British Parliament decide that the doctrine of criminal conspiracy was inapplicable to labor unions.

In the United States, the English common-law doctrine of criminal conspiracy served much the same purpose in restraining the right of workers to organize during the Colonial era. Combinations of workers, it was argued, were apt to be "pregnant with the possibility of public mischief and private injury" and terrorized employers as well as workers. In the early 1800s, there were at least a dozen cases in different states in which workers were convicted of the crime of *collective* action—regardless of the fact that the objective of higher wages was not itself illegal and that no unlawful methods as such had been used.

Freedom from such medieval restraints on the right to organize came finally in 1842 when, in *Commonwealth v. Hunt,* the Massachusetts Supreme Court ruled that the act of union formation by itself was not illegal. In this case, seven members of the Boston Journeymen Bootmakers Society had been indicted and convicted for organizing a strike against an employer who had hired a worker not a member of their union.

If such activity were permitted to continue, the lower court ruled, "all industry and enterprise would be suspended, and all property would become insecure... A frightful despotism would soon be erected on the ruins of the free and happy commonwealth."[1] The union members were defended by Robert Rantoul, Jr., a prominent temperance leader, opponent of capital punishment, and member of the state's first Board of Education. He appealed the case to the Massachusetts Supreme Court, where he argued that the English common law of conspiracy was not in force in Massachusetts. That, he said, had been part of "the English tyranny from which we fled."

In reversing the conviction, Chief Justice Shaw—in a landmark opinion—ruled that the aim of the union was simply to get all those employed in the craft to become union members. This, he said, could scarcely be considered unlawful. Nor, he added, could the mere fact that others might be "impoverished" by this lawful course of action make it unlawful. Supposing, he said, that a group of merchants sold their product so cheaply that their competitors were put out of business. This was surely no conspiracy. Neither was a comparable combination of workers to put whatever price or conditions they chose on their labor.

Thus was the death knell sounded for indictments of unions as criminal conspiracies. And so union growth, no longer stifled by the criminal law, began to spread to almost every trade and to a majority of American cities where tradespeople were establishing themselves.

As judicial attention shifted from the question of whether or not a combination of workers was a conspiracy to the question involving the means they use to gain their ends, unions found themselves confronted with still another legal obstacle, the *injunction.* This is an order of the court to cease and desist from some action, such as a strike, boycott, or picketing. Its use in labor disputes began in state courts during the 1880s when continuing judicial bias against unions appeared to invite litigation.

> For example, an employer, when faced with the threat of a strike or already involved in a work stoppage, would appear before a friendly judge and apply for a temporary restraining order by alleging, in general terms through a loosely worded affidavit, that his or her property rights would be damaged as a result of union action. The judge would quickly grant this request and issue what came to be known as an "omnibus" or blanket injunction prohibiting any and all types of activity. Particularly rankling to labor was the fact that, on many occasions, no union representative was present in court to argue against the imposition of the court order, and the first the union knew about the proceeding was when an officer of the court served notice of the labor injunction upon the labor organization.[2]

Impressed by the success of the Pullman Palace Car Company in breaking its American Railway Union strike of 1894 by obtaining a federal court injunction—subsequently upheld by the Supreme Court—other companies in the decades to follow found the labor injunction to be their most effective weapon in preventing the spread of union organization. Moreover, as the courts became increasingly involved in labor disputes, public disenchantment with the lack of judicial impartiality tended to support growing union complaints of "government by injunction." Eventually, Congress decided that justice had not been served by allowing federal courts virtually unlimited authority to issue injunctions in labor disputes. And so in 1932 it passed the Norris-LaGuardia Act, making peaceful picketing, peaceable assembly, payment of strike benefits, and other union economic weapons nonenjoinable. Equally important, the Act asserted that it was now necessary for Congress to guarantee to the individual employee "full freedom of association, self-organization, and designation of representatives of his own choosing, to negotiate the terms and conditions of his employment... from interference, restraint, or coercion of employers."[3]

And what of the labor movement itself?

By 1860, there was a perceptible trend toward higher wages and shorter hours for workers. The average workday for nonagricultural employees was estimated at 11 hours, and the range of wage rates had advanced from their previous level of $1.25 to 1.50 *per day* to $1.50 to 2.00 *per day.*

The advent of the Civil War brought a new spurt in union membership growth, aided both by labor shortages incurred through military mobilization and by President Lincoln's publicly expressed pro-union sentiment that "labor is the superior of capital and deserves much the higher consideration."[4] By the time the war had ended, the trend toward national and international unions became noticeable, with some 13 unions (plasterers, cigar makers, bricklayers, and masons) making their appearance between 1860 and 1865. More than 50 national unions were in existence by 1879, helping to lay the foundation for the eventual establishment of the American Federation of Labor in 1886.

American Federation of Labor

The first move leading toward the ultimate creation of the American Federation of Labor actually took place at Columbus, Ohio on December 8, 1886, when forty-two representatives of twenty-five craft unions (with a total membership of 150,000) formed a wholly new organization, the American Federation of Labor, and elected Samuel Gompers as its first president.

Who, in fact, was Samuel Gompers? He was the man destined to lead the American Federation of Labor from 1886—with the exception of a single year—to the time of his death at the age of 74 in 1924.

Born in London's East End of Dutch-Jewish parentage, he was apprenticed at the age of 10 to his father's trade of cigar making. At the age of 13 he emigrated with his parents to New York where he joined a local cigar makers' union. Early on, he became known to his fellow unionists as a practical, feet-on-the ground leader who clung as tenaciously to his conviction that all ideas must be tested by their immediate consequences as he later did to his presidency of the AFL. Only

5 feet 4 inches tall, Gompers sported a drooping walrus mustache, a tuft of hair on his chin, and generally gave the appearance of a stubborn, forceful man of inexhaustible energy as he traveled across the country to address labor meetings and conventions. As "one of the boys," he found it easy to relax in the congenial atmosphere of the beer parlors, music halls, showgirls, and smoke-filled saloons of America's playgrounds.

Nonetheless, Gompers succeeded in leaving an indelible mark on the trade union movement in this country. As a staunch defender of the craft-union model of labor organization, he enabled the AFL to become the first such organization ever to achieve permanence, regardless of economic circumstances, by maintaining an unbroken and continuous existence for nearly seventy years, from 1886 until its merger with the CIO in 1955.

While a comprehensive account of subsequent events in the annals of American labor—such as the AFL-CIO merger of 1955 and its "trials, tribulations and tortures of success" ever since—must be sought in literature beyond the scope of this book,[5] it would be a mistake to assume that hotel and restaurant workers remained, until more recent times, wholly untouched by these events.

Unions of Hotel and Restaurant Employees

History records the first local union of people in the catering industry as having been formed in Chicago in 1866. It was called the "Bartenders and Waiters Union, Chicago." Its members, mostly German immigrants who had absorbed their union lessons in Europe, were later caught up in the "crusade of the plain people of America against wage slavery" being led by the Knights of Labor. Their affiliation with the Knights occurred in 1886. At about the same time, other local unions of waiters and cooks emerged in San Francisco, St. Louis, New York City, and Brooklyn—all of them affiliated with the Knights of Labor in the great upheaval of the 1880s.[6]

By the latter part of 1886, however, the waiters' and bartenders' groups were ready to join in the growing protest against the arbitrary leadership of the Knights, for by that time, the national leaders of the Knights of Labor had ordered the Chicago assembly of waiters and bartenders to exclude from their membership all who handled intoxicating beverages.

Not surprisingly, when the Columbus convention that founded the American Federation of Labor was held in December 1886, those attending included representatives from waiters' and bartenders' locals' in New York, Cincinnati, and Boston; all were intent upon seeking new ways to unite their forces along economic lines, as the craft unions of Europe had done. One of their spokesmen, Julius Weiner of the German Waiters Union No. 1 of New York, presented a letter to the convention formally requesting help in the formation of a national trade union of all catering industry workers.[7] Although action to grant a national charter did not occur until 1891, the wages and working conditions of the times were not going unnoticed. Typical of the articles appearing in the *Waiters' Journal (Kellnerzeitung)*, a publication of the New York German Waiters Association, was the following:

> Traffic in black slaves was luckily abolished by the bloody Civil War, but, unfortunately, *white slavery* is still flourishing in various guises... One class of wage earners still suffering from such bondage is, without doubt, the waiters' profession...the general public is unaware of the fact that waiters are very often compelled to work fifteen hours, and even longer, day after day, with hardly enough allowance of time to partake of the hastiest of meals... No man can work for fifteen or sixteen hours and do his work well. The long tedious days and nights make the waiters drowsy... To create incentive to remain keen and alert, a number of proprietors abolished the payment of regular wages and inaugurated payment by percentage. This new method worked well at first, but...as soon as the waiters, by increased activity, earned more money than their former wages, the bosses cut down the remuneration from 10 percent to 5 percent of their sales... The majority managed only to earn about $4.00 a week, and being powerless to help themselves, had to walk the streets...[8]

Keenly aware of the mounting grievances occasioned by such long hours, low pay, and oppressive working conditions, union leaders pressed for the issuance of local charters from the American Federation of Labor. And beginning in 1887, when the first of these was granted to Waiters Union No. 281, New York, some fourteen charters were granted during the ensuing four years to catering-industry locals situated in different cities of the country.

Meanwhile, Julius Weiner's enthusiasm for a national union had continued unabated since his plea at the Columbus AFL meeting. Finally, as a consequence of conferences which he had initiated among waiters' and bartenders' groups in the New York area, he secured agreement, at a meeting on April 23, 1891, upon a provisional constitution for a new union. That same day, after being chosen as the first secretary of the new organization—whose affiliated locals then represented 450 members in all—Weiner forwarded the constitution, together with an application for a national charter, to Gompers at AFL headquarters, then located in New York. The following day Gompers, on behalf of the AFL Council, granted a charter in the name of the "Waiters and Bartenders National Union," thus inaugurating the birthday of the present Hotel & Restaurant Employees and Bartenders International Union.* Shortly afterwards, the AFL Council made affiliation with the new national union compulsory for all locals having AFL charters in the catering industry.[9]

By the time of World War I, the union had become a large and prosperous organization of 65,000 members, composed mainly of waiters,

---

*Effective as of August 24, 1981, in accordance with the instructions of its 39th General Convention held in Chicago, Illinois, this union is known as the Hotel Employees & Restaurant Employees International Union, AFL-CIO.

cooks, and bartenders.[10] But the onset of Prohibition in 1919 marked the beginning of troubles for the HRE Union which were destined to continued undiminished until the repeal of the Eighteenth Amendment in 1933, a date which, incidentally, coincided with a new low in union membership of 24,500 workers.[11] With the advent of repeal of the prohibition amendment and the subsequent passage two years later of the Wagner Act (to which we refer later in this chapter), the HRE union membership multiplied rapidly, reaching a figure of more than 300,000 by the end of World War II in 1945.

Hotel and Restaurant Unionization— 1930-1980

The 1930s and 1940s yielded a rich harvest for the unions in the hotel and restaurant industry. For, despite a year-long strike and an employer lockout precipitated by a "yellow dog contract" dispute in July 1930 between the Cleveland, Ohio Hotel Association and the Waiters, Waitresses and Cooks Union, the years of the New Deal which followed contributed significantly to the success of HRE union organizing campaigns everywhere. The environmental effects of such federal legislation as the National Labor Relations Act (i.e., the Wagner Act) of 1935 and the Fair Labor Standards Act (i.e., the Wage-Hour Act) of 1938 were unmistakable. For example, between 1932 and 1942, when World War II began, HRE membership had increased by more than 700 percent (see Figure 4-1), with a preponderance of union membership among employees of the big city hotels of New York, Chicago, Philadelphia, Boston, San Francisco, and other metropolitan areas.

In almost all major cities in which collective bargaining contracts were obtained, management's side of the agreement took the form of multi-employer bargaining, generally through a local hotel association.

New York City

New York City is a case in point. There, the oldest (1878) and largest organization of hotel operators in the United States—The Hotel Association of New York City—signed its first labor agreement on March 23, 1938; this agreement called for union recognition and for the establishment of machinery for the settlement by conciliation and arbitration of grievances arising between management and employees who were members of the signatory unions. The pattern of citywide bargaining thus established has continued down to the present time, uninterrupted by any strikes among the member hotels of the New York City Association. Elsewhere, most major cities in the late 1930s and early 1940s saw collective action in organizing, in strikes, and in successful campaigns to achieve contractual agreements with some of the nation's leading hotels and restaurants, coast to coast.

San Francisco—and Conrad Hilton

In the West, where union membership had grown rapidly, the San Francisco Hotel Employers Association had been formed during a prolonged eighty-nine-day strike in 1937 when some nineteen hotels were

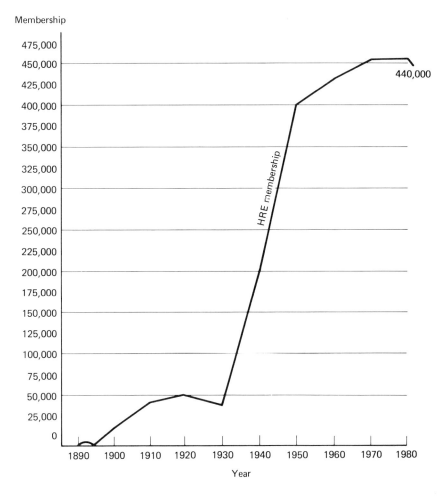

Source: John P. Henderson, Professor of Economics, Michigan State University: Labor
and Manpower Economics, with Particular Reference to the Lodging Industry (unpublished manuscript, December 1973). 1980 membership figure furnished by
the Hotel Employees and Restaurant Employees International Union.

Figure 4-1.   Membership of the Hotel & Restaurant Employees and Bartenders
International Union, AFL-CIO, 1891—1980.

shut down. That strike had been settled with an agreement that was to
last for four years. Well in advance of the 1941 expiration date of that
agreement, it became clear that both sides were girding themselves for
another major test of strength, centering mainly upon the crucial issues
of union security and the nature and extent of union control over hiring.
Following three months of extended negotiations, the unions called a
strike on August 27, 1941. This time the hotels announced that they

would remain open with substitute, nonunion employees instead of closing down as they had in 1937. In response, the union organization
resorted to a "war of nerves" strategy:

> While one hotel was struck, another adjacent to it would be merely
> threatened with a walkout. The transport of food by truck was cut
> drastically by the union's "spotters" and with the help of the teamsters
> and the longshoremen. The style of picketing, as in 1937, was de-
> signed as a dramatic eye-filling spectacle: before the luxurious St.
> Francis Hotel, in the social hub of the city, a huge terrifying figure of a
> robot, clad in iron armor, was posted and displayed a large sign
> reading:

> WE DON'T WANT TO BE TURNED INTO MACHINES!

> The real break for the union came at the end of October when one of
> the biggest of the hoteliers, Conrad Hilton, owner of the nationwide
> hotel chain bearing his name, including the Sir Francis Drake in San
> Francisco, was persuaded to leave the Hotel Employers Association
> and sign a separate agreement with the Unions' Joint Board. By good
> intelligence work the union officers had learned that Hilton, having
> recently made a heavy investment in the Drake, was pressed for cash
> and hence extremely eager to keep his hotel open. The union men
> had avoided picketing his place and offered Hilton strong in-
> ducements to sign a contract.

> Hilton's defection caused a great uproar of protest among the other
> members of the Hotel Association—who were still subject to intermit-
> tent stoppages—and he was denounced in large paid newspaper
> advertisements by the Employers Council as a "traitor" to his class.
> Hilton, in reply, declared publicly that his withdrawal was caused by
> "loss of faith in the intentions and ability of the Association to settle
> the dispute." The Hotel Employers Association actually instituted a
> suit for damages against the Hilton company, which was eventually
> dropped. . . .[12]

In the short run, the unions' attempt to set a precedent with Hilton
that could be used against other signatory employers (commonly known
as "whipsawing") failed, for, at the same time that the Association
dropped its suit, Hilton sold the Sir Francis Drake, not choosing to return
to San Francisco (and membership in the Association) until nearly a
quarter of a century later.

In the long run, the strike dragged on until the attack on Pearl
Harbor caused the U.S. Navy to requisition a number of hotels for its
forces and the War Labor Board settled through arbitration all outstanding issues between the parties.

Miami Beach—and the National Labor Relations Board

One of the longest and costliest hotel strikes took place in Miami
Beach during the twenty-month period from April 1955 to January 1957.
The union spent over $1.5 million for legal fees, soup kitchens, pickets
(including those picketing New York City employment agencies which

were recruiting "strike-breakers," and those picketing at Kennedy Airport where replacement employees were being taken for the flight to
Miami), advertising (warning union members in other cities that they
would be subject to fines and expulsion if they took Miami hotel jobs, and
warning tourists in the North to cancel their prospective travel plans for
Miami Beach), and in successful efforts to get the three television
networks—ABC, NBC, and CBS—to stop originating shows in Miami
Beach as long as the strike continued.

Ultimately, this strike was settled by the signing of a master contract between the hotel association and the union, but not before an important precedent had been established as to the jurisdiction of the
National Labor Relations Board over the hotel industry. During the
twenty years prior to 1955, *both* the hotel industry and the Hotel &
Restaurant Employees Union had opposed the Board's taking of jurisdiction in hotels for the purpose of determining whether or not a majority of
employees wished union representation. But the circumstances of the
Miami Beach strike caused the International Union to reverse its long-
established position—for, in this case, hotel employers had successfully
resisted union recognition by obtaining from a sympathetic Florida
Supreme Court injunctive relief from union picketing. In the end, the
union won its case in the United States Supreme Court, which held that
"dismissal by the National Labor Relations Board of the representation
petition, on the sole ground of the Board's long established policy of not
asserting jurisdiction over the hotel industry as a class, was beyond the
Board's power."[13] Thereafter, hotels could no longer claim immunity
from the processes of the National Labor Relations Board.

Big Mac Under Union Attack

The decade of the 1970s saw a number of attempts, mostly futile, to
unionize the rapidly growing fast-food industry. Not surprisingly,
McDonald's was among the first to draw union attention. Responding to
union insinuations that McDonald's concern for its toiling teenage workers
was something less than altruistic, Chairman of the Board, Ray Kroc,
fired back: "The unions haven't been able to touch us with a ten-foot
pole. Hell, we got employees going to football games, track events,
hockey games. We have picnics for them. We have theater parties. We
have softball games and on and on."[14]

To ward off its employee discontent early in 1972 about low pay
and excessive management control, McDonald's instituted "rap" sessions on a local, regional, district, and national basis. These were led by
home-office personnel staffers, including a former union organizer,
John Cooke.

In January 1973, the company filed an $11.1 million triple-
damages antitrust suit against the Golden Gate Restaurant Association,
the Hotel Employers Association, the San Francisco Hotel Employers
Association, and the San Francisco Joint Board of Culinary Workers,
Bartenders and Hotel-Motel and Club Service Workers; this was a lawsuit

filed ostensibly because of Ray Kroc's contention that labor unions and restaurant owners had "conspired" to pressure the San Francisco Board of Permit Appeals into denying licenses for McDonald's establishments. Even the *Wall Street Journal* was moved to editorialize that somehow San Francisco was being shortsighted for opposing McDonald's "right to free enterprise."

Within a few weeks after launching its suit, McDonald's also became embroiled in a lie-detector controversy. Appearing before San Francisco's Deputy Labor Commissioner, Bryan P. Seale, a group of McDonald's former employees testified during a five-hour hearing that they had been forced to take lie-detector tests and that refusal to take them was grounds for dismissal. While undergoing tests, they claimed they were asked questions about their union sympathies. Further, the ex-employees charged that they were required to turn in all their tips, which were then added to the restaurant's cash receipts.

The Commissioner ruled against McDonald's on both counts, deciding that it was in violation of state law in its use of lie detector tests, and that it had not notified the general public that its employees were required to turn in all tips. Accordingly, Commissioner Seale issued a cease and desist order, requiring McDonald's to stop these practices or face court action. The order was not appealed.[15] Meanwhile, the $11 million lawsuit was dismissed by the Federal District Court as not being within its jurisdiction.

Even though unions were unsuccessful in their early efforts of the 1970s to organize "Big Mac's" employees, they did not give up the struggle. In November 1979, the Detroit Fast Food Workers Union, an independent union (i.e., a union not affiliated with the AFL-CIO), emerged as a threat to the nonunion status of various Burger King and McDonald's restaurants in Detroit.

Detroit Fast Food Workers Union

While details about the Fast Food Workers Union remain sketchy, the following news account, which appeared in the *Detroit Free Press* on February 22, 1980, is instructive:

Fast Food Employee Union Gets First Test

The new union that hopes to organize Detroit's fast food workers will face its first test Friday when 53 employees at the Burger King restaurant at the downtown Greyhound bus station will vote on whether they want to be represented by the union.

The Detroit Fast Food Workers Union, which began organizing drives in November at various Burger King and McDonald's restaurants, hopes to have National Labor Relations Board elections at three McDonald's outlets within the next few weeks.

Danny Cantor, organizing director of the union, said Detroit is the first city where the newly formed union has attempted to organize fast food workers.

"Detroit is where it's at," Cantor said. "If this can be done anywhere it can be done in Detroit."

Cantor said that in the past fast food workers have been ignored by organized labor. "The traditional wisdom is that they're too young, too transient and don't make enough money because the minimum wage ($3.10 an hour) is the only wage at a fast food chain."

"We believe traditional wisdom is wrong. They may be young but they're not naive," he said.

Cantor said he and other organizers for the union began meeting with fast food employes in November and December and found workers felt "if we're going to work like we're on an assembly line, they're going to pay us like we're on an assembly line."

He added that while improvements in wages and benefits were high priority items, equally important was the attitude of supervisors to employees, who are for the most part teenagers.

"We thought wages would be the thing they talked about but the more fundamental issue is respect," Cantor said. "They felt they were not treated with respect and dignity."

Lena Halmon, an employe at the Greyhound Burger King since October, agreed that workers "were upset because many of them are treated with disrespect."

"We're not children anymore," said Ms. Halmon, 19. "The managers should treat us like adults instead of screaming and hollering."

She said her co-workers also believed they are not rewarded for working hard. "Some don't do as much and they get paid the same," she said. "It wasn't fair."

Ms. Halmon said she believes the union will win representation rights because "most of them had been ready for something like this."

Cantor said he is optimistic about the results of the election Friday, which will be announced that night. He said the Greyhound Burger King was chosen for the first election test because the union found its employes "more than interested, they were ready to roll."

A spokesman for the Burger King chain said the restaurant is a franchise under the control of Greyhound Bus Lines and said the corporation had no comment about the organizing effort at its fast food outlets.

The Greyhound company, based in Phoenix, Ariz., and McDonald's could not be reached for comment Thursday.

Cantor said the union plans to keep its organizing drive going and has petitioned the NLRB for elections at three McDonald's locations. He said the schedule for these elections will be decided next week.

He said the union has met opposition from both the Burger King company and McDonald's.

"They're big companies and they're not about to roll over and play dead," he said.

Cantor said supervisors at some organizing locations have held "captive audience" meetings to tell employes that if the union wins representation rights, "a Big Mac will cost $3 and they'll close the store."

"That is clearly not true but they've succeeded in confusing people, which is what they want," he said.

Cantor said whatever the outcome of the election, his union will continue to organize.

"The election won't be the end. It will be the beginning."

Detroit Free Press, 2/22/80.

The final outcome of the National Labor Relations Board election held on Friday, March 7, 1980, at the above-mentioned Burger King establishment has yet to be determined, primarily because of prolonged challenges and appeals by both the company and the union. The actual vote was a close one, twenty-five employees voting for the union and twenty-three employees voting against the union.

Given the high turnover rate in an industry that draws heavily upon teenagers for its supply of labor, many observers doubt whether this union, or any other union, will be successful in the long run in its drive to organize fast-food workers.

Thus far, we have seen something of the role of hotel and restaurant unions as they have maintained a high level of visibility during the past fifty years. This overall picture of union activities would be incomplete, however without some mention of the way in which the union functions.

The International Union

The most powerful unit in the union structure is the International Union, with its headquarters in Cincinnati, Ohio. In terms of staff size and revenue, the office of the International maintains a level of management and financial control not unlike that which we traditionally associate with the operation of any business of comparable size. The executive officers, as of 1983, are Edward T. Hanley, General President, Herman Leavitt, General Secretary-Treasurer, John C. Kenneally, General Vice President, and Paul P. McCastland, Director of Organization.

The Director of Organization has a file containing every contract negotiated by the union's more than 300 affiliated local unions and prepares current background studies of hotel and restaurant industry problems for the use of local union negotiators. Legal counsel represents the International in litigation at all court proceedings and may advise union officials on the respective labor laws governing trade-union activities.

The Constitution of the Hotel & Restaurant Employees and Bartenders International is its fundamental law, a copy of which is included in the appendix to this book.

Figure 4-2 shows the structure of the International Union.

The Local Union

The local union is the one with which members have direct contact. It functions as spokesperson for the interests of its members, processes

Hotel and Restaurant Unions— Structural Organization

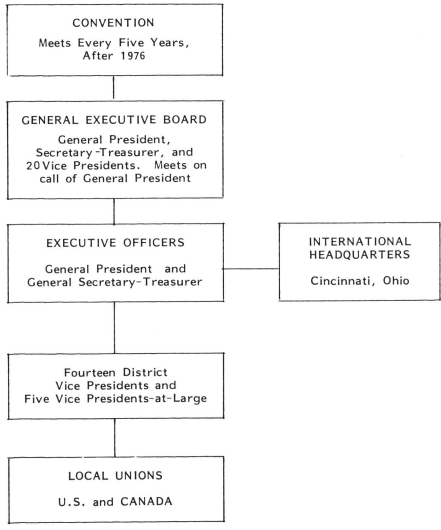

Figure 4-2 Structure of the Hotel Employees & Restaurant Employees international union, AFL-CIO

their grievances, and insures that management decisions are in compliance with the terms of existing labor agreements.

The officers of the local union are typically a president, a vice president, a secretary-treasurer, and a business representative. The latter is usually a full-time salaried member whose responsibilities include the negotiation and administration of the labor agreement. In addition, the business representative is generally responsible for supervising an office staff, collecting dues, recruiting new members, and handling members' grievances. Not infrequently, a business representative is called upon to help the hotel or restaurant employer correct disciplinary problems involving union members.[16]

The Union Business Representative

Typically the union business representative is the person to whom workers can turn in times of trouble. As a link between union members and their employers, the business representative is the one who is "on the spot"; he or she performs the difficult roles of mediator, advocate, and—where possible —preventer of serious labor disputes.

In general, a grievance is defined as a worker's complaint that the company has violated one of his or her rights under the existing labor–management contract. Thus, in any one year, a profile of grievances filed against a hotel or restaurant employer would reflect such typical employee concerns as the following:

○ Days off
○ Cleanliness of employee locker rooms and bathrooms
○ Incorrect wages paid for part-time workers
○ Incorrect computation of overtime pay
○ Seniority in layoffs, vacations, holidays, work-station assignments
○ Quality of employee meals
○ Quota of rooms to be cleaned by maids
○ Employer's refusal to re-employ after layoff, leave, or illness
○ Employer's refusal to show banquet checks as evidence for the amount of banquet gratuities received
○ Hiring of outside nonunion contractors to do work formerly performed by hotel or restaurant employees
○ Employer's failure to supply maid carts
○ Employer's requiring bellmen to handle tour-group baggage without advance guarantee of gratuities
○ Employer's failure to schedule employee mealtime and rest periods
○ Employer's failure to provide, clean, and/or repair employee uniforms
○ Employer's requirement that employee take a lie detector test
○ Employees denied time off with pay for physical examinations required by employer
○ Improper calculation of health, hospitalization, and/or pension benefits due an employee
○ Discharge of an employee for engaging in union organizing activities, or for any other reason not expressly forbidden by the labor–management contract
○ Employer's unauthorized deductions from an employee's pay for breakage or similar violation of "house rules"

Over the years, the role of government in the United States has changed from one of preventing collective bargaining to one of accepting it, and finally to the role of regulating it.

Norris-LaGuardia Act—1932

As we noted earlier in this chapter, public disenchantment with widespread use of court injuntions to halt union organization led to the passage in 1932 of the Norris-LaGuardia Act, or Anti-Injunction Act. This act severely restricted the use of injunctions in labor disputes, made "yellow dog" contracts unenforceable in federal courts, and asserted that Congress must guarantee to the individual employee "full freedom of association, self-organization, and designation of representatives of his own choosing, to negotiate the terms and conditions of his employment ... free from interference, restraint or coercion of employers." Since that time virtually all federal labor laws passed by Congress have embraced this same principle.

Wagner Act—1935

The Wagner Act of 1935, otherwise known as the National Labor Relations Act, declared it to be the public policy of the United States

> ... to protect the exercise by workers of full freedom of association, self-organization, and designation of representatives of their own choosing, for the purpose of negotiating the terms and conditions of their employment or other mutual aid or protection.[17]

The Act established election procedures by which employees could freely choose their own collective bargaining representatives, and in addition, it declared certain employer practices to be unfair. These unfair labor practices are defined as follows:

1. To interfere with, restrain, or coerce employees in the exercise of their rights to self-determination

2. To dominate or interfere with the formation or administration of any labor organization, or contribute financial or other support to it

3. To discriminate in regard to hire or tenure of employment or any term or condition of employment to encourage or discourage membership in any labor organization

4. To discharge or discriminate against an employee who files charges or gives testimony before the NLRB with respect to alleged employer violations

5. To refuse to bargain with the representatives of employees

In the decade that followed passage of the Wagner Act, unions throughout the United States were able to recruit nearly 10 million members. In the case of the Hotel & Restaurant Employees International, membership quadrupled, growing from 80,000 to 320,000.

Taft-Hartley Act—1947

Because there had been no "unfair labor practices" of unions included in the Wagner Act, Congress by 1947 had perceived a need to impose certain restraints on unions for a more balanced approach. Accordingly, it passed the Taft-Hartley Act (otherwise known as the Labor–Management Relations Act) defining the following activities to be unfair union practices:

1. Restraint or coercion of employees in the exercise of their Wagner Act rights

2. Restraint or coercion of employers in the selection of the parties to bargain in their behalf

3. Persuasion of employers to discriminate against any of their employees

4. Refusal to bargain collectively with an employer

5. Participation in secondary boycotts and jurisdictional disputes

6. Attempting to force recognition from an employer when another union is already the certified representative

7. Charging excessive initiation fees

8. "Featherbedding" practices requiring the payment of wages for services not performed

The National Labor Relations Board, which had been established under the original Wagner Act to administer its provisions, was continued as the agency responsible for administering and enforcing the Taft-Hartley Act, with the Board's responsibilities being defined as follows:

1. To determine what the bargaining unit or units within an organization shall be (a unit contains those employees who are to be represented by a particular union and are covered by the agreement with it)

2. To conduct representation elections by secret ballot for the purpose of determining which, if any, union shall represent the employees within a unit

3. To investigate unfair labor practice charges filed by unions or employers and to prosecute any violations revealed by such investigations

One of the principal effects of this Act was to relax the restrictions that had hitherto existed upon an employer's freedom of speech. Henceforth, employers had the right to express their views about unions, provided no attempt was made to threaten, coerce, or bribe employees concerning their decision to join or not to join a union.

Right-to-work clause   Perhaps the most controversial provision of Taft-Hartley is its so-called "right-to-work" clause. This enables states to pass a so-called "right-to-work law" prohibiting labor–management agreements requiring membership or nonmembership in a labor union as a condition of obtaining or retaining employment. The argument goes something like this. Proponents justify such a law on the ground that compulsory union membership violates an individual's basic constitutional guarantee of freedom of association. Opponents claim that majority rule is an indispensable ingredient of democracy, and that when union security arrangements have been negotiated by a union representing a *majority* of employees in an establishment, these arrangements should not be nullified by a state law. Since 1947, twenty states have passed right-to-work laws.

Landrum-Griffin Act—1959

Hearings conducted by Senator McLellan during 1958 disclosed that corrupt practices were occurring within the field of labor–management relations and that existing laws were inadequate to prevent such practices.

As a result, Congress passed the Landrum-Griffin Act (otherwise known as the Labor–Management Reporting and Disclosure Act), one of the most important provisions of which is known as the "Bill of Rights of Members of Labor Organizations." It grants to each union member the right to:

1. Nominate candidates for union office
2. Vote in union elections or referendums
3. Attend union meetings
4. Participate in union meetings and vote on union business

Members who are deprived of these rights are permitted to seek appropriate relief in a federal court. Union members are also granted the right to examine union accounts and records in order to verify information contained in union reports and to bring suit against union officers to protect union funds.

The Landrum-Griffin Act also does the following:

1. Requires the filing of detailed annual reports by unions and corporate officers and labor relations consultants on their financial activities

2. Limits the conditions under which an international union may exercise a trusteeship over an affiliated local union (A *trusteeship* is established when the international union takes over a local union from its officers and places its administration in the hands of a trustee appointed by the International)

3. Requires the maintenance of democratic safeguards in the conduct of union elections

4. Denies the privilege of union office to persons convicted of certain crimes

5. Requires that union officers be bonded for an amount not less than 10 percent of the union funds they handle

6. Prohibits picketing for the purpose of "shaking down" employers, forcing them to recognize a union, or compelling their employees to join a union

What are some of the conclusions to be drawn from this account of union growth and labor-law development? First and foremost is the conclusion that the public attitude toward organized labor and collective bargaining has changed markedly over the years. It has shifted from legal repression to strong encouragement, then to modified encouragement coupled with regulation, and finally, to detailed regulation of union rights and responsibilities.

Union Growth and Labor Laws— Conclusions

In terms of union growth rate, the trend generally, as shown in Figure 4-3, as well as the trend of Hotel Employees & Restaurant Employees International Union membership, as shown in Figure 4-1 (page 104), reflects a leveling off since the 1950s. It is estimated that HRE

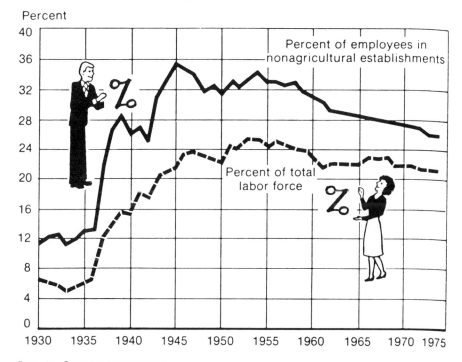

Excludes Canadian membership.

Total labor force includes employed and unemployed workers, self-employed, members of the Armed Forces, etc. Employment in nonagricultural establishments excludes the Armed Forces, self-employed, as well as the unemployed, agricultural workers, proprietors, unpaid family workers, and domestic servants.

Source: Directory of National Unions and Employee Associations, Bureau of Labor Statistics, 1977, p. 62.

Figure 4–3 Union membership as a percent of total labor force and of employees in nonagricultural establishments, 1930–74

membership now comprises approximately 12 percent of the total workforce of the hotel and restaurant industry, whereas organized labor throughout the United States now comprises approximately 20 percent of the total workforce of more than 90 million people.

Collective
Bargaining
and
Unionizing
Campaigns

Virtually all labor unions share at least one fundamental objective—namely, the negotiation of a written agreement with the employer establishing conditions of employment under which the union's members will agree to work.

But before it can negotiate such an agreement, a union must first be chosen as the bargaining representative for a group of workers, either through voluntary recognition by an employer or as the result of an NLRB-conducted secret ballot election. Gaining recognition frequently requires an extensive membership drive by the union; the outcome of this process depends upon many factors. Crucial to its success or failure, however, is the factor of employee satisfaction or dissatisfaction within a hotel or restaurant establishment. Management practices with respect to such important matters as wages, hours, promotion, seniority, discipline, grievances, holiday and vacation allowances, gratuities, health and hospitalization benefits, job security, and other working conditions can either encourage or discourage employees to join the union.

Union Campaign Tactics

In an effort to persuade employees of the reasons for joining, the Hotel Employees & Restaurant Employees International Union will often step up its campaign by circulating leaflets of the type illustrated by Figures 4-4 and 4-5, from the Union in Cincinnati, Ohio.

1. WHAT DO YOU, AS A WORKER, WANT MOST OF ALL?

    You want a steady job that pays a living wage.

    You want a decent livelihood for yourself and family.

    You want a voice in matters which affect this livelihood.

    You want your fair share in the ever-increasing standard of living.

2. HOW CAN YOU, AS A WORKER, GET THESE THINGS?

    You cannot get them alone. If your job is insecure and your wages are low, your employer can tell you "Take it or leave it!"

    But if you join with other workers who have the same problems, your employer has to listen.

    A Union will persuade him to listen.

Figure 4–4

3. WHAT IS A UNION?

It is a group of people like yourself who work for wages or
salary. It is organized to solve work problems which you and
your fellow-workers have in common. It promotes your
interest.

4. WHAT IS THE FIRST THING A UNION DOES?

First, the union gets the employer to sign an agreement setting
standards for wages, hours of work, and other conditions of
employment.

5. HOW DOES A UNION SECURE AN AGREEMENT?

By bargaining collectively with the employer.

This means that union representatives, speaking for the employees,
meet with the employer to discuss wages and working conditions.
Discussion is held round the conference table. When agreement
is reached, it is put in writing like any other contract. The
contract governs relations with the employer until a new agreement
is negotiated.

6. WHAT ELSE DOES A UNION DO?

A union continually improves wages and conditions. Agreements
are usually signed for a year or two. Every time the contract
comes up for renewal, the union tries to get higher wages and
standards.

A union provides a recognized spokesman to adjust grievances
that arise on the job. The union speaks for the worker. Without union representation, the worker is at a disadvantage in
getting a fair settlement of his grievances.

A union helps to assure your future by protecting you from
unjust discharge. It gets you rights in the event of layoffs.

A UNION ALSO WORKS TO GET LAWS WHICH PEOPLE NEED---

Laws to protect health and safety on the job --

Laws to prevent children from being exploited at child labor--

Laws to protect consumers from harmful foods and shoddy
goods--

Laws to get unemployment compensation for workers who
lose their jobs--

Laws for old age benefits, social security, and general
betterment of the conditions of workers and the community.

Figure 4–4   Continued

7. DO YOU <u>HAVE</u> TO JOIN A UNION?

No. But you don't have to vote in elections, either.

However, if you are a good citizen, you make it your business to vote.

And if you want to better your standard of living--

If you want your fair share of the wealth you are helping to create together with other workers--

Then you must do your part by joining the union.

You will not want to stay outside while other workers organize and fight for benefits from which you also gain.

A worker who is honest with himself does not want to be a "free rider" on the "Union train."

8. WHAT KIND OF A UNION DO YOU WANT?

You want a union that will get results.

You want a union with a record of getting results.

You want a solid, stable union affiliated with other established unions in the AFL-CIO.

9. WHAT SHOULD YOU PUT INTO THE UNION?

A union is what the members make it.

When you join, you should attend meetings and express your views.

A union is a democratic organization.

You should take active part in its affairs, to make it even more effective than you find it in serving your needs and the needs of your fellow workers.

10. WHY PAY DUES TO A UNION?

Because the Union needs money to operate.

The union must have officers or business agents who will spend their full time on union work--representing the members, settling grievances, drawing up contracts to better wages and conditions.

There is no friend like the "friend in need." The Union is the worker's friend when he needs action!

Figure 4-4 Continued

11. WHAT ELSE DO YOUR DUES PAY FOR?

Service from the local union . Union business agents help
members find jobs; enforce agreements; bargain with the
employers; speak for the workers in civil affairs to get
schools, parks, playgrounds, low-cost housing. Union
dues also pay for the help of experts like lawyers when
needed to deal with employer experts.

Service from the International Union. This is the parent
body of the local unions. It needs money to pay for
organizing activities, publicity, research. Such services
help the locals in their work. It takes paid officers and
staff employees to furnish these services.

Part of your dues goes into a defense fund. If a local union
has to strike, it must have financial resources to win.

It takes money to buy essential services. A Union cannot
be strong and effective without a treasury.

12. SHOULD YOU JOIN THE HOTEL & RESTAURANT EMPLOYEES
AND BARTENDERS INTERNATIONAL UNION?

Certainly!

This is the only established union in the hotel, motel,
restaurant, cafeteria, and tavern industry.

It has over 450,000 members in the continental United States,
Alaska, Hawaii, Puerto Rico, and Canada.

It is composed of cooks, waiters, waitresses, dishwashers,
bartenders, cafeteria employees, hotel service workers--all
classifications of culinary, catering, and service employees.

It has won for workers in our industry:

The 8-hour day.

One day's rest in seven. (Now the Union is winning
the 5-day week in more and more establishments without
reduction of pay.)

Straight work shifts, in place of the unfair split-
shift workday.
Vacations with pay, holidays, paid uniforms.

Health and Welfare Plans, Pensions financed by the
employers.

And other benefits unheard of before workers organized
a union in our industry.
JOIN THE MARCH OF PROGRESS . . . . BE ONE OF US . . . .
THE UNION WAY IS THE AMERICAN WAY
                        TO GOOD CONDITIONS AND HIGHER PAY!

Figure 4-4 Continued

IT MAY CONSTITUTE AN UNFAIR LABOR PRACTICE UNDER THE FEDERAL LAW, FOR THE EMPLOYER TO SAY OR DO ANY OF THE THE FOLLOWING THINGS. —

THE EMPLOYER CAN'T —

1. Promise employees a pay increase, promotion, betterment, benefit, or special favor if they stay out of the Union or vote against it.

THE EMPLOYER CAN'T—

2. Threaten loss of jobs, reduction in income, discontinuation of any privileges or benefits presently enjoyed or use of any intimidating language which may be designed to influence an employee in the exercise of his right to belong or refrain from belonging to a Union.

THE EMPLOYER CAN'T —

3. Threaten or actually discharge, discipline or lay-off an employee because of his activities in behalf of the Union.

THE EMPLOYER CAN'T —

4. Threaten, through a third party, any of the foregoing acts of interference.

THE EMPLOYER CAN'T —

5. Threaten to close or move the plant, or to drastically reduce operations if a Union is selected as a representative.

THE EMPLOYER CAN'T —

6. Spy on Union meetings. Parking across the street from a Union hall to watch employees entering the hall would be suspect.

THE EMPLOYER CAN'T —

7. Conduct himself in a way which would indicate to the employees that he is watching them to determine whether or not they are participating in Union activities.

THE EMPLOYER CAN'T —

8. Discriminate against employees actively supporting the Union by intentionally assigning undesirable work to the Union employee.

THE EMPLOYER CAN'T —

9. Transfer employees prejudicially because of Union affiliation.

THE EMPLOYER CAN'T —

10. Engage in any partiality favoring non-union employees over employees active in behalf of the Union.

THE EMPLOYER CAN'T —

11. Discipline or penalize employees actively supporting a Union for an infraction which non-union employees are permitted to commit without being likewise disciplined.

THE EMPLOYER CAN'T —

12. Make any work assignment for the purpose of causing an employee who has been active on behalf of the Union to quit his job.

THE EMPLOYER CAN'T —

13. Take any action that is intended to impair the status of or adversely affect an employee's job or pay because of his activity on behalf of the Union.

THE EMPLOYER CAN'T —

14. Intentionally assign work or transfer men so that those active in behalf of the Union are separated from those believed not interested in supporting a Union.

THE EMPLOYER CAN'T —

15. Select employees to be laid off with the intention of curbing the Union's strength or to discourage affiliation with it.

THE EMPLOYER CAN'T —

16. Ask employees for an expression of their thoughts about a Union or its officers.

THE EMPLOYER CAN'T —

17. Ask employees how they intend to vote.

THE EMPLOYER CAN'T —

18. Ask employees at time of hiring or thereafter whether they belong to a Union or have signed a Union application or authorization card.

THE EMPLOYER CAN'T —

19. Ask employees about the internal affairs of Union, such as meetings, etc., (Some employees may, of their own accord, walk up and tell of such matters. It is not an unfair labor practice to listen, but he must not ask questions to obtain additional information.)

THE EMPLOYER CAN'T —

20. Make a statement that he will not deal with the Union.

THE EMPLOYER CAN'T —

21. Make statements to the employees to the effect that they will be discharged or disciplined if they are active in behalf of the Union.

THE EMPLOYER CAN'T —

22. Urge employees to try to persuade others to oppose the Union or stay out of it.

THE EMPLOYER CAN'T —

23. Prevent employees from soliciting Union membership during their free time on Company premises so long as such does not interfere with work being performed by others.

THE EMPLOYER CAN'T —

24. Give financial support or assistance to a Union, its representatives or employees.

THE EMPLOYER CAN'T —

25. Visit the homes of the employees for the purpose of urging them to reject the Union.

If the Employer says or does any of the above in your presence, please report such incidents immediately to your Union Business Representative.

Figure 4–5

Management Campaign Tactics

Similarly, an employer may undertake to counteract these unionizing efforts by a variety of actions that are within the range of those deemed to be lawful. For example, the letter to employees shown in Figure 4-6 is a good illustration of an employer campaign tactic aimed at weakening the union's position.

To straighten out a rumor . . . not one job is at stake if the union gets in or does not. This is my third time around in union attempts to organize and I know the rules all the way . . . I never have nor do I intend to violate them.

The NLRB is a government agency which guarantees your right to be organized or not and I or anyone else cannot stop you from making your own decision. In a free society no one should have to pay someone else's dues for the <u>right</u> to hold the job of their choice, the one you applied for, got and kept for yourself.

There are 108 employees on the eligible voters list that we filed with the NLRB. At a monthly charge of at least $5.00 per employee, for dues, the union would collect $540.00 per month or $6,480.00 per year. How would you like to receive $6,480.00 without doing one days' work on the premises? What a gold mine! That is why there are a few people working hard to get their hands into your pockets.

The question of benefits has come up . . . the biggest benefit is that in 32 years under my ownership and management of the Ideal Corporation, there have been no lay-offs and not even one payless payday and no strikes. SICK BENEFITS . . . you might ask Bernice, in the laundry, about receiving $70.00 per week for several months while ill . . . perhaps a year ago Helen Jones, our 2nd floor maid, missed several weeks of work at similar pay, Loretta, our payroll clerk, recently died--her sister received over $4,000.00 in insurance benefits. Wayman, one of our bell boys, now laid-up from an automobile accident received hospitalization and $36.00 per week in benefits.

For more than twenty years our employees have received a week's paid vacation after one full year of employment. Look around you and see the great number of fellow employees who have worked here for 5, 10, 12, 15, 20 . . up to 32 years . . . people who have never missed a paycheck and have benefited from working here.

One other ugly word is strike . . . the union can use this tactic, should they get in, to call a strike to get me to agree to a contract. With a strike you lose pay and may be ORDERED to be in a picket line.

Figure 4–6 Open letter to all employees of the Ideal Hotel & Restaurant Corporation

REMEMBER TO VOTE AND . . .

IF YOU HAVE SIGNED A UNION CARD YOU CAN STILL   <u>VOTE NO</u>

IF YOU DO NOT WANT THE POSSIBILITY OF A STRIKE   <u>VOTE NO</u>

IF YOU DO NOT WANT DUES, FINES, ASSESSMENTS   <u>VOTE NO</u>

IF YOU DON'T WANT UNION DOMINATION   <u>VOTE NO</u>

IF YOU DO NOT WANT TO PAY FOR SOMETHING
YOU ALREADY HAVE   <u>VOTE NO</u>

My record speaks for itself.

BE ON RECORD YOURSELF   VOTE NO   FEBRUARY 2nd   <u>VOTE NO</u>

Sincerely,

Oscar Waldorf, President

Figure 4–6 Continued

Some Do's and Don'ts for Employers in the Hotel and Restaurant Industry

Regardless of the vigor of the union organizing campaign, there are important rules of thumb which hospitality industry employers bear in mind as they seek to avoid any disruption of their operation while an organizing campaign is in progress. Given the dimensions of most union–management relationships today, it would not be unreasonable to suppose that the first thing any hotel or restaurant employer does in these circumstances is to consult an experienced labor lawyer. Indeed, failure to obtain competent legal advice is a mistake few companies can afford to make. Nonetheless, past experience suggests that employer–union confrontations sometimes occur so unexpectedly that "first aid" in the form of the following "Do's and Don'ts" often serves as a useful guide:

Some management "don'ts"

1. Don't get provoked into any arguments with union sympathizers.

2. Don't imply in any way that union organization may result in discharges, layoffs, sale, or lockout.

3. Don't promise any rewards if the election beats the union.

4. Don't ask employees if they have signed union cards or attended union meetings, or how they are going to vote.

5. Don't call individuals into your office to discuss union organization.

6. Don't interfere with employees who distribute Union literature in non-work areas. You can, however, prevent any union activity in work areas where the activity interferes with the regular course of business.

7. Don't interfere with the right of any employee to wear a union button.

8. Don't change working conditions of employment unless you can document a valid reason for making such change.

9. Don't threaten or promise benefits depending on how employees vote.

10. Don't ask employees what they think of the union.

11. Don't punish employees for union activities, or imply that you know of such activities.

12. Don't get names of employees who attend union meetings or spy on the union or on the union "ring leaders."

13. Don't ask a job applicant about his or her union affiliation.

14. Don't bribe anyone.

15. Don't try to get an anti-union employee to act as your agent in encouraging others to vote against the union ... but be sure that employee does vote, himself.

16. Don't predict that you will lose business because of unionization or that the hotel will shut down.

17. Don't announce your refusal to bargain with the union.

Some management "do's"

1. Do give your personal opinion of the union, its leaders and organizers, but be careful not to engage in libel or slander.

2. Do warn employees to carefully read anything the union asks them to sign. Advise them that they don't have to sign cards and that they can vote in any election held whether they sign cards or not.

3. Do caution that a union may force an employee out on strike even though he or she is happy with an offer the employer has made.

4. Do state that the union organizers or the employee's friends will not know how an employee voted in a secret ballot election. URGE all employees to VOTE.

5. Do tell employees that hotels and restaurants provide jobs and unions cannot prevent layoffs if they become necessary.

6. Do warn that union seniority and production quotas may penalize ambitious employees who want to progress as fast as their capabilities permit.

7. Do advise that union dues may be considerable and may increase at a greater rate than wages.

8. Do tell employees that they have a free choice not to join a union and that you hope they will not. You can say that their best interest lies in the union's defeat.

9. Do urge employees to report union coercion to supervisors, and inform employees that they don't have to talk to union organizers if they don't want to.

10. Do explain that unions, if they win, usually seek to require membership or a dues equivalent of all employees, whether they want to join or pay or not.[18]

Union Representation Election

Union representation elections are conducted by the National Labor Relations Board, or by a state labor board if it is determined that the election is under the latter's jurisdiction.

If the union's petition to hold an election is not contested, the election can be conducted by secret ballot. Such an election is known as a *consent election*. If, on the other hand, the petition is contested either by an employer or by a rival union, then pre-election hearings must be held to determine voting choices to appear on the ballot. If the resulting *formal election* does not yield a majority of votes for any one of the available choices on the ballot, then a *runoff election* must be held between the two choices receiving the largest number of votes. Unless the majority of employees vote for "no union," the union that receives a majority of votes in the election is the one certified by the National Labor Relations Board as the bargaining agent for a period of at least one year, or for the duration of the labor contract. The group of employees thus designated by the NLRB as appropriate for representation by, for example, a local of the Hotel Employees & Restaurant Employees International Union, is thereafter identified as the *bargaining unit*.

Evolution of the Collective Bargaining Relationship

Recognition by a hotel or restaurant employer of a union representing employees of his or her establishment is simply the first step in building a joint, cooperative relationship between the two parties. Once the dust has settled as a consequence of the differences, rivalries, and hostilities generated during the heat of the unionizing campaign, the primary concern of the parties is to engage in the collective bargaining process.

At the Bargaining Table—A Simulation Exercise

Whatever concrete demands a union may seek from a hotel or restaurant employer, the fundamental goal of every union is to negotiate with that person a written agreement covering wages and working conditions on terms that are agreeable to both parties. This is what is meant by the *collective bargaining process*.

Once the agreement has been reached, each party then has the responsibility of administering its provisions and insuring that the other party keeps its part of the bargain. This means also that the two sides must continue to cooperate in resolving any differences arising from subsequent interpretations of the agreement.

Based upon a decade of classroom experience with collective bargaining, the authors believe that a simulation exercise is the best way—short of actual "real-world" experience—for you to learn about what happens at the bargaining table. Accordingly, we have included in the appendix an operationally tested model for simulating real-life negotiations between a big-city commercial hotel and a union representing its employees.

This model assumes that you will be able to complete the requirements of simulated bargaining in not more than six classroom sessions of one hour each. Student teams representing management and union positions learn quickly to negotiate, to decide what tactics and strategy must be used, and ultimately to come to an agreement over what may initially appear to be insurmountable issues. The instructor, during this exercise, functions as a resource person and as a "stage manager" of the learning experience. For example, he counsels students on their preparation for negotiations and the sources of bargaining information. He also sees to it that the simulation takes place in a classroom composed of tables and chairs arranged in such a way that four members of each management team sit across the table from the four opposing members of each union team. There is no allowance for student spectators in this exercise. Everyone must be a participant.

As we have noted elsewhere in this chapter, the union–management relationships that most frequently get public attention are those characterized by strikes, violence, and conflict. Seldom do the news media focus upon the fact that most union–management relationships are peaceful ones, resulting primarily from bargaining experiences and skills exercised by negotiators for each side. Hence, a primary reason for involving you in this simulation is to show that with imagination, knowledge of hotel and restaurant operations, and the ability to be both rational and flexible, you are likely to reach an agreement in which both parties can cooperate.

For those of you who may never intend to be involved in unionized hotels or restaurants, the importance of this exercise should not be underestimated, because, as countless students before you can confirm, there is always the possibility that your hotel or restaurant may someday be subject to an unexpected unionizing effort. In that event, what you will have learned *now* about how to handle yourself at the bargaining table will surely serve you to great advantage then.

Summary   Although unions of working people have existed since the fourteenth century in England and in this country since the Colonial era, it was not until the 1930s that they began to achieve significant bargaining power. Much of that power has been gained as a result of a basic change in the public attitude toward organized labor and collective bargaining. We have seen this attitude shift from legal repression to strong encouragement as reflected in the Wagner Act, then to modified encouragement coupled with regulation as reflected in the Taft-Hartley Act, and finally to detailed regulation of union rights and responsibilities as reflected in the Landrum-Griffin Act.

In recent years, membership in the Hotel Employees and Restaurant Employees International Union, AFL-CIO has been leveling off in common with the general membership pattern of all unions. Approximately 20 percent of the U.S. workforce is now unionized. In the case of the hotel and restaurant industry, it is estimated that 12 percent of the work force is unionized.

Because the rights of employees to unionize and to bargain collectively over their wages and working conditions are now firmly established, it is in the best interests of everyone who may sometime be required to deal with a union to develop the ability to bargain effectively. To this end, an exercise in collective bargaining for the hospitality industry has been included at the end of this book in Appendix A. The principal parts of a labor agreement are typified by the hotel contract shown in Appendix B.

Questions for Discussion

1. What is the meaning of a "Bill of Rights" for union members?

2. Under the Taft-Hartley Act, which unfair practices apply to both unions and employers?

3. What are the pros and cons of the likelihood of unionization being successful in the fast-food industry?

4. Assume that you are representing a large nationwide company that is negotiating a union contract in the hotel–restaurant industry at the present time. What economic, legal, social, and political factors might you expect to exert some influence on your negotiations? Explain.

5. From your viewpoint, is there anything to be said in favor of picketing? Or of strikes? Explain.

6. Of all the personal attributes which you have found it important to have at the bargaining table, which *one* do you consider to be the most important? Why?

7. Would you describe successful collective bargaining as an *art* or as a *science*? Discuss.

Key Terms

○ AMERICAN FEDERATION OF LABOR

○ BARGAINING UNIT

○ CONSENT ELECTION

○ FORMAL ELECTION

○ INJUNCTION

○ INTERNATIONAL UNION

○ KNIGHTS OF LABOR

○ LANDRUM GRIFFIN ACT

○ LOCAL UNION

○ MULTI-EMPLOYER BARGAINING

○ NATIONAL LABOR RELATIONS BOARD

○ NORRIS-LAGUARDIA ACT

○ UNION BUSINESS REPRESENTATIVE

○ TAFT-HARTLEY ACT

○ TRUSTEESHIP

○ WAGNER ACT

○ WAITERS AND BARTENDERS NATIONAL UNION

○ WHIPSAWING

A Case
Study: The
Airport
Motor Hotel*

The Airport Motor Hotel is located near the major airport of one of America's largest cities. As part of the service to its customers, the hotel has always provided service to and from the airport by means of small buses which are operated by hotel employees. Since the hotel is located some distance from the airport, it is necessary for the buses to travel over busy freeways to reach either the airport or the hotel.

On May 1, 1968, Samuel Wilson was employed by the hotel as a bus driver. From that date until April 5, 1971, his work record showed that he had never been involved in a serious accident. On April 5, 1971 while at the wheel of a company bus, he was involved in a catastrophic accident which resulted in the death of four persons, injuries to five others, and considerable property damage. As a result he was indicted by a grand jury for involuntary manslaughter and placed under bail for his appearance in county court. After several conversations between union and company representatives, it was agreed to suspend Wilson from his job as driver and provide other employment at the same rate of pay pending his trial in county court. It was further understood that the entire matter would be reviewed by company and union officials after the completion of Wilson's trial. Mr. Smith, manager of the Airport Hotel, attended the trial and after hearing the prosecution's case testified under oath for the defendant. Transcript of the trial shows that he stated: "Samuel Wilson is one of our best employees." He further testified that "if Samuel Wilson

* Adapted from John R. Abersold and Wayne E. Howard, The Foster Motor Freight Company Case, Cases in Labor Relations (Englewood Cliffs, N.J., Prentice-Hall 1967), pp. 26–29.

doesn't lose his driver's license we will retain him in our employ as a driver."

Sam was convicted of involuntary manslaughter and was sentenced to a prison term, but the sentence was immediately suspended by the court. The grievant's license to drive was not revoked by the state. Immediately thereafter, the company discharged Sam on the basis of his responsibility for the accident as determined by the county court. He then filed a grievance protesting his discharge, contending that the company discharged him without justifiable cause and requesting his reinstatement with full seniority rights and restitution of all monies lost by reason of his discharge. No satisfactory settlement was reached by the parties and the union filed a demand for arbitration.

Applicable Contract Provisions

Article X—Section 1   The company shall have the right to discharge an employee for justifiable cause.

Position of the Union

The union contends that industry practice is not to discharge a driver on the basis of one accident, but that three chargeable accidents normally constitute basis for discharge. The company is aware of this practice and is bound by it. Under this standard the grievant's record is not one which merits his discharge, since he was never previously involved in a chargeable accident.

The testimony under oath of the company's manager at the grievant's trial stops the company from subsequently claiming that it had justifiable cause for Wilson's discharge, since his license was not revoked by the state. Furthermore, the manager testified under oath that the grievant was "one of our best employees." This statement occurred after the accident and, indeed, after all of the prosecution's testimony had been revealed at the grievant's trial.

The agreement between company and union representatives to permit the grievant to return to his job pending the trial of his case was not intended by the parties to make the decision reached in the trial determinative of his right to continued employment with the company. It was merely agreed that the parties would again meet and discuss his future status with the company following the trial and after a careful review of all the circumstances bearing on the case. No restrictions were placed on the driving of the grievant during this interim period, except the restriction to drive only within the state—a restriction required by the conditions of his bail bond. Under these circumstances, the mere fact that the grievant was convicted of involuntary manslaughter as a result of his one unfortunate accident does not constitute justifiable cause for discharge.

Position of the Company

The company argues that there can be no question of just cause for discharge since the county court found the grievant guilty of criminal negligence. The mere fact that the court suspended Wilson's prison sentence in no way dilutes the court's findings. Moreover, as a result of this negligence, four persons were killed, five others were injured, and considerable loss of property resulted.

The action of the grievant also subjected the company to damage suits amounting to many hundreds of thousands of dollars, not to mention the loss of its vehicle. Though it is covered by insurance, its insurance rates for future liability coverage will increase considerably as a result of the grievant's negligence, and retention of the grievant is likely to cause them to rise even more.

Moreover, the company has a responsibility to the public at large. The public should not be subjected to the hazard of encountering a negligent driver on the highway. The company's responsibility in this regard is all the greater by reason of its knowledge that the grievant's negligence caused the catastrophic accident which gives rise to this case. The incident undoubtedly has also reduced the competence of the grievant with respect to future driving, since he will always carry with him the grim memory of his past negligent action.

The company made no agreement with the union to maintain the grievant in its employ. Rather, it agreed to review the situation after the outcome of the court case. The verdict of involuntary manslaughter returned by the jury released the company from any further obligation to maintain the grievant in its employ.

The company is unaware of any industry practice that would prevent it from discharging a driver before involvement in three chargeable accidents. Nor can it be bound by such practice in the absence of evidence that it agreed to be bound. The company further submits that none of its drivers has ever been found guilty of criminal negligence in an accident. Regardless of the grievant's prior record, this fact alone constitutes just cause for discharge.

Case Questions

1. Was the hotel justified in discharging Sam Wilson? Why or why not?

2. Was the union justified in demanding Sam's reinstatement? Why or why not?

3. If you were the arbitrator, how would you decide this grievance? State the reasons for your position.

Notes

1. Arthur M. Schlesinger, Jr., *The Age of Jackson* (Boston: Little, Brown, 1945), pp. 339–41.

2. Eugene C. Hagburg and Marvin J. Levine, *Labor Relations: An Integrated Perspective* (St. Paul, Minn.: West Publishing Co., 1978), p. 16.

3. Norris-LaGuardia Anti-Injunction Act, March 23, 1932, Public Law 65, 72nd Congress, 29 U.S. Code, Sec. 2.

4. In Arthur A. Sloane and Fred Witney, *Labor Relations*, 3rd ed. (Englewood Cliffs, N.J.: Prentice-Hall, 1977), p. 63.

5. For an excellent study of the rise of the CIO and its constituent unions, see Walter Galenson, *The CIO Challenge to the AFL, A History of the American Labor Movement* (Cambridge, Mass.: Harvard University Press, 1960); also, see Irving Bernstein, *Turbulent Years, A History of the American Worker, 1933–41* (Boston, Mass.: Houghton Mifflin, 1971), especially pp. 116–25, for an account of the Hotel and Restaurant Employees and Bartenders International Union, AFL-CIO.

6. Matthew Josephson, *Union House, Union Bar: The History of the Hotel & Restaurant Employees and Bartenders International Union, AFL-CIO* (New York: Random House, 1956), pp. 3–9.

7. Ibid., p. 13.

8. Ibid., pp. 13–14.

9. Ibid., p. 15.

10. Bernstein, *Turbulent Years*, p. 116.

11. This decline, it should be noted, mirrored the general decline in strength of the American labor movement from its high point in 1920, when it included 12 percent of the country's workforce, to its low point in 1933, when unions represented barely 2 million members, something less than 6 percent of American workers.

12. Josephson, *Union House, Union Bar*, pp. 295–96; the author's newspaper quotes are from the *San Francisco Chronicle*, November 6 and November 9, 1941.

13. 101 US APP DC 414 249F (2nd) 506.

14. Max Boas and Steve Chain, *Big Mac, The Unauthorized Story of McDonald's* (New York: E. P. Dutton, 1976), p. 96.

15. Ibid., p. 109.

16. For an excellent, down-to-earth explanation of the various roles of a labor union representative, see these two paperback publications: Duane Beeler and Harry Kurshenbaum, *Roles of The Labor Leader* (Chicago, Ill,: Roosevelt University, Labor Education Division, 1969), and Duane Beeler and Harry Kurshenbaum, *How To Be A More Effective Union Representative* (Chicago: Roosevelt University, Labor Education Division, 1965).

17. 49 Stat. 449 (1935).

18. The following paperback books are excellent source materials to consult for information about both the management and union sides of unionizing campaigns: *What to do When the Union Knocks* (U.S. Chamber of Commerce, Washington, D.C., 1975), *How to Be A More Effective Union Representative*, by Duane Beeler and Harry Kurshenbaum (Chicago: Roosevelt University Press, 1965); and *Roles of the Labor*

Leader by Duane Beeler and Harry Kurshenbaum (Chicago: Roosevelt University Press, 1969).

Behavioral Architecture

When you finish this chapter, you should understand:

1. The evolution of the American first-class hotel

2. What is meant by the psychological impact of motels

3. What contemporary architects mean by "tuning in to the chore-ography of human activities"

4. Each of the five important stages of the life cycle

5. How the life cycle of multisite hospitality establishments pro-vides opportunities for adapting successfully to future change

> Time was when the "grand hotel" was a stage setting for the idle rich. Now it is a stage setting for business promotion—conventions and tourism. ... The new grand hotels are places for people to notice, enjoy and remember. ... The hotel you stay at may be one of the things you come to see—and to experience. ...
>
> Restaurants and bars have always been stage sets—whether places to see and be seen or romantic hiding places. ... Not only convenience and functional comfort, but a setting which provides a sense of occasion—whether it's "fast food" with the kids or New Year's Eve in a nightclub—are required ... in the increasingly competitive world of restaurants, bars and clubs. ...
>
> Jeanne M. Davern, *Places for People*
> (New York: McGraw-Hill, 1976), Preface.

Places to stay and places to eat and drink are, by definition, places for people. Yet when you look at some of the older hotels and restaurants around today, you wonder if they were really designed as if people mattered.

In retrospect, it is plain that builders early on tended to concentrate their attention on the structure of a building simply as a static object or monument. Thus, in ancient times, rulers built the great pyramids to signify their political domination. People could not look up without seeing the tomb of their king, symbol of the status quo.

In modern times, even so commonplace an American institution as the hotel has been seen as an architectural monument designed to symbolize the reach of our urban frontiers. Ever since the early days of the nineteenth century, hotel buildings grossly disporportionate to their surroundings were built in this country not to serve cities but to create them.

Evolution of the American First-Class Hotel

Memphis' Gayoso House, completed three years before the city had been incorporated and ten years before it had a railroad, was being advertised in 1846 as a "spacious and elegant hotel," even though it then stood in the heart of a dense forest.

Writing to his wife in November 1858 from an almost vacant site that was to become Denver, one William Larimer optimistically predicted, "We shall have a good hotel here by spring." Construction had already been started, he said, and a hotel manager was on his way from Omaha.[1]

Summing up his impressions of a visit during the early 1860s to these urban outposts, British novelist Anthony Trollope concluded:

> In the states of America the first sign of an incipient settlement is a hotel five stories high, with an office, a bar, a cloakroom, three gentlemen's parlours, two ladies' parlours, a ladies' entrance, and two hundred bedrooms. ...Whence are to come the sleepers in those two hundred bedrooms, and who is to pay for the gaudy sofas and numerous lounging chairs of the ladies' parlours? In all other countries the expectations would extend itself simply to travellers—to travellers or to strangers sojourning in the land. But this is by no means the case as to these speculations in America. When the new hotel rises up in the wilderness, it is presumed that people will come there with the express object of inhabiting it. The hotel itself will create a population—as the railways do. With us the railways run to the towns; but in the States the towns run to the railways. It is the same thing with the hotels.[2]

To all appearances, therefore, the wedge of urbanism being driven into America's nineteenth-century wilderness was powered by something recognizably new, an American-style hotel. Of course, the mere possession of a "grand hotel" was not enough to guarantee a successful metropolis. By all accounts the West, as early as the 1820s, was littered with ambitious towns that never grew. Around 1823, a group headed by Nicholas Biddle, president of the Bank of the United States, and Saunders Coates, editor of the *Mobile Register*, set about constructing the town of Port Sheldon, near Holland, Michigan. Not surprisingly, their first major project was a "large and commodious hotel," named Ottawa House. It opened just before the Panic of 1837, and closed barely five years later when the projected town itself failed.

Whence came the new-style American first-class hotel? The design, which became the prototype for decades of hotels here and abroad, came out of New England. It was the work of Isaiah Rogers (1800–1869), the world's first hotel architect.

Isaiah Rogers, the First Hotel Architect

If the reality of hotel architecture today is in real estate—as the *New York Times* seems to suggest[3]—the architectural realities of nineteenth-century hotels in America rested in the rich traditions of the Greek Revival movement, of which Isaiah Rogers was the most brilliant exponent. Paradoxically, the age of upstart towns and cities became the age of the "Greek Revival"; this period extended roughly from 1820 to 1860. "These decades from the twenties to the sixties were vital in every phase of development," wrote Leopold Arnold, Dean of Columbia University's School of Architecture in his introduction to Talbot Hamlin's classic text.[4] He continued:

> Politically, the system of government was crystallizing, and at the same time gaining flexibility to administer to the needs of an increasingly complex society. Economically the expansion was fabulous, for the seemingly limitless natural resources were being developed (and also exploited); and the industrial power which has since carried us to national greatness was being established. The population, increasing rapidly, pressed relentlessly to the West, converting successive frontiers into settled territories. ...
>
> There was a spirit of confidence, which if over-youthful, was nonetheless inspiring. The people had embarked upon a great experiment in government, and had made it work. They had conquered a continent and were beginning to profit from the fruits of their labors. They were witnessing the miracles of science changing the world before their eyes, and they were sure that change was progress. They looked upon government not as a mere agent for policing and defense, but as an institution for the administration of human welfare; Science and Government should solve the problems of the world. It was a phase of adolescent optimism preceding the confusion, conflict, and disillusion through which the nation passed before reaching maturity.[5]

As the curtain of wilderness was being lifted in the America of the early 1800s, so too was the desire surfacing for intellectual encounter with literature and the arts. A society whose way of life was sufficiently cultivated to spawn the prolific writings of Emerson, Thoreau, and Hawthorne as well as the "Hudson River" school of artists led by Durand and Cole could scarcely be expected to stifle its appetite for unfettered architectural expression. The resulting hotel structures, of which the first and most influential example was the Tremont House, bore decorative detail clearly rooted in classic Greek precedent. This did not mean an unalterable allegiance to the traditions of the past, but rather, as Dean Arnold is careful to point out, it reflected the "enthusiasm which the whole Western World, and particularly the new republic, showed for the struggles of Greece during her wars of independence"—hence the names that were given to the then new towns, such as Athens, Troy, Ithaca, and Ypsilanti.

Tremont House—The First Modern Hotel

It remained for Isaiah Rogers, a young, self-educated architectural prodigy, to ignite the fires of the entire Greek Revival movement with his epoch-making design of the Tremont House in Boston. The son of a Plymouth, Mass. shipbuilder, Rogers left home when he was 16 to become an apprentice carpenter in Boston. Seized with a wanderlust not uncommon to teenagers, he left for the South as soon as his apprenticeship was over, spending the years 1820 and 1821 in Mobile, Alabama. Although it is uncertain as to who was his employer, he did have the good fortune to enter and win a contest for the design of the first theater in Mobile. From that time on, he apparently considered himself an architect, for he returned to Boston to work during the ensuing four years for the well-known designer and builder of the Bunker Hill Monument, Solomon Willard. At the age of 26, Rogers opened his own architectural office and shortly thereafter was commissioned by a group of Boston merchants to design the Tremont House. When it opened in Boston on October 16, 1829, it was apparent that he had scored an architectural breakthrough. With few models to follow, Rogers had succeeded in designing what critics called the first modern hotel.

With an exterior so simple as to be almost austere and its architectural detail based upon Greek forms, the Tremont House exuded an air of elegance and public purpose. Its facade of Quincy granite was dominated by a colonnaded portico and pilasters at the corners. There were 170 guest rooms; a dozen richly furnished public rooms (unknown previously); a lavish, formal dining room with a deeply coffered ceiling and a screen of Ionic columns at either end; and other such distinctive innovations as room service, a free cake of soap in every guest room, a reading room with newpapers from around the world, printed menus in the dining room, and food prepared by a continental French chef—all served to please so many of the public that Rogers quickly achieved fame and fortune as the country's leading hotel architect. His subsequent work included many of the best-known hotels of the era: the Bangor House in Bangor, Maine; the Astor House in New York; the Charleston Hotel in Charleston, South Carolina; the Burnet House in Cincinnati; the St. Charles Hotel in New Orleans; the Battle House in Mobile; and the Maxwell House in Nashville.

Admiration by its patrons aside, the Tremont House's advanced mechanical equipment was the envy of designers and engineers the world over: "In this building," wrote Talbot Hamlin, "for the first time in America if not indeed in the whole world, mechanical equipment became an important element in architectural design."[6]

The Rogers design had pioneered the incorporation of inside plumbing into what architectural historians were calling the world's first modern building. Even though plumbing above the ground floor was still unknown, the Tremont featured an elaborate ground-floor battery of eight water closets located at the rear of the central court and, in the basement, a series of bathrooms with cold running water. Remarkable as it was, this rudimentary development was simply a forerunner of what was in store for hotels of the future.

Nothing, it seemed, accelerated the growth of American hotels so much as their readiness from that early day to become laboratories and showcases of technological progress. In one hotel after another inventions were first tried out and then widely adopted by the rest of the lodging industry. Thus, by the turn of the century, hotels had ushered into American life such conveniences as central heating, private bathrooms, passenger elevators, electric lights, and telephones.

From the outset, this new-style American hotel had been viewed in terms of its physical structure and mechanical improvements. Little or no attention had yet been paid to the *people* who were its users. Our imperfect statistics suggest, however, that the needs of one influential group of Americans, the ubiquitous traveling salesmen, could no longer be disregarded.

Rise of the Modern Commercial Hotel

In a time of burgeoning populations and expanding economies, the lack of commercial hotel facilities to accommodate the rapidly growing numbers of traveling salesmen ("drummers") prompted the birth of the nation's first commercial hotel in Buffalo, New York, on January 18, 1908. It was the brainchild of Ellsworth Milton Statler, an enterprising young hotel man from Wheeling, West Virginia, who early on had perceived the need for a scaled-down version of the nineteenth century luxury hotel at a price which the commercial traveler could afford ("A room and a bath for a dollar and a half"). Undeniably, the Buffalo Statler and other Statlers following in its wake had inaugurated a new era in American hotels. They not only gave impetus to ongoing improvements in building structure and design (as, for example, the design of back-to-back guest rooms using a common shaft for plumbing, heating, and electrical conduits—known as the "Statler plumbing shaft"); more importantly, as hotels were opened successively in Cleveland, Detroit, St. Louis, New York, and Boston, Statler proclaimed their triumphs as proof of his conviction that the three most important factors in a hotel's success are location, location, location. Indeed, few competitors seemed to disagree, as they vied with one another from coast to coast in corroborating Statler's proposition, that it pays to set up shop where the customers collect. There was no denying that cities as the centers of commercial gravity had become the natural magnet for hotels, for "that pile of solemn but exuberant shapes that for so long has been the emblem of man's hospitality to man."[7]

Resort Hotels on the Wane

By the time that Statler was beginning to dot the urban landscape with commercial hotels, many of the country's fashionable resorts for the well-to-do were already in eclipse. As far back as the seventeenth century, society-minded Pilgrims had patronized the Colonies' first resort, Stafford Springs, Connecticut—a favorite watering-hole for New England Indian tribes. "In second and third position for resort age honors were two Pennsylvania Springs, the Yellow Springs in Bucks County and the Bath Springs at Bristol," writes Cleveland Amory in his entertaining book, *The Last Resorts* (Harper & Row, N.Y., 1952, p. 17). These were soon followed by many other "springs" hotels, all catering to the rich and near-rich of ninteenth-century America.

Today, two resorts survive—the Homestead at Hot Springs, Virginia and the Greenbrier at White Sulphur Springs, West Virginia. Probably the most famous is the Greenbrier, originally known as the White Sulphur Springs Hotel, scene of the renowned encounter between the governor of South Carolina and the governor of North Carolina, when one is reported to have said to the other: "It's a long time between drinks."

Now a property of the Chesapeake and Ohio Railroad, the Greenbriar no longer serves as a gathering place for the great generals, famous statesmen, and reigning belles of yesteryear. They are solemnly commemorated with a dignified monument on the rear lawn of the hotel. Instead, it is the site of high-level corporate meetings, trade association conferences, and national conventions. The old order has clearly given way to the new. Gracious hospitality, beautiful surroundings, and healthful springs are now the domain of the convention delegate and the packaged-tour customer.

Motels

Though nearly a half century was to pass before the Statler paradigm reluctantly gave way to the motel and motor inn, lesser remnants of its architectural legacy still endured. Noting their standardized similarity to telephone booths and gasoline service stations, Reyner Banham, Professor of Architectural History at University College, London, described the Caribe Hilton (architect, Edward D. Stone) and the Istanbul Hilton (architect, Skidmore, Owings & Merrill) as "an eight or ten-story slab of accommodation, with a corridor down the middle of each floor, rooms on either side, and bathrooms tucked in between the rooms and the corridor. It is as classic and conventional as a Georgian terrace house."[8] Somewhat less charitably, the British *Architectural Review* characterized the contemporary hotel structure as "a Corbusian machine for staying the night in."[9]

By the 1950s, however, the mood was changing. Though hardly a novel idea,[10] the motor inn concept as typified by Holiday Inns helped discourage the notion that hotels were costly to build, costly to stay in, and costly to operate. Oddly enough, it was an architect, Eddie Bhrestein, who suggested the name, Holiday Inn, to founder Kemmons Wilson;

it was a name obtained from an old Bing Crosby movie he had once seen.

As competition increased, the basic motel image that emerged was one of a place where "you get a clean bed and a bath and somewhere to hang your clothes and a door to lock against the world. The unmonumental motel, made of one- or two-story blocks around a parking yard (with the office and restaurant—if any—in a separate block at the front) dealt with problems of service in an equally radical way; there wasn't any . . . apart from the clerk at the front office."[11]

With the postwar proliferation of in-city and along-the-highway accommodations giving way to such competitive features as high-rise construction, heated swimming pools, and other amenities attractive to convention-goers and vacation travelers, the distinctions between the urban and suburban hotel–motel establishments were becoming less discernible.

What *was* discernible in the motel boom of the fifites and sixties, however, was the impact these hostelries were having upon the persons using them. Hadn't the resort to pastiche architecture and slapstick design, it was asked, resulted in a serious threat to our concept of personal authenticity?[12] Wasn't man being reckoned as inauthentic when the world treats him as "anybody" or "everybody," as a creature of circumstance at the mercy of the ready-made suit or the packaged tour?

Motel and Hotel Design

With no little disdain, Mary Warnock provided a graphic answer:

> ...there remains a hard core misery in hotel life which makes one wonder whether the tourist industry does not thrust inauthenticity on its customers more than it needs to. Part of the trouble is the general low level of aesthetic appeal in the interior decoration and furnishings of hotels. It is not so much that heavy flock wallpapers and dark moquette-covered chairs are not to one's *own* taste; they do not appear to be in anyone's taste in particular. They are there for all to gaze on or to use, and nobody ever seriously chose them. This is the very essence of inauthenticity in which the concept of an individual choosing for himself has quite dropped out.
>
> In my particular hotel, above the doors, there was a kind of clouded glass, with an asymmetrical snakelike line engraved on it, in a vaguely Art Nouveau style. I found myself obsessed with the question of who decided to have it there ... who said: "We cannot have plain glass; there must be some decoration." The answer seemed to be that probably no one said it. Somehow the glass was put up independently of anyone's actual decision. ...
>
> Then, in the hotel lounge, there was, from about six o'clock onwards, continuous piped music—one tune vaguely followed on from another, unremarked and hardly heard, played on unidentifiable instruments. ... Nobody seemed to mind, or not to mind these sounds, and if one raised the question who had actually chosen to have them going on, rather than silence, it would seem no one had; the sounds were for anyone, produced by anyone, specially chosen by no one.

... Moreover, if the idea has somehow got about that it is preferable to have piped music rather than not to have it, it is extraordinarily difficult to imagine a way to dislodge this idea, and in any case, perhaps one of the characteristics of inauthentic man, for whom the tourist trade caters, is that he doesn't care much either way.

It is also impossible to avoid inauthenticity in the hotel dining room. There is something particularly dispiriting about paying a great deal for a meal which one knows is not prepared for oneself as an individual, nor even for all the guests in this particular hotel, but for the whole food-eating public, and then deep-frozen until it should be wanted.[13]

Measured in terms of personal identity and unaffected sincerity, the hotel–motel creation of the postwar decades seemed less a triumph of design process than a capitulation to the "plastic esthetic of tacky assembly line lookalikes," in the words of Ada Louise Huxtable. Writing in the architecture feature section of the Sunday *Times*, Huxtable, that paper's architectural critic, brought the decisive reminder that the swing from cheap expediency to cheap pretense in hotel design were part and parcel of an ominous game plan— one in which the environment is the loser, and the consumer the sucker:

The new American landscape is made of plastic pretensions and false dreams. The unfulfilled promise is the American way of life, from the oversize restaurant menu suggesting farm-fresh succulence and delivering dreary precooked fare to the die-stamped motel with its celebrated plumbing that is already beginning to fail and synthetic Elizabethan pubs with styrofoam beams and food. ...

Caveat emptor, as they used to say, only the buyer is no longer in the position to beware. He takes what he gets. ...

... I never approach a trip requiring an overnight stay without a sinking heart. It's not that I won't be reasonably comfortable ... things like beds, baths, ice and Coke are the preoccupations of the American "hospitality" industry ... it's that I will be so depressed. ... It is that one is forced into a banal, standarized, multibillion-dollar world of bad colors, bad fabrics, bad prints, bad pictures, bad furniture, bad lamps, bad ice buckets, and bad waste baskets of such totally uniform and cheap consistency of taste and manufacture that borax or camp would be an exhilarating change of pace.

All this is arranged in identical, predictable layouts smelling of stale smoke and air-conditioned at a temperature suggesting preservation of the dead no matter what the climate outside. Like the roads leading to airports everywhere, you never really know where you are. It is a complete loss of identity—both personal and place. Ask any psychiatrist about that.[14]

Apparently, these were judgments few professionals would have contradicted. "I find recent hotel architecture dismaying," wrote Harry Mullikin in the *Architectural Record*, observing that most contemporary hotels were difficult to distinguish from office buildings.[15] Moreover, it was feared as late as 1976 that the contagion of cold impersonality so characteristic of office buildings had infected even the newest monuments to southern hospitality in Atlanta, the Peachtree Center Plaza and the Omni International hotels:

> Having just returned from two weeks traveling in England where I stayed in a different place every night, I thought a few comparisons between English and American facilities might prove of interest. ...
>
> In most American hotels, including the two ... in Atlanta, once the guest leaves the public areas and closes the door behind him for the night, he finds himself in a formula-designed space. None of the essentials is lacking, to be sure. The ubiquitous television set rests on the dresser, and there might be a Gideon Bible in the drawer of the nightstand. But there is no sense of place. ... The rooms are like hundreds of other rooms in hundreds of other hotels. They are cold and impersonal and rarely give any clue as to where one is.
>
> In England, on the other hand, the guest is treated very much as he might be if he were visiting a private house. The decor would win no prizes, and the furnishings may be a little shabby, but there is always a "home-like" quality about the rooms.[16]

To those accustomed to regard hotel structures as absolutely reflective of distinguished architectural achievement, Sherman Emery's *Interior Design* editorial had been incomplete.

Lamenting the "slapstick" effect of hotels generated by Britain's Development of Tourism Act of 1969, a critic for the *London Architectural Review* looked darkly at the whole lot as "a very undesirable accretion to our architectural heritage." Why undesirable? Because, said the *Review*, in our society a long delay in building the necessary hotels "lays the environment open to the unmitigated scourge of the developer. ... He is a scourge because, by getting between the architect and the man who is to own and use the building, he frustrates the ordinary processes of design. Architecture happens as a result of the collusion between a client who fully understands his own enterprise and an architect who is able to respond to his needs. It cannot happen when the real client is some third party who has no real interest in, or knowledge of, the enterprise he is endeavoring to house. ... The buildings which result have the same overall character; at once faceless, thoughtlessly standardized and brash."[17]

Even the superb confidence of the internationally known hotel architect, William B. Tabler, seemed to be faltering as he addressed hotel students at the University of Massachusetts early in the 1970s:

> Something is going very wrong with the relationship between architects and hotel administratiors; and we both need to understand what it is or it will get worse. What is going wrong is that a wedge is being driven between the professional architect who is designing or renovating a hotel and the professional hotel administrator who is going to have to operate that hotel. That wedge is being driven,

perhaps unknowingly and certainly unwisely, by the developer, the man who has the money or knows where to get the money.[18]

To Tabler, it looked very much as if architects' dreams of great hotels could never be realized unless hotel administrators could rid themselves of the notion that an architect needs at least two bosses, the hotelier and the developer. The solution, he felt, was to "put your trust in a good architect, and be a good client." For, in his view, "good architecture is the reward of good clients."

To another architect, Atlanta's John Portman, the task could be best achieved if the architect himself were the developer. For, he wrote, if architecture is ever to succeed in shaping the environment, it must not only keep control of both the real estate and the architectural aspects of a building project. Most importantly, the architect must assume responsibility for improving the quality of urban life so that cities would be desirable places for *people* to work and live in.

Tuning in to the Choreography of Human Activities

To make such progress possible, according to Portman, the architect's work must inevitably reflect a "total life involvement":

> We cannot afford to abandon the cities; it is a course of action that makes no sense either economically, politically, or socially. And if we do not intend to abandon our cities, we must stop acting as if that is what we are going to do. ...
>
> A city is a living entity that is changing all the time. ...
>
> Every city has to go back and say: "OK, this whole thing is for that little guy who is walking around down there. How can we have this huge mass of density, and profit, and all the rest of it and still create a livable environment?"
>
> My ideas about cities began to expand and change in the mid-1960s, when I made my first journey to Scandinavia. The Tivoli Gardens in Copenhagen were a revelation to me. ... When you walk through Tivoli, you see that almost everyone is smiling. I have given much thought to just which ingredients create the magic of the place. It has taught me much about the effect that environment can have on one's feelings. ...
>
> The overall experience ... led me to realize that the way you should go about designing and evolving an environment is by thinking about what people want and need on a day-to-day basis.[19]

As for the resulting forms and structures, Portman believes that each building must be part of an urban coordinate unit ... a "pedestrian village where people can and want to live, work, shop, and walk without recourse to wheels."[20] And further, for a coordinate unit to succeed, he is convinced that it must "lift the human spirit" while at the same time functioning as an economically feasible investment.

Above all, what Portman wants is to make "architecture more responsive to people, and people more responsive to architecture":

Architects in the past have tended to concentrate their attention on the building as a static object. I believe dynamics are more important: the dynamics of people, their interaction with spaces and environmental conditions ... I am naturally interested in the latest structural techniques, in innovative building materials and the technology of my craft; but I am more interested in people. Buildings should serve people, not the other way around.[21]

An Architecture for People and Not Things

In Portman's opinion, an architecture for people and not for things is not so much a controversial theory about architecture—as some have claimed—as a dramatic concern for the way people will experience and react to a building. Thus, he believes that when people move through a spectacular hotel their journey should be orchestrated:

When you enter upon an escalator the space should unfold rather than explode upon you all at once. Pulling the elevator out of its shaft and opening it up with walls of glass makes it another way of experiencing architectural space. ... When people step into an ordinary elevator, all conversation tends to stop. When people ride in a glass-enclosed elevator they are much more likely to go on talking."[22]

To Portman, the whole idea has been to open everything up—to take a hotel from its traditional closed, tight position and to explode it into an elaborate atrium structure with its hanging sculptures, interior sidewalk cafes, glass elevators, and revolving roof-top restaurants. These have been some of the more arresting developments bearing his distinctive architectural signature.

George J. Wimberly's Culture-Oriented Architecture

The Innovative Approach

Of the three architectural firms of the world specializing in hotel architecture (i.e., those of Portman, Tabler, Wimberly), the one most renowned for its innovative approach to user and environmental considerations is the firm of Wimberly, Allison, Tong & Goo. The founder of this Hawaiian-based resort-design firm, George J. "Pete" Wimberly, whose philosophy closely mirrors that of the behavioral architecture school, has designed more than twenty hotels which dot the exotic resort areas of Hawaii, Japan, and the South Pacific (including the countries of Southeast Asia). As the designer of hotels in such culturally diverse places as Tahiti, Fiji, Samoa, Okinawa, Singapore, Indonesia, and Manila, and as tourism consultant to the governments of Pacific area territories and countries, Wimberly has never deviated from his belief in "people-oriented" and "culture-oriented" hotels. Writing in the *Cornell Quarterly*, he contrasts this deep-rooted conviction with the proliferation of "architectural bad neighbors" in the post–World War II era when many hastily built hotels came to resemble "ugly racks of shoe boxes dropped into exotic locations."[23]

Expanding further upon the importance of building hotels that "make a positive contribution not only to the economy but to the culture and social fabric of the community as well," Wimberly told fellow conferees at the island of Tonga in 1976:

> To give the best of oneself to any endeavor is not easy, but it is the only road open to those who value their culture and their environment. ... The local culture, way of life, the songs, the dances, the chants, the handicrafts and the architecture should be preserved at all costs; .... every effort should be made to see to it that only the best of any of these should be presented to the visitor, and to this end, the government and the industry itself must work to see that this is done.[24]

For his part, Wimberly intends to continue this reinforcement of local culture by designing and integrating resort hotels in such a way as to give the strongest possible sense of *people* in their cultural milieus. Wimberly's resort creations are indeed at the forefront of today's—and tomorrow's—architectural "good neighbors."

Life Cycle of Hospitality Establishments

Thus far, we have seen how hospitality establishments have emerged from early beginnings as inanimate paeans of Greek Revival architecture, American plumbing, and urban sprawl to today's multisite facilities behaviorally suited to the needs of their users. Whether those needs are

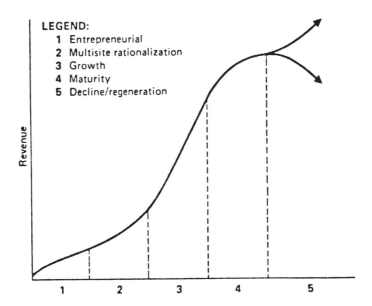

LEGEND:
1 Entrepreneurial
2 Multisite rationalization
3 Growth
4 Maturity
5 Decline/regeneration

Source: W. Earl Sasser, R. Paul Olsen, and D. Daryl Wyckoff, *Management of Service Operations*. Reprinted with permission. © 1978, Allyn and Bacon, Inc., Boston, p. 535.

Figure 5–1   The multisite service firm life cycle and functional areas of corporate activity

met through designing contemporary hotels and restaurants in the Portman–Wimberly idiom or through the "cookie-cutter" prototypes of McDonald's and Holiday Inns, it is important to recognize that the resulting structures and operations tend to follow a predictable *life-cycle* pattern (see Figure 5-1).

The concept of a life cycle in the hospitality industries, as researchers have recently demonstrated, involves a predictable series of stages which every multisite restaurant or hotel is destined to go through.[25] It is divided into five major stages: entrepreneurial, multisite rationalization, growth, maturity, and decline/regeneration. A description of each stage follows. At the end of this chapter we have included a case study of Victoria Station, Inc., in which you are to identify the various life-cycle stages.

Entreprenurial Stage

The *entrepreneurial stage* occurs when an individual owner has recognized a market need and offers a hospitality service, usually at one location. During this stage, the dominant design for the services being offered tends, as we have already seen, to reflect the owner's interest in building an imposing monument.

The emphasis is not so much on who the customers are or how well their needs are served as on the architectural identity of the building and its technological innovations—hence the classic Greek Revival architecture of Boston's early Tremont House, the bright orange roof of a Howard Johnson's, the "great sign" of Holiday Inns, and the golden arches of a McDonald's.

Multisite Rationalization Stage

The *multisite rationalization stage* occurs when the entrepreneur begins thinking of additional facilities, once the original facility has reached its physical limit or its market area limit. During this stage of geographic expansion, site selection comes into sharper focus, reflecting not infrequently the owner's uncanny "feel" for ideal locations. As noted earlier, Ellsworth Statler once observed that the three most important factors in the success of a hotel were location, location, location; and in the exercise of this skill he had few peers. Today, the chairman of the board and founder of LaQuinta Motor Inns intuitively performs a similar function for his company—with remarkable success.

In the 70-billion-dollar restaurant industry, long dominated by individual entrepreneurs, multisite operators like Howard Johnson's, Kentucky Fried Chicken, and McDonald's now account for over 40 percent of all dining revenues—indicating rather convincingly that once the dominant design has been selected and reproduced in multiple geographic areas, the "cookie-cutter" concept foreshadows the rapid growth phase to follow.

Since one requirement for future success is both increased revenues and profitability, it is not surprising to see concern for market share surfacing prominently by the end of this stage.

Growth Stage

The *growth stage* occurs when firms fuel their sales and profit push with rapid construction of new company-operated facilities (sometimes at the rate of one new opening each day, or each week), the expansion of franchising or licensing arrangements, and the purchase of competitors. For many hotels and restaurants, this is the "golden age" of accelerated sales and swollen profits. It is the time when esprit de corps is high; a time when people are excited about "getting in on the ground floor" of a rapidly expanding enterprise; as well as a time when substantial economies of scale are produced.

However, toward the end of this stage, the euphoria associated with the hectic pace of one grand opening after another is dimmed by the pressures arising from a variety of problems. Escalating costs often exceeding expected revenues, overexpansion, declining profits, and loss of focus upon the managerial complexities of multisite operations are some of the more pressing problems that affect the growth process.

A 1976 study of the fast-food industry has asserted that managing a food service chain through its growth stage is like maneuvering a ship through the Bermuda triangle.[26] Interviews which Harvard Business School researchers conducted with the presidents or chief operating officers of thirteen fast-growing food service chains indicated that most of them change course only after hitting one of nine particular obstacles, any one of which is sufficient to "sink the ship" or at least to require extensive repairs. The nine obstacles are:

1. Failure by management to understand that there are four basic, but quite different, functions to manage:

   New unit development
   Operations
   Marketing
   Concept development

2. Failure of the founder(s) to delegate responsibility.

3. Failure of the management team to develop the skills required to manage a larger firm.

4. Lapse of management motivation.

5. Haphazard growth.

6. Not changing a mature concept.

7. Diversifying too quickly.

8. Breakdown of communication.

9. Poor franchisor-franchisee relations.

A contemporary example of a chain in trouble is that of the 101 railroad-motif restaurants, Victoria Station, Inc. The *New York Times* of January 3, 1980, reported that the company had locked itself into a single theme—that of reconditioned boxcars and cabooses—an apparent "cookie-cutter" predicament from which it is still trying to extricate itself. As for the question of future growth, Victoria Station's vice president of operations appeared to echo the Bermuda Triangle theory with his statement to the *Times*: "We'll have to make it through the current rough sailing before we think about opening many new restaurants."[27]

Maturity Stage

The growth stage ends and the *maturity stage* begins when one or more of the following factors come together to create tough operating problems. For one thing, market share (i.e., percentage of the market) levels off. For another, keen competition from upstart competitors threatens the profitability of the enterprise. Then too, this is the stage when managerial complexities—not hitherto faced—emerge to confront the unwary navigators of the "Bermuda Triangle."

Above all, the maturity stage occurs when many hospitality firms blindly follow their market expansion goals with an out-of-date concept. Thus, after a decade of phenomenal growth during which the novelty of Victoria Station's boxcars adorned with nineteenth-century British railway memorabilia attracted customers, it was apparent to nearly everyone except the management that the concept was passé.[28] Nonetheless, despite an anticipated loss for the 1980 fiscal year, as well as a sharp drop in the market price of its common stock, the operating vice president told the *New York Times* that "the basic railroading theme is not the problem. . . . What we're going through is the indigestion of too rapid growth."[29]

In a word, this can be described as the stage of major shakeouts; a time when gnawing doubts as to the viability of the concept are fueled by press reports of lackluster earnings or even more serious troubles, as in the 1980 examples of Sambo's, Wendy's, Pizza Hut, Victoria Station, and Jack-in-the-Box.[30]

Those who adapt successfully to changing market conditions do so by revitalizing the old concept, as in the case of the Holiday Inns expansion into casino gambling in Nevada and New Jersey; or by generating a newer concept, as architect John Portman did in his design of atrium hotels for Hyatt and Western Hotels.

In some instances, notably Sheraton Hotels in the late 1960s and Howard Johnson's in the late 1970s, inability to change a mature but obsolescent concept leads to a merger with another, larger organization better able to breathe life into the system.

In others, failure to modify a dying concept leads downhill to decline, the last stage in the life-cycle process.

Decline/Regeneration Stage

The final stage of the life cycle is often delayed, if not avoided entirely, by prolongation of the maturity stage through a series of market expansions, concept modifications, and management development changes. McDonald's, Burger King, and Sheraton are examples of multisite chains which appear to have executed such changes successfully. Undoubtedly, there are others you can identify. Those are the firms that are devoting attention to ways of attracting and appealing to new market segments, as well as to ways of renewing and recapturing the loyalty of existing customers in the face of new competitor challenges.

When, however, a hospitality firm does find itself in a tailspin, the consequences are almost always irreversible. This is true because awareness of its decline seldom surfaces until a hotel or restaurant company has incurred major losses of market share, along with serious erosion of its profit margins. At this point, it becomes impossible to mask further decline by desperation "turnaround" attempts to remodel, refinance, or recycle the company's total package. Unless it is lucky enough to be acquired in a "distress sale" to a new owner, the company's only alternative then is to undertake bankruptcy proceedings.

Importance of the Life-Cycle Concept

The life-cycle concept as it applies to places to stay and places to eat and drink is important for three reasons.

First, because of the inevitable sequence of stages through which companies are destined to pass, management's responsibility is to anticipate the changes at each stage and to adapt to them successfully. Even though the hospitality industry evidence accumulated thus far has been based solely upon the experience of multisite firms, there is little reason to doubt the applicability of the life-cycle concept to single-site firms. By identifying what stage of the life-cycle pattern they are in, hospitality establishments can plan smooth shifts from one stage to the next instead of reacting in panic to a set of conditions that could have been predicted in advance.

Second, by looking at the future through the magnifying glass of the life-cycle process, one can better assess the state of the present than one can by simply analyzing the present alone. One gains a greater and more useful perspective this way.

And finally, as we recognize that the time between the entrepreneurial stage and the end of the maturity stage is becoming progressively shorter in every sector of the hospitality industry, it means that we can never afford to get locked in to a particular building design, or menu offering, or operational philosophy. Always, we must be able to adapt promptly to the innovative, free-wheeling changes of the marketplace while at the same time holding profitability at levels sufficiently adequate to insure survival in an industry that puts a heavy premium on the ability to cope with change.

Summary   In this chapter we looked in broad perspective at places for people to stay and to eat and drink.

We saw that the message of the long historic process of urbanization in this country is one that is closely related to the location and

structure of those buildings that we readily identify as hotels. Early on,
hotels became the entering wedge being driven into America's wilderness
primarily for the purpose of creating cities themselves—but not always,
of course, with singular success. There were lots of failures. Later, as
cities and their burgeoning populations grew, the number of hotels
multiplied, bringing into focus a myriad of political, economic, and
social undercurrents of American life. In consequence, there emerged
distinctive patterns of hotel architectural design and technological innovation destined to dominate the hospitality horizon until the mid-
twentieth century. Given the rise of the post–World War II phenomenon
of multisite motel and fast-food restaurant chains—as symbolized by the
nationwide "cookie-cutter" prototypes of McDonald's and Holiday Inns—
it was inevitable that the question of their life cycle should arise. As the
pace of the economy accelerated in the postwar decades, it became apparent that hotels and restaurants, like other industries, tend to follow a
predictable life-cycle pattern.

 We have found the life-cycle concept to be important because by
utilizing different strategies at different stages of life-cycle development
it is possible to plan a smooth transition from one stage to the next and
thus avoid the "panic button" approach that usually results in a fatal
tailspin. In the face of turbulence and uncertainty that are likely to continue well into the twenty-first century, an understanding of the life-cycle
concept will help you to anticipate the changes required in order to sustain profits at each of the five stages.

 1. Explain the symbolic significance of the great pyramids in rela- **Questions**
tion to design and location of early hotels in the United States. Do you **for**
think hotels and/or food service establishments today can justifiably be **Discussion**
described as "sterile obelisks," a phrase used by architect Clovis Heimsath
in a May 1978, article appearing in the *Cornell Hotel and Restaurant Administration Quarterly*? Why, or why not?

 2. Explain the significance of Isaiah Rogers' contribution to hotel
design. Comment upon what you consider to be "blind spots" of his
hotels and their imitators.

 3. Discuss the impact upon people of the "cookie-cutter" concept
as reflected by the multisite development of motels and restaurants in
the post–World War II era. Have you ever felt that these facilities were
conspicuously insensitive, in their design or operation, to the people who
use them? Explain.

 4. What do you see as the principal disadvantages to the idea of
"tuning in to the choreography of human activities"? Can you give examples from your own experience? In your opinion, are atrium-style
hotels, Holiday Inns, and McDonalds' fast-food restaurants "where it's at"
in the 1980s? Defend your position.

 5. Why is it important to understand the concept of the life cycle as
it applies to the hotel and restaurant industry?

6. Discuss the stages of the life cycle in multisite hospitality establishments.

7. How can one determine at what stage a hospitality firm is in its life cycle? Illustrate. Some multisite operators think that the best method of determining where a company is in the life cycle is to predict the next stage first and then work backwards. Why do you think that this might be considered a useful approach?

8. How do you think the life-cycle concept can be effectively utilized as a management tool in strategic planning for hospitality establishments?

9. Some companies believe the life cycle concept to be inappropriate for them since they have been in existence for long periods of time—sometimes for nearly a century—and they are continuing to operate profitably. Discuss why "Established in 1776" may no longer be a passport to survival in today's complex and competitive world of multisite chain operations.

10. Discuss what is meant by the "Bermuda Triangle" concept.

Key Terms
- COMMERCIAL HOTEL
- CULTURE-ORIENTED ARCHITECTURE
- DECLINE/REGENERATION STAGE
- ENTREPENEURIAL STAGE
- GROWTH STAGE
- LIFE CYCLE
- MATURITY STAGE
- MOTEL
- MULTISITE RATIONALIZATION STAGE
- RESORT HOTEL
- TREMONT HOUSE
- TUNING IN TO THE CHOREOGRAPHY OF HUMAN ACTIVITIES

A Case Study: Victoria Station, Inc.*

In early fall of 1973, the three founders of Victoria Station, a chain of railroad theme restaurants, had completed the initial phases of their development strategy. They had opened 17 restaurants with an additional 5 under construction, and approximately 10 more on the drawing boards. . . . Sales in the year ending March 31, 1973 were $11,350,089. . . . In addition, the company had made a very successful initial public of-

* Prepared by D. Daryl Wyckoff, Lecturer in Business Administration, as the basis for class discussion rather than to illustrate handling of an administrative situation (revised by W. Earl Sasser, Assoc. Professor of Business Administration). Used by special permission of Connors Investor Services, Inc., Reading, Pennsylvania. Copyright © 1973 by the President and Fellows of Harvard College. Reprinted by permission of the Harvard Business School.

fering of its stock. The founders wre preparing for the next phase of their growth by developing operating controls and reporting procedures to maintain the profits from the existing units, while continuing to open new units. Observers in the restaurant industry were watching to see if these "youngsters would clear the next hurdle."

Company Background

Victoria station was founded by three classmates of the Cornell University School of Hotel and Restaurant Administration. . . . Richard Bradley, president, said that the original intention of the venture was to create "a top-notch operating company." The three were prepared to undertake nearly any business if operations were critical to success; however, "the restaurant opportunity presented itself first": Bradley, Peter Lee, and Robert Freeman felt that they had the ability to operate nearly any type of business. The question was, where did they feel they could gain the maximum leverage? Finally they decided on entering the limited-menu, theme-restaurant, medium-priced market. . . .

The concept of Victoria Station was based on "a carefully thought-out program involving the elements crucial for success in the restaurant business: concept and uniqueness, quality control, and financial control."

Uniqueness of Concept

The basic concept at Victoria Station was to serve the rapidly growing number of singles, couples, and families who enjoyed well-prepared food, but who could not afford high prices. Victoria Station featured prime rib of beef served in a unique railroad atmosphere utilizing actual rolling stock (i.e., boxcars) converted into restaurants. Authentic artifacts and memorabilia from the British Railways further enhanced the decor of the restaurants. . . .

The original Victoria Station had facilities to seat approximately 156 persons. However, through additions this was later expanded to 205 places.

Tables were waited on and bussed by male college students, with young women providing cocktail service at the tables and in the waiting areas. Each waiter started as a busboy, progressed to lunch waiter, then advanced to dinner waiter; each step provided a significant increase in earning capacity. All tips were pooled and divided on a prearranged formula among waiters, busboys, cocktail waitresses and cooks. As a result, service was a self-policing, team affair, rather than a divisive competition. For a restaurant that thrives on volume and turnover, the atmosphere at Victoria Station was considered to be unusually relaxed.

The menu was relatively limited. . . . Entree prices ranged up to $7.50, but 80 to 90 percent of the main courses were purchased for $4.75 or $5.75 ($4.95 or $5.95 in some locations). While beverages and a la carte items such as baked potato and sauteed mushrooms increased the average dinner check substantially, it was possible for a couple to enjoy

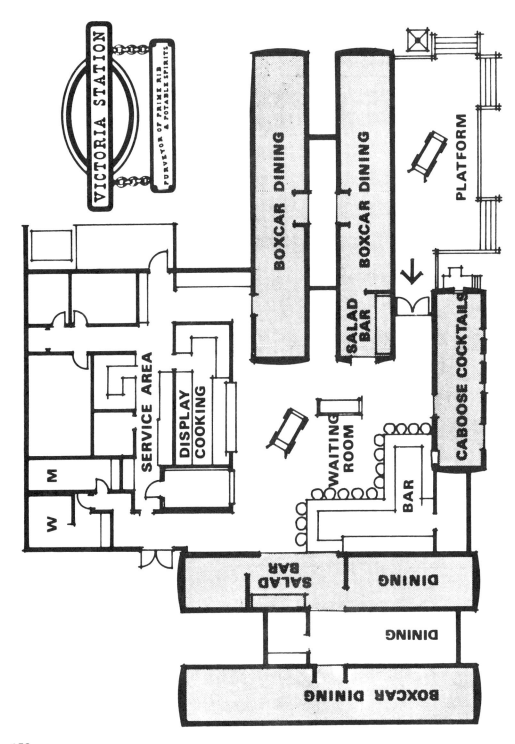

Victoria Station, Inc., Layout of typical 205-seat restaurant

prime-rib dinner with salad and wine for approximately $15.00, including tip. The average lunch check (not including tip) was $4.00. . . .

The company employed no advertising or paid promotion, and therefore relied entirely on initial publicity before opening and word-of-mouth advertising for its marketing success. Simply being open for lunch, particularly in downtown areas, was considered by management as a form of advertising for couple or family dinner business.

Quality Control

Richard Bradley felt that "if you can control the [food] specs, then your only remaining problem is one of execution." He believed that the first job of management was to ensure that the supply of raw materials at all locations was of uniformly high quality.

To achieve this, all beef was purchased nationally, cut to specification and shipped directly to each location. Besides prime-rib roasts, Victoria Station used controlled-portion filets and top sirloin butts. The latter item appeared on both the lunch and dinner menus, providing a minimum of waste. Luncheon ribs (a noon-time specialty) were derived as a by-product of the least expensive prime rib dinner, which was served without the bone.

Shrimp were purchased nationally and shipped to all restaurants. Produce and most service items and accessories were purchased locally from an approved purveyor list. All invoices were paid from the San Francisco headquarters. A computerized checking system assured that the names of vendors not on the approved list would be brought to the attention of operations management.

Execution was primarily a matter of careful management supervision to ensure strict adherence to clearly defined standards. Each prospective restaurant manager was put through three months of on-the-job training, followed by a ten-day seminar at headquarters and nine months as assistant manager.

Standards were defined in a comprehensive operations manual. Appearance, food preparation and service, beverage preparation and service, atmosphere, equipment maintenance, safety, inventory control and other matters were set down in detail, together with complete job descriptions for all managers.

For example, there was a checklist which was used by each regional manager in evaluating restaurants and managers in his area. Included on the list were such details as the level of lighting, and whether the beans at the salad bar were properly drained. In addition to providing the regional manager with a useful vehicle for correcting deficiencies (which might otherwise be picked up by his superiors in one of their periodic visits), the checklist formed the basis for determining whether the manager and his two assistants would be eligible for the semi-annual performance bonus. Failure to qualify for the performance bonus eliminated an individual from participation in the profitability bonus.

Financial Control

Financial control of restaurant operations was maintained through several detailed reports. Daily meal counts; sales receipt and expenditure reports; and sales breakdowns for food, house and bottle wine and other beverages were tallied for each waiter at both lunch and dinner. Sales and collections were reconciled on the same report. Daily inventories were taken of ribs, steaks and liquor, with other items inventoried no less often than monthly. . . .

Bar stock was replenished on the basis of one full for one empty. A profit and loss statement was prepared monthly for each restaurant. Computer operations to be introduced shortly would soon provide financial analysis of similar-sized restaurants by region, budget/actual variance, man-hours, revenues per seat and revenues per square foot.

While it was believed by top management that these control procedures enabled them to spot potential problems such as waste or pilferage before they got out of hand, they felt that the continued good will of a capable employee group could not be overemphasized. In this regard, management had set up a stock-purchase plan to augment its bonus system and tip-pooling program. It was the feeling of management that the stockholder-employee was a vigilant employee, because the broken stack of dishes or the purloined loin was potentially money out of his pocket.

Because meat costs represented 70 percent of food costs, management constantly monitored meat prices. There were some debates among observers as to the general trend in meat prices. While all felt that prices were on an upward trend, some felt that there might be a slight short-term down trend due to imports. However, most felt that there was an increase of as much as 12 to 18 percent due over the next 12 months. It was felt that this would magnify the need for a very well-executed cost control program.

Organization

. . . The three officers . . . were described as a "management team" in which each member had special responsibilities. Lee was oriented toward the controller function and the development of management information systems. He was also responsible for quality control. Robert Freeman was primarily responsible for operations. Under Freeman was a director of operations and four regional managers. It was believed by the top management team that the overall success of Victoria Station operations depended heavily on the performance of the regional managers. These managers were selected from highly experienced Victoria Station unit managers, as were nearly all of the members of middle management. The purpose of the regional-manager organization was to provide localized management and relieve [the director of operations] from heavy involvement in day-to-day operating decisions as the number of units grew. . .

Restaurant Expansion Activities

"New activity is the primary challenge—new restaurants, businesses, and locations. People have a pride of working with a well-respected growth company," was said by Peter Lee. Victoria Stations numbered 17, with an additional 5 under construction, and 10 more committed to or being designed.

Members of the financial community described the Victoria Station growth record as "most impressive." The market price of the stock was running about $18/share, which reflected a price-earnings ratio of approximately 59 times last year's earnings. Market analysts felt that such a price was justified based on past and anticipated growth. However, one market observer pointed out that such a favorable price–earnings ratio was dependent on a continued record of growth in the number of units and profitablity.

Peter Lee described the process of new site selection, construction, and opening in the following general terms:

> . . . We have tended to depend on outside architectural firms to provide a design and a certain degree of project management during construction. Fairly early in the game, we established a basic standard design for our stores. However, we have had to make some modest modifications of the design for each location. These architects that we have worked with have tended to be captives. The first firm we worked with did some very good work with us and was instrumental in helping us develop some of our basic concepts. When we really started to grow about 2 years ago, our business outgrew his capacity. He simply did not care to expand, so we changed architects. The present firm is keeping up, but there is a real question in the minds of some around here why we don't have our own in-house capability on this.
>
> We have handled construction in a number of ways. Originally, we tried to use the same contractor at all locations . . . As we expanded geographically, it has become necessary to use local contractors in each area. We still tend to minimize the number of companies we work with to reduce the hassle.
>
> The local legal work can be very tedious . . . We thought that building permits, liquor licenses, and other necessary legal details would progress much more quickly than it has. As of right now, we are about one year behind schedule on that project. We are still not sure why the delays have been so great. . . . Now and then you simply get stalled — that really has hurt us . . . We are finding good locations more difficult to secure, and we have at least one location that has been a disappointment . . . We are also finding that construction time is creeping up, after a period when we were actually shortening it. Building costs are also drifting up—probably partially due to the inflation in building materials.

Review of Objectives and Strategy

The following summarizes several quotations from the letter to the shareholders in the annual report for the year ended March 31, 1973.

It is gratifying to report that Fiscal Year 1973 which ended March 31, 1973 was unquestionably the most successful in the history of Victoria Station. In many ways, 1973 was truly a spectacular year, particularly for so young a corporation. Challenges, often severe and frequently beyond our control or that of any lone corporation, also abounded during fiscal 1973. Sharply rising costs in virtually all areas, frequent frustrating construction delays, and significantly increased competition, often from vastly larger organizations, were major problems we faced most of the year. Nevertheless, we close out 1973 by all standards a far stronger company than we were twelve months ago. Perhaps then, the true measure of 1973 is the height of our achievements, given our rapid rate of growth and the challenges created by it and a host of other factors. . . .

We are tending increasingly to view our management activities as a series of delivery systems with, of course, restaurant operations in the center of the picture. For example, the real estate, construction and maintenance functions deliver to operations a completed restaurant; the human resources and training functions deliver trained management people and in-restaurant training services along with wage, salary and benefits programs, payroll and other administrative services; the accounting and data processing functions deliver financial procedures, systems and data; the operations analysis and quality control functions deliver interpretive feedback and analysis; and the operating restaurants deliver our product and service to the customer as well as sales and earnings to the corporation and its shareholders. Additionally, specialists on the operations staff are able to provide help and guidance in such areas as food operations, beverage operations and internal control. The advantages of this approach include streamlining the flow of information, pinpointing responsibility for various activities and providing a basis for measurement of results.

At a meeting with Richard Bradley, Peter Lee, and several other members of the Victoria Station organization in San Francisco, the following remarks were made.

We have built the foundations for a much larger company. The cost controls, quality controls, and organization we have installed are intended for the future. If we were planning to stay at our present size, these expenditures would not be necessary.

The financial community has high expectations for Victoria Station. They expect fast, steady, profitable growth. How fast a growth is necessary to satisfy the financial community and our investors? However, the real question is, what growth rate is necessary to satisfy ourselves? To what extent are we willing to sacrifice day-to-day operations to maintain growth just to please others? We are concerned that we are losing our objective.

Case Questions

1. Explain what has happened in each stage of the life cycle.

2. What stage do you think the firm is in by January 1983?

3. What would you have done in 1973 if you were responsible for charting the company's course?

4. What are the essential elements of the Victoria Station concept?

5. Is the railroad motif vital to the success of this chain? Does the boxcar theme keep people coming back, or is it simply a gimmick?

6. Is growth a matter of increasing sales within existing units, or of adding new units? Is it possible that the financial community could stampede a firm into a stage of uncontrolled growth?

7. What about the personal aspirations of the founders? Are they interested only in building a monument?

8. How would you advise Victoria Station to go on from the point at which the business stood as of March 31, 1973 if you were dealing with the three young founding investors? Would your advice be different if the top management had *not* been the young founding investors? Why?

Notes

1. From Daniel J. Boorstin, *The Americans: The National Experience* (New York: Random House, 1965), p. 143.

2. Ibid., p. 141. Quoted by Boorstin from a Trollope book on North America, not otherwise identified.

3. See Paul Goldberger's review of *The Architect as Developer* by John Portman and Jonathan Barnett (New York: McGraw-Hill, 1976), in the *New York Times*, January 5, 1977.

4. In Talbot Hamlin, *Greek Revival Architecture in America: Being an Account of Important Trends in American Architecture and American Life Prior to the War Between the States* (New York: Oxford University Press, 1944, pp. xi–xvii).

5. *Ibid.*, p. xvi.

6. *Ibid.*, p. 112.

7. H. J. Dyos and Michael Wolff, "Monuments of Modernity: The Victorian City," *New Society*, August 23, 1973, p. 447.

8. Reyner Banham and Peter Hall, "The Late Twentieth Century Hotel," *New Society*, August 23, 1973, p. 451.

9. Ibid.

10. As far as is known, the first use of the word "motel" was in 1924. In that year, James Vail provided accommodations for motorists on the north side of San Luis Obispo, California, on Route 101 at the foot of the Questa grade. He called it Motel Inn and erected an electric sign . . . OTEL. The first letter flashed "H" and "M" alternately. See White, *Palaces of the People* (Taplinger Publishing Co., N.Y., 1970, p. 168).

11. Banham and Hall, "The Late Twentieth Century Hotel," p. 451.

12. Mary Warnock, "Packaged Inauthenticity," *New Society*, July 22, 1971, p. 159. The author draws upon the theories of Martin Heidegger, the German philosopher, to explain that human authenticity is attained only when an individual takes hold of the direction of his or her own life as opposed to letting it be dominated by impersonal external forces. Thus, inauthentic man does not treat himself as a unique individual facing other individuals, but rather as "anybody" or "everybody."

13. Ibid.

14. Ada Louise Huxtable, "Hospitality and the Plastic Esthetic," *The New York Times*, October 14, 1973.

15. Harry Mullikin, "Hotels and Motels Reflect a Changing World," *Architectural Record*, August 1966, p. 137. When he wrote this, Mullikin was vice president of Western International Hotels. Currently, he is chairman of the board and chief executive officer of Westin Hotels, the company formerly known as Western International Hotels.

16. Sherman R. Emery, editorial, "At Home—Abroad," *Interior Design*, July 1976, p. 83.

17. "Hotels—Inquest on a Defeat," *Architectural Review*, September 1972, pp. 131–43.

18. William B. Tabler, "American Hotel Design Today," 1971 Statler Lectures at the University of Massachusetts, Department of Hotel, Restaurant and Travel Administration, p. 1.

19. John Portman and Jonathan Barnett, *The Architect as Developer* (New York: McGraw-Hill, 1976), pp. 23, 130–31.

20. Monica Geran, "An Interview with John Portman," *Interior Design*, July 1976, pp. 95–97.

21. Portman and Barnett, *The Architect as Developer*, p. 64.

22. Ibid., Part 2, *"Architecture as a Social Art,"* pp. 57–143.

23. George J. Wimberly, "Resort Hotels: The Challenge of Gracious Design," *The Cornell Hotel and Restaurant Quarterly*, November 1977, p. 27.

24. George J. Wimberly, "An Architect's View of the Environmental and Cultural Impacts of Tourism Development in Pacific Countries," address of September 2, 1976 to PITDC Conference at Tonga.

25. W. Earl Sasser, R. Paul Olsen, and D. Daryl Wyckoff, *Management of Service Operations* (Boston: Allyn & Bacon, 1978), see ch. 7, "The Multisite Service Firm Life Cycle," pp. 534–66. For a discussion of the life-cycle concept generally, see E. Jerome McCarthy, *Basic Marketing: A Managerial Approach*, 6th ed. (Homewood, Ill.: Richard D. Irwin, 1978), pp. 240–57; William R. Davidson, Albert D. Bates, and Stephen J. Bass, "The Retail Life Cycle," *Harvard Business Review* (November–December 1976), pp. 89–96; Barrie G. James, "The Theory of the Corporate Life

Cycle," *Long Range Planning,* June 1973, pp. 68–74; Theodore Levitt, "Exploit the Product Life Cycle," *Harvard Business Review* (November–December 1965), pp. 81–94.

26. W. Earl Sasser and Ivor P. Morgan, "The Bermuda Triangle of Food Service Chains," *The Cornell Hotel and Restaurant Administration Quarterly* (February 1977), pp. 56–61. The term "Bermuda Triangle" is here used to describe the stage of development of a company during which the managerial complexities it faces are greater than its capacity to handle them. This article pinpoints nine obstacles to be avoided in the growth process and recommends ten strategic steps which the food service industry can take in charting a safe course for the future.

27. *New York Times,* January 3, 1980, "Boxcar Restaurants Hit Brakes," a feature story by Steve Lohr.

28. Ibid.

29. Ibid.

30. *New York Times,* January 17, 1980, "Restaurants Brace for a Slump," a feature story by Steve Lohr.

Important Elements of Pre-Opening Management

When you finish this chapter, you should understand:

1. The critical path method (CPM)

2. The uses of the critical path approach in establishing a sequence of deadlines for all activities associated with the pre-opening management of both small and large hotels

3. The purpose of a pre-opening staffing plan and how it relates to organizational charting

4. The five key features of a sound cost reporting system

5. The principal pre-opening activities falling within each of the eleven time periods outlined for the innkeeper of a small property

6. The principal licenses and permits that are required before a new hotel can open for business

In Chapter 5 we saw that in the entrepreneurial stage of a hospitality firm's life cycle, recognition of a compelling market need usually points the way to its economic health and competitive survival long after its first customers begin to arrive.

In this chapter we shall see that no less essential to the firm's future economic life are the decisions made and the strategies adopted during the lengthy incubation period preceding the grand opening.

Moreover, recent research has shown the importance of pre-opening game plans in forestalling such familiar traumas as:

○ The conflict that arises when the building and construction trades (i.e., plumbers, electricians, painters, plasterers, etc.) and the furniture, fixtures, and equipment delivery people and installers are all fighting for the use of the same elevator.

  ○ The costly delays occasioned by a general contractor who falls behind the contract completion date, while at the same time furnishings and equipment are being delivered on schedule—with no place to put them. This frequently necessitates having to build expensive temporary storage space or incurring additional costs for transportation and warehousing until construction has been completed. (Incidentally, there is also a high incidence of pilferage and theft when furniture, equipment, and supplies are temporarily stored on the site.)

  ○ The crunch that occurs when 200 headboards for king-size beds are delivered to a new hotel where installers discover that they do not fit through the guest-room doors. Accordingly, the 8-foot-high by 6-foot-wide headboards must be sawed in half and then reassembled in the guest rooms.

  ○ The serious gap that occurs when a general contractor who is paid a bonus for completing hotel construction a month ahead of schedule earns his bonus by beating the contract completion date ... but, at the same time, the completed hotel must stand idle until the carpeting which had been ordered for delivery on the contract completion date arrives as originally scheduled—but not ahead of time.

  ○ The problem of installing quickly and economically the furniture, fixtures, and equipment in a 500-room hotel with 110 different shapes and sizes of bedrooms and 13 separate furniture and design layouts ... with almost every room having a different location for its furniture or a different positioning of its pictures and mirrors.

  Traditionally, hotel grand openings have seldom been models of integrated planning. As one perceptive journalist has noted:

> Anyone connected with the opening of a new hotel knows that under
> the best of conditions it is an exercise in organized chaos and under
> the worst of circumstances, a time of pressure-packed panic.[1]

  In point of fact, few operating executives today would deny that the acid test of managerial competence in the lodging industry occurs *not* in the first, second, or third year of operation but rather in the critical months and years immediately preceding the opening of a new hotel.

  Nonetheless, while some managements have come a long way in their acceptance of the pre-opening phase as the most important period in the economic life of a new hotel, much corporate activity continues to reflect the traditional shortcomings of nineteenth-century entrepreneurial behavior. W. Earl Sasser and his associates believe that this explains, in part, the distinctive lag exhibited by service industries in adopting new management techniques long since successfully employed in the manufacturing sector. "In most cases," Sasser notes, "the entrepreneurs have had little training or inclination for the discipline of industrial engineering or operations research. They have been more typically 'promoters' and 'developers' of business than 'refiners' and 'rationalizers.' "[2]

Whatever the forces may be which tend to retard acceptance of innovation in the hotel industry, there is little doubt that during the decade of the 1970s much progress was made by some companies in their grasp of the strategic planning process involved in pre-opening management.

In the sections that follow, therefore, you will become familiar with some of the more important tools for plotting and monitoring the pre-opening management process. It should be borne in mind that while the process we are about to describe will vary according to the size and complexity of the particular establishment, the general pattern is typical for all new lodging and restaurant facilities.

But first, a word about the impact of architectural plans upon this process.

Once determination is made that the proposed hotel is feasible and funding has been completed, the architect can proceed with working drawings for the site and for the exterior of the building. One does not have to be an architect, however, to realize that these drawings represent more than the documentary nitty-gritty upon which preliminary construction cost estimates are based. Invariably, they are the reflection of the personal philosophy of the individual architect.

**Architecture
and Design**

Nowhere has this idea been better expressed than in a recent book by John Portman and Jonathan Barnett:

> The people who are drawn to the practices of architecture have quite different temperaments from those who are attracted to real estate, and the two professions are unreceptive to the subtleties of each other's work. The result is a lack of communication, to put it mildly. ...
> Portman has learned to think of real estate architecturally, and architecture entrepreneurially. ... His approach to environment design is based on observations of the way people behave in public places. He tries to anticipate the psychological reaction of the building's ultimate users. ...[3]

Happily, the news about architectural breakthroughs in recent hotel design is good news; we became familiar with the highlights of these new developments in Chapter 5.

Thus, even though the architectural plans are underway to design an impressive hotel, and final construction details are being hammered out with the general contractor, the perceptive hotel developer at the same time must face another fact of life that is no less important. And that is to provide a system for continuous monitoring and coordination of the entire project from day one down through the grand opening.

Tools for
Monitoring
Pre-Opening
Progress

It is, perhaps, a truism that discontinuities in today's business environment have made obsolete the intuitive practices of an earlier day upon which hotel operators so confidently depended during the time between the ground-breaking ceremony and the day of the grand opening.

For too long, appropriate technology for monitoring new hotel construction has eluded even some of the more progressive firms. There are few episodes that are more painful or explosive than those unpredictable crises associated with the entire pre-opening phase of a new hotel. In the case of larger hotels (i.e., those with more than 1,000 rooms), the crises become increasingly acute when, as the scale broadens, it becomes progressively more difficult to manage all the interrelated parts of the project. "Muddling through" is the way some companies describe their methods for coping with such complexities.[4] Other companies more attuned to the concepts of the production-line approach[5] have discovered that technology can be modified to suit the needs and resources of a particular situation, even one so traditionally haphazard as the building and opening of a new hotel.

One development having a beneficial impact on the management of new construction in the lodging industry involves the application of the so-called critical path method (CPM).

The Critical
Path Method

Simply stated, the Critical Path Method (CPM) involves listing all the steps involved in the project; organizing them sequentially in a flowchart spanning the period from the beginning to the end of the project; and setting time limits on each step so as to create a "critical path" or a series of deadlines which affect the completion time of the project.[6]

Whether the technique is catching on generally in the hospitality industry is as yet too early to tell. But the indications are that since the late 1970s, the idea has not gone unnoticed by some hotel organizations. As far as we know, the earliest reference in hotel management literature occurred in November 1972, when the *Cornell Hotel and Restaurant Administration Quarterly* headlined on its cover page an article titled, "CPM for Resort Condominiums." Written by Peter M. Gunnar, president of Condominiums Northwest, Inc. (Salem, Oregon), it set forth briefly—in two pages of text and two pages of diagrams—the author's experience in developing three condominium resort hotels with a total of 775 rentable rooms. In the diagram shown here as Figure 6–1 Gunnar developed a master plan covering the nine-month period from the initial site offering to the start of unit sales and the signing of construction contracts. Simply stated, "Its purpose is to pinpoint areas of concern well in advance and to help the developer plan for crisis areas ahead."[7]

Emphasizing the need to improve the innkeepers' professional approach to the complexities of accommodation management, the Canadian Government Office of Tourism in 1976 published a remarkably informative book, *The Inn Business,* in which prospective operators were urged to chart their course carefully before buying land for an inn, or

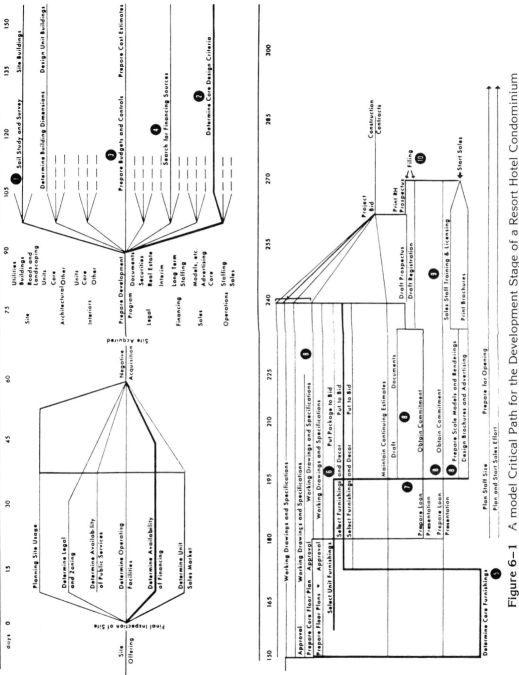

Figure 6-1 A model Critical Path for the Development Stage of a Resort Hotel Condominium

*Circled numbers are keyed to explanations in the article.

165

Timing of activity Prior to opening date	Activity
13-20 months and subsequently:	• Preliminary architectural design completed. • Contact local or regional planning authority to confirm that design and construction practices conform to basic planning criteria and regulatory requirements e.g. height restrictions. • Contact and make preliminary application at appropriate liquor licensing authority. • Engage electrical and mechanical engineers to provide design advice on such things as elevators, electrical systems, air conditioning, heating, plumbing, etc.
12-19 months:	• Begin search and application procedures for financing the project. • Construction tenders called for (takes usually 3-4 weeks to select contractor). • Where desirable engage interior designer (3 or 4 weeks) kitchen and bar design specialists (3 or 4 weeks); and landscape architect, if necessary, (3 or 4 weeks).
11-16 months and subsequently:	• Final design completed. • Have planning authority, fire marshall and other government agencies, as required, approve final design plans (takes about 2 weeks if plans meet all their criteria). • Apply for building permit. • Ask interior designer, if one is hired, for final drawings and specifications on furniture, fixtures, etc. (2-8 weeks). • Ask kitchen and bar specialist for final layout specifications for kitchens and bars (2-8 weeks). • Call for tenders on furniture, fixtures and equipment (2-3 weeks after specifications received).
10-14 months:	• Begin construction.
6-12 months:	• Set up working office (usually off-premises) and establish permanent telephone number for the inn. Engage secretary if necessary. • Hire a manager for the inn (if the owner does not plan to manage it himself). • Get in touch with the Post Office to establish the exact mailing address for the inn. • Establish rate structure. • Develop the marketing program and have preliminary promotional literature printed (stationery, brochures, direct mail and group business packages). • Prepare pre-opening costs. • Update sales and cash flow forecast. • Oversee tenders on furniture, fixtures and equipment. • Begin to establish self with community, tourist association, local industrialists and provincial tourism department.
6 months:	• Should have opening date targeted and begin confirming reservations. • Intensify promotional campaign (e.g. spot radio advertising, newspapers, etc.). • Draw up organization chart, carry out job analysis. Prepare job descriptions and specifications.
3-6 months:	• Search and advertise for necessary department heads and interview applicants.
2-4 months:	• Department heads to be on hand for interviewing and selection of staff, supervising the installation of equipment, ordering of departmental supplies. • Menu designs formalized and submitted for printing. • All necessary staff should be hired. • Service contracts establish for necessary equipment and services, e.g. TV's, window washing, laundry and dry cleaning, vending machines, etc.
1 month:	• Finalize plans for official opening party and send out invitations. • Delivery of all operating supplies should be scheduled and confirmed. • Carry out final staff scheduling.
1-3 weeks:	• All staff should be on hand for orientation and training. • Dry runs should be carried out, i.e. on equipment and service.
Opening date 2-3 weeks after:	• Hold official opening ceremony.

Figure 6-2 Pre-Opening Schedule of Activities for Operators of Smaller Inns

acquiring an existing inn, or expanding one already owned. Thus, to chart one's course, it was suggested, meant to organize all the steps involved in a particular inn project so they could be shown in sequence on a flowchart. Then, time limits should be set for the completion of each step, consequently creating a *critical path* or series of deadlines.[8] Although deadlines obviously vary with the size and complexity of a given establishment, *The Inn Business* in Figure 6–2 furnishes its estimates of the time operators of smaller inns should allow for each step prior to opening.[9]

CPM in Restaurants and Hotels

Recent research has shown that as the scale of restaurant and chain hotel projects grows, it becomes increasingly important not only to identify and keep track of all the activities comprising a particular new project but also to recognize the interrelationships of the various pre-opening tasks that must be accomplished on schedule.

As Sasser, Olsen, and Wyckoff suggest, the Critical Path Method represents a useful tool for managing service industry projects provided three criteria are met:

○ First, the project must be complex and large enough to justify this level of control. CPM contributes little to trivial projects with a few very simply monitored activities.

○ Second, the project must consist of clearly defined separable activities that have identifiable "starts" and "finishes," and when all of the activities are completed, the project is completed.

○ Third, the activities must have a defined, logical order or sequence.[10]

In the case of chain operations with computer-assisted capabilities, periodic printouts not only make needed information instantly visible as a project progresses but, perhaps more importantly, serve as "early warning" devices to facilitate work-activity changes promptly in the face of adverse circumstances.

The point is that, regardless of the size of scope of your pre-opening operations, you should plot your course of action. A basic approach, such as that used by the executive housekeeper of a large California hotel, would include the preparation of a "Countdown for Opening" chart similar to the one shown in Figure 6–3.

But this, in turn, would require detailed preparation, each week or month, of performance charts and graphs showing how long each work activity should take, and when it should be started and completed. Such analyses frequently encompass hundreds, if not thousands, of isolated work activities showing those which can be done concurrently and others which must be done sequentially. If it is clearly impossible to accomplish some of the tasks in the time allotted, this fact will become clear in the charting process and adjustments can be made. This might be necessary

Time prior to opening	Discussion & planning with top management	Activity by executive housekeeper or department	Purchasing	Interviewing and hiring
8 months		Plan and lay out office Plan linen room equipment		
7 months	Submit office plans for approval Submit linen room plans for approval	Lay out uniform room (costume control)		
6 months	Discussions re bath linens Discuss uniforms Submit uniform room plans for approval	Order office equipment Order linen room shelving if millwork		Executive housekeeper moves to actual location
5 months	Discuss contract cleaning (whether permanent or temporary) Discuss major cleaning equipment	Sample uniforms Order uniform room equipment or millwork	Order linens (bed, bath, cafe, banquet)	
4 months		Prepare "punch list" for acceptance of housekeeping department Check guest room "punch list" with engineering, rooms division and management	Order linen room equipment Order Gideon Bibles	
3 months	Discuss guest room supplies	Research guest room and bathroom supplies and test samples Design forms to be printed Decide number of keys needed for each area Make organization chart	Order uniforms Order major cleaning equipment Order keys Order light cleaning equipment—shelving, baskets, brooms, dust pans, carpet sweepers, etc.	
2½ months	Discuss which items will be made in sewing room for housekeeping, cafe and banquet departments	Lay out floor linen rooms and select equipment (carts, baskets, etc.) Become highly conversant with union regulations	Order forms to be printed Order sewing room equipment	Hire clerk-typist

Source: *Institutions Magazine*, January 1970

Figure 6–3 Countdown for opening chart

Time prior to opening	Discussion & planning with top management	Activity by executive housekeeper or department	Purchasing	Interviewing and hiring
2 months	Decide on special equipment for guests (hairdryers, razors, etc.) Decide on signs in rooms (room rates, razor blade disposal, air conditioning instructions, etc.)	Set up payroll procedures Make staffing chart Write job descriptions Do a rough maids' and housemen's manual (revise after opening) Establish labor pars for housekeeping department	Order guest room and bath-room supplies and hardware Contracts for cleaning	
6 weeks	Report progress on previous decisions and activities	Write up house and department rules (prepare to change)	Order temporary "clean-up" supplies Order special equipment for guests Order Stock metal shelving for linen rooms Order sewing room supplies	Interview assistants and hire (one assistant housekeeper hired to be training supervisor)
5 weeks	Review and revise standards where necessary	Test and select cleaning supplies	Order room signs made up	Hire people for cleaning up after construction
4 weeks	Confer with sales and rooms departments about opening occupancy Check with rooms division on furnishings "punch list"	Clean public areas Prepare complete list of room furnishings and color schemes	Order telephone directories	Interview employees Hire linen room clerk, seamstress, uniform room attendant
3 weeks		Supervisor trained Diagram of bathroom and guest room items for maids' reference Prepare cart "layout"	Order cleaning supplies	
2 weeks		Uniform room set up Linen room set up Sewing room set up Training of maids and housemen for cleaning Start clean-up cleaners in guest rooms		Hire supervisors, maids, housemen—to be hired gradually as needed, depending on when rooms are ready
1 week		Set up system of lost and found Training of second group of maids and housemen by supervisors Uniforms issued and fitted		

Figure 6–3 (Continued)

if, for example, the electrical workers go on strike during the construction phase and thereby increase the time needed for completion of the project by two months—at an added cost that could run as high as $200,000. On the other hand, early completion can greatly increase potential revenues. For example, approximately half of the 1,120 guest rooms of the Atlanta Peachtree Hotel were turned over to the owner five weeks ahead of schedule, resulting in additional room revenues of $1 million generated by that early completion.[11]

While describing the nature and scope of work activities embraced by the "big picture" of a pre-opening master plan far exceeds the limitations of this text, we want to bring our discussion of pre-opening management down to earth, first, by adding time-related details to an actual staffing plan for a 180-room hotel constructed in the 1970s; then, by showing diagramatically how each employee group fits into the chain of command; and finally, by indicating some of the key success factors which today guide the pre-opening plans of major corporations in the hospitality field.

Pre-Opening Staffing Plan: Time-Related Details

Basically, a pre-opening staffing plan is prepared for the purpose of showing how many weeks ahead of the "grand opening" employees are to be hired. Figure 6–4 is an example of such a plan used by an international hotel chain in scheduling its people's lead time for the pre-opening operations of a 180-room hotel. Without such a visual aid, it is easy to neglect some hiring tasks until the last minute or, in the alternative, to hire more people than are needed to accomplish the work available. Some companies with computer capability extend the information shown by this visual approach to include the following additional items:

1. Shift time assigned to each employee
2. Employee's salary
3. Employee's moving costs to be paid by the company
4. Employee source (i.e., whether recruited from outside the company or transferred or promoted from within the company)

Clearly, by planning ahead, aided by graphical techniques of this character, you have a greater chance of minimizing the risks inherent in the whole range of pre-opening activities and of completing the entire project within budget—and *on time.*

Organizational Structure: The Chain of Command

Having preplanned the type and number of employees needed and their respective lead times, you should also design an organization chart showing how each employee group fits into the chain of command. While such a chart was not prepared by the management of the aforementioned 180-room hotel, chains of authority and areas of responsibility do vary

Position	Lead time (number of weeks an employee is needed on the payroll prior to hotel opening)	Total no. employees
Rooms department		
Front office mgr.	4	½
Ass't. front office mgr.	3	1
Room clerks	2 × 3 weeks	
	3 × 2 weeks	5
Reservation clerk	3	1
Secretary/machine operator	3	1
Bell captain	2½	2
Bellboys	2	12
Doormen	2	3
Parking attendant	1	2
Security	4	5
Executive housekeeper	6	½
Housekeeper	4	1
Supervisors	4	4
Linen/uniform attend.	3	1
Seamstresses	2	2
Maids	10 × 3 weeks	
	5 × 2 weeks	
	5 × 1 weeks	20
Night maids	2	5
Housemen/cleaners	3	10
Total rooms department		76
Food & beverage department		
Food & beverage mgr.	8	½
Ass't. F & B mgr.—banquets	5	1
Secretary	5	1
F & B cost controller	8	1
Food controller	5	1
Beverage controller	5	1
Store clerks	6	3
Head cashier/checker	3	1
Cashiers/checkers	2½	7
Executive chef	6	½
Garde manager	4	1
Tournant	4	1
Pastry chef	4	½
(Roast cook) butcher	3	1
1st cooks	1 × 3 weeks	
	3 × 2 weeks	4
2nd cooks	1 × 3 weeks	
	3 × 2 weeks	4

Figure 6-4 Pre-opening staffing guide for a 180-room hotel

Position	Lead time	Total no. employees
Pastry/baker/helper	3	3
Vegetable/pantry	1 × 3 weeks	
	1 × 2 weeks	2
Empl. cafeteria cooks	3	2
Empl. cafeteria helper	2	1
Chief steward	4	1
Dishwashers/potwashers/cleaners	3 × 4	
	6 × 3	
	2 × 2	11
Main Restaurant		
Headwaiter	4	1
Captain	3	2
Waiters	2½	13
Busboys	2½	5
Coffee shop/swimming pool		
Hostess/headwaiter	4	2
Captain	3	2
Waiters	2½	13
Busboys	2	4
Room service		
Captain/order taker	3	2
Waiters	2½	8
Banquet		
Headwaiter	3	1
Set-up waiter/housemen	2	2
Bars		
Head bartender	4	½
Bartenders	3	3
Barboys	2	2
Bar waiters	2	6
Total food & beverage department		115

Administrative & general

General mgr.	5 months	½
Executive ass't. mgr.	10 weeks	1
Secretary (exec.)	15	1
Chief accountant	10	½
Ass't. chief accountant	6	1
General cashier	2	1
Income auditor	2	1
Accounts receivable	2	1
Accounts payable	2	1
Payroll clerk	2	1
Secretary	6	1
Night auditor	2½	1

Figure 6-4 (Continued)

Position	Lead time	Total no. employees
Front office cashiers	2½	4
Personnel mgr.	8	½
Personnel sec.	6	1
Timekeeper	4	4
Drivers	1 × 8 weeks	
	1 × 4 weeks	2
Purchasing agent	5	½
Purchasing clerks	4	2
Head storekeeper	6	1
Receiving clerk	4	1
Total administrative & general		27
Heat, light, & power department		
Chief engineer	8	½
Engineer (shift)	6	1
Electric Eqpt.	3½	2
Refrigeration men	3½	2
Boiler men	3½	2
Total h, l & p department		7½
Repair & maintenance department		
Storeman	2	1
Carpenter	2	1
Painter	2	1
Plumbers	2	2
Electricians	2	2
Mechanics	2	2
Gardeners	4	4
Total repair & maintenance department		13
Advertising/promotion department		
Sales mgr.	10	½
Secretary	8	½
Total advertising & promotion department		1
Telephone department		
Chief operator	4	1
Operators	3 × 3 weeks	
	2 × 1 week	5
Total telephone department		6
Laundry department		
Laundry mgr.	4	1
Washers/sorters/extractor	3	4
Shaker/feeders/folders	3	4
Drycleaners/steam press	2	3
Checker/marker	2	1
Valet delivery	1	1
Total laundry department		14

Figure 6–4 (Continued)

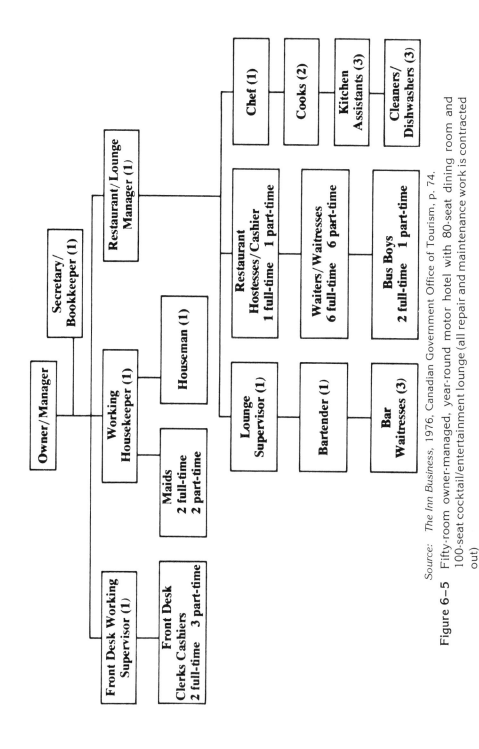

Owner/Manager

Secretary/Bookkeeper (1)

Front Desk Working Supervisor (1)

Front Desk
Clerks Cashiers
2 full-time   3 part-time

Working Housekeeper (1)

Maids
2 full-time
2 part-time

Houseman (1)

Restaurant/Lounge Manager (1)

Lounge Supervisor (1)

Bartender (1)

Bar Waitresses (3)

Restaurant
Hostesses/Cashier
1 full-time   1 part-time

Waiters/Waitresses
6 full-time   6 part-time

Bus Boys
2 full-time   1 part-time

Chef (1)

Cooks (2)

Kitchen Assistants (3)

Cleaners/Dishwashers (3)

Source: *The Inn Business*, 1976, Canadian Government Office of Tourism, p. 74.

Figure 6–5 Fifty-room owner-managed, year-round motor hotel with 80-seat dining room and 100-seat cocktail/entertainment lounge (all repair and maintenance work is contracted out)

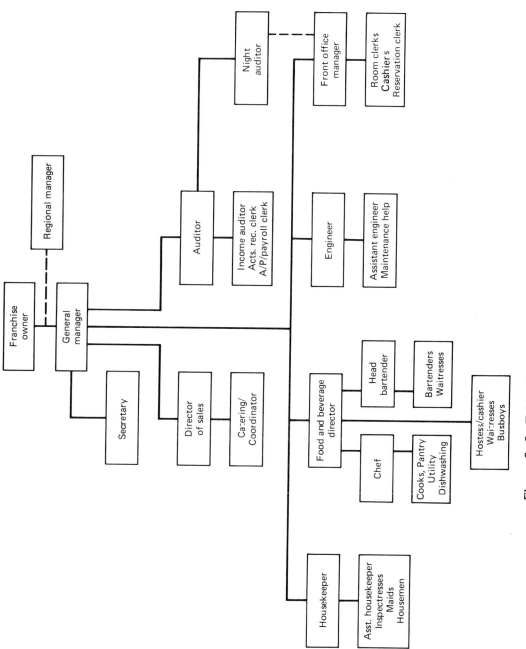

Figure 6-6 Table of organization of a franchise motor inn

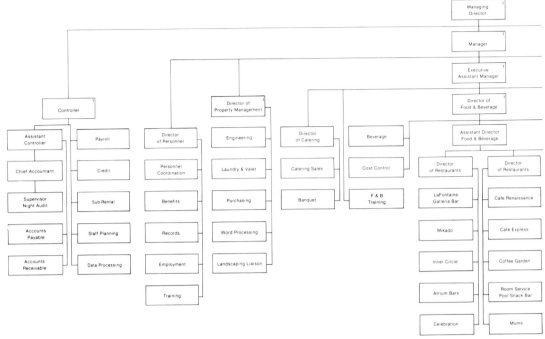

Figure 6–7   Detroit Plaza Hotel: Table of organization

significantly as an organization enlarges. To demonstrate this we include three examples in Figures 6–5, 6–6, and 6–7.

Key Success Factors

Perhaps the major differences between the old pressure-packed, panic approach to new hotel and restaurant openings and the current emphasis upon rigorous strategic planning is that managers are now being rated in terms of their demonstrated planning skills rather than for their "grand-opening" rave notices or press clippings.

In eloquent support of the need for such skills, the American Hotel and Motel Association's Financial Management Committee, under the leadership of its chairman, Joseph F. Cotter, executive vice president and controller of the Sheraton Corporation, recently sponsored a series of informative articles entitled, "Controlling Construction and Renovation Costs."[12] Drawing upon their extensive experience in controlling the cost of new-hotel construction projects, the authors make many practical recommendations for effective schedule control (i.e., completing construction on time and within budget) that are singularly instructive. For example, by use of a "Time Is Money" chart, shown in Figure 6–8, it can be easily seen that a month's delay of a $50-million project could cost more than a half-million dollars.

Moreover, use of the Critical Path Method is urged as an eminently desirable means of predicting and identifying which activities can delay the entire project and thereby increase the time needed for completion.

176

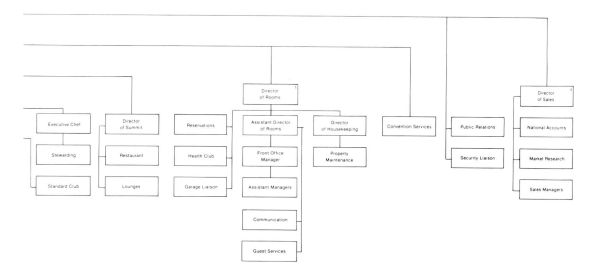

Normally, not more than 10 to 15 percent of all the tasks on any new-hotel project are critical to its timely completion; this means that the remaining 85 to 90 percent of the work need not be scheduled on a "crash" basis.

Cost reporting system The one tool which the authors regard as being the most indispensable in minimizing the financial risks of construction is a cost reporting system embracing such key features as

    1. Designation of high-risk areas of anticipated construction cost so as to capture subsequent spending variances at a level permitting instant identification and diagnosis of problems as they occur.

    2. Reliance upon the design-to-cost technique to insure rigorous application of every structural design to the budgeted cost for the total project.

    3. Preparation of periodic risk summaries to pinpoint actual and anticipated problems, and to establish a range of cost or schedule exposure (see Table 6–1).

    4. Monthly cost analysis reports showing budget, dollar commitments, actual expenditures to date, estimated cost to complete, and variances from budget. (The authors view this as the most important cost report of all, since it summarizes all the data pertaining to the current status of each account as well as the projected final cost of construction. See Table 6–2.)

177

TIME IS MONEY			
TOTAL PROJECT SIZE	COST PER DAY	COST PER WEEK	COST PER MONTH
$50,000,000	$25,635	$125,100	$541,650
30,000,000	15,381	75,060	324,990
10,000,000	5,127	25,020	108,330
5,000,000	2,564	12,510	54,165
1,000,000	513	2,502	10,833
500,000	256	1,251	5,417

Direct dollar loss for construction project time delays based on 13% annual construction inflation.

Source: *Lodging*, July 1980, p. 19.

Figure 6-8 "Time Is Money" chart

Table 6-1 Risk summary report

Description	Probability (%)	Schedule impact	Cost impact
Carpenters' strike	75	Up to 60 days	$100,000–300,000
Smoke detectors (new safety law)	100	None	$25,000–40,000
Prospective lawsuit by disappointed suitor for newsstand/gift shop concession	50	None	$500,000

Table 6-2 Monthly cost analysis summary ($000's)

Description	Budget	Dollar commitment	Expended to date	Estimate to completion	Variance to budget
Locker rooms	$ 637	$ 684	$ 644	$ 684	($47)
Carpet	$ 890	$ 950	$ 635	$ 950	($60)
Swimming pool	$ 100	$ 75	$ 40	$ 75	$25
Totals	$1627	$1709	$1319	$1709	($82)

Table 6-3   Variance report

Projected variance	Responsibility	Reason	Corrective action taken
$200,000	A. Jones	Faulty design	Architect to redesign
$135,000	V. Lacey	Cement finishers' strike	Second shift authorized to make up lost time
$ 40,000	G. Rowan	Defective conduit for electric cable	Claim submitted to supplier who has agreed to replace conduit

5. A variance report with projected variances in excess of a predetermined amount arrayed in descending order of magnitude to focus attention on those items having the greatest impact on the cost to complete. As illustrated in Table 6-3, this report also explains the reason for the variance and shows the corrective action to be taken.

Pre-opening licenses and permits   No less important than these techniques for controlling costs of new construction are the licenses and permits that must be obtained before a new hotel can open up for business. While most experienced operators instruct their attorneys to apply for a liquor license and an innkeeper's license as soon as financing for a new property has been obtained, they frequently are unaware until the eleventh hour of the licensing requirements of other governmental agencies. Figure 6-9 provides a list of licenses and permits typically required by such agencies in a major metropolitan area.

To illustrate how the coordination of the whole pre-opening takes place, we have combined the pre-opening instructions of a number of international–hotel companies (along with a few adaptations of our own) into Appendix C at the end of the book. To do the job effectively, management must see to it that all of the pieces of the pre-opening jigsaw puzzle fit together so as to present a total picture. The appendix, therefore, represents some of the ways in which companies insure this result.

Summary

Pre-opening management is not infrequently thought of as a laundry list of activities to be hurriedly checked by the general manager twenty-four hours or so before a grand opening. Others—especially those companies with burgeoning franchise establishments in mind—have been moved to see each of their pre-opening activities as part of a whole and hence have sought to furnish franchise-holders with pre-opening guides outlining the basic steps from groundbreaking to ribbon cutting. Except for such concerns, few hospitality establishments would be able to make it to opening day. Even so, many people—especially those in the hotel business—have learned through bitter experience that panic and chaos at the end are inevitable unless profound attention is paid in advance to the strategic

Federal
  Federal identification number
  IRS special liquor tax stamp
  Federal Communications Commission

State
  Liquor licenses
  Swimming-pool operating permit
  Sales & use taxes—operation
  Sales & use taxes—fees & payroll

City
  Health Department inspection permit
  Occupancy permit
  Refrigeration permit
  Laundry equipment
  Elevator/escalator permit
  Hot water tank/pressure vessels permit
  Flammable liquid storage permit
  Garage permit
  Certificate of license to operate as a hotel
  Cabaret "A" & restaurant license
  Certificate of compliance
  Sign license
  Spa license
  Massage license

Other permits and licenses
  Broadcast Music, Inc. (BMI)
  American Society of Composers and Publishers (ASCAP)
  Dry cleaning license

Figure 6–9 Licenses and permits required

resources for building the road over which management must travel on its pre-opening journey.

Much, therefore, that has been discussed in this chapter suggests that such worries are needless if one makes certain to (1) adhere to the practice of those management skills which make needed information more visible as new construction progresses; (2) facilitate risk assessment so as to avoid all "surprises"; (3) track costs accurately through a sound cost and schedule control system; and (4) monitor performance carefully so as to permit corrective action without delay.

As a starting place for developing more effective techniques for handling pre-openings, managers can make use of such tools as the critical path method (CPM), staffing plan and organizational charts, and cost reporting systems—all of which we have discussed in this chapter. Even though you may not be able to achieve a "failsafe" level of a risk-free pre-opening, you may be able to make better judgments about the key status indicators so that your particular project is completed on time and within budget.

1. Why has the critical path method not been used more widely in pre-opening management game plans for hotels and restaurants?

2. Why is it important to set a time limitation on each event in the pre-opening flowchart?

3. What points should be considered when one is preparing a critical path for the pre-opening management of a hotel?

4. What, in your opinion, are some of the difficulties you might encounter in introducing and using CPM as a tool for controlling pre-opening management?

5. What is the purpose of a project master plan?

6. It has been said that one way to establish a critical path covering the pre-opening period of a hotel or restaurant is to begin with the "grand-opening" target date and then back up from there. Do you agree? Explain.

7. You have just been designated as the general manager of a new 200-room hotel to be built in a university community. Explain in narrative form the sequence of activities that you visualize taking place beginning about one year prior to the opening and continuing down to the grand opening.

- COUNTDOWN
- CRITICAL PATH METHOD
- LICENSES AND PERMITS
- PRE-OPENING SCHEDULE
- PRE-OPENING STAFFING PLAN
- RISK SUMMARY REPORT
- TABLE OF ORGANIZATION
- TIME IS MONEY CHART
- VARIANCE REPORT

1. Author unidentified, "Making a Smooth Move," *Hotel & Motel Management,* May 1974, p. 30.

2. In W. Earl Sasser, R. Paul Olsen, and D. Daryl Wyckoff, *Management of Service Organizations* (Boston: Allyn & Bacon, 1978), p. 73.

3. John Portman and Jonathan Barnett, *The Architect as Developer* (New York: McGraw-Hill, 1976), pp. 4–5.

4. See Roger A. Golde, "Muddling Through: The Art of Properly Unbusinesslike Management," published in New York by Amacom, a Division of American Management Associations, 1976, p. 13. Not unsympathetically, Golde says: "The key to muddling through is that one thing leads to another. ..."—a fate, one suspects, that is seldom blessed with consequences devoutly to be desired.

5. See Theodor Levitt, "The Industrialization of Service," *Harvard Business Review,* September–October 1976.

6. Strictly speaking, this is a modified version of the Critical Path Method usually associated with PERT (Program Evaluation and Review Technique) developed by the U.S. Navy in connection with its Polaris missile program. To build the Polaris, the Navy developed an intricate plan that consisted of a series of interrelated steps, some of which could be completed simultaneously and some of which had to be finished before others could begin. If, for example, inspection of the total time for each sequence indicated that the entire project would require 30 weeks, that sequence—the one requiring the most time to complete—was called the Critical Path. It was regarded as "critical" because it determined the completion time of the project. Therefore, once the critical path was known, managers could focus on those particular activities that were most likely to delay the project.

7. Peter M. Gunnar, "Development of a Resort Hotel Condominium," *The Cornell Hotel and Restaurant Administration Quarterly,* November 1972, pp. 17–20.

8. Office of Tourism, Department of Industry, Trade and Commerce, *The Inn Business*, p. 1, Ottawa, Canada, 1976. Information in this report was prepared by Pannell Kerr Forster & Co., Toronto.

9. Ibid., *Management of Service Organizations,* pp. 50–51.

10. Sasser et al., p. 87.

11. Brian M. Baker, William L. Sheehan, and Michael D. White, "Controlling Construction and Renovation Costs," *Lodging,* May 1980, p. 43.

12. Ibid.; also Brian M. Baker, Robert L. Elmore, and Michael D. White, "Controlling Construction and Renovation Costs," *Lodging,* June 1980; Brian M. Baker and Michael D. White, "Controlling Construction and Renovation Costs," *Lodging,* July 1980.

The Feasibility Study

When you finish this chapter, you should understand:

    1. Why feasibility studies should be prepared for proposed hotel projects and who the principal users of the study are

    2. The seven steps typically taken in the conducting of an economic feasibility study

    3. How to determine the strength of at least three market segments which generate demand for hotel rooms

    4. The meaning of the terms "fair share" and "market share" and their role in the feasibility study

    5. Some of the sources and techniques frequently used to prepare financial projections for a proposed hotel project

    6. The factors to ultimately be considered when determining whether or not a proposed hotel project is feasible

From a simplistic viewpoint, it can be said that the success of any hotel is determined by the following five factors:

    1. A strong market with a proper mix of supply and demand

    2. A good site

    3. The proper facilities and amenities for the market offered to the public at the right price

    4. Management expertise

    5. Proper financing

    It is equally true that in most cases, if the first three factors are not working for the hotel, neither management expertise nor financing can

183

make it successful. Indeed, it is becoming increasingly true that most lenders will not finance a project without the proper site in a strong market offering facilities and services commensurate with market demand. The art and science of determining whether a proposed project is a good investment from both the lender's and developer's point of view is known as *project feasibility analysis.*

Definition of a feasibility study   A feasibility study can be defined as "a systematic method for evaluating the economic factors at work and the likely results of operations before they are begun."[1] Under this definition, the objective of a feasibility study is to look four to five years into the future and predict the most likely operating results if a hotel were constructed on a specific site in a specific market. For those of you who follow the U.S. government's or private econometric forecasting firms' attempts to forecast just one component of the economy even one year in advance, this sounds like a tall order. Happily, however, feasibility analysis is not as complex as forecasting the macro economy, and has evolved into a fairly sophisticated art that is relied upon by most lenders and developers today.

The purpose of this chapter, then, is to provide some insight into why and how feasibility studies are prepared. While it is probably not reasonable to expect that readers will be able to prepare a feasibility study after completing this chapter, they should have an understanding of its importance to the development process, as well as a grasp of how the results should affect the ongoing operations once the hotel is open for business.

Why Prepare a Feasibility Study?

Investment Capital

Strategic planning—usually defined as the process of determining how a business may make the best possible use of its resources in the future—has rightly been characterized as "still largely an art, with firms doing varying amounts of planning. (Actually, most do very little, failing even to make their objectives explicit.)"[2] Paradoxically, large lending institutions, the traditional source of investment capital for lodging enterprises, were found not long ago to have approved loans without adequate industry analysis or comprehensive data about borrowers.[3] This was particularly true for some of the large Real Estate Investment Trusts (REITS) which were forced to call many real estate loans during the 1974–1975 recession. This experience has awakened most lenders to the necessity of having a professionally prepared feasibility study submitted as part of the loan package before deciding on whether or not to provide investment capital to a specific project.

Investment capital, then, is one reason to prepare a feasibility study. If the developer intends to finance a portion of the hotel project through loans with a third party, such as a large insurance company or mortgage banker, the lender will generally require a feasibility study to help assess the risk and probable return on the loan.

Return on Owner's Equity

A second and equally important reason to have a feasibility study prepared for a proposed project is to give the developer insight into whether the project is a good investment as well as what he should expect the project to return after it is open. The analysis should not only tell the developer something about the risk and return associated with the project; it should also describe his market segments and recommended product to increase the chances for success from the development.

In Chapter 1 we introduced the idea that a property's market segmentation has an impact on occupancy, room rates, profitability, and product. Clearly, if market segmentation determines the product and amenity levels that a hotel should offer to maximize the probability of success, then one role of the feasibility study should be to determine what market segments are currently generating demand for rooms in the market and the optimum product/amenity mix for capturing the largest and most profitable segments.

The Competitors

The market study will also tell the eventual manager of the hotel who his or her primary competitors are and how successful they are. A property's primary competition can be defined as those hotels which will be competing for the same market segments as the proposed hotel and/or those hotels which are currently serving the demand that the proposed property hopes to penetrate.

For example, if 40 percent of the area demand is generated from the group-meetings segment and two competitive properties are currently capturing 80 percent of this demand, the manager will be able to assess his relative service and facilities advantages and disadvantages. This can be utilized when trying to sell to this market segment if the hotel is determined feasible.

Determination of Budget and Marketing Plan

The methodology used to determine a project's feasibility can also be used by the manager of an existing hotel as a basis for the annual budget and marketing plan. Thus, the feasibility study should be an ongoing process that keeps management informed about the dynamics of the economy in which the property is located. Holiday Inn, Inc., for example, requires its managers and assistant managers to perform ongoing market analyses for the hotels they manage.

As part of the ongoing feasibility study, hotel owners use financial projections that are supported by a market study to determine whether to buy, sell or refinance an existing hotel. The financial projections help to establish the economic value of the property and are used to determine the selling price or the amount of money that can be borrowed to refinance the hotel. If two or three years of stable operating history is available and future projections reflect the past, then management's projections are usually acceptable. In the event that future projections vary from recently observed operating history, then the projections should be prepared by a qualified third party and supported by a market study. Such was the case in 1979 when a major Texas real estate developer sought to purchase the Sheraton Fort Worth. The property, which is a classic Fort Worth landmark, had been operating for several years at below-market average occupancies and average rates. The developer's plan was to totally renovate the hotel and have Hyatt Corporation of Chicago, Illinois, manage it. In this case, the historical operating performance of the hotel was of marginal value. An independent market study with financial projections was commissioned to be used as a cornerstone in the developer's mortgage loan request.

In summary, then, a feasibility study is really more than a crystal ball to determine whether or not a proposed hotel will make money. The smart developer and manager will use it to provide insight into the available market segments, the facility and amenity needs, and as a monitoring device of the dynamic economy in which the hotel must compete.

General Components of a Feasibility Study

The typical feasibility study can be divided into seven components, as illustrated in Figure 7-1.

The feasibility report itself is usually limited to the first five steps shown in Figure 7-1. This is commonly referred to as a *market study with financial projections.* The estimation of the amount to be invested in the project (Step 6) should be subject to the anticipated income from operations. Many hotel developers commission market studies after a considerable amount of time and money has already been spent on the acquisition of the proposed site, architectural renderings, and in some cases, unfortunately, after the developer has announced the project to the media.

The proper time to commission a market study is after the developer has gained control of the proposed site. A site can often be controlled for the required length of time through the use of a *purchase option*, which is a nonrefundable payment made to the land owner and has the following characteristics:

○ The purchase price is determined and fixed to the buyer during the option term

○ The property cannot be sold to another party during the option term

○ The price of the option is relatively low, typically ranging from $100.00 to 10 percent of the purchase price

It should be emphasized from the beginning that the feasibility-study report is only a summary of the salient facts and analyses that result from the actual research. Care should be taken not to assume that if a particular piece of analysis is not included in the example study, it

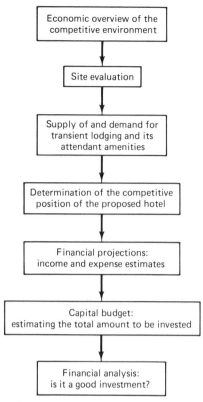

Figure 7-1 Flowchart of steps typically taken in the conduct of an economic feasibility study of a proposed Hotel

was not performed. Most feasibility studies are backed up with a significant amount of research which is organized into workpapers and kept in files at the office of the firm that prepared the study.

One of the first steps in preparing a feasibility study is to survey the general market area in which the proposed hotel will be competing. More specifically, the research examines the statistical area first and the market sector that contains the site second. A recent study conducted jointly by Laventhol & Horwath and Pannell, Kerr, Forster & Company[4] concluded that between 53.4 and 54.5 percent of the hotel rooms occupied in airport, suburban, and highway locations in the United States were generated by individuals traveling on business. Thus, the economy of the standard metropolitan statistical area (SMSA) is of key importance to most hotels. One must determine how self-contained the market will be. This means judging whether the market is stable or growing and if this economic condition is due to the strength of local factors such as a growing industrial base, or whether the market is dependent upon another geographical area for stability and growth. Smaller towns and communities can be substantially dependent upon larger geographic areas,

General
Market
Overview

whereas larger cities often seem so self-contained as to be independent of external influences other than those affecting the economy as a whole.

Smaller communities that are independent of a larger metropolitan area are frequently dependent upon one or two companies for the majority of their employment and hotel room demand. Greenville, Texas is an example of a small community whose hotels are substantially supported by one electronics manufacturer. Hotel-room demand fluctuates dramatically with the granting and completion of each government defense contract. If the manufacturer were to build its own hotel or provide living quarters to its visitors, this would have a serious impact on the existing hotel community. This kind of vulnerability is not limited just to small communities. It is also the case with the Tandy Corporation in Fort Worth, Texas and Amway in Grand Rapids, Michigan. These two companies are the largest hotel-room demand generators in their respective communities, and both are either building or renovating their own hotels to house their visitors. The impact of this business decision will negatively affect nearly every hotel in each market.

Larger metropolitan areas are favored by most mortgage lenders for hotel investments because they are less susceptible to the business cycles of any one business or industry. Further, overbuilding is viewed as a temporary phenomenon due to ongoing economic growth and attrition within the hotel community itself. This was the case in Atlanta, Georgia, which in 1976 was viewed by many industry observers as hopelessly overbuilt—yet by 1979, it was commonly agreed that more hotels were needed to service the market.

Current trends suggest that the independence of larger cities is changing. As the nation evolves toward a network of megalopolises, larger cities are becoming vulnerable to conditions outside city limits. In addition, the significant economic shifts that are occurring within larger cities can significantly affect the overall success of a hotel. Even though a city's economy may be stable, areas within the city may be exhibiting growth in population, retail sales, office space, and industry at the expense of another area within the same city. This has occurred in many cities recently with "suburban flight," where the economic base of a city is leaving the downtown or central business district and moving to nearby suburban areas.

Thus, while most studies begin by addressing the salient economic and demographic features about a city because of the availability of data, the market area may not necessarily be defined by a city's legal boundaries. For example, many hotels have been built near major airports in recent years; and while the feasibility study will begin by discussing the economic conditions of the city, the more detailed analysis and fieldwork will be conducted on the airport geographical sector of the city. Further, convention hotels need to be evaluted as much on the economy of the region and the host city's competitiveness relative to other cities in the area as on the dynamics of the host city itself. Convention planners have an entirely different set of decision-making criteria they use when deciding where to hold their conventions. (These criteria will be discussed later in this chapter.)

The objectives of the market overview, then are fourfold:

1. To determine the market's general economic health

2. To provide growth projections that can be associated with particular market segments and thus develop a separate growth factor for each segment

3. To characterize the market's population, its spending abilities, its stability, and its vulnerability to economic fluctuation

4. To provide a background for considering the relative market for hotels and motels

Evaluating a market's ability to support hotel rooms

There are literally hundreds of specific generators of hotel-room demand, making an all-inclusive listing impractical and probably impossible.

However, understanding that hotel demand in general is generated from a relatively small number of market segments and then attempting to analyze the market's environment in terms of attracting, retaining, and stimulating the growth of these segments should help you picture the rationale behind the market overview.

The market segments we are most concerned with here include the commercial business traveler, the tourist and pleasure traveler, the person traveling on government business, and the meeting and convention attendee. While this list is not all-inclusive (other relatively prevalent segments include local demand and college or university demand), it does represent a major portion of demand in most markets.

The commercial business traveler. As pointed out in Chapter 1, the commercial business traveler is typically the mainstay of a lodging establishment's business. His or her purpose for travel is to transact business. Therefore, in the market overview, the research is interested in two points for this source of demand:

1. The number, size, and diversity of the local industrial, commercial, and retail establishments which would attract the commercial traveler to the market area

2. The local environment's attractiveness to existing and new industrial, commercial, and retail establishments

Some of the most common generators of commercial demand include commercial or industrial firms either headquartered or with plants in the area; retail outlets, particularly shopping malls; government complexes; colleges and universities; medical complexes; and military bases.

The research and feasibility report will generally not only identify these demand generators, but will also evaluate their ability to generate transient room nights. For example, a large office building with the regional headquarters of a large insurance company as the largest tenant will generally be a higher-quality generator of commercial room night demand than an equally large office building with a large law firm or accounting firm as the lead tenant. This is because the insurance company will generally be frequently bringing its field staff and new employees into the office for meetings and training. In addition, because insurance companies are a major source of capital for commercial and real estate ventures, they are regularly visited by developers and businesspeople seeking money.

The accounting and law firms generally do much of their work locally and when out-of-town clients require them, the employees of the accounting or law firm often visit the client.

In larger market areas, it is often unrealistic to identify and interview all of the commercial demand generators. In these cases, the research will often look for barometers which indicate the degree of growth. While there are many such barometers, we shall discuss three of the more common ones: office space absorption, employment, and building-permit valuation.

Office Space Absorption—This economic indicator illustrates the amount of office space that has been built over a specific period of time and the amount that is occupied. Looking strictly at the amount of space constructed can be misleading, because it may lead the researcher to conclude that businesses are locating in all the new space when, in fact, it may be either empty or filling at the expense of other space within the market.

Assume, for example, that a given market had 14 million square feet of commercial office space available in 1981, and it was 87.3 percent occupied. Assume that the same market in 1982 had 15.4 million square feet of commercial office space available, and it was 84.0 percent occupied.

The office space absorption rate for 1982 would be computed as follows:

Amount of office space (millions of square feet)	1981	1982	Change Sq. Ft.	Change Percent
Available	14.0	15.4	1.4	10.0
Percent occupancy	87.3	84.6	—	-3.1
Amount occupied	12.222	13.0284	.8064	6.6

There are several aspects that should be considered in interpreting this table. First, notice that the office-space occupancy declined from 87.3 percent to 84.6 percent. As can be seen, this decline is very misleading by itself, because while it did decline, the amount of space occupied actually increased. The reader should be careful to remember this principle when looking at year-to-year occupancy changes for hotels within a market as well.

Second, notice that the supply of space increased faster than the demand for office space. This illustrates how simply calculating the increase in the supply of space can also be misleading.

Finally, it can be seen that the amount of additional space that was occupied in 1982 compared to 1981 was 806,400 square feet, or a 6.6 percent increase over the prior year. This is the true absorption-rate figure and is able to reflect what actually occurred despite the larger increase in supply and the declining occupancy levels.

To translate office-space absorption to commercial rooms growth, the researcher must interview all the significant hotels in the market area and determine the total number of rooms occupied, on a daily basis, by business-motivated travel. (This frequently involves interviewing the managers of all the hotels in the statistical area.) A ratio is then established that correlates commercial room demand and occupied office space. In the above example, there were 13,028,400 square feet of office space occupied in 1982. If there were 1,303 commercial rooms occupied on an average daily basis, then the correlation would be one hotel room occupied for every 10,000 square feet of office space occupied $(13,028,400 \div 1,303 = 10,000)$.

The potency of office space as a commercial-rooms-demand generator depends upon the quality of the companies located in the office buildings. Again, in the above example, the 864,000 square feet absorbed in 1982 should have resulted in 86 additional rooms demanded daily by the commercial sector $(864,000 \div 10,000 = 86)$. Since every city is different, this ratio must be established by original research. This author has observed the spread to be as much as one room per 30,000 square feet occupied in the Dallas central business district (CBD) to one room per 6,600 square feet occupied in the Gallaria area of Houston.

Employment—Employment is generally an excellent macro-economic indicator, particularly in small to medium-sized markets. When looking at employment statistics, it is the change over a given period of time, usually several years, that is important rather than the absolute number in any one year. This will show the magnitude of any increase or decrease in the labor force, thus giving an indication of the expanding and contracting nature of the local industrial base.

One important aspect to the industrial base is its diversity. This gives an indication of how much a local market relies on one employer and/or one industry. Clearly, the broader the industrial base, the less susceptible the market is to either economic fluctuations or the continued strength of one manufacturer or employer.

To give an indication of the diversity of the employment base, the research will generally involve an investigation of the distribution of employment over different standard employment categories. The following table shows how this distribution was presented in an Austin, Texas feasibility study.

As illustrated, the Austin economy was not highly dependent upon any one employment category, indicating a diverse employer base. In fact, being the state capital, the largest employer was the government sector, usually a stable employer regardless of economic conditions.

Employment distribution, Austin metropolitan area, April 1972

Category	Number employed	Percent of total employed
Manufacturing	13,060	8.9
Construction	10,710	7.3
Trade	29,370	20.1
Government	52,500	35.9
Other	40,600	27.8
Total employed	146,240	
Unemployed	2,860	1.9% of labor force
Total civilian labor force	149,100	

Source: Texas Employment Commission

In summary, then, employment figures can give insight into the strength of a market from several standpoints:

1. The trends in the number of people employed from year to year show the degree to which the market's employer base is growing or contracting. In periods of economic slowdown, these trends can also show how hard the local economy has been hit.

2. The distribution of the employment base over different employment categories illustrates the diversity of the employer base and the market's potential reliance upon one employer or industry. Generally, a decreasing reliance upon an agricultural employment base as well as growth in the finance, insurance, and real estate sector is a positive trend. Government is also generally a very stable employer, particularly when the base is relatively large and is likely to remain in the market.

3. Often, the demographics and trends in the demographics of the labor force can give important insight into the market's potential viability. For example, the primary employment base generally consists of people between the ages of 25 and 49. Looking at the changes in the number of people in this age category, perhaps even by educational level, will often give insight into the growth of local industry and its future. This is because the employment base will generally locate in markets where the employer base is growing. In addition, when industry is searching for a market to construct a new plant, regional office, or in which to relocate, one of the important factors in the decision is the size, training, growth, and quality of the local labor force.

Building-permit Valuation—A third indicator of commercial activity in a market concerns building-permit valuation. Building permits are generally a good barometer because all commercial, industrial, and residential construction that takes place must have a building permit.

Therefore, to track both the amount of construction and the value of it in dollars over a period of time gives an indication of the growth and strength of the commercial market.

The following chart shows the building-permit activity from 1960 through 1971 in Austin, Texas:

Building permits issued

Year	Number	Value	Average value
1960	3,341	$ 46,239,657	$13,840
1965	4,002	71,491,537	17,864
1967	4,455	131,640,835	29,549
1969	4,613	150,972,872	32,728
1970	4,914	134,229,838	27,316
1971	5,983	202,463,278	33,840

Source: Building Inspection Division, City of Austin

As illustrated, in 1971 the building activity in Austin was strong and growing, with over $200 million worth of development authorized through building permits.

In summary, the research and analysis undertaken in a feasibility study to determine the size and strength of the commercial market involves looking at individual demand generators such as manufacturing plants, corporate headquarters, shopping centers, etc., and the trends in the economic indicators which correlate with commercial activity. The purpose of this research is to determine the strength, diversity, and location of the market's commercial base as well as to enable the researcher to predict the probable growth rate of this sector into the future.

The tourist/pleasure traveler The pleasure-travel market is important to a hotel's demand because of its seasonality and the higher room rate a property receives as a result of having more than one person in the same room. This is commonly referred to as double or multiple occupancy.

We illustrated the seasonality of the pleasure or tourist market segment in Chapter 1. Understanding these travel patterns is important to estimating the strength of this segment for any given market. For example, in many areas in the northern part of the United States, particularly those areas with either natural or tourist attractions, demand from the vacation-market segment is very strong from approximately Memorial Day through Labor Day. This is the period when most schools are out for the summer, and consequently the time when many families take their annual vacations. During this period of time, it is not unusual for the well-placed, well-run hotels to run at or near capacity every day. However, as illustrated below, this is not enough to give most year-round hotels enough occupancy to break even.

Assume that you are preparing a feasibility study for a proposed 150-room motor hotel in the Northeast. Your research indicates that the property can achieve a 100 percent occupancy because of the vacation market from Memorial Day through Labor Day (98 days). In addition, it shows that the best the property will be able to do the remainder of the year is a 40 percent occupancy. What is your recommendation?

Perhaps the best way to determine the answer is to calculate the annual occupancy of the proposed property under the demand assumptions provided above. This would be done as follows:

$$\text{Occupancy} = \frac{\text{rooms demanded}}{\text{rooms available}}$$

$$= \frac{(98 \text{ days} \times 100\% \text{ occupancy} \times 150 \text{ rooms}) + (267 \text{ days} \times 40\% \text{ occupancy} \times 150 \text{ rooms})}{150 \text{ rooms} \times 365 \text{ days}}$$

$$= \frac{14,700 + 16,020}{54,750} = \frac{30,720}{54,750}$$

$$= 56.1\% \text{ occupancy}$$

Under these circumstances, you would probably have to recommend that the property not be built. An exception to this seemingly obvious conclusion can be seen in markets like Ruidoso, New Mexico and Bassier City, Louisiana, where the summer season corresponds with the highly successful horse-racing season. Large room-price premiums are charged for overnight accommodations during the racing season which allow the hotel owners to realize profits at relatively low annual occupancies.

There are basically three ways that a property can penetrate the pleasure-travel market segment, none of them necessarily exclusive to the others:

1. It can capture "transient tourists"—people who are en route to another destination and require overnight lodging along the way. This generally requires that the property be on or proximate to an interstate or principal highway. It is also beneficial for these hotels to have a commonly recognized franchise affiliation and have moderate room rates.

2. It can capture "destination tourists"—people who are within their destination markets and require overnight lodging while they enjoy the various activities then intend to pursue. Examples of these types of markets include:

Disney World (Orlando, Florida)
Disneyland (Anaheim, California)
Cedar Point (Sandusky, Ohio)
Galveston Island (Galveston, Texas)

3. It can *be* the destination by offering the facilities and amenities which attract tourists to the hotel for the purpose of utilizing the hotel. This usually requires that the hotel be near a relatively large population base or be near a strong recreation area such as a resort. Examples of this type of hotel include:

Marriott's Great America outside Chicago, Illinois
Marriott's Great America outside San Francisco, California
Inn of the Mountain Gods (Ruidoso, New Mexico)
The MGM Grand (Las Vegas, Nevada)

The Feasibility Study/195

Typically, the research for the pleasure-travel segment involves gathering attendance figures for the area attractions, looking at highway traffic patterns and discussing the seasonality and strength of the market with the local chamber of commerce, visitors' and convention bureau, and the local existing hotels. Hotels that would be too dependent on "transient tourists" for operating revenue have not been considered good investments since 1973 by hotel companies and hotel investors. An example that illustrates the source of this skepticism is the operating history of a group of relatively small, moderately priced, franchised motor hotels located at the intersection of Interstate 10 and Interstate X in Slidell, Louisiana. The transient tourist segment was the primary demand source for the motor hotels, and they enjoyed occupancies that were near capacity until the Arab oil embargo of 1973. Within a few weeks of the embargo, occupancy levels dropped over 50 percentage points in each property.

Most "transient tourist"–oriented hotels across the country were negatively affected in a similar manner. Recognizing that the potential exists for future embargos or shortages in petroleum supplies, lenders and investors are seeking hotel projects with a combination of different demand sources.

The government traveler   In certain markets, federal and state government business can represent a substantial amount of a market's room night demand. In addition, where the government installation is stable, such as within a state capital or large agency, it does not exhibit a significant amount of seasonality. This means that demand levels are fairly constant year-round and therefore provide a stable source of business.

The strength and stability of government-related demand is usually determined through interviews with the various demand sources. Such sources often include state governments, military bases, federal agencies such as NASA, HUD, or IRS offices, etc.

One particularly important aspect of government demand is that most government employers are given a per diem expenditure limit for food and lodging. Therefore, this segment is generally room-rate–sensitive and if a hotel hopes to penetrate government demand, it must be willing to charge room rates that fall within the per diem limit.

The meeting and convention attendee   The meeting and convention market can represent a significant source of demand for a property. However, this market is not uniformly spread throughout markets. Rather, the competition for this segment is somewhat intense between cities, and it therefore tends to concentrate. In addition, to penetrate this market segment requires that a property invest in facilities and amenities additional to those that are required for the market segments discussed earlier. Therefore, it is important that the market study thoroughly research the strength of the meeting and convention market before recommending that a property attempt to penetrate it.

We know from Chapter 1 that the meeting and convention market can generally be divided into two subsegments:

1. Conventions and associations
2. Executive conferences

In addition, conventions and association meetings can be classified into size categories. These size categories are usually dependent upon whether the convention or association meeting is national, regional, state, or local in scope.

The ability of a market or hotel to penetrate the larger convention and association market is highly dependent upon several factors:

1. The meeting and exhibit facilities within the city. Most larger conventions require a significant amount of space that can only be provided by a convention center or a grouping of large properties with extensive public space.

2. The number and quality of hotel rooms within the city. Even with enough exhibit space, it is not unusual for the larger conventions to require 20,000 or more hotel rooms. Today, there are very few cities that can provide this many rooms at one time. Even with the smaller conventions and association meetings, the market must be able to provide a relatively large room *block*. A feasibility study for a proposed Hilton Inn in Austin, Texas (see appendix D) pointed out, for example, that even though most of the state associations were headquartered in Austin, the city did not have enough available hotel rooms to fully penetrate the market. In Austin's case, much of the problem was due to both a limited number of rooms available and strong demand filling those rooms so that room blocks were not available.

3. The solicitation effort of the city and/or the hotels within the city. Since conventions are generally highly profitable to not only the hotels but also the retail establishments, the competition between cities is often intense for the more lucrative groups. Many cities are imposing a rooms sales tax on the local hotels to help fund the local convention bureau. It is important, then, for the researchers to investigate the annual solicitation budget of the city for conventions and to compare it to the budget of competitive areas.

4. Other factors that are important to capturing out-of-town meetings are the transportation into and around the city and the quality of the night life or recreational facilities.

The convention segment is somewhat seasonal in demand patterns. The following table shows the monthly distribution of major conventions for 1981.

Distribution of major conventions:
Percentage occurring each month

	%		%
January	5	July	6
February	5	August	8
March	9	September	7
April	10	October	13
May	13	November	7
June	15	December	2

Source: *Meetings and Conventions Magazine,* Research Department

As illustrated in the table, more than one-half of the total demand occurs in the months of April, May, June, and October. This is important because while the convention segment can represent a signigicant amount of business for a hotel, it is generally not steady business and must be supplemented with other demand sources.

The executive conference market is totally different in nature from the convention segment, and as we saw in Chapter 1, this market is not always complementary in facility and amenity needs. Most feasibility studies for transient hotels will examine the smaller executive-type-meeting business in terms of the demand emanating from local corporations. The research is prepared by interviewing representatives from local industry as well as the existing hotels and motels in the market area.

The methodology for determining the feasibility of a total executive conference center is much more extensive and frequently involves sending questionnaires and conducting interviews with the larger companies in the entire region. This region might be determined, for example, by identifying the major cities with nonstop airline service to the city in which the feasibility study is being conducted. In summary, it requires a more intensified research effort if a property is to specialize in one market segment, and the facilities and amenities will be built almost exclusively to serve the one-market segment. This is true for resorts as well as executive conference centers.

Summary of General Market Overview

There are many approaches to understanding the market overview; we have presented one here. The important point is that the research is undertaken to understand the strength of the existing economic base, to determine how and where it is likely to be growing and its vulnerability to economic fluctuations. This is done by analyzing the trends, by comparing the statistics of the market to other markets, and by determining the amount of current activity that is taking place which will sustain the economic viability in the future.

This research and analysis will play a very important role later in terms of quantifying the future strength of the economy and of each of the market segments.

The next step of a feasibility study is to quantify the existing demand and to evaluate the quality of the existing hotels. Then, by combining this with the market overview, projections of supply and demand can be estimated.

Site Evaluation   The actual site on which the hotel is placed is one of the most important determinants of its ultimate success. History is filled with examples of hotels that opened in strong markets but were unsuccessful because of poor location.

There are numerous factors that should be considered when one is evaluating the strength of a hotel site. A few of the more important ones include:

- Size and shape of the site
- Zoning
- Access
- Visibility
- Sign ordinances
- Highway and road developments
- Labor availability
- Proximity to demand sources

While it is beyond the scope of this text to discuss the details of each of these factors, the importance of the site evaluation should not be discounted.

Supply and Demand Analysis   We have previously discussed the calculation of a hotel's occupancy. It is based upon the number of rooms demanded or occupied and the number of rooms available. This principle can be expanded to an entire market's occupancy and is calculated in the exact same manner:

$$\text{Market occupancy} = \frac{\text{Rooms occupied}}{\text{Rooms available}}$$

Just as in a single property, the numerator and denominator are often dynamic. Therefore, the supply and demand analysis attempts first to quantify the supply and demand at a given point in time, and then to predict how each is likely to change in the future.

Quantifying the existing supply and demand is relatively easy. The supply inventory can be determined through directories, interviews with local public officials, and observation.

Demand is quantified by interviewing the managers or owners of the existing properties. During these interviews, the researcher determines the mix of business (market segments), the occupancy of each hotel, the seasonality of demand, the source of demand, and the utilization of each of the amenity offerings. By physical inspection, the researcher can also determine which hotels represent the primary competition in the market and which hotels are only secondary competitors. For example, in one study, it was pointed out that while there were 4,343 rooms available in the proposed city, only 1,725 were considered competitive.

Projecting the supply of rooms is done by interviewing the local officials, developers, and operators to determine if any hotels are under construction, announced, or rumored. Once these have been identified, follow-up research is made to determine the nature of the development, including location, amenities, number of rooms, chain affiliation (if any), estimated opening date, and the probability of the property opening at all.

This last point is important because many hotels that are rumored or announced to be opening in fact never do. Since the projected supply is an integral component of projected occupancy, the research must be as thorough as possible in determining the best projection of supply entering a market.

Projection of demand is based upon the economic growth rates projected for the city or market. For example, in one feasibility study, the following historical growth rates were determined for selected economic barometers:

Historical growth rates of selected economic barometers

Barometer	Historic growth rate
Building-permit values	25–28%
Business activity	20–22%
Airline passengers	20–22%
Convention delegates	10%

This information, of course, was identified through the general market overview. Then, based upon the projected activity for these and other economic generators, the study projected the following growth rates for each of the different market segments.

Projected growth by market segment

Market segment	Percent of market	Projected growth rate
Individual commercial	70.0	15%
Convention group commercial	18.0	15%
Transient/tourist	12.0	10%

Why don't these growth rates equate to the historical growth rates of the selected barometers? Without the work papers to the feasibility study, it is difficult to determine; but let's follow the possible logic for one of the market segments, the convention and group commercial.

We know that the historical growth rate for this segment was 10 percent. In addition, from the market overview, we know that much of the potential existing demand is going to other cities because of the lack of available rooms. The overview also points out that with the addition of new rooms to that particular city's market, convention activity should exhibit a significant growth rate. While we cannot illustrate how 15 percent was determined, the rationale is clear. This example shows the importance of the market overview and how it relates to the projected growth rates for demand.

Combining the individual growth rates for each market segment into one overall growth rate for room night demand is simply a matter of calculating the weighted average for each segment. For example, from the table on p. 199, to calculate the weighted average:

Market segment	Percent of market	×	Projected growth rate	=	Weighted growth
Commercial	70		15%	=	.105
Group	18		15%	=	.027
Tourist	12		10%	=	.012
Total				=	.144
				=	14.4%

Therefore, the overall growth in demand for the city's market was projected to 14 percent (rounded) of the 1972 demand level.

Summary of Supply and Demand Analysis

There are essentially four ways that a property can receive demand for room nights:

1. From the strength and growth of the general economy

2. From the strength and growth of the sector in which the property will be built

3. By penetration of the existing demand within the market

4. From derived demand—that is, from a created demand which would not ordinarily be in the market but is "created" by the property itself. This frequently occurs, for example, when large convention hotels are built and the internal sales force is able to sell meetings and conventions which normally would not come to the market. It also frequently occurs for executive conference centers and resorts.

All of the research and analysis presented to this point has been concerned with identifying the sources, strengths, project growth rates, and quantification of demand for hotel rooms. The remaining portions of the chapter deal with the specific proposed hotel itself: its competitive position, the recommended facilities and amenities, and the projected financial results that the hotel should achieve.

Competitive Position

Once the future supply of and demand for hotel rooms has been estimated, the researcher must determine how effective the proposed hotel would be in capturing the individuals seeking overnight accommodations. Factors that contribute to a hotel's attractiveness include:

1. Site
2. Facilities
3. Management
4. Pricing
5. Franchise affiliation
6. Proximity to major demand generators

The positive and negative aspects of these factors, when viewed collectively, determine the proposed hotel's competitive position. Ideally, the feasibility study should dictate each of these six factors. Typically, however, the developer has already determined where he would like to build the hotel, how many rooms and the kind of facilities he would like to offer, who will manage the hotel, and the kind of franchise affiliation he would like to seek. Thus, the researcher is generally asked to determine how this type of hotel would perform in the marketplace, rather than recommend the optimum product.

The next section of the chapter discusses some of the factors contributing to a hotel's competitive position and demonstrates some of the analytical tools used to project occupancy.

Facility Recommendations

The decision concerning recommended facilities and amenities should be based upon the market segments that the property expects to serve. We provided some insight into this subject in Chapter 1. With the cost of construction and real estate rapidly increasing, it is important that the study not recommend amenities or facilities that are likely to remain unused. This means, for example, that extensive meeting space should not be recommended unless there is enough demand for it to make a profit center, or unless the meeting space will generate enough incremental demand to become a profit center. This determination is often made by the developer and/or an architect and is not always a part of the feasibility study. However, it is an objective of the study to be sure that the recommended facilities are commensurate with the needs of the major market segments.

There are two terms that need to be defined and discussed before we describe how to determine how well a proposed property will do in a market. The terms are "fair share" and "market share."

Fair Share

The concept of fair share refers to the amount of room nights a property would receive if demand were distributed based upon the number of rooms in each property, rather than upon location, product, management, etc. It is calculated by dividing the number of rooms available in a property by the total number of rooms in a market.

For example, if a 200-room hotel were located in a market that has 2,000 competitive rooms, its fair share would be calculated as follows:

$$\text{Fair share} = \frac{\text{Property rooms available}}{\text{Market rooms available}}$$

$$= \frac{200}{2,000} = 10\%$$

If the 200-room property were under construction in a market that had 2,000 existing rooms, its fair share when it opened would be 9.1 percent ($200 \div 2,200$).

While the concept of fair share does not reflect actual performance, it is useful in determining how well a property is or will do within a market relative to its competitors. We will illustrate this shortly.

Market Share

Market share refers to the amount of room nights a property actually captures relative to the total number of rooms demanded within the market. It reflects actual results and is broadly used in business as a measure of success relative to competition. It is particularly meaningful when measured over time to discern the trends in market share and the impact of various marketing programs.

Market share is calculated by dividing the number of rooms occupied in a given property by the total number of rooms demanded within a market. For example, if a 175-room hotel were running a 74 percent occupancy in a market that has 1,400 rooms with a market occupancy of 68 percent, market share would be calculated as follows:

$$\text{Market share} = \frac{\text{Property rooms occupied}}{\text{Market rooms occupied}}$$

$$= \frac{175 \times .74}{1,400 \times .68}$$

$$= 13.6\%$$

In this example, the property's fair share is 12.5 percent ($175 \div 1,400$), so it is enjoying a 1.1 point premium over fair share ($13.6 - 12.5$).

This principle is very useful for existing properties as well as for estimating the expected market penetration of a new hotel.

Perhaps the most subjective part of a feasibility study is determining the projected occupancy a proposed property will achieve when it opens. While there are several methods commonly utilized, the end result is the researchers' professional training and familiarity with the market.

Estimating Market Penetration

One commonly used technique is to start with the proposed property's fair share and then assign premium and discount points based upon its advantages and disadvantages relative to the existing competition. Some of the more common factors considered include:

- Site
- Chain affiliation
- Property and amenities
- Management
- Proximity to the major demand-generators

The net result of this analysis is the determination of a percentage of fair share which the proposed property is anticipated to capture when it opens.

Certainly, the ultimate test of the feasibility of any proposed hotel project is whether or not the project will achieve the financial objectives of the interested parties. For the lender, the financial objective is covering the debt service* and other fixed charges. For the developer and owner, it is the achievement of an expected rate of return of investment or a certain amount of cash flow.

Financial Projections

The objective of the financial analysis section of the feasibility study is to project the operating results of the proposed hotel given the anticipated occupancy and average rate it is expected to receive. Owing to the weight that is placed on the financial projections in the determination of whether or not to proceed with the project, it is important that they be prepared by a knowledgeable and independent third party who does not have a vested interest in the proposed hotel.

Different methods exist for projecting both revenues and expenses for each operated department. The desired goal is to arrive at an income amount that fairly represents the probable future operating results of the proposed hotel. Some of the resources that researchers use when preparing financial projections include:

- The Laventhol & Horwath U.S. Lodging Industry Study
- The Pannell, Kerr, Forster & Company U.S. Lodging Industry Study
- Actual financial statements of similar hotels in the same region of the country

---

* "Debt service" means the interest and charges currently payable on debt, including payments on the principal.

○ Actual financial statements of similar properties operated by the company that will manage the proposed hotel

○ Wage and hour studies for hotel employees conducted in the city under study

○ Utility rates for the city under study

○ Historical room-rate increases in the city under study

○ Federal government guidelines for future minimum wage increases

○ The design of the proposed hotel

Using these resources and the researcher's knowledge of the industry as guidelines, the future operating performance will be projected based on the following techniques:

○ Actual modeling of the departmental revenues

○ Amounts per guest room available

○ A percentage of another department's revenues

○ An amount per guest room occupied

○ An amount per square foot

○ An amount achieved by a similar hotel in a comparable market

Capital Budget / Financial Analysis

Up to this point in the chapter, the concept has been to present some of the major components of a feasibility study to provide an understanding of the research behind and importance of each. The summation of all of these parts should add up to the ultimate determination of whether or not the project is feasible and the attendant risks of pursuing construction.

One set of criteria commonly applied to determine whether or not a project is feasible includes the following:

1. The market either exists or can be developed.

2. The necessary technology exists or can be developed.

3. The financial returns and risk are satisfactory to all those who will invest funds in the project.[5]

Another set of criteria says:

1. Build for a known market, existing and future.

2. If you can't build to operate profitably—today and tomorrow—don't do it![6]

Regardless of which set of criteria is selected, the feasibility study should answer all of the market and risk considerations. In terms of the financial consideration, while the financial projections will provide insight into the probable results of operations, the answer depends upon the comparative attractiveness of alternative investment opportunities which the individuals providing funds for the hotel have before them. Thus, the final step in the feasibility study, which is almost always calculated after the completion of the market study and financial projections, is the determination of debt-service coverage and return on owner's equity.

The capital budget should include all the expenses that will be incurred during the development of the hotel. The list of expenses includes:

1. Land acquisition costs
2. Market study and financial projections
3. Architectural and engineering costs
4. Interim interest
5. Fixed-asset construction
6. Furniture, fixtures, and equipment
7. Pre-opening expenses
8. Consulting
9. Loan origination fees
10. Miscellaneous (travel expenses, permits, licenses, filing fees, etc.)

The sources of funds to pay for these expenses generally come from either debt or equity contributions. Therefore, as mentioned earlier, the decision to proceed with the project will be based on the lender's confidence that the project will be able to pay debt-service and other fixed charges and the developer's anticipated achievement of a desired rate of return on investment.

Notes

1. Kenneth I. Solomon and Norman Katz, *Profitable Restaurant Management* (Englewood Cliffs, N.J.: Prentice-Hall, 1974), p. 208.

2. E. Jerome McCarthy, *Basic Marketing: A Managerial Approach* (Chicago: Richard D. Irwin, 1978), p. 37.

3. W. Earl Sasser and Robert L. Banks, "Lender Attitudes Toward Hotel Financing," *Cornell Hotel and Restaurant Administration Quarterly*, February 1976, pp. 30–31.

4. Laventhol & Horwath, *U.S. Lodging Industry, 1979*, p. 21.

5. David S. Clifton, Jr. and David E. Fyffe, *Project Feasibility Analysis: A Guide to Profitable New Ventures* (New York: Wiley & Sons, 1977), p. 175.

6. C. Dewitt Coffman, *Marketing for a Full House,* ed. Helen J. Rechnagel (Ithaca, N.Y.: Cornell University, School of Hotel Administration, 1975), p. 110.

Energy Conservation: A Priority

When you finish this chapter you should understand:

1. The potential sources of energy that will be needed in the 1980s and 1990s for hotels and restaurants

2. The meaning of such energy concepts as cogeneration and retrofit

3. Specific energy conservation measures being undertaken by hotels and restaurants

4. What is meant by the statement that "conservation suffers from the least momentum and the weakest advocacy"

5. The reasons for the widespread view that we are in an energy emergency likely to last for a decade

> The main sources of energy available to us on the earth are chemical fuels, uranium and sunlight . . . In the very long run we shall need energy that is absolutely pollution-free; we shall have sunlight. In the fairly long run we shall need energy that is inexhaustible and moderately clean; we shall have deuterium (from the ocean). In the short run we shall need energy that is readily usuable and abundant; we shall have uranium. Right now we need energy that is cheap and convenient; we have coal . . .
>
> Freeman J. Dyson,
> "Energy in the Universe,"
> *Scientific American*,
> September 1971

In our discussion of "behavioral" architecture—hotels designed as places for people (Chapter 5), we considered how the hospitality industry can, in the design of its buildings, tune in to the "choreography of human activities." Implicit in this is the supposition that, having mastered the art of designing buildings "inside out" (i.e., based on the idea that people matter), we can continue to participate in the largest of the world's resources. But can we? To what extent must we take into account the fact that the production of oil, the fuel that furnishes most of the world's energy, is likely to level off—perhaps in the 1980s—and that alternative measures will have to be developed to meet our growing energy demands? In our view, this is a fundamental question facing the hospitality industry in the period at least to the end of this century. Accordingly, this chapter attempts to provide the necessary background on the present state of the art as we face the challenges of the critical energy transition, away from oil as the world's dominant fuel.

Energy Outlook for the 1980s

Quoting an irate automobile driver in a gasoline line during the 1979 gas shortage, *Business Week* reported: "There's good news and bad news. The bad news is that gas will cost $2 a gallon."

"And the good news?" asked another driver.

"There won't be any gas," answered the first, "so we won't have to line up for it."[1]

If, in substance, that is the energy message for all of us in the remaining years of the twentieth century, it is fair to ask: Where can we get all the energy we will need for the rest of this century to keep our hotels and restaurants going with heat, light, air conditioning, and refrigeration? Not from conventional sources of energy (i.e., oil, natural gas, coal, and nuclear power) here at home, nor from foreign oil, say the experts.[2] Rather, we must lessen our dependence on increasingly high-priced oil imported from the unstable, unpredictable Middle East by accelerating—on an all-out emergency basis—our development of energy conservation methods and of solar power, a renewable energy source. In other words, the present outlook forces us to ask: How, in the 1980s, can the hospitality industry maintain its economic growth while at the same time experiencing zero energy growth?

Industrywide Efforts to Conserve Energy

The awesome prospect of being compelled by the government to close down, as a nonessential industry, in the event of either a national emergency or energy rationing, prompted the American Hotel & Motel Association (AH&MA) in 1976 to institute a $200,000 energy program with a threefold aim:

1. To motivate employees of the lodging industry to participate actively in the effort to eliminate wasteful energy consumption

2. To make available to hotel and motel operators the information on which they can act to significantly reduce energy consumption in their

properties without adversely affecting present guest services and comfort (the improved efficiency should lead to an effective level of reduction of 15 to 30 percent by the end of the program's first year)

3. To provide operators with the means of monitoring and evaluating the success of their efforts[3]

While it is yet too early to claim any measurable results from this program, enthusiasm for discovering viable alternatives to the rapidly accelerating costs of fuel and power has spawned the creation of two "firsts" for the AH&MA: (1) the establishment of an ongoing research facility, the Energy Technical Center (ETC) in San Antonio, Texas; and (2) the publication of a looseleaf handbook, the *Energy Conservation Manual.*

Describing its ETC as "the biggest new ballgame in the lodging industry" since the opening of its Washington office and the establishment of its Educational Institute on the campus of Michigan State University, Wallace W. Lee, Jr., president of the Hospitality, Lodging & Travel Research Foundation—ETC's parent organization—and Richard E. Holtzman, president of AH&MA, jointly announced in 1977 the following ETC functions to be performed under the Foundation's direction, by a five-member staff of specialists:

1. To operate as an information center for the hotel/motel industry, equipment manufacturers, and governmental groups

2. To revise and expand the *Energy Conservation Manual* on a continuing basis

3. To monitor city, state, and national energy legislation as it would affect hotel/motel operations

4. To establish lodging industry liaison with the utility industry, government agencies and trade associations

5. To expand the foundation's library and to publish quarterly additions to the bibliography[4]

The most arresting aspect of this research venture was described in *Lodging* in October 1977 when Robert Aulbach, Energy Management Consultant to AH&MA, in a feature story on cogeneration,[5] recommended that serious consideration be given to installation of cogeneration plants in hotels and motels "where electrical and thermal loads are very high." Leaving no doubt as to where he stood on this matter, Aulbach underscored the importance of his recommendations with this closing editorial comment:

For you, the lodging industry owner or operator, to understand the concept of co-generation at this time is to take a timely step in the direction of rethinking survival methods in the midst of a crisis that will not end . . . [6]

Despite apprehensions by some that energy conservation would tilt too much toward more insulation, turning down thermostats, recaulking windows, and dimming lights, the economic as well as the political necessities of more effective energy management were not going unnoticed by other leaders in the industry. After all, energy costs were getting out of hand as early as 1975–1976. One 600-room hotel reported an annual utilities cost increase of $90,000. A New York City owner of three large hotels disclosed that for a six-month period the combined energy costs of these hotels increased by more than a million dollars. Another major hotel corporation reported that its energy costs for one year had exceeded its net profit figure by nearly $7 million.

Consequently, it came as no surprise that coincident with the publication in 1976 of the AH&MA *Energy Conservation Manual,* several of the larger chains, including Holiday Inns, astutely issued their own instructions elevating energy use and control to the same level of importance as other key management functions, while noting at the same time that holding down energy use and energy costs without disrupting operations would immediately generate greater profits.[7]

E-CAT at Holiday Inns In sharpening its particular focus on the practice of good energy management, Holiday Inns repeatedly emphasizes the necessity of creating in each one of its inns not another committee but instead an Energy Conservation Action Team (E-CAT) to implement an action program geared to the following objecctives:

1. Establish commitments from all department heads

2. Identify energy wastes

3. Set goals and establish action programs

4. Continue energy conservation efforts

	CURRENT PERIOD				YEAR TO DATE		
	THIS YEAR	LAST YEAR	VARIANCE	PCTG	THIS YEAR	LAST YEAR	VARIANCE
ELECTRICAL (KW)	150104	141704	8400-	5.9-	654008	654778	770
PER OCCUPIED ROOM	67.10	63.49	3.61-	5.7-	42.55	43.10	.55
TOTAL COST-ELECTRICAL	$4,530	$3,288	$1,242-	37.8-	$20,366	$15,882	$4,484-
PER OCCUPIED ROOM	$2.03	$1.47	$.56-	38.1-	$1.32	$1.05	$.27-
NATURAL GAS (CUBIC FEET)	377	223	154-	69.1-	2700	2239	461-
PER OCCUPIED ROOM	.17	.10	.07-	70.0-	.18	.15	.03-
TOTAL COST-NATURAL GAS	$397	$220	$177-	80.5-	$2,762	$2,145	$617-
PER OCCUPIED ROOM	$.18	$.10	$.08-	80.0-	$.18	$.14	$.04-
WATER (GALLONS)	455	250	205-	82.0-	1792	1510	282-
PER OCCUPIED ROOM	.20	.11	.09-	81.8-	.12	.10	.02-
TOTAL COST-WATER	$204	$98	$106-	108.2-	$869	$635	$234-
PER OCCUPIED ROOM	$.09	$.04	$.05-	125.0-	$.06	$.04	$.02-
TOTAL UTILITY COST	$5,131	$3,606	$1,525-	42.3-	$23,997	$18,662	$5,335-
PER OCCUPIED ROOM	$2.29	$1.62	$.67-	41.4-	$1.56	$1.23	$.33-
OCCUPANCY PERCENTAGE	93.6	96.0			88.2	87.3	
AVAILABLE ROOMS	2324	2324			17430	17402	

Source: Holiday Inn, *Energy Conservation Manual,* 1976, Section VI, p. 3.

Table 8–1. Holiday Inns Inc.—Food and Lodging Division Utility consumption and cost analysis for 07/76

1. Calculate your goal each month by multiplying the % reduction you estimated after your first survey times the consumption per occupied room figure for last year, year-to-date.

Energy
Conservation/
211

Example: if you set a goal of 20% reduction and your consumption per occupied room for last year year-to-date was:

Electricity	_____	1	43.10
Natural Gas	_____	2	.15
Water	_____	3	.10

Calculate your goal by multiplying each figure by .80.

Electricity	43.10	x.80 =	34.48
Natural Gas	.15	x.80 =	.12
Water	.10	x.80 =	.08

2. Compare the figure you calculated above with the figure recorded as your actual consumption per occupied room this year year-to-date.

	actual		goal
Electricity	4 42.55	vrs	34.48
Natural Gas	5 .18	vrs	.12
Water	6 .12	vrs	.08

3. Plot both figures on a monthly basis on the tracking charts.

Source: *Energy Conservation Manual*, p. 2.

Table 8-2. Method of calculation used to develop actual vs. goal = performance figures

These objectives are underscored in a series of instructional guides, one of which broke new ground in the application of computer technology to the measurement of energy conservation effectiveness in hotels. Each month a "Utility Consumption and Cost Analysis Report" is produced at the Memphis computer center of Holiday Inns and sent to each Holiday Inn. The figures shown on the report are based upon the monthly utility bills, and are illustrated in the sample printout shown in Table 8–1. The method of calculation employed in developing actual versus goal-performance figures is reflected in Table 8–2. By using a tracking chart to plot actual electricity, natural gas, and water consumption for each month and the calculated goal figure computed from the Utility Consumption and Cost Analysis Report, innkeepers are enabled to visualize trends and to see graphically whether they are *over* or *under* their respective goals. Examples of tracking charts may be seen in Tables 8–3, 8–4, and 8–5.

As first one, then another of the companies in the hospitality industries activated ambitious conservation programs, the word of their accomplishments began seeping into the trade press. Thus, Doubletree Inn in Tucson, Arizona reported savings of $29,000 in its 1976 electric bill as a consequence of an aggressive employee motivation and training program enabling it to pare 739,000 kilowatt hours off its energy use in that year. Similarly, Hilton Hotels reported a saving of $28,000 in waste from previously unsuspected steam leaks in individual hotels. One hotel, the 300-room Mount Laurel Hilton in New Jersey, reported early in 1980 that it had reduced its energy costs from 13.2 percent of sales to 7.6 percent of sales in a two-year period during which the occupancy rate rose 50 percent over prior levels.

For the years 1974 to 1977, Burger King reported a 17 percent reduction in energy use. Fifty percent of these savings came from improved housekeeping—i.e., better heater maintenance, careful adjustment of lighting, and prompt repair of leaky steam traps—all of which were accomplished with little or no investment.[8]

At the same time, a multiplicity of heat recovery systems, pilot-light-less gas ovens (50 percent of the gas used by gas ovens is consumed by the pilot light!), energy management consultants, scores of checklists ("12 Ways to Save Energy in Swimming Pool Operations"; "29 Ways to Save Energy in Meeting and Function Rooms"), more efficient kitchen vents, etc.—all were being exhibited with increasing prominence at the annual trade shows in New York and Chicago. As of this writing, innkeepers and restaurateurs alike hope that the ultimate payoff will equal the promised performance.

In a time of volatile travel-related markets, accelerating rates of obsolescence, rising labor rates, and debatable productivity, it was perhaps not surprising that the industry elected to concentrate on those conservation opportunities requiring little or no capital investment instead of

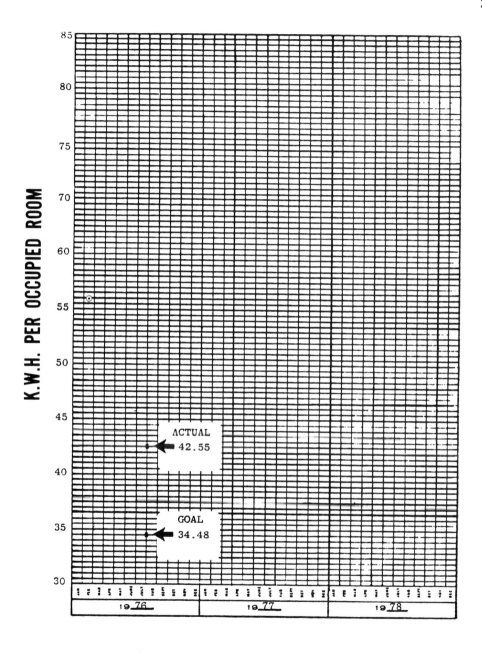

K.W.H. PER OCCUPIED ROOM

ACTUAL 42.55

GOAL 34.48

19 76   19 77   19 78

Source: *Energy Conservation Manual, p. 1.*

Table 8–3. Electrical Tracking Chart

NATURAL GAS TRACKING CHART

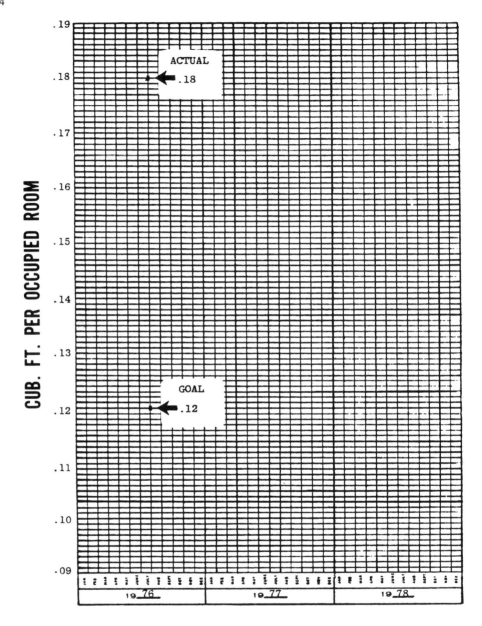

Source: *Energy Conservation Manual, p. 2.*

Table 8–4. Natural Gas Tracking Chart

WATER TRACKING CHART

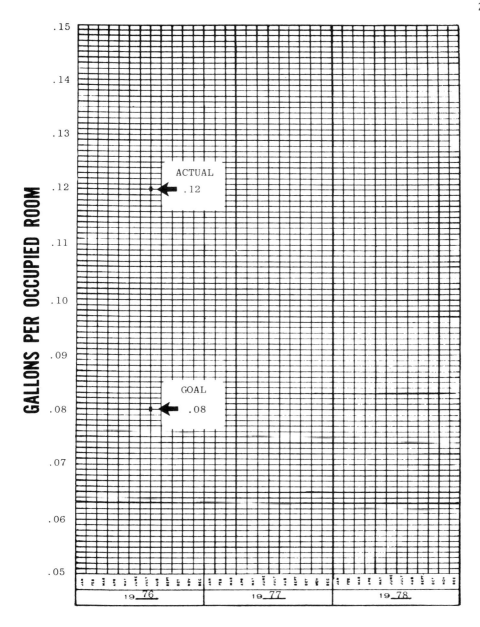

Table 8–5. Water Tracking Chart

those energy-saving designs and devices in which the anticipated savings fail to offset the heavy capital investments involved in the technology of solar energy.

Nevertheless, a few pioneers managed to preserve the industry's reputation for being a showcase of technological progress.

Solar Power at La Quinta Motor Inns

As early as 1976, the La Quinta Motor Inn of Dallas, Texas became the nation's first hotel to install a solar system for space heating and hot water. In its account of this industry "first," *Lodging* magazine explained:

> LaQuinta corporation failed to get a grant as applied for from the Energy Research and Development Corporation (ERDA). So they paid their own way. ERDA came to help them celebrate the achievement.
>
> The solar system operates in conjunction with conventional water-to-air heat pumps located in the [26] rooms of the new addition. These heat pumps perform both heating and air-conditioning functions. The heating cycle of the heat pump is the only function that is solar-assisted.
>
> In cold weather, the pumps transfer heat from water circulating in a closed loop to the air in the rooms. In warmer weather, they reverse the process and cool the rooms by transferring heat from them to the circulating water.
>
> The system has 19 flat-plate collector panels that are 400 square feet and black-lined to absorb the sun's heat. The panels are mounted on the roof facing south. Thus, they receive maximum sunlight in this latitude.
>
> The sun heats a solution of water and antifreeze that is in contact with the panels. This solution, in turn, becomes a heat exchange medium for warming water in a 2500-gallon insulated storage tank that is a part of the circulating loop mentioned above.
>
> This substantially improves the efficiency of the heat pumps in warming the rooms and reduces the amount of energy required. The hot water in the storage tank is also used to preheat the regular water supply for the inn.
>
> Another energy-saving feature of the system is the use of large amounts of heat taken from the rooms during warm weather (by the heat pumps) to heat the domestic water supply for the motor hotel and adjacent restaurant. Very few commercial heat installations put recovered heat to effective use.[9]

Although the total cost was not indicated (except that it cost $15,000 more than a conventional heating system), the LaQuinta owners anticipate recovering their investment in the system by 1983.

Solar Energy Systems at Days Inns

In October 1979, Days Inns announced plans to install solar-energy water-heating systems in eleven of its inns, with approximately half of the cost to be funded by the U.S. Department of Energy.

In principle, the solar hot-water plant is a system composed of flat-plate collectors arranged in parallel rows facing south. The collectors are placed on the roof of a Days Inn, with a total collector area of not less than 1,000 square feet. Each installation includes a storage tank of not less than 1,000 gallons of water. The system is designed to heat approximately 65 percent of the daily hot-water needs of a Days Inn or a Days Lodge complex. The payout of capital expenditures for each system installation is projected to be seven years.[10]

In fact, only five Inns actually completed solar energy installations. By the end of 1982, Days Inns' Energy Conservation Director had reported that one of the five Inns had been sold; three others were not performing satisfactorily; and the remaining Inn was operating right on target. In the company's view, the return on investment from such solar systems has been insufficient to justify their installation in other Inns.

Since nearly 80 percent of a hotel's energy consumption occurs in heating, ventilation, and air conditioning (only 10 percent of energy costs is for lighting), Hilton Hotels Corporation in 1978 undertook an engineering study of the feasibility of having its own power plant at the New York Hilton. It was planned to be included in the design of a new 850-room tower addition to the hotel. A preliminary study by consulting engineers had indicated an attractively short payback period of five years for a cogeneration system that utilized waste heat for the hotel's hot-water and laundry needs.[11]

As of 1979, however, the general manager of the New York Hilton reported that the entire project had been suspended indefinitely for reasons that were not disclosable.[12]

Cogeneration for the New York Hilton

Restaurants—Solar and Wind Power

As reports increased of solar systems being installed in Carribean and Pacific resorts,[13] other segments of the hospitality industry began to take notice. Thus, the Cattlemen's Restaurant chain of California opened its first solar restaurant, in Washoe City, Nevada, in late 1977, noting that the estimated fuel savings would yield a 100 percent return on its energy investment in five years.[14] Meanwhile, a restaurant and motel complex known as "Pea Soup Anderson's" in Santa Nella, California successfully capitalized on the marketing advantages as well as the power savings generated through the operation of its newly constructed windmill. In San Francisco, a restaurant newly opened in 1977, The Sundance, advertised its solar energy heating and cooling system under the name "Enersense." That system reduces fossil energy supply by more than 50 percent when compared with conventional heating and cooling systems, and is designed to heat or cool different parts of the building independently by transferring stored energy through two heat pumps situated on the premises.[15]

By the late 1970's, industrywide tools for energy management were becoming generally accessible through trade publications and governmental information services. Particularly useful in helping to save energy are the approaches described for hotels and restaurants in the following works:

○ *Energy Conservation Manual,* published by the Hospitality, Lodging & Travel Foundation, Inc., an affiliate of the American Hotel & Motel Association, 888 Seventh Avenue, New York, NY 10019. See especially Section VI, "Energy Inventory and Review, Hotels and Motels."

○ *Energy Audit Workbook for Restaurants,* September 1978, U.S. Department of Commerce. This 72-page booklet is available from National Technical Information Service, U.S. Department of Commerce, 5285 Port Royal Rd., Springfield, VA 22161.

○ *Lodging,* a monthly publication of the American Hotel & Motel Association. It features a monthly special section on energy management containing a checklist of practical suggestions for controlling energy costs.

In substance, these specialized publications stress the positive impact energy conservation steps can have on the "bottom line."

Thus, a typical restaurant can save as much as 15 percent of its utility costs—without any appreciable capital outlay—simply by identifying the obvious opportunities for energy savings through an energy audit. For example, most HVAC (heating, ventilating, and air conditioning) systems designed before the 1974 Arab oil embargo operate when the outside temperature is only 50 to 55 degrees F. A simple change in the controls so that the chiller (i.e., air conditioner) will turn on at 63 degrees, instead, yields obvious savings when you take into account hourly energy costs, demand charges, fuel-adjustment charges, and taxes.

Very often, an energy-hungry restaurant eats away at profits unless close attention is paid to the obvious wastes. Methods to avoid such waste include turning off the hot water faucet, shutting the door to the walk-in refrigerator, turning off all powered equipment not in use, fully loading ovens and dishwashing machines, and turning off unneeded lights. These, as well as other energy-saving steps frequently shown as checklists in hospitality industry publications, are just a few of the obvious ways to reduce restaurant energy costs.

Similarly, hotels can reduce their energy costs in places other than their restaurant/kitchen operations by implementing such measures as installing room-status systems which turn the HVAC unit on or off as a guest checks in or out; installing peak-power demand controls, soft-start lighting, and photoelectric sensing to control lighting intensity. These steps, along with others outlined in the *Energy Conservation Manual* mentioned previously, are estimated to reduce energy consumption by 15 to

30 percent by the end of the first year following completion of an energy inventory and audit.

In a word, these conservation guides for the hospitality industry aim simply to make available the various methods by which one can analyze energy uses, determine areas in which energy savings can be made, and develop action plans to make the energy savings one has accomplished both visible and ongoing.

To enable you to conduct your inventory and audit with a minimum of problems, the following conversion factors are listed. From them, your fuel requirements can be rapidly calculated based on Btu input, or by multiplying the amount of fuel input by Btu value (if known), the hourly Btu value can be obtained.

Conversion factors

Natural Gas

1 cubic foot = 1,000 Btu
1 Therm = 100 cubic feet = 100,000 Btu
1 Mcf = 1,000 cubic feet = 1,000,000 Btu

Liquefied Petroleum Gases

Butane: 1 gallon = 102,000 Btu
Propane: 1 gallon = 92,000 Btu

Fuel Oil

No. 2: 1 gallon = 140,000 Btu
No. 5: 1 gallon = 148,000 Btu

Electricity

watt = 3.412 Btu
kilowatt = 1,000 watts = 3,412 Btu

Steam

1,000 lbs. = 1,000,000 Btu

Coal

Since there are various types of coal and the Btu value varies considerably, the value should be obtained from the coal supplier.

Electricity

Assume electricity = $0.05/Kilowatt-hour (Kwh)
Cost of 1,000,000 Btu of electricity, therefore is:

$$(1 \text{ Kwh} = 3,412 \text{ Btu}) \ \frac{1,000,000 \text{ Btu}}{3,412 \text{ Btu}} = 293.08 \text{ Kwh}$$

293.08 Kwh × $0.05 = *$14.65 per million Btu*

Fuel Oil

Assume that both No. 2 and No. 5 fuel oil costs
$0.40/gallon
Cost of 1,000,000 Btu is calculated as follows:
No. 2 fuel oil = 140,000 Btu/gallon

$$\frac{1,250,000 \text{ Btu}}{140,000 \text{ Btu}} = 8.92 \text{ gallons}$$

(1,250,000 Btu = input to boiler at 80% efficiency
to get 1,000,000 Btu output) 8.92 Gallons × $0.40
= *$3.57 per million Btu*

No. 5 Fuel oil = 148,000 Btu/gallon

$$\frac{1,250,000 \text{ Btu}}{148,000 \text{ Btu}} = 8.44 \text{ gallons}$$

8.44 gallons × $0.40 = *$3.38 per million Btu*

Natural Gas

Assume that natural gas costs $3.50 per Mcf,
or $0.35 per therm.
Cost of 1,000,000 Btu is calculated as follows:
1 Mcf = 1,000,000 Btu = *$3.50 per million Btu*
1 Therm = 100,000 Btu = $0.35

$$\frac{1,000,000 \text{ Btu}}{100,000 \text{ Btu}} = 10 \text{ therms}$$

10 therms × $0.35 = *$3.50 per million Btu*

Commonly used abbreviations

Bbls—Barrels (42 Gallons)
kw—Kilowatt
kwh—Kilowatt-hour
mcf—1,000 cubic feet
mw—Megawatt (1 million watts)
Btu—British thermal unit
Therm—A unit of energy used for natural gas equal to 100,000 BTU

Source: Energy Conservation Manual, The Hospitality,
Lodging and Travel Research Foundation, Inc.,
New York, 1977, vol. 1, pp. g8–9.

At the end of this chapter, we have included a practical illustration
of a way in which energy conservation measures may be undertaken. "A
Case Study in Energy Management: Controlling the Cost of Utilities" and
applies to motor inns ranging in size from 75 to 200 rooms. While the
emphasis in this illustration tends to be upon recognized areas of energy

waste in motor inns, it is important to remember that every building, whatever its function, has a distinct energy-use pattern. Accordingly, the approaches suggested for saving energy should be used selectively.

As the decade of the 1980s begins to unfold, the influence of the energy problem in the hospitality industry is gaining visibility in at least three ways. *First,* we are seeing the creation of energy manager positions in some of the larger hotel and restaurant corporations; these positions call for both technical and operations expertise. In addition to engineering know-how, an energy manager's training and experience must demonstrate a successful grasp of customer needs, employee motivation, and bottom-line performance. *Second,* the design and construction of new hotels and restaurants—as well as the remodeling of older properties—are reflecting increased sensitivity to energy conservation as the number-one priority. With nearly 40 percent of energy consumption going for space heating, hot water, air conditioning, and lighting, many companies are now engaged in what is called "retrofit"—a process that involves changes in structure and equipment that "button up" buildings to improve their thermal and lighting efficiency. The third, more sophisticated tools are not emerging to help us predict energy consumption accurately and appraise the effectiveness of all our ongoing energy conservation efforts.[16]

Nonetheless, it would be a mistake to let these modest gains lull us into complacency. The present energy emergency in our country can scarcely be overstated. Stobaugh and Yergin have warned that "our whole industrial system is like a vehicle built to operate on $3 oil, puffing along with an inefficient engine and with a body leaking vast amounts of energy. Each drop wasted drives higher the price of future oil purchases, which in turn makes it easier for OPEC to cut production and raise prices even more. Now that we have $30 oil, correcting this situation is the nation's first order of business."[17] It is, say these authors, an emergency that will persist throughout the 1980s.

Assuming therefore that conservation is the principal key of achieving the cheapest, safest, most productive energy alternative readily available, the question arises as to what handicaps the hospitality industry faces as it seeks to accelerate its energy-saving efforts in the future.

First is the matter of our own inertia. In the past it didn't matter greatly how much energy was used for heating, lighting, or cooling our restaurants and hotels. It was often cheaper to leave the heat on in our unoccupied guest rooms and dining rooms than to install expensive thermostatic controls. But now that the world is changing so rapidly that we can no longer ignore the possibilities for greater energy efficiency. As Stobaugh and Yergin pointed out, the question arises: "Which is cheaper—a barrel of oil from distant and hostile terrain, with the risk of a dramatic increase in price—or a barrel saved by insulation?"[18]

Second, conservation suffers from "the least momentum and the weakest advocacy." As one former assistant federal energy administrator has observed, "The oil companies and utilities are busy talking up how much they need to produce. But no one's out there wholesaling conservation by the ton and barrel."[19] Indeed, the Texas Railroad Commission has darkly questioned the wisdom, if not the patriotism, of those who would encourage conservation by asserting: "This country did not conserve its way to greatness. It produced itself to greatness."[20]

Third, the energy decision making and action at the point of end use of energy is becoming highly decentralized, "involving millions and millions of actors, often poorly informed, without easy access to capital or to the requisite skills, and for whom energy Is only one of a myriad of concerns rather than the central organization focus."[21]

What to do? We favor reliance upon a company energy policy to guide the transition from dependence upon imported oil to the equivalent production of millions of barrels per day of *conservation* energy. For example, AT&T has set an internal goal of negative energy growth—aiming to use less energy in 1984 than in 1973—even though its business is projected to double. To paraphrase Stobaugh and Yergin, what is good, in this case, for AT&T is also good for the hospitality industry.

Summary

In this chapter we have seen that unless we curb our gluttonous appetite for imported oil, we will continue to drive its price up and—with the traumas of the Middle East producers continuing to plague us—in all probability reduce the supply as well as its dependability.

During the decade of the 1980s, therefore, we are going to have to rely less on conventional energy sources and more upon conservation. Indeed, our hospitality industry leaders today no longer think of energy conservation as simply a highly desirable practice. Rather, it is regarded as an absolute necessity.

Thus, under the auspices of the American Hotel & Motel Association, we have seen the emergence of an energy conservation and information program designed to help hotels and motels significantly reduce their energy consumption without adversely affecting guest services and comfort. Also, the U.S. Department of Commerce in its *Energy Audit Workbook for Restaurants* describes some simple methods by which an owner, manager, or operator of a restaurant can analyze energy uses and determine how energy can be saved.

In addition, we have highlighted not only the commitments to energy conservation programs being made by hotel and restaurant companies generally but also some of the pioneering experiments with solar and wind power in this industry ... with emphasis upon the range of reductions being made in energy consumption.

Finally, we have taken note of such encouraging trends as the creation of energy management executive positions; the emergence of energy-conscious designs in new hotels and restaurants along with the "retrofit" concept for updating older properties; and the application of sophisticated mathematical tools for predicting energy consumption and appraising conservation effectiveness.

Above all, this chapter stresses that despite the handicaps under which all hotels and restaurants labor, setting a meaningful goal—like that of AT&T—will serve to guide our transition from imported oil at ever-increasing prices to *conservation* energy. At the very least, our aim for the 1980s should be zero energy growth.

Questions for Discussion

1. What forces in hotels, restaurants, fast-food establishments, and other institutions seem to account for the creation of energy manager positions?

2. Identify three ideas that you would recommend for incorporation into a restaurant operation to reduce energy demand.

3. What is the meaning of cogeneration? Discuss its possible application to hotels and restaurants.

4. What are the functions of the Energy Technical Center?

5. Is a solar system for space heating and hot water practicable for the hospitality industry? Explain.

6. Discuss the handicaps to greater energy conservation efforts and indicate how you personally would seek to overcome them if you were a hotel or restaurant manager.

Key Terms

○ COGENERATION
○ E-CAT
○ ENERGY AUDIT
○ ENERGY CONSERVATION
○ ENERGY INVENTORY
○ ENERGY TECHNICAL CENTER
○ SOLAR POWER
○ TRACKING CHART

La Quinta Motor Inns, San Antonio

A Case Study: Controlling the Cost of Utilities*

La Quinta Motor Inns, Inc., is a San Antonio–based chain of approximately 100 motor inns, ranging in size from 75 to 200 rooms, but averaging about 130 rooms.

Design evokes Old Mexico in flavor, the New Southwest in efficiency. Construction, however colorful, is nonetheless streamlined. Lobbies are small. Restaurants—not operated by La Quinta—are nearby. Appeal is to the business traveler.

---

*Reprinted from *Lodging,* the official publication of the American Hotel & Motel Association, June 1979.

Source of the material presented here is Nancy Palmer of La Quinta's Dallas offices. She worked with Robert S. Noyes, senior vice president–motor inn operations. She also worked with AH&MA's Energy Technical Center, also located in San Antonio.

La Quinta spends an average of $347 per room per year on utilities. Nothing that goes into the room costs more.

The chain learned from AH&MA's Energy Technical Center that electric costs are expected to rise by 11.8 percent this year [1979], gas by 17 percent and oil by 19 percent. La Quinta decided that "we couldn't control utility prices but we could control utility consumption."

The corporation decided in 1978 to approach utility cost reduction in two ways: (1) more practical operations control, and, (2) better utilization of energy-saving technology in construction.

Operations Control

Motor inn management is now held responsible for keeping all equipment properly cleaned, insulated and maintained. Managers are asked to think of motor inns as they would think of their own cars. "You wouldn't think of driving your car without giving it a periodic tuneup."

Heating, ventilation and air conditioning equipment, such as coils, compressors, controls and filters, are cleaned thoroughly and consistently. Policy requires that each filter be cleaned every 30 days.

Special emphasis is put on keeping the building envelope air-tight. That means paying special attention to caulking, weather-stripping and insulation.

All water pipes are being insulated. Plans even call for an extra layer of insulation throughout most of the buildings.

Extra heavy blackout draperies are used in each guest room. During summer months, draperies are kept closed so that rooms will not get so hot from sunlight that they'll require excessive energy to cool when guests arrive.

In the laundry, says Noyes, "we have designed a two-inch-thick insulating cover that fits over each dryer front. It is painted white and is hardly noticeable." The extra layer of insulation keeps heat that might otherwise escape from the dryer inside where it belongs. Less energy is used to get linens dry and less cooling is necessary in the laundry area.

Conversion of outside lighting to low pressure sodium lights has been in progress for nearly two years. Sodium lights cut electrical consumption by as much as 80 percent.

Fluorescent lighting is replacing incandescent lighting in guest rooms as fixtures are replaced. Fluorescent lighting provides the same amount of illumination with a 46 percent energy reduction (Figure 1).

Bulb wattage has been reduced to an appropriate operable level in all light fixtures. For example, bathroom vanity lights have been reduced from two 75-watt incandescent lights to a 60-watt fluorescent light. Even with this reduction, La Quinta provides 3½ watts per square foot—considered a high lighting level.

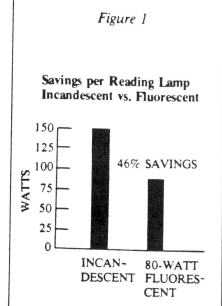

Figure 1

**Savings per Reading Lamp
Incandescent vs. Fluorescent**

46% SAVINGS

WATTS

INCAN-
DESCENT

80-WATT
FLUORES-
CENT

Estimated use per occupied room 4
hours/day. 4 hours/day x 70 watts
saved/day/room x 100 rooms
equals 28,000 watts divided by
1,000 equals 28 KWH x
$1.035/KWH equals $0.98 x 365
days/year equals $357.70/savings
per year per 100 reading lamps or
$3.58 per year per lamp.

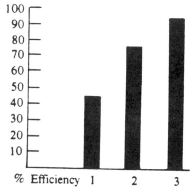

Figure 2

**Improvements in domestic hot
water heating as a result of
cleaning combustion chambers,
adjusting firing rate, insulating
hot water piping.**

% Efficiency   1   2   3

(1) Percentage of efficiency of
domestic hot water system prior to
program efforts. (2) Improvements
in efficiency after cleaning
combustion chambers and
adjusting firing rate. (3) Further
improvement after the insulation of
hot water piping. Note that
percentage of efficiency in what is,
in most hotels and motels, the
biggest factor in energy costs, was
approximately doubled.

Time control clocks are now used on all exterior lights as well as on
some motor-powered equipment. For example, the booster water pumps
that keep the hot water supply at a constant temperature throughout the
piping loop are turned off during slack periods (later night) and turned
back on during peak demand periods (early morning).

Central heating and air conditioning is used at many of the first-
built La Quinta Inns and Rodeway Inns now operated by La Quinta. At
these inns, La Quinta has designed and tested a heat recovery exchange
that will assist in the preheating of the domestic hot water supply.

The chain also discovered that it can save approximately 30 percent
of natural gas costs by cleaning and properly adjusting the burners in the
water heaters and gas dryers (Figure 2).

Flow restrictors are used on toilets, lavatories and showers to conserve water; leaky faucets are repaired as soon as leaks are discovered.

As equipment wears out, La Quinta replaces it with the latest energy efficient product on the market. They recently bought 500 new television sets that cost a little more than previous models but operate at a lower energy level.

Energy Audits

La Quinta computerizes energy audits. Printouts show, for each calendar month, and for each property and for all properties:

○ Energy costs for the chain
○ Costs per property
○ Costs per room and per guest
○ Btu's consumed per square foot
○ Consumption per cubic foot
○ Consumption per inn, room and guest

Printouts contain projected utility costs through 1988 based on current inflation rates and thus assist management in forecasting future costs. The 10-year cost projections include listings for (1) water; (2) electricity; (3) gas, firm; (4) gas, interruptible, and (5) fuel oil.

Printouts also serve a trouble-shooting function. They provide continuous monitoring, spotting unusual costs or consumption and allowing for prompt corrective action. One property, for example, showed a large increase in water consumption. Investigation revealed that the makeup valve in the cooling tower had not been replaced after repairs and therefore was wasting water. Without the energy audit, it may never have been discovered.

Construction Technology

La Quinta has been widely publicized as one of the few lodging chains that is experimenting broadly with solar energy. Where new inns are not equipped with a solar system as an alternative source, the type of HVAC (heating, ventilating and air conditioning) hardware used will make the retrofit use of solar energy possible at a later date for a fraction of the cost.

La Quinta is also one of the few chains to use heat pumps extensively in new construction. Waste heat is reclaimed from heat pumps during the cooling cycle to help heat the domestic hot water.

Other energy-saving construction techniques are also used; among them:

○ Thermopane glass and solar screens on all windows.
○ Windows recessed for partial shading.

○ Recirculating fan units in bathrooms (the units contain sanitizing and deodorizing filters that provide clean, sterile air with an absolute minimum of bacteria).

○ A reflective roofing surface membrane in warm climates to reflect heat.

○ Main electrical feeders that are oversized to eliminate possible overheating of electrical systems.

○ Infrared heat lamps with timers in baths to reduce wattage and amount of energy used.

○ Rooms painted a light color for maximum reflective lighting conditions.

○ Translucent white lamp shades rather than opaque shades to allow light to be more evenly distributed through the room.

○ A large domestic hot water storage system used to keep water temperature as low as possible and to minimize peaks in energy consumption. (A separate booster boiler is provided to increase the temperatures of stored domestic water to levels required by the laundry on an as-needed basis only, thereby avoiding the necessity of having to store large quantities of high-temperature water on a 24-hour basis).

Guest Involvement

Guests as well as inn managers and staffs must be involved to achieve maximum energy conservation. Attached to the mirror in each lavatory at La Quinta inns is a message asking guests to help the chain conserve energy. It reads:

> The energy you save belongs to you, tomorrow, next year, at home and on the road. Thanks for conserving energy during your visits with us. Because of your efforts plus our own companywide programs, La Quinta has been able to maintain and, in some inns, even reduce energy expenditures this year versus last year. This is being achieved without reducing our guests' comforts and services and in spite of the higher cost of energy and higher occupancy levels at our inns.
>
> "You're making it happen. And it means our country's energy resources will last longer. Thanks for turning the heat/air conditioner, lights, radio and TV off and checking to see that all water faucets are turned off when you leave.

"We feel that it's important for our guests to know that by helping us control our energy consumption now, they are actually helping themselves," says Robert Noyes. "By helping us control our costs, they are helping us keep our rates as low as possible and, also, helping to conserve fuel for all of us."

"We can't find an answer to the energy problem overnight because so much planning and coordination go into a program of this magnitude." "It will probably take us three years to implement our entire program throughout the chain, but at least we've taken the first steps."

1. What are three ways for keeping the building envelope air tight?

2. How many layers of insulation are put over most water pipes?

3. What is the purpose of heavy blackout draperies?

4. In the laundry, what energy-saving device is used on the dryer front?

5. How much is saved by using low-pressure sodium lighting outside?

6. Compare fluorescent to incandescent room lighting cost.

7. Name two places where La Quinta uses time control clocks to advantage.

8. At what type of property is La Quinta testing heat recovery exchange?

9. How much is saved by cleaning and properly adjusting burners in water heaters and gas dryers?

10. Name three places where flow restrictors are used.

11. Name five out of the six types of information on energy use revealed by monthly computer printouts.

12. How far in advance does La Quinta project energy costs?

13. Name four out of the five categories of projection of future energy costs.

14. What is the trouble-shooting function of computer printouts?

15. In new construction, what provision does La Quinta make for future solar installations?

16. Why are heat pumps used extensively by La Quinta?

17. Name at least five of the nine energy-saving devices (thermopane windows, etc.) La Quinta is using in new construction that are mentioned here.

18. What are the purposes of the chain's hot water storage system installations at new motor inns?

19. How would you evaluate La Quinta's message to guests to encourage joint involvement in energy saving?

Notes

1. *Business Week,* July 30, 1979, p. 4.

2. Among the numerous "experts" on the energy problem, none are more persuasive—nor more scholarly—than Robert Stobaugh and Daniel Yergin. Robert Stobaugh is Professor of Business Administration at the Harvard Business School and director since 1973 of the school's Energy Project. Daniel Yergin is a former faculty member of the Harvard Business School who is now a lecturer at the Kennedy School of Government at Harvard University and Director of the International Energy Seminar at the Center for International Affairs, Harvard University.

Together they have authored the following definitive works on the energy problem:

- ○ *Energy Future: Report of the Energy Project at the Harvard Business School* (New York: Random House, 1979). Others who served as co-authors of this book are: I. C. Bupp, Mel Horwitch, Sergio Koreisha, M. A. Maidique, and Frank Schuller.
- ○ "The Energy Outlook: Combining the Options," *Harvard Business Review,* January–February 1980, pp. 57–73.
- ○ "Energy: An Emergency Telescoped," *Foreign Affairs,* February 1980, pp. 563–95.

3. *Energy Conservation Manual, 1976,* The Hospitality, Lodging & Travel Research Foundation, Inc., 888 Seventh Avenue, New York, NY 10019.

4. "ETC: A Whole New Ballgame," *Lodging,* July 1977, p. 13.

5. *Cogeneration* is a term that deserves special attention because it is a major concept in energy conservation. Applied to a hotel, restaurant, or other hospitality establishment, it usually means the combined production of electricity and steam from a single fuel source at the building site. It can scarcely be characterized, however, as an inexpensive system. For, as energy experts point out, the component parts of a cogeneration system—such as turbines, engines, boilers, piping, and controls—can cost millions. Writing in the *New York Times* (April 1, 1982, p. D2), Barnaby J. Feder reported that

> Fifty-four industrial cogeneration facilities are known to be in various stages of planning or construction, and 23 such projects are under way at commercial sites, such as shopping centers, or institutions, such as hospitals or universities, with many more projects unreported. [Feder concluded that] technical improvements continue to make investments more attractive, albeit no less expense initially. One key technical goal is incorporation in cogeneration systems of recently developed fluidized bed boilers, which burn coal more efficiently and emit less air pollution.

6. Robert Aulbach, "Co-Generation: Does This Apply to Hotels/Motels?" *Lodging,* October 1977, pp. 37–38. An excellent explanation, complete with schematic diagram of what cogeneration is and how it works.

7. More than one-half of AH&MA's *Energy Conservation Manual* is devoted to a section titled: "Part IV, Energy Conservation Opportunities without Major Cost." It is therefore a key part of the manual, filled with specific information on operations and maintenance that can help reduce the amount of wasted energy. For example: "Did you know that when you serve a guest an unwanted glass of ice water, you waste 8 oz. of water in the glass, 8 oz. in the icemaking, and 16 oz. heated to 180 degrees in the glass washing? Did you know that supplying hot water to guests costs hotels and motels more than anything else involving energy use except

heating and cooling, and yet 90 percent of hotel and motel hot water lines are uninsulated—causing an energy waste of 60 to 80 percent?"

8. Stobaugh and Yergin, *Energy Future*, p. 154.

9. "Solar Energy for Hotels and Motels," *Lodging*, June 1977, pp. 10–12.

10. *Motel/Hotel Insider, Weekly Newsletter,* October 29, 1979, p. 3.

11. *New York Times,* August 9, 1978, p. D14.

12. Letter dated January 12, 1979, from Jorgen H. Hansen, general manager of the New York Hilton.

13. *Lodging,* June 1977, pp. 13–15; see also *Pacific Business News,* June 6, 1977.

14. *Detroit Free Press,* October 5, 1977, p. 5.

15. "The Karas Executive Report for Foodservice Decision Makers," 7, no. 8 (February 1977).

16. See especially "Gauging Energy Savings: Further Applications of Multiple-Regression Analysis," by Michael H. Redlin (School of Hotel Administration, Cornell University) and Jan A. deRoos (Sheraton Corporation) in *The Cornell Hotel and Restaurant Administration Quarterly,* February 1980, pp. 48–52.

17. Stobaugh and Yergin, "Energy: An Emergency Telescoped," p. 594.

18. Stobaugh and Yergin, *Energy Future,* p. 180.

19. Stobaugh and Yergin, "'The Energy Outlook," p. 71.

20. *Newsweek,* April 18, 1977, p. 73.

21. Stobaugh and Yergin, "The Energy Outlook," p. 71.

Pricing and Analyzing Profitability

When you finish this chapter, you should understand:

    1. The major revenue centers in a hotel

    2. The historical relationships between changes in occupancy (covers) and changes in prices for both the rooms department and food and beverage departments in hotels and motels

    3. The various formal and informal approaches to setting room rates

    4. Discounting situations in a hotel and the principles underlying determination of equivalent occupancies

    5. The potential average rate and achievement factors in a hotel

    6. The importance of support services in a hotel and factors that should be considered when support services are being designed

Within any hotel or motel there may exist several different revenue centers; their number varies depending upon the size and complexity of the property and the markets it is attempting to serve. In fact, one common approach to classifying lodging properties into motels, motor hotels, and hotels is by "inventorying" the services and amenities that the property offers to its guests.

    The following chart shows one approach to these services and in which classification they would typically be expected to be found:

Facility/service
Property classification

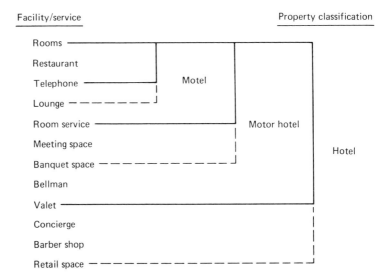

Rooms
Restaurant
Telephone — Motel
Lounge
Room service — Motor hotel
Meeting space
Banquet space Hotel
Bellman
Valet
Concierge
Barber shop
Retail space

The facilities and services offered by a well-run property are design-ed to contribute to the hotel's revenue. This contribution may be made either directly or indirectly.

An example of an amenity indirectly contributing to revenue would be an indoor swimming pool. Even though most hotels do not charge registered guests a fee to use the pool, additional revenue can be in-directly generated in several ways:

○ The hotel may be able to sell more escape weekend business because of the availability of a "year-round" pool

○ The hotel may be able to charge a little higher room rate because the guest perceives a higher price-value relationship with the pool

Services or amenities for which there is a charge for use—such as telephone, food and beverage, and meeting rooms—directly contribute to a hotel's revenue.

Hotel managers hope that in addition to contributing to revenue, the services and amenities offered will contribute to the overall pro-fitability of the operation. Those services which directly produce revenue should be profit centers—that is, the revenue directly received from each service will exceed the expenses directly attributable to those revenues. However, often this is not the case and, in fact, many services within the average hotel or motel are actually not cost-justified. This is becoming a more common situation owing to increasing construction and operating costs.

In the next section we will examine the historical perspective of the lodging industry's sources of revenues and the expenses associated with these revenues. Later, we will discuss the major source of revenue—that arising from rooms—in greater detail.

As mentioned above, in the typical lodging facility, in addition to selling rooms, the operator offers other services and amenities for which the guest is often charged. Needless to say, it is hoped that each of these revenue centers will also be profit centers. As we have said, this is not always the case, as we shall see. A classic example of a revenue center that is often not a profit center is the telephone department. Even though guests are often charged for each phone call they make, whether local or long distance, the average property incurs more telephone-related expenses than revenue. This is illustrated by the following figures:

Revenue and expenses
Telephone department, 1980

	Transient hotels	Motels with restaurants	Resorts
Revenue per available room	$549	$371	$346
Expenses per available room	703	427	509
Profit (Loss)	($154)	($ 49)	($163)

Source: 1981 Trends in the Hotel Industry, Pannell, Kerr, Forster & Co., New York, NY pp. 29, 42, 54.

As illustrated, regardless of property type (i.e., hotel, motel, or resort), the average lodging facility lost money in the telephone department in 1980.

Our historical perspective will only address rooms, food, beverage, and other revenue. This is because the revenue components of other revenue such as laundry, purchase discounts, and valet service comprise a relatively small percentage of total revenue, as is shown below:

Hotels and motels, ratios to total revenues, 1980

Revenue category	Percent of total revenues
Room revenue	60.2 ⎤
Food revenue	24.3 ⎥ 93.5
Beverage revenue	9.0 ⎦
Other revenue and income	6.5

Source: 1981 Trends in the Hotel Industry, Pannell, Kerr, Forster & Co., New York, NY, p. 10.

Room Revenue

Room revenue is comprised of two components: the average room rate the property receives for each occupied room, and the number of rooms occupied. For example, if a 200-room property operated at a 75 percent occupancy last year and the average room rate was $55.50, the annual room revenue would have been:

$$\text{Annual room revenue} = 200 \times .75 \times \$55.50 \times 365$$
$$= \$3,038,625$$

Trends   The table shown below gives the annual trends of occupancy and average room rates for hotels and motels from 1959 through 1980. A study of the table will make several conclusions apparent:

○ Occupancy levels for hotels and motels have remained relatively stable over the twenty-year period. This can be interpreted to mean that the supply of rooms has generally increased at the same rate as demand for lodging has increased.

○ Average room rates have not been stable. In fact, the average annual increase in room rates has been over 7 percent during the twenty-year period.

○ The rate of change for room-rate increases has accelerated in recent years compared to the earlier years in the period under study. The following tables provide some insight into why this is true.

Trends in occupancy and average room rates:
hotels and motels, 1959-1980

Year	Occupancy Percentage	Average Room Rate
1959	69.2	$13.63
1960	68.2	13.95
1961	67.2	14.06
1962	67.5	14.17
1963	67.8	14.30
1964	69.2	14.63
1965	70.5	14.97
1966	71.5	15.49
1967	73.1	16.29
1968	72.9	17.41
1969	72.8	18.76
1970	68.6	19.92
1971	66.5	20.56
1972	68.2	21.03
1973	69.2	22.07
1974	68.2	23.68
1975	65.1	26.12
1976	68.3	28.23
1977	70.2	30.76
1978	72.7	34.69
1979	72.8	39.26
1980	69.9	45.55

Source: 1979 *Trends in the Hotel-Motel Business,* Harris, Kerr, Forster & Company, New York, New York, p. 53, and *1981 Trends in the Hotel Industry,* Pannell, Kerr, Forster & Company, New York, New York, p. 10.

Transient hotels, increases in average room rates
compared to departmental costs and
expenses, selected years

Year	Average room rate		Departmental costs and expenses	
	Amount	Percent change from previous year	Amount per available room	Percent change from previous year
1960	$14.48	2.2	$4,532	2.0
1961	14.44	− 0.3	4,453	− 1.7
1962	14.63	1.3	4,503	1.1
1963	14.56	− 0.5	4,372	− 2.9
1964	14.80	1.6	4,384	0.3
1965	14.95	1.0	4,378	− 0.1
1974	25.04	8.5	5,942	5.7
1975	27.55	10.0	6,091	2.5
1976	29.85	8.3	6,675	9.6
1977	32.50	8.9	7,197	7.8
1978	36.65	12.8	8,113	12.7
1979	42.00	14.6	9,011	11.1
1980	49.52	17.9	9,724	7.9

Source: *1979 Trends in the Hotel-Motel Business,* Harris, Kerr, Forster & Company, New
York, NY, pp. 55–56.

Average annual rate of change

Period	Average room rates	Departmental costs and expenses
1959–1965	0.5%	− 0.6%
1973–1980	14.0%	9.1%

From the tables, it can be seen that until recently, the changes in
room rates appears to parallel changes in departmental costs and expenses.* In 1979 and 1980, room rates increased more rapidly than
departmental expenses while occupancy levels remained essentially the
same. Therefore, it appears that the industry has used increases in room
rates to offset inflation and maintain or improve profit margins. There is
no problem with this as long as the customer is willing to pay the increased rates. However, if the disposable income of the consumer fails to keep
pace with the increases in room rates, there may be some softening in demand overtime.

Food and Beverage Revenue

As with room revenue, food and beverage revenue is comprised of
two component parts: the amount of money each customer spends and

---

*Departmental costs and expenses include expenses from all departments, not just
rooms. However, the major components of these expenses are quite comparable between
departments.

the number of customers served. For food, the average amount spent by the customer is referred to as the average check or receipt. Each customer is referred to as a cover.

The following table shows the trends in room revenue, food revenue, beverage revenue, number of food covers, and the average food check for hotels and motels from 1959 through 1978. The numbers shown are indexed with 1958 equal to 100. This means that numbers less than 100 exhibit a decline, while numbers over 100 show an increase from the 1958 base year.

Hotels and motels, trends in food and
beverage revenue, 1959–1978
(1958 = 100)

Year	Room revenue	Food revenue	Beverage revenue	Food covers	Average food check
1959	105	104	105	102	102
1960	106	105	104	101	104
1961	105	104	106	98	106
1962	107	105	108	97	108
1963	108	104	105	95	109
1964	113	101	104	92	110
1965	118	106	110	93	114
1966	124	111	116	94	118
1967	133	114	121	92	124
1968	143	118	124	91	130
1969	153	123	131	89	138
1970	153	119	128	82	145
1971	152	119	130	80	149
1972	161	129	139	84	154
1973	170	141	149	87	162
1974	181	150	156	85	176
1975	189	152	159	80	190
1976	215	165	168	81	204
1977	242	178	181	80	222
1978	280	198	199	80	248

Source: *1979 Trends in the Hotel-Motel Business,* Harris, Kerr, Forster & Company, New York, NY, p. 54.

As illustrated, the trends in food and beverage revenue are quite similar to the trends in rooms revenue in that the increases in pricing have been responsible for the increasing revenues. However, there is one important difference. Occupancy for hotels have remained relatively stable while there is a distinct declining trend in food covers in hotels and motels. There are many possible reasons for this. One might be that the tremendous increase in the competition for food away from home by fast-food, family, and specialty restaurants has negatively impacted the food volume in hotels. A second reason might be that the optimum location for a hotel and motel may be a marginal location for food and beverage facilities. We will discuss this point in much more detail in Chapter 10.

With the number of covers declining at hotels and motels and competition from free-standing restaurants increasing, what is happening to the profit margins for the food and beverage department in hotels and motels? While we do not have any definite data which completely separate the food and beverage departments into a total profit center including the allocation of undistributed expenses, it is generally believed by experts in the industry that most food and beverage operations in hotels are marginally profitable at best. Of course, there is some danger in this generalization because many hotels receive substantial profits from the food and beverage operations. However, to the degree that declining cover counts and inflation in expenses are not offset by price increases, many properties will face declining profits or increasing losses in the future. We will discuss some of the implications of this shortly.

Other Revenues and Income

Other revenues and income have been increasing in absolute terms. However, as a percentage of total revenue, it has shown a slight decline, going from 7.8 percent in 1958 to 6.5 percent in 1980 of total sales. Because there are so many possible income-producing services included in this category, a good history of the expenses associated with this revenue category is not available. However, since it comprises such a small part of total revenues, it can be assumed that the profit contribution is generally small.

Conclusions

What can be concluded about the trends in lodging revenues? Some of the more important conclusions include the following:

○ While room revenue has shown steady increases over the twenty-year period, it was almost entirely attributable to increases in room rates as occupancy levels remained relatively stable. This, in turn, leads to the conclusion that industry supply is relatively efficient—that is, as demand increases, the supply of rooms also increases, keeping occupancy levels stable.

○ Food and beverage revenue increases have been solely the result of menu price increases. In fact, the trend has been for food covers in hotel and motel restaurants to decline. When this trend is coupled with increasing competition from free-standing restaurants and rising inflation rates, the profit margins for food and beverage departments are under significant pressure.

○ To the degree that the auxiliary services and amenities, including food and beverage, face reduced profit margins and/or losses, there will be increased pressure to offset these declines by increasing the profit margins from the rooms department.

○ If the market remains efficient, with the pace of new rooms supply keeping pace with the anticipated increase in room demand, these increased profit levels will have to come from increases in room rates.

Of course, this scenario is predicated upon the continuing general decline in non-rooms patronage as well as increases in demand for rooms being generally diluted by increases in new supply. The factor left out is management expertise in increasing occupancy as well as food, beverage, and other revenues. And so the rationale for the remainder of this chapter will be to address the management of room revenues and departmental profits. In Chapter 10, the management of food and beverage operations will be addressed.

This text's approach to these topics is at variance from that of classical textbooks. The emphasis is upon the management of the revenues for rooms rather than how to check in a guest or what are the duties of the housekeeper. Food and beverage trends and ways to select market segments and keep them happy will be a focal point of the discussion. The intention is to fill a gap in current literature that will assist the hotel operator in filling rooms and restaurant seats in addition to keeping the cost down once the customer arrives.

The
Management
of Room
Rates

In Chapter 7, we addressed the topics of the feasibility study and selection of a market and location that is and will continue to exhibit relatively strong demand for overnight accommodations. As a by-product of the feasibility analysis, it can be determined who the competition is, their strengths and weaknesses, and which market segments offer the most potential given the market, location, and facilities of the proposed hotel.

The first part of this chapter examined the importance of the price of rooms in relation to the continuing profitability of a lodging property. The following table amplifies this by showing the direct contribution margin of the three main revenue-producing departments in the typical lodging facility.

Comparative departmental income, hotels and motels
percentage statement, 1980

	Rooms	Food and beverage	Telephone
Revenues	100.0%	100.0%	100.0%
Departmental costs and expenses	25.3	79.9	128.0
Departmental income	74.7%	20.1%	−28.0%

Source: *1981 Trends in the Hotel Industry*, Pannell, Kerr, Forster & Company, New York, NY, p. 10. Telephone by calculation.

From the table it is clear that the largest profit contribution for the typical hotel or motel is generated by the rooms department. This is because there are relatively few variable expenses involved in renting each room, so that once these variable costs are covered, most of the incremental revenue goes directly to departmental profit.

If rooms really are so profitable, why do not hotels and motels simply sell rooms only? Or why do they not simply charge each customer more for each room and earn a higher profit? The answer to the first question will be addressed later in this chapter under the heading of "Support Services." The second question can be addressed through a discussion of pricing, demand elasticity, and discounting.

Pricing Theory

The basic theory of pricing for rooms in a lodging facility should be to maximize profit margins while offering the customer the highest perceived price–value relationship relative to competition. The rationale for this theory is that it allows the owners to receive a satisfactory return on their investment while keeping the customer happy because he believes that the price is fair—given the amenity and service levels offered.

Currently, the hospitality industry is utilizing either informal pricing methods or sophisticated quantitative methods. A brief review of each follows:

Informal pricing methods

Intuitive—This method basically consists of charging what the market will bear. It is not based upon any market research or return-on-investment analysis. When successful, it is generally because of luck, rarely achieving either goal of maximizing profit margins and return on investment or of price value to the customer.

Competitive—The competitive pricing method involves setting the prices based upon rates the property's competitors are charging. There are two problem assumptions with the method. First, it assumes that the property has the same amenities, advantages, disadvantages, and financial requirements as the competition. Equally as dangerous, it assumes that the competition has properly priced their rooms. While better than the intuitive method because it does take competition into account, it generally does not achieve the objectives stated above.

Follow the leader—This method is commonly used in other industries, particularly the steel and automotive. Here the leading competitor (largest, most successful, etc.) sets its prices and then everyone follows likewise. This, however, is not a good idea for the same reasons stated for the competitive pricing method.

Trial and error—Under this method, various prices are tried and the volume achieved under each price level is recorded. Then, the highest volume level is selected and the pricing levels associated with that volume are published. The problem with this method is that it completely ignores the seasonality of demand, the mix of business, and competition. In addition, as we will see under the section "Discounting," it is not always best to maximize occupancy at the cost of room rates.

Formal pricing methods   There are some formal pricing methods that attempt to consider the investment in the property, the expected volume level (occupancy), the anticipated costs of doing business, and the owner's expected return on investment. While these methods tend to ignore the competition and the customer if followed blindly, they do take financial considerations into account.

Two of these methods are briefly discussed: the Hubbart formula and the Horwath and Toth method.

Hubbart formula—The Hubbart formula was developed in the late 1940s by an American Hotel & Motel Association (AH&MA) committee headed by J. Roy Hubbart of the Sturm-Bickel Corporation. The goal of the formula is to "back into" the average room rate based upon the following factors:

- ○ Initial investment
- ○ Financing costs
- ○ Projected occupancy
- ○ Desired return on investment considering the owner's income tax bracket
- ○ Departmental costs
- ○ The anticipated profit (loss) from other departments.

The advantage of this method is that it considers most of the relevant financial inputs; and if the assumptions are correct, it provides the owner with his expected earnings.

Horwath and Toth method—The Horwath and Toth method involves a well-accepted rule of thumb that is supported by a mathematical theorem. The basic rule is that for each $1,000 invested in the hotel, there is a $1.00 required average room rate. For example, if a hotel costs $70,000 per room to construct, this method would suggest that the average room rate should be $70.00. The assumptions behind this rule are that the property will average a 70 percent occupancy and that the operation will result in a 55 percent house profit.

It should be clear, however, that the proper way to price must take the owners, the customer, and the competition into account. None of the above methods properly do this. Certainly, the quantitative methods are a good place to start because if the property is not profitable, it will not be in business long enough to please the customers. However, once the quantitative methods suggest a pricing range, it should be checked against competitive pricing levels, the expectations of the primary market segments being served, and the service and amenity levels offered. The final pricing can then be set based upon all of these considerations.

The next section deals with demand elasticity, which should assist in both the pricing decision and the maximization of occupancy levels.

Demand Elasticity

The theory behind the principle of elasticity of demand is that the quantity of rooms sold is affected by the price charged for those rooms. In other words, demand is sensitive to pricing levels; as prices increase, demand will decrease, and vice versa.

Elasticity of demand can be expressed by the following formula:

$$\text{Elasticity of demand} = \frac{\text{Percentage change in quantity sold}}{\text{Percentage change in price}}$$

If the resulting number is greater than one, demand is said to be elastic or sensitive to price. An elastic demand is one in which a change in pricing will result in a greater change in volume—i.e., if prices are raised by 10 percent, volume will decline by more than 10 percent. An inelastic demand is one in which the change in volume is less sensitive to changes in pricing—that is, that a change in price will result in a less than proportionate change in volume.

The degree of elasticity depends upon how much the result of the formula is greater than or less than one. Knowing this elasticity for your particular market and market segments is important. For example, if it is known that demand is relatively inelastic, then prices can be raised with little fear of volume showing significant declines. Inelastic demand normally occurs, for example, when there is relatively little competition and demand is strong for rooms in the market.

Is demand elastic in the lodging industry? Certainly it depends upon local market and competitive conditions. However, in general it is relatively elastic, although the formula would probably produce a value less than one. This does provide some pricing flexibility in most operations. However, for the aggressive pricer, it may cause the customer to "trade down" or to switch to a lower-priced facility if he or she believes the price–value relationship is out of line.

It also means that it is not always a good strategy to lower prices when occupancy levels are falling. With less than optimum elasticity, demand will generally not increase in a greater proportion, if at all, than the percentage decrease in prices. The following section discusses average room-rate management techniques, including discounting or price-reduction strategies.

Maximizing Rates

It has been shown that setting the proper room rates, commonly referred to as the rack rates, is of key importance to the profitability of the hotel. However, it would be a serious mistake to assume that once the room rates are set, management can turn its attention to another aspect of sales or cost control and let the average rate take care of itself. The actual average rate achieved is dependent upon many factors, including the method in which the front desk or reservationist sells the rooms to the customers, the mix of business the hotel receives, the amount of rate discounting that takes place, and the customers' acceptance of the posted rack rates. Each of these factors is, for the most part, controllable. They all include a decision on the part of either management or the hotel employees. Each has a bearing on what the ultimate average rate will be.

The Hotel Royale is a hypothetical hotel containing 385 rooms. The following table illustrates the room mix and price structure of its rooms and provides the information necessary to evaluate the impact of each of the components of average room rate on profitability.

Hotel Royale, room mix and price structure

| Room type | Number | Rate structure | |
		Single	Double
1 Bed	125	$53–$55	$58–$60
2 Bed	240	$53–$55	$62–$64
Suite A	15	$70	$70
Suite B	5	$85	$85

Selling the Rooms   The method and degree in which a room is sold to a customer is probably the easiest way to raise or lower the average room rate. Frequently, the quality of rooms within a given hotel will differ depending upon the room appointments, view, size, and proximity to amenities such as the pool or, in the case of a high-rise hotel, the floor level. Such is the case in the Hotel Royale, and as can be seen, the average price range for any given room type is $2.00. Consequently, unless the hotel is running a very high occupancy and has no choice as to which room in which to place a customer, the average rate can vary on a particular night by as much as $2.00. The amount of selling the front desk clerk or reservationist does when assigning a customer a room will determine the variance.

Generally, the selling of higher-priced rooms is merely a matter of properly training hotel personnel. Recognizing the value of this, most hotel chains with central reservation numbers instruct their salespersons to first quote the higher price range of each room type when asked the room rate. If there is hesitation on the part of the customer, they then quote the lower price ranges. Consequently, it is generally the case that the average rate of rooms reserved in advance is higher than the average rate of rooms sold to walk-ins.

Mix of Business

The mix of business refers to the relationship between the number of single occupied rooms sold and the number of double occupied rooms sold. The percentage of multiple business (double occupancy divided by total occupancy) is a key statistic in both the forecasting and managing of the average room rate. For example, in the Hotel Royale, the rate spread between a single room and double ranges from $3 to $11. The amount of additional expense incurred by the hotel to rent a $64 double instead of a $53 single is minimal (sheets and towels for the second person plus the maid's extra time to clean the larger room). Therefore, nearly all of the $11 difference between the two rooms will contribute to departmental profit on the operating statement. The impact of the mix of business will be illustrated in detail later in the section "Potential Average Room Rate."

Discounting

Discounting is the practice of charging a rate less than the posted rack rates to customers who generate a large amount of revenue to the hotel through frequent usage. It is a necessary aspect of the hotel business and usually prevents a hotel from attaining its potential average rate. Discounts are typically given to convention groups that reserve a large block of rooms for several days; to corporate clients who fly their personnel in frequently and either house them overnight in the hotel and/or use the meeting-room facilities frequently; and to local government agencies or similar groups upon whose repeat business the hotel depends for a continuing occupancy base. It should be thought of as a cost of doing business, and before a discount is given to anyone, its impact and necessity should be carefully evaluated.

Assume, for example, that the average room rate in the Hotel Royale is $52.75. A discounting grid can be prepared to assist management in evaluating the revenue impact of different pricing decisions. The grid in the following example will show the equivalent occupancy that must be achieved in order to maintain a certain room revenue level as the amount of discounting is increased or decreased.

To prepare the discounting grid, one first needs to calculate the marginal cost of renting a room—i.e., the direct cost incurred as a result of renting the room. This would include a maid to clean it, clean laundry and linen, new supplies such as soap, and electricity to heat or air condition and light the room.

How about the front-desk clerk who checks the guest into the hotel? Or the bellman who carries the guest's baggage to the room? Or the waitress in the restaurant waiting to serve the guest dinner?

None of these staff personnel are a direct cost of renting the specific room to the specific person we are discussing. All of these employees would be scheduled to work regardless of whether or not the specific room we are analyzing is rented. Therefore, the only marginal costs of renting the room would be the maid, supplies listed above, and electricity.

In the Hotel Royale, a maid earns $32.80 per day including benefits. Each maid cleans fifteen rooms during her shift, so the marginal payroll cost is $2.19 ($32.80 ÷ 15). In addition, other marginal costs total $3.10 per room. Therefore, the total marginal cost per room is $5.29 ($3.10 + $2.19). The formula to calculate the equivalent occupancy required to maintain the same revenue level after discounting compared to the revenue level with no discount is as follows:

Equivalent occupancy =
$$\text{Current occupancy} \times \frac{\text{Rack rate} - \text{Marginal cost}}{\text{Rack rate} \times (1 - \text{discount \%}) - \text{Marginal cost}}$$

With the Hotel Royale currently operating at a 65 percent occupancy, the equivalent occupancy required if the rates are discounted by 10 percent would be computed as follows:

$$\text{Equivalent occupancy} = 65\% \times \frac{\$52.75 - \$5.29}{\$52.75 \times (1 - .10) - \$5.29}$$

$$= 65\% \times \frac{\$47.46}{\$47.48 - \$5.29}$$

$$= 72.9\%$$

The discounting grid for the Hotel Royale for discounts of between 5 and 20 percent would appear as follows:

Hotel Royale, Discounting grid

Current occupancy level	New occupancy level required to maintain profitability if rack rates are discounted by			
	5%	10%	15%	20%
80%	84.7	90.0	96.0	102.9
75%	79.4	84.2	90.0	96.4
70%	74.1	78.6	84.0	90.0
65%	68.8	72.9	78.0	83.6
60%	63.5	67.3	72.0	77.1
55%	58.2	61.7	66.0	70.7
50%	52.9	56.1	60.0	64.3
45%	47.6	50.5	54.0	57.9
40%	42.4	44.9	48.0	51.4
35%	37.1	39.3	42.0	45.0
30%	31.8	33.7	36.0	38.6
Average rate $52.75	$50.11	$47.48	$44.84	$42.40

Once the discounting grid has been prepared, it can be utilized as a management tool for different types of pricing decisions, including the effects of discounting. For example, the Hotel Royale has historically achieved a 35 percent occupancy on Saturday nights. The hotel management turned to the marketing department for some ideas on how to bolster sales on these nights. Marketing approached the general manager with an "Escape Weekend" package that worked as follows:

The purchaser of the package would receive a double room, a bottle of champagne, and two cocktails for one package price. The internal pricing discount was to be twenty percent of the rack rate for the room, the champagne at retail value, and the cocktails complimentary.

The marketing department estimated that an average of 35 couples would take advantage of the package on any Saturday night and that the original customers would switch to the package. This would yield a projected revised occupancy of 44 percent. However, by referring to the discounting grid, it is apparent that the breakeven occupancy if rates are discounted at 20 percent and the occupancy before discounting is 35 percent would be 45.0 percent.

$$\text{Equivalent occupancy} = 35\% \times \frac{\$52.75 - \$5.29}{\$52.75 \times (1 - .20) - \$5.29}$$
$$= 45.0\%$$

Since the additional 35 rooms would only bring the occupancy up to 44 percent, the hotel is better off at 35 percent occupancy with the $52.75 average rate. At least 39 additional rooms would be required before the hotel would receive an equivalent amount of room revenue after direct costs if the package were to be adopted. Therefore, it would be a better management decision to reject the proposal from a financial viewpoint, under the assumptions provided.

Of course, there may be some sales or marketing reasons to continue with the package anyway. The grid should not be used blindly because it only addresses the financial aspects of average rate management. As we pointed out earlier, an equally important aspect is the customer and his or her continuing price–value perception of the hotel.

The discounting grid approach to rate management is highly useful, but only provides part of the picture. It does not provide a method for the ongoing measurement of the discounting that is taking place and the "cost" of that discounting. One management tool which addresses this issue involves the potential average room rate.

The Potential Average Room Rate

Theory The potential average room rate can be thought of as the average rate that would be achieved if all of the occupied rooms in a hotel were sold from the top price down and no discounting occurred. It is a standard by which to measure the actual average rate achieved. It is based upon the posted rack rates and the mix of business which the hotel experiences.

The variables used to calculate the potential average rate include the potential average single rate, the potential average double rate, the percentage of multiple business, and the rate spread.

Potential average single rate—The potential average single rate is defined as the average rate that would be achieved if all the rooms were sold at the single rate with no discounts given. Since the room rate for one person is typically the lowest undiscounted rate available, the potential average single rate represents the minimum potential average rate that the hotel can achieve.

Potential average double rate—The potential double rate is the average rate that would be achieved if all the rooms were sold at the double rate with no discount given. If suites and special rooms are ignored for the moment, the potential average double rate represents the maximum potential average rate a hotel can achieve. When suites and special rooms, which normally have a higher charge associated with them, are included in the potential double rate, they merely increase the potential rate and are accounted for in exactly the same way.

Percentage of multiple business—The percentage of multiple business is a function of the number of single and double rooms occupied and is the relationship between double occupancy and total occupancy. Generally, it is desirable to have a high percentage of double occupancy because of the higher average rate associated with it.

Rate spread—The rate spread is simply the difference between the potential double rate and the potential single rate. It, therefore, represents the scale between the minimum and the maximum potential average rate.

Calculating the potential average rate   As we have said, the potential average rate represents the average room rate that would be achieved if all of the occupied rooms in a hotel were sold at the rack rates. It is a function of the mix of business and is calculated by multiplying the percentage of multiple business by the rate spread and adding this result to the potential average single-room rate. For example, assume that the Park Palace Hotel has the following rooms mix and rack-rate structure and wants to determine its potential average rate:

$$\text{Potential average single rate} \ = \ \frac{\$5,500.00}{250 \text{ rooms}} \ = \ \$22.00$$

$$\text{Potential average double rate} \ = \ \frac{\$7,200.00}{250 \text{ rooms}} \ = \ \$28.80$$

$$\text{Rate spread} \ = \ \$28.80 - \$22.00 \ = \ \$6.80$$

Assume that the projected occupancy is 70 percent and the projected multiple occupancy is 35 percent. The percentage of multiple occupancy would then be 50 percent (35% ÷ 70%) and the potential average room rate would be calculated as follows:

Potential average room rate = Potential average single rate + (% Multiple occupancy × Rate spread)

$$= \$22.00 + (.50 \times \$6.80)$$

$$= \$25.40$$

As can be seen in the equation, the minimum potential average rate the Park Palace Hotel could have, assuming that no discounting occurs, is $22.00 and the maximum average rate is $28.80. The potential average rate, then, is a function of the percentage of multiple business the hotel expects to receive. These relationships are shown graphically in Figure 9–1.

	Number of	Rate structure		Revenue at 100% occupancy	
Room type	rooms	Single	Double	Single	Double
1 Bed	75	$22.00	$26.00	$1,650.00	$1,950.00
2 Bed	175	22.00	30.00	3,850.00	5,250.00
	250			$5,500.00	$7,200.00

Park Palace Hotel, room mix and rate structure

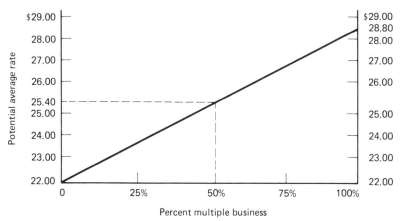

Figure 9–1   Park Palace Hotel

Achievement Factors   It is typical for most hotels to give discounts to groups that guarantee a significant number of rooms during a period of time. Therefore, a hotel will seldom achieve its potential average rate. However, one can easily calculate an achievement factor (AF) which gives management an indication of how close the hotel is coming to achieving the potential average room rate. This provides a means for evaluating rack rates, salesmanship, and discounting.

The achievement factor is computed by dividing the actual average rate by the potential average rate and multiplying the result by 100 percent:

$$A_f = \frac{\text{Actual average rate}}{\text{Potential average rate}} \times 100\%$$

Assume, for example, that in February, the Park Palace Hotel's percentage of multiple business was 50 percent and its actual average rate was $23.62. The achievement factor would be computed as follows:

$$A_f = \frac{\$23.62}{\$25.40} = 93.0\%$$

This can be interpreted to mean that in the month of February, the Park Palace Hotel discounted its rack rates an average of 7 percent (100 − 93). If the hotel had run a 70 percent occupancy, the 7 percent discount "cost" $8,722.00 in lost revenue, determined as follows:

250 rooms × 70% occupancy = 175 rooms occupied per day

175 × 28 days = 4,900 rooms occupied during month

Potential revenue, 4,900 × $25.40 = $124,460

Actual revenue, 4,900 × $23.62   =   115,738

$ 8,722

It is not known whether it was necessary to discount the rates 7 percent to achieve the 70 percent occupancy. However, we can provide some general guidelines on interpreting the achievement factor to help management decision making.

Achievement factors greater than 100 percent—Although rare, this occasionally occurs because of additional room charges due to rollaway beds or charges for extra people not included in the published rack rates. This situation indicates that front-desk personnel are probably selling the most expensive rooms first, no discounts are being given, and there is little or no consumer price resistance. If occupancy is strong, room prices can probably be increased; or if occupancy is low, management should consider discounts to help build occupancy.

Achievement factors 95 percent to 100 percent—This indicates that the "average" amount of discounting is taking place as a result of corporate rates, group business, and other high-patronage markets. It would indicate that room rates could probably be raised in the future if occupancies are high. However, management should be careful with industry averages. Frequently, the environment of a given hotel may prescribe entirely different discounting procedures and therefore different target achievement factors. This will be discussed in more detail in the next section.

Achievement factors 90 percent to 95 percent.—This could be interpreted as an acceptable amount of discounting if the hotel is either group-business and/or commercial-traveler–oriented. If occupancies are strong, management should consider revising discounting procedures. In any case, an analysis of the mix of business by market segment should be undertaken to determine if this much discounting is necessary to maintain present occupancy levels.

Achievement factors less than 90 percent—Heavy discounting is taking place, room clerks are probably selling the cheaper rooms first, and there is possible consumer resistance to the rack room rates. Unless the mix of business is almost entirely group-oriented, management should amend either the discounting procedures or the prices.

Setting target achievement factors Although there are general guidelines for interpreting achievement factors, much depends upon a hotel's particular market mix. It is, therefore, important that management set internal discounting policies and target achievement factors. From the targets, actual results can be evaluated and action plans implemented when negative variances occur.

Target achievement factors should be set for each month in the coming fiscal year. Probably the best time to do the analysis is during the period when the hotel's annual plan is being formulated, because much of the internal and external review of the various factors affecting the hotel is being evaluated. Most of these factors play a role in the achievement factor.

Some of the factors that should be considered when a hotel is evaluating its projected average rate, and a brief discussion of their role, follows:

1. *Projected monthly occupancy*—The basic principles of supply and demand would indicate that as the demand for rooms increases in relation to supply, a hotel will generally have to discount less to fill its rooms. Although this depends somewhat on the type of business demanding rooms, achievement factors should be higher during those months when occupancy is high.

2. *Historical achievement factors*—Since occupancy and room-mix cycles generally follow a consistent trend from year to year, the historical achievement rate is an important factor. The components of the historical occupancy (customer mix) should be evaluated as well as the reasons for the discounts given. Were they necessary? Assuming there is several years of history, is there much fluctuation in that month from year to year? Is the historical discounting policy going to be continued next year? If the discounts have been given to group business and conventions, are the same or similar-size conventions expected to return next year? Basically, what type of environment historically existed? Did the discounts yield the expected amount of business? Is that same environment expected to exist next year?

3. *Market segmentation*—The types of market segments being served by the hotel and the relative mix of each is another important variable in setting a target achievement factor. It makes sense that the higher the percentage of tourist business a hotel receives to total business, the less discounting the hotel will have to give. This assumes that the tourists are not coming in organized tours with discount packages booked by intermediaries such as travel agents.

Market segmentation, then, is a major ingredient in discounting and average rate. Each market must be analyzed by month as to what percentage of the hotel's total market it will comprise. The expected amount of discounting given to each market can then be evaluated.

4. *Competition*—The competition cannot be overlooked when average rate and discount factors are being estimated. Competitors should first be classified into primary competitors and secondary competitors.

Insight into the competition should be provided by the sales department, since it will be aware of how successful each competitor is with each market segment and the relative advantages and disadvantages they have.

From the competitor analysis, management can factor in the amount of estimated discounting that will be necessary to successfully compete for the blue-chip business and maintain profitability.

It should be noted that much of the above analysis is a necessary component of the pricing decision. Although discounting and potential average rate are an integral part of room-rate pricing, the setting of the target achievement factor should come after room rates have been finalized.

Up to this point, we have discussed the profitability of the rooms department. We have seen that if the twenty-year trend of rising costs and declining patronage continues for the hotel and motel food and beverage business, continued pressure may be placed on accelerating room rates to maintain profit margins. Several methods for pricing and then managing room rates have been presented.

Earlier the question was raised: If rooms are so profitable, why not build a property selling only overnight accommodations, leaving the support services off? This is precisely what one motel chain has successfully done. Its typical property consists of nicely appointed rooms with a free-standing restaurant that is leased to one of several major coffee-shop chains. All of its management focus is on the rooms department.

The remainder of this chapter addresses support facilities and the balancing act that must be maintained between these services and amenities and the highly profitable rooms department.

Support Services

For purposes of this chapter, we are defining support services as any service or facility other than rooms. This category would include, for example, restaurants, lounges, meeting rooms, tennis courts, room service, etc. The question becomes which, if any, of these support services should a lodging facility offer in addition to its basic rooms package? One answer is to think of each service or amenity as a module that can be added to the facility, and then ask the question, How will the addition or deletion of this module help attract a higher share of the primary target market segment? Or, How will the addition of this service module help capture a secondary market segment that is complementary to the primary market segments? Under this approach, each service module becomes a profit center—that is, it increases profits through one or more of the following ways:

○ It receives revenues from the guests utilizing it, and these revenues are greater than the direct departmental costs associated with offering the service or amenity.

○ It represents an amenity that is attractive to a target market segment allowing greater penetration and increased occupancy levels.

○ It allows the hotel to charge a higher room rate because the service or package of services is offered.

The danger with the last point is keeping the consumer's perception of price and value in balance. For example, it may be perceived as desirable to offer recreational facilities in an executive conference center. However, if the expense levels of such recreational facilities are increasing and are totally offset by increases in room rates, the guests may begin to look at competitive properties. This is because their perception of the price–value relationship is no longer positive. This situation frequently occurs, for example, when expensive meeting-room space is built but it is either poorly marketed or there is no market for it. In an attempt to cover costs, management turns to increasing the room rates.

Of course, the opposite situation can occur. This is illustrated in the following excerpt from an article appearing in the *Harvard Business Review:*

> A resort operator decided to increase the number of rooms in a lodging facility and not to expand the central services required to support the additional guests. The fact that room rentals contribute up to 90 percent of total revenue and that tennis courts, swimming pools, meeting rooms, parking areas, and so on contribute next to nothing, or nothing, convinced the operator to create an imbalance in favor of revenue-producing activities. However, the number of guests adjusted itself to the level of occupancy that the central services could support, not to the level of room capacity. The room capacity beyond the level supported by the central services was wasted.[1]

So, what is the answer to selecting the proper mix of support services? In earlier chapters we discussed the fact that different market segments have different expectations and needs. To capture the convention and meeting market, a facility must offer banquet and meeting space. However, before constructing that space, the developer should be sure that it is cost-justified—that is, that the space will be sufficiently utilized to cover the costs associated with it and not put pressure on the rooms department to cover its losses.

Now, back to La Quinta Motor Inns. We briefly discussed their strategy earlier in this section: to offer attractive rooms only. The restaurant is not operated by the motel chain, and there are no bellhops, no meeting rooms, and no gift shops—only rooms. In conjunction with this strategy, La Quinta's stated target market segment is the per diem business traveler. By marketing only to this traveler, who wants a clean room and a coffee shop with no other frills, La Quinta has managed to maintain its construction and operating costs at attractive levels, thus keeping room rates in line. The perceived price–value relationship from the per diem businessperson toward La Quinta is quite positive.

Summary

During the last twenty years, the lodging industry has experienced declining patronage in its restaurants. Other support facilities have met with mixed results. Some have been highly profitable, some have incurred significant departmental losses. One answer to the mixed results seems to be matching facilities and amenities with the expectations and needs of the property's target market segments.

Also during the twenty-year history, the supply of new roooms has kept pace with increased demand. This has resulted in relatively stable occupancy levels. Whether this will continue to occur in the future as demand increases remains to be seen. However, the result of this situation in the past is that most of the industry's increases in room revenue have come from increases in room rates. These increases have essentially paralleled increases in departmental costs and expenses, thus maintaining profit margins.

The importance of room rates to the lodging industry provided the rationale for focusing on several management tools for managing the average room rate. These included sales techniques, discounting, and the potential average room rate.

The next chapter focuses on food and beverages. As has already been shown, while the food-away-from-home business is showing strong growth, the lodging industry has not participated in this growth. In fact, the undeniable trend has been a declining cover count, offset only by menu price increases. The long-term results of this phenomenon have been the need to re-examine the target market's expectations on a case-by-case basis.

Notes   1. W. Earl Sasser, "Match Supply and Demand in Service Industries," *Harvard Business Review,* November–December 1974, p. 135.

Food Service Industry: Trends and Feasibility Analysis

When you finish this chapter, you should understand

1. The major industry segments in the food service business and the characteristics of each

2. Why hotels and motels in general have not done well in food and beverage volume and profits

3. Three schools of thought about future growth potential within the food service industry and the rationale for each school

4. The contrast between each of the major steps in a restaurant feasibility study compared to a hotel feasibility study

5. The definition of the vital and peripheral meal periods and the importance of each to the success of a restaurant

6. How to prepare a breakeven analysis for a proposed restaurant

The food service industry has been around as long as or longer than the lodging industry. As is true of the lodging business, the food-away-from-home business undoubtedly had its beginnings with the travel industry. Consequently, as the travel industry entered its era of high growth during the 1960s and 1970s, parts of the food service business prospered too. During this time period, the food service industry was one of the most visible growth industries on Wall Street. However, we saw in the previous chapter that not all sectors of the food service industry were necessarily exhibiting unprecedented growth. In fact, food sales in the hotel and motel industry have actually had declines in cover counts during the past twenty years. It was only the increases in menu prices that have allowed the food and beverage revenues in hotels and motels to show any growth at all.

Why the contrast? Did Wall Street misread the industry or did the hotel industry simply fail to capitalize on an excellent opportunity? What, in fact, caused the growth of the industry, and is it likely to continue?

Historical Perspective

In order to understand why the restaurant industry has grown and whether it will continue its strong growth rates, it would be helpful to review where the industry has come from in its recent history and the nature of its growth.

At the beginning of the century, the U.S. was still basically an agrarian society; most of the population still lived in small towns or in the country. Eating meals away from home, except at the homes of neighbors, was a special event that only occurred two or three times each year, if at all. World War I began the movement to the cities as the country geared up to produce the arms and equipment necessary to sustain an army in Europe. Between the first and second world wars, the number of food service establishments within the United States doubled to 300,000. By 1966, there were 442,207 establishments, excluding bars and taverns.[1]

Much of the reason for the increase in the food service industry can be attributed to some specific trends which followed industrialization. Industrialization resulted in a significant increase in the disposable income of American families. Of course, the rise in the number of working women has further enhanced income, increasing the propensity to eat out.

The following table illustrates the growth in expenditures for food away from home as a percent of total food expenditures between 1940 and 1980.

Food away from home as a percent of total food personal consumption expenditures

Year	Away from home ($ billions)	Total food ($ billions)	1 ÷ 2
1940	3.1	16.2	18.7%
1950	9.4	46.0	20.4%
1960	14.2	70.5	10.1%
1970	27.7	114.6	24.2%
1980	80.0	302.3	26.5%

Source: U.S. Department of Commerce, *Survey of Current Business.*

The figures indicate that the amount of food consumed away from home has grown substantially both in dollars and as a percentage of total food expenditures since 1940. In 1980, over one fourth of all food expenditures were made for food away from home.

What about future growth in the restaurant industry? We have seen in earlier chapters that the demographic and income trends will provide a long-term favorable environment for continued growth. In addition, some of the psychographic trends that should favorably impact the industry include the following:

○ Assets have been replaced by experience as a measure of prestige.

○ Increasing travel has developed the awareness of the public about restaurants.

○ The increasing incidence of two-worker families means that the amount of time available for preparing home-cooked meals has been significantly reduced.

○ The "Me Generation" and the movement away from traditional family patterns have caused more people to eat out more often.

Within the food service industry, three distinct market segments are identifiable: the restaurant market, the travel and lodging segment, and the contract feeding market. **Major Industry Segments**

Restaurant Market

The restaurant market is the largest segment of the food service industry in terms of dollar volume and numeric units. It also is the most responsive to changing lifestyles and values. In addition, it is highly competitive because not only are there more competitive establishments in this segment, but the customer decision to eat out is generally discretionary. The restaurant competes directly with the grocery-store market for the food dollar.

Within the restaurant market, there are several different types of restaurants. The major categories include:

○ Fast food, generally characterized by
    Limited menu
    Fast service, generally self-service
    Limited self-seating
    Very low check average due to inexpensive pricing
    Primarily chain or franchise

○ Coffee shops, generally characterized by
    Inexpensive menus, relatively extensive but characterized by convenience foods*
    Limited counter service
    Low to moderate check average
    Longer operating hours—generally 18 to 24 hours each day

○ Family restaurants, characterized by
    Extensive menus
    Low to moderate average checks
    Table service
    Light atmosphere

○ Atmosphere/specialty restaurants
    Extensive decor and service
    Alcoholic beverages and entertainment often provided
    Moderate to expensive average check
    Generally independently owned

Travel and Lodging Market

The travel market for food service has been characterized by particularly fast growth because of the increased mobility of the populace. As the travel industry has changed from rail and bus to automobile to airline, so have the growth rates and competitive entry into each of the different travel-market categories.

The travel food service market is somewhat different from the restaurant market in that the competition for the consumer is not as intense. This is because the segment serves a more captive market in that patrons generally do not have the alternative to eat at home, nor do they have as wide a selection of alternative restaurants to choose from.

The major categories and a brief description of each include:

○ Railroad and bus food service, characterized by
    Limited menu
    Low check
    Fast, self-service, often stand-up tables
    Declining patronization

○ Highway restaurants, characterized by
    Coffee shop or family-restaurant–type menu and service
    Longer hours
    Low to moderate average check

○ Lodging-establishment restaurants

○ Airline passenger feeding

---

*The term "convenience foods" generally refers to foods that are partially or wholly prepared off the restaurant premises by a manufacturer with the final heating and servicing taking place at the restaurant.

It is difficult to generalize about lodging-establishment restaurants. As a segment of the industry, restaurants within hotels and motels do not have a good reputation for quality. Additionally, as we illustrated in Chapter 9, patronization and earnings have shown a declining trend.

There are a number of reasons for these characteristics, including the following:

○ Restaurants are significantly more management- and labor-intensive than the rooms department of a hotel. Food and beverage is also less profitable than rooms. Consequently, many hotel and motel operators have viewed their food and beverage operations as "necessary evils." This attitude has resulted in a reluctance to put trained managers and employees in place. This results in poor quality, low or no profits and further justification not to expend the effort, required time, and money to properly operate the restaurant.

○ Many hotel feasibility studies do not adequately address food and beverage potential. Consequently, the developer and architect do not put large enough facilities in place to justify the cost of competent management for the food and beverage area. This shortcoming in the feasibility study most likely stems from the industry stigma that this is not a high-profit area. It also stems from the fact that the information required for a restaurant feasibility study differs from that needed for a hotel feasibility study. To do the proper research would significantly increase the time, effort, and cost of this "total" feasibility study, and this is a cost many developers are unwilling to pay.

○ Frequently, a good location for a hotel or motel is not also a good location for a restaurant. As will be illustrated later in this chapter, restaurants depend on a population base and demographic factors for demand. Hotels, on the other hand, depend upon transient travelers and access from transportation arteries to the site. For example, a roadside motel on Interstate 95 may do very well in room occupancy but suffer in food and beverage volume because there is a small local population base.

However, there is a bright spot for restaurants within hotels. In recent years there has been a national resurgence in the renovation of large, older hotels in certain cities. For example, the Adolphus Hotel in Dallas, Texas which was built in 1912 by Adolphus Busch as a posh getaway for the wealthy was recently restored to its former glory by developers. The Peabody Hotel in Memphis, Tennessee, once the grand hotel for the rich in the South has been reopened, completely restored. This trend is occurring throughout the United States.

In an effort to derive as much revenue as possible from all public areas, developers and operators are re-emphasizing the food and beverage aspect of the hotels.

Will it work? The jury is still out. We will readdress this question later in this chapter after developing the techniques of the restaurant feasibility study.

Airline-passenger feeding, although categorized with the travel-market segment, is unlike any segment discussed so far in this chapter. The meal is generally included in the price of the airline ticket and generally does not include a choice of menu items. However, as one would suspect, the growth of this segment has been impressive as the trend toward more air travel has exhibited strength.

Contract Feeding and Vending Market

The final market segment is the contract feeding and vending market. This market primarily consists of four categories:

1. Business and industry feeding
2. School and college feeding
3. Health-care feeding
4. Recreation feeding

The impetus behind the existence and growth of the contract feeding market is the cost reduction and administrative burden associated with an institution providing the service itself. In addition, as the food service industry becomes more technologically complex and people demand more quality in their food service, institutions and industry are turning to contract feeders, which have demonstrated the expertise to maintain cost and quality levels.

The contract feeding industry has exhibited a great deal of competitive consolidation in the past ten to fifteen years, since the economies of scale have favored the giants while hurting the smaller, independent feeders. Because of economic and technological strength and the economies of scale, the contract feeding industry has been forced to consolidate competitively in the past ten to fifteen years.

Growth in Multiple-Unit Restauants

Earlier in this chapter we reported that during the first part of the century the number of food service establishments exhibited relatively strong growth. During the initial growth years, the industry was characterized by few chains and a relatively high failure rate. Much of this failure rate was due to poor management, poor locations, and the inability to change with the trends. The last twenty years, however, have been characterized by a period of significant consolidation within the industry. While the number of new restaurants opening each year has been strong, the fact is that the number of restaurants in the country has been nearly the same and has actually declined on a per capita basis.[2]

If the number of establishments in the food service industry has remained stable and yet the growth in the meals-away-from-home market has been exhibiting above-average growth, where has the growth been coming from? While the industry is still somewhat fragmented, the chain operations have shown a majority of the growth in recent years. This is due to several factors:

○ The fast-food chains have demonstrated substantial growth due to their large capital resources, real estate and property development expertise and perhaps most importantly, their ability to franchise their stores. From the restaurant developer's standpoint, it is generally much more attractive to affiliate with a national brand such as Wendy's or McDonalds, who have large advertising campaigns, a proven product and are more financiable than an unknown name.

○ There has been an increase in the number of chains, both regional and national in recent years. This tends to overstate the growth in chain restaurant sales.

○ On the higher end of the restaurant market, e.g. family and specialty restaurants, the cost of opening a new restaurant has inflated dramatically. The costs of land, construction and furniture, fixtures and equipment are now so high that it requires substantial capital to construct a new restaurant. What was once a relatively easy-entry business is more and more falling to the chains with the capital resources to finance a new business.

○ The restaurant business has always had one of the highest failure rates of any industry in the United States. This is due to many factors, including the significant expertise required to successfully manage a restaurant, the extreme competitiveness within the industry and the fickle nature of the customer base. In recent years, lenders have been reluctant to finance new restaurants which do not have a proven track record in both concept and management. This attitude favors the chains and franchises of an established brand, adding fuel to the growth of chains relative to independent restaurants.

So where is the restaurant industry headed? Will it continue to grow throughout the remainder of the 1980's or are the demographic and psychographic trends which have fueled past growth slowing down? Will the industry continue to consolidate to the chain affiliations or is there a renewed opportunity for the entrepreneur? There has been a lot of discussion among industry observers, analysts, and executives regarding these questions. Some of the more common beliefs regarding growth in the industry are presented below.

Fast-Growth Theory

There are many who believe that the recent growth in the food-away-from-home market will not only be sustained but will, in fact, accelerate. Proponents of this school of thought point to the fact that restaurants have taken a significant portion of the family total food dollar over the past ten years. As pointed out earlier, in 1960 20% of the total food dollar was spent for food away from home. By 1980 this jumped to 26%. Proponents of this school project that 50 percent of the average American's food dollar will be spent on meals away from the home by the end of the 1980's.

What is driving this trend toward accelerated growth? In addition to the economic and demographic trends, the psychographic trends are providing a significant impetus. These combined forces have brought us to the point where eating several meals each week in a restaurant is a way of life that will likely continue.

Moderate-Growth Theory[3]

Some people believe that while the restaurant industry will show above-average growth, it will not nearly achieve the rate predicted by the fast-growth school.

Some of the arguments advanced by the moderate-growth school include the following:

○ Much of the growth of the restaurant industry, particularly the fast-food sector, was due to the novelty of the product and suburban migration. Now that there are fast-food establishments in nearly every American community, including the once-void suburbs, the rate of growth cannot be sustained.

○ The demographic and economic trends that worked so well in the past for the industry will slow its growth in the future. For example, between 1960 and 1975, the percentage of women 16 years and older employed in the work force rose from 36 to 44. However, according to the Bureau of Census projections, this percentage will rise to only 45.9 percent by 1990.

○ The disposable income increases of the 20-to-30-year-olds could actually decline in the 1980s as couples who postponed childbearing in their twenties start families. The addition of children to the household will not only reduce income available for meals away from home, it will also reduce free time available to drive to the nearby restaurant for a meal.

○ Past eating-out patterns could be altered by the increasing convenience of eating at the home. For example, the microwave oven and product improvements in convenience foods have made it increasingly convenient to prepare home meals. Encouraged by consumer purchases of home microwave ovens, food retailers are aggressively marketing a return to eating meals within the home.

In summary, then, those in the moderate-growth school believe that some of the very same economic and demographic trends which helped the restaurant industry in the past will combine with technological developments and family responsibilities to slow the growth in the 1980s and beyond.

Retail Life-Cycle Theory

In Chapter 1, we introduced the concept of the retail life cycle, which holds that every major form of retailing must evolve through four stages of growth:

- ○ Early growth
- ○ Accelerated development
- ○ Maturity
- ○ Decline

As a retailing concept reaches each of the identifiable stages in its evolution, certain patterns become apparent. Each pattern, in turn, prescribes a management response to prolong the positive stages and diminish the negative stages.

Much of the focus on the restaurant industry and its future has revolved around the fast-food chains. Let's examine them from the retail life cycle perspective to determine at what stage the industry was, in the early 1980s, and the strategies that top management is currently implementing as a result of this stage.

The fast-food industry entered the 1970s with a relatively small number of national chains in each menu category—i.e., hamburgers, pizza, chicken. Each of these chains was generally exhibiting very strong growth patterns in customer counts and sales.

During the 1970s, a relatively significant number of chain competitors entered the market, many achieving national acceptance. At the same time, the dominant chains continued to expand at a record-breaking pace. From Chapter 1, we recognize this stage of evolution as *accelerated development*. New competition was rapidly entering the market. Real growth in sales approximated a strong 7 percent annually. Profits grew substantially as Wall Street investors flocked to the fast-food chains.

It was in the latter part of the 1970s that talk of maturity and saturation began to be heard among some industry observers. By 1979, real annual growth in the fast-food industry had slowed to less than 1.0 percent, according to the National Restaurant Association. Stock prices for the former glamor chains such as Wendy's and McDonald's began to decline.

Those espousing the retail life-cycle theory would argue that the fast-food industry either had entered or was entering the third stage of the life cycle—*maturity*. During this stage, sales and profit levels decline due to the existence of too much capacity and stable or declining demand levels.

One common management strategy to help offset the declines in customer patronage during the maturity state is to modify the concept in an attempt to capture new market segments and strengthen position with existing segments. How did the fast-food industry react? The strategies appear to be focusing on several areas:

1. *Expanded menus.*—Some of the major chains have added new items to their menus and actively promoted them. These items range from salad bars to new-product introductions. The strategy was to add more variety to the menu, thus appealing to a broader market segment.

2. *Additional meal period.*—More of the chains have entered the breakfast market so successfully penetrated by McDonald's.

3. *New decor packages.*—In an effort to broaden their appeal as well as justify rapidly increasing prices, new, more up-scale decor packages are being put into place.

Admittedly, it may be too early to determine if the fast-food industry has actually reached maturity. The retail life-cycle school of thought provides a convincing rationale for why top management within the major chains has chosen the strategies they are implementing.

If the fast-food industry has, in fact, reached maturity, look for even more product, location and pricing innovations throughout the 1980's in a effort to postpone the final retail life cycle phase.

So, where does this bring us? We would propose that while the food-away-from-home industry does hold opportunity, regardless of segment, the successful operators in the future will have a combination of location, product, and management expertise in their favor. It is the first of these areas that we will address next in this chapter.

Restaurant Feasibility Studies

The feasibility study is becoming increasingly important to the success of a proposed restaurant. The process that we will present not only forces the developer to take a disciplined approach to the market characteristics; it also involves a relatively in-depth study of the following areas:

1. The competition, their market segments and sophistication

2. The strength of the proposed concept with special analysis of each serving period; this provides insight into the vulnerability of the concept

3. A financial and marketing analysis of the vital and peripheral serving periods

4. The breakeven point for the restaurant

Our approach to the presentation of the restaurant feasibility study will be to first compare the market analysis techniques for restaurants and hotels and then to explain each of the concepts outlined above.

Hotel/Restaurant Comparison

In chapter 7 we studied the process for determining the feasibility for hotel and motel projects. In some ways, the process for selecting markets for restaurants is similar. However, there are some important differences.

Economy. Restaurants are generally less susceptible to regional and national economic conditions than are hotels. In contrast, however, it is probably true that the economy of the primary market area has a more important effect on the volume in restaurants, because most hotel customers are transients, originating outside the immediate market area. It is the opposite situation for restaurants. Local economic conditions typically have a greater impact on dinner houses (specialty) and luxury restaurants than on fast-food and family eating places. *

Supply and demand. When new hotel rooms enter a market, there is generally a dilution in occupancy. Hotels are vulnerable in a quantitative sense to competition. The restaurant market, on the other hand, is much trendier, particularly in the higher-receipt properties. Therefore, the restaurants have a higher "conceptual vulnerability" than hotels. The state of the art in an area is important. In some markets, restaurant concepts and menus are very sophisticated. Additionally, the local population base which patronizes restaurants is very experienced and demands this in order for a restaurant to survive.

In other markets, the population is not as demanding and restaurateurs can thrive with a much simpler menu and concept. The restaurant feasibility study must consider the state of the art or level of sophistication that exists within the market area to insure the proposed concept and menu are not obsolete or will become so in the near future.

Demand generators. Generally, market (demand) generators are more diffused for restaurants than for hotels. As we said in Chapter 7 hotels need clusters of demand generators such as office space, industry, interstate highways, etc. to thrive. Restaurants receive business from many of the same sources but also enjoy business from the local populace. Therefore, within an SMSA or market, the number of potential locations for restaurants is usually greater than for hotels. In addition, within a market, trends in the hotel business will generally be more uniform than in restaurants.

Labor intensity. Restaurants are much more labor-intensive than hotels. Therefore, the analysis of labor cost, availability, and talent is a must in the restaurant study. For hotels, these factors are generally looked at, but not with the same intensity.

The table following exhibits some of the aforementioned as well as other similarities and differences between the hotel and the restaurant market evaluation process.

---

*"Economies of scale" refers to the decrease in unit cost of a product or service owing to large-scale production. For a restaurant chain, the major economies of scale would accrue in advertising, purchasing of food, equipment, and other items. Other economies of scale might include management and accounting expertise, research into new products and recipes, central food preparation, and storage such as in a commissary.

Hotels Versus Restaurants: Market
Evaluation Approaches

	Hotels	Fast food	Coffee shop/ family	Specialty	Luxury
Importance of economic conditions	5	2	2	3	4
Speed with which customer perceives product changes	2	3	3	5	5
Importance of limited-access highway near site	5	3	3	2	1
Visibility from major traffic carriers	5	5	3	2	1
Importance of skilled labor force	3	3	3	4	5
Relevance of prevailing wage rate in market area	3	5	4	4	3
Potential for customer segmentation	3	3	3	5	3

5 ——————— 1
High   Low

Competition

In the restaurant feasibility or selection process, there is generally a much closer focus on the competition than is true for hotels. In hotel feasibility studies the interest is in quantifying demand within the market area. This is accomplished by interviewing the primary competitors. In addition, one looks at the market segments as well as the strengths and weaknesses of each property. However, the primary goal is to quantify demand.

For the restaurant feasibility, the competitive review is much more qualitative. This is because it is difficult to quantify the number of "covers" demanded in the market area. Even if this could be quantified, it would not necessarily be meaningful. Unlike hotels, restaurants can create demand to a degree. That is, a well-executed concept providing good value can get consumers out of their homes and into the restaurant. In addition, it is often difficult to identify directly competitive restaurants. One restaurant may be a major competitor for lunch business but not for dinner. Another restaurant may only be competitive for the cocktail crowd. Therefore, the competitive analysis for the restaurant feasibility will focus on the following general areas:

○ *The volume levels and seat turnover ratio* by revenue period.* — Revenue periods may include breakfast, lunch, cocktail hour, dinner, late snack and post-dinner cocktail hour. Most restaurants won't have all of these periods, but they should be analyzed to determine the strength of each within the market area.

○ *The quality of the implementation and the concept from the customer's viewpoint of each competitor.* —If those properties with reasonably good concepts and quality levels are all doing well, this is a very positive sign. On the other hand, if well-executed concepts are not enjoying high levels of patronization, this is a clue that either the market is overbuilt or there is a very high risk of concept vulnerability.

○ *The ability of the market to absorb new restaurants.* —If during the past several years new competitive restaurants have opened with little long-term effect on the volume of competitors, one would conclude that the market is still strong. If, however, competitive restaurants experienced a permanent decrease in volume when competitors opened, a caution flag should be raised about the market's ability to withstand more restaurant entries.

○ *The "state of the art" of the restaurants in the area.* —Generally, the more sophisticated the restaurant market within a city, the higher the concept vulnerability and therefore the risk a new restaurant will face. The following chart depicts four levels of sophistication:

Concept Vulnerability

○	If located in sophisticated restaurant cities such as Los Angeles, Chicago, San Francisco, or New York
○	If located in suburbs of sophisticated restaurant cities
○	If located in less sophisticated restaurant cities
○	If located in communities of 100,000 or less

Degree of vulnerability ↑

It is generally true that the concept will have to be more adaptable to changing competitive concepts and consumer preferences in the more sophisticated markets if it is going to survive and thrive over the long term.

Once the competitive analysis has been completed, an objective review of the concept for the proposed restaurant is made. Is the proposed concept, menu, and value superior to the market? Where does the concept fit within the market? Are similar concepts (those currently serving target market segments) doing well? Are their concepts sophisticated? Is the market a sophisticated restaurant market?

---

*The seat turnover ratio is a common ratio used in the restaurant industry. It is computed by dividing the number of seats available into the number of covers served. For example, if a 150-seat restaurant serves 350 covers for lunch, the seat turnover ration would be 2.33 (350 ÷ 150).

The answers to these questions form the prescreening process and tell the analyst or developer whether or not to proceed with further study. Ideally, the proposed concept should be two to three years ahead of the market in concept sophistication. This becomes increasingly important as the average check moves out of the low to moderate range.

Strength of the Concept

As we mentioned above, once the competitive analysis in completed, the strength of the concept for the proposed restaurant should be evaluated. Generally, this is done by revenue period. This will help to determine the concept's vulnerability in its vital and peripheral periods.

The vital period for a restaurant can be defined as that revenue period (breakfast, lunch, or dinner,etc.) upon which the restaurant will depend for survival. All other periods, while important, are defined as peripheral periods. This is because if the concept is not successful during the vital period, it probably will not be profitable. We will discuss how to identify and analyze the vital period in a following section.

The following table shows the "typical" serving or revenue period segmentation for different restaurant categories:

Typical serving period segmentation

Restaurant category	Typical relevant serving periods
Luxury restaurant (no enter-tainment)	Lunch Dinner (sometimes dinner only)
Concept dinner house	Lunch Cocktail hour Dinner Evening entertainment
Moderate check, average family restaurant	Lunch Dinner Other (may have distinct cocktail hour or evening lounge business)
Coffee shop	Breakfast Lunch Dinner Other (for example, after midnight if open 24 hours)
Fast food	Lunch Dinner Other (many fast-food restaurants are successfully penetrating the breakfast market)

The analysis of the concept's strength will include the identification of each serving period the restaurant will hope to penetrate. Then, a review of the strength of the market, the competition, and the proposed restaurant's ability to penetrate the market is completed.

Proximity to Demand For hotels, it is important to be located as close to the primary demand-generators as possible while maintaining easy highway access. In the restaurant selection process, this can be equally true, although people will drive a little further for their meal.

The following table shows the average driving time customers take to reach their restaurant.

Average driving time to reach restaurant

Restaurant type	Average minutes
Fast food	11
Family	14
Coffee shop	11
Dinner house (theme)	16
All restaurants	13

Source: National Restaurant Association

An important aspect of the above chart concerns where the people are coming from—that is, what were their activities immediately prior to or after driving (or walking) to the restaurant.

The following table shows the activities or origination/destination points prior and subsequent to eating out:

Prior and subsequent activities to eating out

Category	From home	From work	Shopping	On business trip or vacation	Other*
Type:					
Fast food	26%	32%	17%	7%	18%
Family	37	31	10	12	10
Coffee shop	22	46	9	11	12
Dinner house	37	28	9	11	15
Occasion:					
Breakfast	47	16	1	25	11
Lunch	15	51	14	8	12
Dinner	50	17	9	10	14
All restaurants	29	35	12	9	15

Source: National Restaurant Association

*Other includes at school or at recreation (movies, bowling, etc.)

The table provides some interesting insight about location. For example, if the proposed restaurant is a dinner house or theme concept, with dinner being the vital period, locating near a residential area with the proper demographic and income characteristics is important. On the other hand, if the restaurant is a coffee shop with lunch as the vital period, locating close to where people work is important.

A final interesting consideration is when people generally patronize a restaurant: during the weekdays or on the three-day weekend. The following table lends some insight into this aspect. While all restaurants appear to be dependent upon the weekend trade (based on the figures in the table), some, such as dinner houses, are more dependent than others, such as coffee shops.

Weekday versus weekend eating out patterns
(% of Eating out occasions)

Category	Weekday	Weekend
Fast food	50%	50%
Family	44	56
Coffee shop	59	41
Dinner house	45	55
All restaurants	47	53

Source: National Restaurant Association

One important conclusion that can be made regarding the three tables presented relates to gasoline shortages. It is likely that the United States will face, from time to time, gasoline shortages until an alternative automobile fuel is widely available. From the tables, however, we can see that the impact of these shortages is not likely to be as severe on the restaurant business. This is due to the fact that many people go to restaurants while pursuing activities (such as work) that they will do anyway. In addition, the average driving time to most restaurants is not significant.

Commitment to Quality   Perhaps the most important ingredient in a restaurant's ultimate feasibility is the commitment to quality by the management. This becomes increasingly true as the price level increases. In fact, the luxury restaurants are so quality-intensive that physical location and decor are often quite secondary to their success.

To illustrate, New York City is considered by many connoisseurs to have some of the country's greatest restaurants. Joseph Baum, a New York restaurant giant who created the Four Seasons and Windows on the World describes the ingredients of good and great restaurants as follows:

> A good restaurant elevates a human need into a subtle and sophisticated pleasure; it is only by going from craft to art that a restaurant becomes great. It is not simply exoticism, or experimenta-

tion, or even originality; it is performance, performance that allows the client-customer to participate in the experience of creation.

If the customer is aware of the security of professional execution, if he knows that the finger is going to hit that note, then he feels a tension; not a tension of confusion, but of anticipation. Then he is past the notes and he is now singing. That is a great restaurant.[4]

Baum's description is admittedly somewhat elusive and romantic. Andre Sultner, chef and owner of Lutece, considered by many to be one of the world's finest restaurants, describes the elements of a great restaurant in more definable terms:

I need good chefs. I need good ingredients. I need good waiters. I need good dishwashers. On one night I will serve 100 dinners. If this evening my dishwasher is not 100 percent, the whole evening is ruined. If the plates are not ready on time, if they are not warmed, if they are not placed precisely right, then it will not work. Our secret is that it works well most nights. Lutece is not a restaurant of the chef but of the whole crew.[5]

Thus, while the research and analytical process that has been described for restaurant feasibility studies remains important for all types of restaurants, there is a certain quality level when the restaurant moves from good to great, where specific location becomes less of a factor to success. In fact, it is sometimes part of the mystique of the evening when one has to drive to an "out-of-the-way" location to enjoy a truly great dining experience.

Financial Analysis

Perhaps the most important part of the restaurant selection process is the financial and ratio analysis. By this time in the analysis, the study will have determined the market's strength and degree of sophistication. In addition, the concept of the proposed restaurant will have been evaluated in terms of expected longevity and ability to compete.

Frequently, the chain restaurants are able to proceed to financial analysis directly from the market and competitive review. This is because the criteria for location selection will have already been established. The chain will have experience in the ability of the concept to be viable within various types of markets.

Before we proceed with the specifics of the financial and breakeven analysis, a brief review of some key concepts will be presented.

The Income Statement   Following is an annual income statement for a theoretical 150-seat restaurant. The statement illustrates income and expenses to the unit profit level, which we define as profit before income taxes.

Income Statement[6]

150-seat restaurant

Sales		
Food	$ 810,000	70%
Beverage	350,000	30
Total sales	$1,160,000	100%
Cost of sales		
Food	$ 307,800	38%
Beverage	87,500	25
Total cost of sales	$ 395,300	34%
Gross profit	$ 764,000	66%
Controllable expenses		
Payroll	$ 243,600	21%
Employee benefits	58,000	5
Direct operating expenses	69,600	6
Music and entertainment	23,200	2
Advertising and promotion	23,200	2
Utilities	46,400	4
Administrative and general	69,600	6
Repairs and maintenance	23,200	2
Total controllable expenses	$ 556,800	48%
Income before rent or occupation costs	$ 207,900	18%
Rent or occupation costs	23,200	2%
Depreciation	34,800	3
Total occupation costs	$ 58,000	5%
Unit profit	$ 149,900	13%

The percentage figures next to each dollar amount reflect the ratio to total sales in the case of expenses (except for cost of sales). It is important to understand that these percentages are not fixed. That is, depending upon the classification of the expense as fixed, semivariable, or variable, they will change as the volume level changes.

A definition and brief generic description of each expense category follows.

Fixed expenses—Fixed expenses are those which are presumed to be totally unresponsive to changes in volume. A good example of a fixed cost would be depreciation. In the illustrated income statement, depreciation expense is $34,800. Being fixed means that this cost remains the same regardless of sales level.

The graphic relationship between fixed costs and volume is shown below:

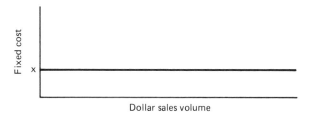

This means that as sales volume increases, the percentage of fixed expenses to sales will decrease. This is depicted graphically as follows:

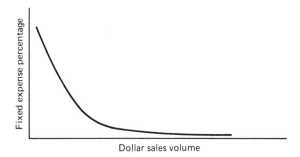

Variable expenses.—Variable expenses are those which are presumed to be proportionately responsive to changes in sales volume. An example of a variable expense would be the cost of food sold. In the theoretical income statement, it cost $.35 to receive $1.00 in food sales. This is true regardless of whether sales are 1.00 or $1,000,000.

The graphic relationship between variable expenses and sales volume is shown below:

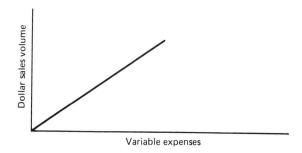

Semivariable expenses.—Semivariable expenses are those which contain two components: a fixed portion and a variable portion. For example, the cost of service personnel (waiters, waitresses, and busboys) in a restaurant are semivariable. This is because it requires a minimum staffing level regardless of how much volume the restaurant does. However, as volume increases, it requires more service personnel to adequately service the increased volume.

The graphic relationship between semivariable expenses and sales volume is depicted as follows:

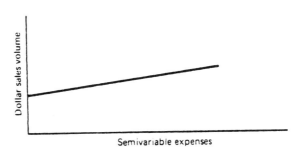

Semivariable expenses

Breakeven Analysis

One more analytical tool is helpful in a restaurant feasibility study—the breakeven analysis. This can be defined as the sales volume level where revenues (sales) and expenses are equal and the profit is zero. While it is true that few restaurants operate at the breakeven point, it is a highly useful concept in the feasibility process.

To calculate the breakeven point, a determination must first be made as to what are the total fixed costs and the variable cost percentage. Once this task is completed, the breakeven point is simply calculated as follows:

$$\text{Breakeven point} = \frac{\text{Fixed expenses}}{1 - \text{Variable expenses }\%}$$

For example, if it is known that the fixed cost for a restaurant is $175,000 and that the variable cost percentage is 55%, the breakeven point would be:

$$\text{Breakeven point} = \frac{\$175,000}{1 - 55\%}$$

$$= \frac{\$175,000}{.45} = \$388,889$$

Now, let's turn to a theoretical restaurant and see how these tools can be utilized in the feasibility analysis.

A Mini-Case

Assume that the theoretical restaurant had the following background:

○ The restaurant has 150 seats and serves lunch and dinner. Cocktails are available either in the dining room or in the cocktail lounge, which features live entertainment.

○ The restaurant averages 274 covers for lunch with an average check of $7.00. Lunch is served during the weekdays all year.

○ Dinner averages 296 covers with an average check of $12.50. This figure includes the liquor sales. Dinner is served 360 days each year.

○ Sales and direct costs have been divided into two profit centers, day and evening. The following schedule shows this breakdown:

150-Seat restaurant

Day	Total	Fixed component	Variable component	Variable %
Sales	$ 498,680			
Cost of sales	(189,498)		$ 189,498	38%
Payroll and related	(103,000)	$ 84,460	18,540	18%
Other direct costs	(29,500)	27,124	2,376	8%
Profit contribution	$ 173,182	$ 111,520	$ 213,978	64%
Evening				
Sales	$1,332,000			
Cost of sales	(506,160)		$ 506,160	38%
Payroll and related	(135,400)	$ 124,568	10,832	8%
Other direct costs	(97,200)	90,396	6,804	7%
Profit contribution	$ 593,240	$ 214,964	$ 523,796	53%
Total profit contribution				
Unallocated expenses				
Payroll and related	$ 91,534	$ 91,534		
Other operating costs	109,841	109,841		
Occupation costs	146,454	146,454		
Total unallocated	$ 347,829	$ 347,829		
Unit profit	$ 422,093			

The first thing that should be clear after a little analysis is that the vital period is during the evening. This is when the highest profit contribution occurs. This can be seen by the fact that the profit contribution from the evening period more than covers the fixed costs from the day period and the unallocated expenses—i.e.,

$$\$593,240 - 111,584 - 347,829 = 133,827$$

This is not true for the day period, when the profit contributions are only $176,682.

Another useful analysis is to calculate the breakeven point in covers for each serving period. This would be done as follows:

$$\text{B.E. lunch} = \frac{\$111,584}{1-.64} = \frac{\$111,584}{.36}$$

$$= \$309,996$$

To translate this to the number of daily covers necessary to breakeven, we need to divide the required sales by the average check and the number of serving days each year:

$$\text{B.E. covers} = \$309,996 \div \$7.00 \div 260 \text{ days} = 170 \text{ covers}$$

$$\text{B.E. Evening} = \frac{\$214,964}{1-.53} = \frac{\$214,964}{.47}$$

$$= \$457,370$$

$$\text{B.E. covers} = \$457,370 \div \$12.50 \div 360 \text{ days} = 102 \text{ covers}$$

As can be seen, the risk involved with each serving period is slightly higher for the lunch period. This period currently is averaging 1.18 times the number of covers necessary to break even.

The evening period, on the other hand, is exceeding a requisite breakeven number of covers by 2.9 times. Therefore, a decline in evening-period covers would more quickly place the period in a breakeven or loss position than for the day period. We already know that the evening period is generating enough profit contribution to cover all of the fixed costs of the restaurant and still maintain a profit margin. We can calculate the number of covers that would be necessary on a daily basis during the day period to allow the restaurant to break even. This would be done as follows:

$$\text{B.E.} = \frac{\$674,377}{1-.64} = \frac{\$674,377}{.36} = \$1,873,269$$

$$\text{B.E. covers} = \$1,873,269 \div \$7.00 \div 260$$

$$= 1,029 \text{ covers}$$

In other words, the restaurant would have to increase the number of covers served each day by over three times to cover all of the expenses for the property. Even if this was realistic, it would not be a good risk for an investor or lender approached for a loan on this project.

From the foregoing analysis, we can draw the following conclusions about our theoretical restaurant:

○ Although the restaurant is profitable, the vital period is during the evening. This is the only period when large enough sales and profit levels are generated to cover the fixed expenses of the restaurant. The day period is referred to as the peripheral period.

○ Since the evening period is the vital period, it is here where the concept becomes the most vulnerable. During the market and competitive analysis portion of the feasibility study, much of the research will focus on how well the evening concept stands up to competition, as well as how well it is likely to be received by the market.

    ○ While the day period does make a profit contribution under the assumptions provided above, we would be less concerned about a volume decline during this period. This would allow the management to experiment with new concepts during the day period with less risk, if desirable.

Chain Indentification

The top 100 chains are gaining an increasing share of the total restaurant sales market. How does this relate to the selection process? Is it always an advantage to have a chain identification, as is generally the case with hotels?

Many of the advantages of a chain stem from standardization and economies of scale.[7] The fact that consumers know that they can expect a standard product, standard decor, and consistent delivery each time they visit McDonald's, regardless of location, is a significant advantage to McDonald's.

However, as the average check and decor package increase past the family restaurant state, it can be argued that chain identity begins to lose some of its advantages. This is because consumers are looking for more than a meal at higher level prices. They want an experience, a uniqueness in the product. Therefore, from the customer standpoint, it is not always advantageous to identify with a chain. This might also explain why there are few, if any, national chains of luxury restaurants. It also explains, in part, why many multi-unit restaurant companies often change the name and identity of each restaurant unit. In this way, they are able to enjoy the economies of scale associated with running many units while avoiding the problem of the consumers bypassing chain restaurants in their search for uniqueness and individuality.

Restaurants Within Hotels Revisited

We have seen that the trends for restaurant patronization within hotels has been declining over the past decade. We have also discussed the trend toward the renovation of older hotels in urban locations. Armed with the discipline of restaurant feasibility analysis, let's review the potential future of restaurants within hotels.

A portion of a hotel's food sales is driven by hotel occupancy. This is particularly true of breakfast and, to a lesser degree, dinner. As larger, downtown hotels increase occupancy and upgrade their food and beverage operations, food sales during breakfast should increase substantially.

Lunch sales are dependent upon proximity to office buildings and other concentrations of employers. This, of course, is a strength of most downtown areas of large cities. Consequently, luncheon food sales should increase for those operations that successfully promote to this market.

That leaves dinner, the period when most hotels probably have the greatest opportunity for increasing food sales. It would be difficult to generalize about the potential for increased dinner sales in hotels. However, we can provide insight into some of the ingredients for success.

○ Hotels located in urban areas with a downtown residential population have increased potential for dinner sales.

○ Hotels located in the sophisticated cities have a good opportunity if they keep the concept up-to-date and viable.

○ Hotels with higher occupancies, particularly during the weekdays have some opportunity because of "built-in" market.

In summary, it appears that those operators of large hotels who renew their focus on restaurant facilities have the potential to increase food and beverage sales. Of course, the ultimate test comes in the quality of the food and the service delivery when the customer orders a meal.

Summary

As with hotels, there are several approaches to the restaurant selection process. We have presented one which emphasizes the risk of conceptual vulnerability and market sophistication. The advantage to this approach is that it provides both a quantitative and a qualitative evaluation of a new restaurant's ability to succeed in a market.

There is another important advantage in understanding this approach. We have mentioned that restaurants face a high degree of risk from new competitors entering the market with a better concept. This would imply two things to the smart operator:

1. His or her concept should be flexible, particularly as the average receipt increases.

2. He or she should remain in "touch" with the market to be sure his product is not facing obsolescence. This is particularly true for the vital period.

One excellent way for the operator of a restaurant to continually update his or her knowledge of the dynamics of the market is through the continuing feasibility study. This would require that every one to three years, depending upon the market, a new feasibility study be prepared for the existing restaurant. During this study the following questions would be answered:

○ If this restaurant were not here, would the study recommend that one be built?

○ Would there be any modifications in the concept?

○ Has the vital period changed? Is the current concept still the best in the market during the vital period? If not, what changes should be made?

○ Who is the current competition, by revenue period, and what are their strengths and weaknesses?

1. John W. Stokes, *How to Manage a Restaurant or Institutional Food Service* (Dubuque, Ia: Wm. C. Brown Co. 1972), p. 2–3.

2. "The Frantic Fast Food Fracas, "*Financial World,* August 1, 1978, p. 36.

3. For an interesting and more in-depth analysis of this school, see "Exploding the Myth: The Truth About Food Service Growth," *The Cornell Hotel and Restaurant Administration Quarterly,* February 1978.

4. Fred Ferretti, "The Art of Creating Great Restaurants," *New York Times Magazine,* November 25, 1979, p. 30.

5. Ibid., p. 44.

6. It is suggested that the reader who is unfamiliar with the restaurant income statement review the *Uniform System of Accounts for Restaurants,* prepared by Laventhol & Horwath for the National Restaurant Association. The statement illustrated is also known as the Statement of Income and Expenses or the Summary Profit and Loss Statement.

7. Economies of scale refer to the decrease in unit cost of a product or service due to large-scale production. For a restaurant chain, the major economies of scale would accrue in advertising, purchasing of food, equipment, and other items. Other economies of scale might include management and accounting expertise, research into new products and recipes, central food preparation and storage such as is common in a commissary.

Strategic Planning

When you finish this chapter you should understand:

1. The definition of strategic planning and why it is important to any organization

2. The eight components of strategic planning and the role of each component

3. The two critical elements of an objective

4. At least five steps in budgeting

5. The six tasks within the planning process

6. The key elements to a good business-mission statement

7. Three alternative ways for setting objectives and the pros and cons of each method

We do not yet have a genuine theory of business and no discipline of business management. But we know what a business is and what its key functions are. We understand the functions of profit and the requirements of productivity. Any business needs to think through the question, "What is our business and what should it be?" From the definition of its [goals and mission] a business must derive objectives in a number of key areas; it must balance these objectives against each other and against the competing demands of today and tomorrow. It needs to convert objectives into concrete strategies and to concentrate resources on them. Finally, it needs to think through its strategic planning—i.e., the decisions of today that will make the business of tomorrow.

Peter F. Drucker, *Management: Tasks, Responsibilities, Practices*
(New York: Harper & Row, 1974), p. 49.

The concept of strategic planning, under a variety of different names, has spread rapidly throughout organizations around the world during the past two decades. Small wonder! For the words themselves connote adventure—adventure in prediciting the future, in assessing the strengths and weaknesses of an organization or business relative to its competition, and adventure in making decisions today that will determine the success or failure of the business in the future.

There are many reasons why a business needs to define an objective, an identity, and a philosophy about what the purpose of the business is and where it is going. One simple one is survival. As Joel E. Ross and Michael J. Kamie so aptly point out:

> We can say beyond any reasonable doubt that a well-directed effort by the top management of an organization can make it grow at a faster rate than the economy in general, and also at a rate faster than the competitive firms in the industry. The real basis for this effort by top management is organizational strategy. Without it, failure is a matter of time.[1]

Strategic planning is a powerful tool that can lead to success when properly utilized and well executed; long-term failure is almost guaranteed if it is ignored. This is the reason for this chapter. We will discuss the definitions of strategic planning and a simple approach. We will delve into the planning process itself and describe what a strategic plan looks like and how it is prepared. Finally, we will discuss selected examples to understand how this tool can be applied within the hospitality industry.

Strategic Planning Defined

There are many definitions of strategic planning. Most of the better ones include an explanation of the goals and mission of the business. Most incorporate the necessity of examining the strengths and weaknesses of the organization; studying the environmental, competitive, legislative, and social trends and assessing their potential impact on the organization; and, based upon this analysis, making a few crucial decisions which allocate scarce resources to deal with selected threats and opportunities.

For us, the concept of strategic planning has a very precise definition which encompasses all of the above processes. Strategic planning is *the process which provides the framework from which all decisions that will impact the future nature and direction of the organization are made.* These decisions can confront the business at any time; they are about market segments, pricing, product changes, capital allocations, and human resources.

It is clear that these decisions can and will affect the long-term strength of the organization. It should also be clear that when they are made within the framework of a well-thought-out direction from top management, the decisions will be consistent and will move the business toward a common set of objectives. If the decisions are made without the guidance of a strategic plan, the direction may be uncoordinated and in conflict with other department decisions. Worse yet, the future of the business may be determined by a series of short-term "fire-fighting" decisions made by middle managers with no coordination of direction from top executives. This is how businesses fail. From small businesses to corporate giants, the failure to provide a strategic framework for decision making can be fatal.

Strategic planning is not an art nor a set of equations to be solved. It is a process for making decisions. Moreover, strategic planning is a framework for assessing a changing environment and assuring that long-term directives can be made that are consistent with management's expectations. To effectively manage a hospitality business, an effective set of controls must be in place. The controls we speak of can be likened to the instruments a pilot uses. They provide the means of knowing where one is going (goals and missions); rules to maintain a safe course (policies); a means of knowing where one is going (objectives); a flight plan for getting there (strategies, tactics and programs). Once in the air, the pilot has methods for monitoring progress; instruments for checking out the equipment (internal analysis); an idea of what weather conditions to expect (environmental analysis); and a radio to report progress (reporting). Our concept of strategic planning is shown in Table 11–1 and discussed in the following pages.

A Concept of Stratetic Planning

Table 11–1. Components of Strategic Planning

Goals	Economic incentives for being in business—what? For whom?
Business mission	Definitions of the basic product (narrowly) and the market (broadly)—What? To whom?
Policies	Statements of the values of the organization and its posture toward risk.
Objectives	Key achievements—What? When?
Strategies	Broad courses of action to achieve the objectives—How?
Tactics and programs	Documenting and formalizing the efforts and resources needed to carry out strategies.
Annual budgets	Identifying the specific inputs required to meet the objectives, closing the five prior components, which define the output desired.
Monitoring	A continuing formal review of performance where adjustments can be made to improve performance.

Goals

An economic entity must have economic incentives for existing. This fact is often overlooked and usually relegated to the status of an afterthought in the mission statement. It is the reason for doing business. More than that, it is the way investors will get their money back. Some individuals may seek short-term tax losses to defer the tax on other income to later years. Venture capitalists desire a potential start that can be later sold, privately or publicly, for a multiple of earnings (and investment). Some investors want dividends. Others, willing to accept the risk of time, desire capital gains.

The major factor influencing the choice of goals is the legal entity embracing the firm and the after-tax return to the owners. Proprietorships and partnerships are usually concerned with their after-tax cash flow. Private corporations may be more concerned with dividends or liquidation value, and some private forms of ownership may not be at all concerned with returns, but with monument building for ego satisfaction. With publicly held companies, the problem of goal setting becomes confusing. Should today's investors or the shareholders of tomorrow be addressed? Is the goal stated as price per share, or market price compared to book value of stock? The polarity of these options is the reason that economic goals are usually ignored or buried in a far too general statement. Nevertheless, establishing goals is the most important step in strategic planning. How can alternative strategies be compared or rejected without a goal? How can a company or individual choose a business to pursue without a goal? How can it establish objectives for strategy development without a goal? How can effective financial policy be established for the business mission without goals?

Business Mission

The second fundamental step in the strategic planning process is the development of a business-mission statement. A mission statement communicates the underlying design or thrust of a company. Thus, it is usually long-term in nature. The goals and mission statements drive all plans, long-and short-range.

Mission statements should address both the product and the market of the business. However, they must not be too vague. For example, a hotel company which states that it is in the travel business faces both increased opportunities and increased threats, for there is an unwritten law in business that says that the further a company strays from its main areas of marketing and management expertise, the less likely it is to be successful. Look at the high-growth conglomerates of the 1960s. Investors flocked to purchase their stocks, driving prices to unrealistically high levels. However, in the early 1970s, these giants rapidly fell from favor and investors lost millions of dollars. Why? One commonly offered reason is they did not have a well-thought-out mission statement. Consequently, they did not know who they were or where they were going. This identity crisis resulted in an over taxation of their existing management expertise.

Our hotel company with the travel-business mission statement could conceivably acquire a travel intermediary, a car rental business, an airline, or a fleet of luxury liners. All of these acquisitions would be congruent with the mission statement. Yet each would require a different set of management systems, marketing programs, capital and financial assumptions, and technical expertise. Perhaps a meaningful mission statement for this company would read as follows:

> To be recognized as the industry leader in quality hotel development, ownership, and operations by providing first-class accommodations that represent prestige and value to the up-scale business- and pleasure-travel markets throughout the United States.

From this mission statement, management has a clear idea of the product and market thrust of the organization. The major key to an effective mission is to define the product narrowly and the markets broadly. However, it must be specific enough to develop meaningful policies and objectives.

Policies

Policies are statements of the organization's values and attitudes toward risk. In a new and developing company, policies are few. But as the company grows and later matures as a business, the number of policies increase. This increase is necessary to better define the limitations that are placed on a growing number of decision-makers and establish the management style that is expected throughout the organization. Classically, policies are divided into five categories:

○ *General principles*—A set of basic beliefs that transcend the organization itself and become a timeless statement of the basic beliefs to guide management in the day-to-day conduct of their business. An example of this concept was extracted from IBM's statement of principles:

> The underlying meaning of these [general principles] was best expressed by Tom Watson, Jr., in his McKinsey Foundation Lectures at Columbia University in New York in 1962, when he said:
>
> I firmly believe that any organization, in order to survive and achieve success, must have a sound set of beliefs on which it premises all its policies and actions.
>
> Next, I believe that the most important factor in corporate success is faithful adherence to those beliefs.
>
> And finally, I believe that if an organization is to meet the challenges of a changing world, it must be prepared to change everything about itself except those beliefs as it moves through corporate life.
>
> In other words, the basic philosophy, spirit, and drive of an organization have far more to do with its relative achievements than

do technological or ecomomic resources, organizational structure, innovation, and timing. All these things weigh heavily in success. But they are, I think, transcended by how strongly the people in the organization believe in its basic precepts and how faithfully they carry them out.

Now, what is this set of beliefs he was talking about? There are three:

Respect for the individual. Respect for the dignity and the rights of each person in the organization.

Customer service. To give the best customer service of any company in the world.

Excellence. The conviction that an organization should pursue all tasks with the objective of accomplishing them in a superior way.

○ *Organization*—A definition of the organization structure and responsibilities assigned to individual positions and committees as well as the means of making decisions.

○ *Human resources*—Policies that are established to govern the management of employees and to express the principles and practices underlying the relationship between the company and its employees. Specific items usually identified include: recruiting and placement, equal employment opportunity, benefits, compensation, employee conduct and training.

○ *Finance*—Limitations on the financial structure of the company need to be established primarily to identify the level of risk that it is willing to accept. Generally, these policies are stated as ranges or maximum levels of leverage, lease obligations, fixed-charge coverages, dividend-payout ratios, credit parameters, limitations on spending, and appropriate control systems.

○ *Operations*—This type of policy establishes the nature of the contract between general business management and unit operations management. It should define the authority limits, responsibilities, and expectations of each party.

Objectives

The objectives of the business describe the "what" of planning. They are the results that are to be achieved. There are two critical elements to any objective: a number and a date. Simply, objectives should be measurable. In fact, it is the achievement or nonachievement of these stated objectives and subobjectives that will ultimately be used to measure management performance.

Consider, for example, the marketing manager whose objective is solely to increase market share. How can his performance be measured? If his objective is to increase market share by 5 percent within the next twelve months, his performance can then be measured.

In what areas should objectives be set? Peter Drucker, a well-known management philosopher and consultant, believes that objectives are required in every area in which results significantly affect the continued survival and profits of the enterprise. These areas are commonly referred to as *key result areas.* Eight of them have been identified that apply to any business organization:

○ Marketing
○ Innovation
○ Human organization
○ Financial resources
○ Physical resources
○ Productivity
○ Social responsibility
○ Profit requirements[2]

Objectives can be set by top management early in the planning process or developed through research by either the planners or middle management and presented to top management for approval. Regardless of how they are developed, they must be consistent with the mission statement, they should be quantified, they should challenge the company's management and employee team, and they should be agreed to by those people who will be charged with the task of executing them.

Strategies

Strategies refer to those broad directions designed to achieve objectives. They do not refer to specific action plans or programs.

Strategy development in larger companies generally evolves from extensive research into the product, the competition, market potential, etc., such as what we will be describing shortly. All proposed strategies, however, should be constrained by the company's mission statement and the specific objective it is seeking to achieve.

Tactics and Programs

Tactics and programs are the specific action plans that are developed to achieve objectives within a strategic framework. Being action-oriented, they should include quantifiable check points to allow frequent monitoring. They should identify who is responsible for implementing each program so that management can evaluate individual performance. Finally, they should include any significant assumptions that should also be monitored. This will provide an early warning system should the key assumptions prove to be erroneous, resulting in the program potentially going astray.

Often, a business will have a cluster of objectives, subobjectives, substrategies, and subprograms, all designed to move the results toward the primary objectives.

Annual Budgets

Budgeting analyzes in detail the many functions or activities that must be performed and identifies the associated costs involved in reaching these goals. Necessarily, budgeting requires the following steps:

○ *Marketing plan*—Defines specific market share increases and the associated pricing considerations

○ *Income budget*—A combination of the sales projections and associated costs

○ *Capital budget*—Defines the investment needs

○ *Nonfinancial objectives*—Identifies specific accomplishments that will be completed that are necessary to carry out the long-term strategies

○ *Cost-reduction analysis*—A continuous review and improvement of the application of resources in the operation and staff departments

○ *Contingency plans*—Proposed reaction steps to possible changes in the environment

Monitoring

After specifying the strategies, programs, and budgets, the next step is to confirm that all is going as expected by checking progress along the way. If things are going awry, then either the program or the tactic was inappropriate and it should be rethought, or operational changes must be effected to bring things back on track. An important part of monitoring consists of timely accounting and operations analysis reports. However, it is equally important to track the assumptions that went into the plan to be sure that the basis for the strategies is still valid.

The Planning Process

The actual planning process is an in-depth look at the business, its environment, and the future. It is designed to answer three key questions: Where do we want to go? Will we need to make operating changes in response to a changing environment? What are the strategic choices that will get us where we want to go?

Planning is an orderly process in which facts relevant to the business are amassed and then organized into options so that a *few* strategic decisions can be made and a long-term "blueprint" can be set up. The process, once established, becomes a basic management tool that will be the driving force of change throughout the company in the future. But strategic planning must be supported and used by the chief business officer (or owner) or it is doomed to failure and the business will be wrought with indecision, nondecision, and constantly reversing decisions.

A simple conceptual model (Figure 11–1) has been developed to present the various phases of the planning process. In this model, we have introduced the idea of business managers and operating managers. Business managers are charged with setting the goals and objectives of the organization to insure the direction is correct. Operating managers, on the other hand, are charged with seeing that the right strategies are executed so that the goals set by the business managers are achieved. The six major tasks and the management interaction required are discussed in the following sections.

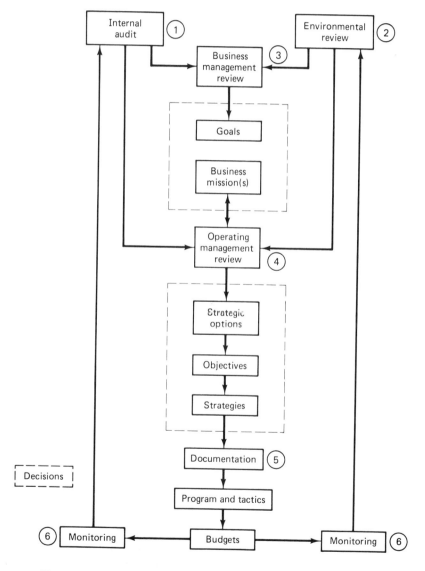

Figure 11-1. Strategic planning process: Conceptual model

Task 1: The Internal Audit

The internal audit is a critical review of the business which includes analysis of past performance, historical trends, current position, and how the business has performed against previous objectives. The purpose of the audit is to determine the major strengths and major weaknesses of the business (compared to key competitors) and to outline programs of action to correct any weaknesses or identify potential opportunities. In addition, the audit should reveal the profitability of current operations against other investment opportunities.

How is this done? First, notice that we talked about identifying strengths and weaknesses relative to key competitors. This implies that it is first necessary to identify those key competitors. We must also determine which categories we will be evaluating the business against—i.e., market share, market segments, product, financial performance, or human resources. Certainly all of these areas are critical to the ongoing success of a business. A brief discussion of each of these factors follows:

Market share. The question here is What is the market share and what is the share of each of the key competitors? Has the trend been a growth or decline in share? The answers to these questions are critical. The following example illustrates a hotel whose occupancy grew while it actually lost market share.

Hotel X market share analysis

	Rooms available		Rooms occupied		% Occupancy	
	1981	1982	1981	1982	1981	1982
Total market	1,500	1,500	1,080	1,145	72.0	76.3
Hotel X	200	200	148	150	74.0	75.0

Hotel X market share

| 1981 | 13.7% |
| 1982 | 13.1% |

As illustrated, market share for Hotel X declined by 0.6 percent in one year, even though occupancy increased. Why should the hotel be concerned? Because it lost customers to competition. What if the hotel suffers the same share loss in the following year and the market occupancy declines? What if the trend continues? On the fact of the above information, Hotel X has a weakness compared to competition which must be identified and corrected.

Market segments. In Chapter 10 we discussed the concept of vital and peripheral meal periods for restaurants. We can use the same principle with market segments. It is important to know what the primary market segments of the business are and who the competition is for each of them. For a single hotel property, it is also necessary to know who the primary customers are and who the competition is. Then a review of strengths and weaknesses relative to the needs of the target market segments (customers) and relative to key competitors can be undertaken. This review should include an assessment of price, product, service, location, and people.

Product. In the two areas for review presented above, we are looking for symptoms of a problem or a strength. In the product review, which is defined as both the physical product and the service quality, we begin to look for causes of strengths and weaknesses. This review implies a knowledge of what services and what product the customer wants.

Financial performance. It is relatively easy to obtain the financial statements of publicly held competitors; for others, it is probably unrealistic or illegal. However, to the degree one can determine how the business is doing financially compared to the key competitors, it can be a very worthwhile undertaking. It may illuminate a potential opportunity to capture a market segment that is more profitable than the existing market segments. It may bring to the surface a potential acquisition candidate. Or it may initiate a reassessment of existing products and markets and then evolve into new segments.

Another aspect of the financial review might include determining the profitability of each of the existing market segments. Assume, for example, that the Granada Hotel believes that a large part of its business is from truckers. Because of the contract signed with a trucking firm, the guaranteed rate for overnight truckers is $30.00, a $15.00 discount from the rack rate. Upon close review, the hotel found that the truckers were generating about 60 rooms per week, year round. In addition, it was requiring about $100,000 per year in parking lot repairs to service this segment. Let's see if all this is worthwhile.

Granada Hotel	
Trucker revenue	$ 93,600
Departmental expenses (26%)	24,336
Departmental profit	$ 69,264
Less: Parking lot repairs	100,000
Contribution to profit	($ 30,736)

This analysis shows that the Granada Hotel would be better off without the overnight truckers under the current contract and volume. It is this type of review that would reveal this problem to management, which could then formulate a corrective action program.

The other aspect of financial performance that must be evaluated is the return to the investor. As mentioned in the goals-setting section, there must be a way for an investor to get his money back. This is the time for an analysis of competitor, industry, and "money market" returns.

Human resources.   In any hotel or restaurant operation, there are three types of resources: physical, human, and financial. The best-managed companies put human resources in front and build the other two around it. Why? Because the only real difference in a continuous competitive advantage is human resources and human resource development. Too many companies spend too much time focusing on their financial and physical resources. Yet in many industries, particularly service industries, it is the human resources that determine the long-term viability of the business. Within the human resources section of the internal audit, the following areas should be addressed:

○ What is the organizational climate within the business? Are the company's policies, the management style, and the values of top management promoting a healthy work environment and a dedication to excellence?

○ How strong are managers and supervisors? Have all of them been provided with an assessment of his or her strengths and weaknesses along with a development program to correct key weaknesses?

○ What is the turnover ratio in employees? How does it compare to the industry and the competition? Are good employees being lost to competitors?

○ Is there a succession program for each of the key people? If the general manager leaves next month, can he or she be replaced from within?

○ Do all employees have tangible objectives to work toward? Do they know how the top management is keeping score?

Remember, the purpose of this audit is to determine strengths and weaknesses within the company and to develop corrective action programs to repair the weaknesses. It is our opinion that the human resource audit is the single most important review in the entire planning process, because it is the organization itself that leads people to outstanding accomplishments or failure.

The results of the internal audit will be a critical assessment of the organization's strengths and weaknesses in those areas that are vital to business survival and growth. The next step in the planning process, then, is to look at the business environment, to study the *existing* external trends and assess their potential impact on the business.

Task 2:   The Environmental Review

The primary focus of the environmental review is to assess the existing external trends that are not ordinarily within management's control, but will influence the future of the business. Its purpose is to clearly identify the dynamic forces and factors that are moving customers to and from the business. For example, the increase in airline travel may be a positive business trend that is moving customers to a hotel located close to a regional airport. On the other hand, the increasing cost and declining availability of gasoline may be an unfavorable trend for a hotel located on an interstate highway.

The purpose of the environmental review is to segregate those trends that could have an impact on the key areas of a business into favorable, neutral, and unfavorable classifications. Clearly, if this review is to be orderly and disciplined, it must revolve around key categories. While these categories should be determined according to the specific business, some general areas that demand research include product and service; customers, both current and new; the competition; the industry in general; government legislation and actions; and resources. The larger the business, the greater the number of factors that must be reviewed.

The following list of environmental categories should be monitored in detail, depending upon the size of the organization:

- Demographics
- Values/lifestyles
- Resources
- Technology
- Public attitudes
- Government
- International
- Economy

The large corporation will spend large amounts of capital and effort in environmental scanning—looking for threats, trends and/or opportunities in each of these areas. But even the small restaurant or hotel must be attentive to specific environmental changes as shown in our next example.

Whenever a trend is identified, there should be a written description of whether it is an increasing or decreasing trend, its magnitude, and how long the trend has been going on. Then each trend must be categorized as to potential impact on the business and at what point it will trigger a new action plan. A favorable trend will trigger a new strategy when it achieves a certain point, such as a 5.0 percent growth rate. On the other hand, an unfavorable trend will trigger a contingency plan at a given point in time.

All of this implies that the environmental and business review is not a once-a-year program. It should be ongoing, with specific individuals assigned the duties of tracking each target trend and updating management on a regular basis as to its status. In larger companies, research departments are set up to perform this task. In a small business such as a hotel, a task force or group of individuals can prepare the requisite research and reports.

In earlier chapters we looked at some general trends that could impact a business. Following are several more:

○ The biggest borrower of capital in the 1980s will be the federal government. This will cause one of the biggest capital crunches in history, driving up interest rates and slowing growth.

○ Foreign companies are putting forth a significant development effort in the United States. Since many foreign corporations are either partially owned or subsidized by their government, they can often offer lower prices than American companies.

○ Government regulation in the United States is costing American businesses billions of dollars a year—and it looks as if this may get worse. In Murray L. Weidenbaum's words:

> It is hard to overestimate the rapid expansion and the almost infinite variety of government involvement in business which is now occurring in the United States. The new type of governmental regulation is not limited to the traditional independent regulatory agencies, such as Interstate Commerce Commission, Civil Aeronautics Board . . . Rather, all the operating bureaus of government—the Departments of Agriculture, Commerce, Energy, Interior, Justice, Labor, Transportation, Treasury and Health, Education and Welfare—are now involved in actions that affect virtually every firm in every industry.[3]

○ Energy.

Task 3: Business Management Review

Armed with both the internal and external research facts, management people can now put on their "business hats" and answer some very gutsy questions. The first of these is: Are we in the type of business that will yield acceptable returns? This question really demands two answers. The first is to decide what the financial goals of the company are and, second, if those goals can be achieved from this type of business. Ideally, this analysis will consider the business cycle discussed in Chapter 1 and what phase the organization is in. The answer to this question determines successive planning steps. A decision tree of some possible outcomes is shown in Figure 11–2.

The next set of discussions deals with preparing the business mission. The resulting decisions should be a combination of both business managers' and operating managers' opinions. In our previous example (see Figure 11–2) Cases A, B, and D would lead to the same business mission, but Case C may lead to an entirely different mission. (Case B is just a change in financial policy, although a specific objective and associated strategies may be warranted to achieve the needed leverage.)

For example, the business mission for the continuing operations cases of a restaurant-lounge could read something like:

> To own and operate a competitively priced restaurant-lounge in the "Old Town" center of Memphis, Tennessee, that will appeal to the college student as well as the 23-to-30-year-old residents nearby.

This mission almost seems too simplistic. However, its power is in the limitations it imposes on operating management. Those limitations fall into the following areas:

1. Target-market segments
2. Pricing
3. Concept

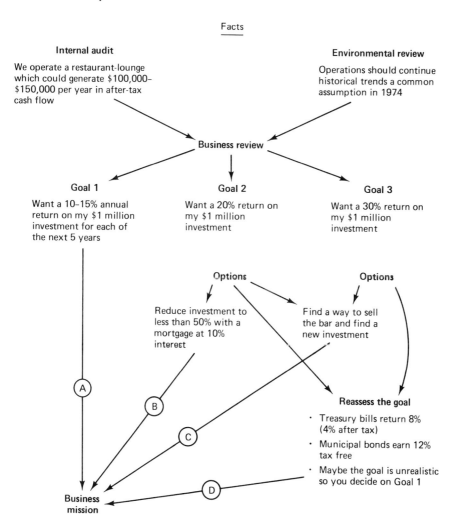

Figure 11–2 Business management review, possible decision outcomes

Task 4: Operating Management Review

By now, we have determined what business we're in through the mission statement and the financial goals of the organization. It is now time to answer another question: What can we do? In many organizations, this question is countered with a responding question: What do you want? This response is not planning, it is averting the major planning objective of *generating options.* For example, if the plan stated: "We could do this, but . . .," the *but* is the option. It may require capital expenditure (sometimes small, but often large) or it may have a short-term increase in profits with a long-term risk (a reasonable alternative if a sale of the property is the goal), or it may require depressing short-run profits for long-term survival (cut prices or increase advertising to gain market share). These strategic options incorporate both objectives (What, by when?) and strategies (How?). Generally, options are very polar, but there can be subtle distinctions. Theoretically, options fall into three classes: *superiority* (involves the best, most luxurious, highest service, at a high price); *equivalence* (involves matching price and offering with the competition—usually in response to competitive action to maintain share); *inferiority* (involves budget-type products—trading price versus service or taking a "low profile" and reallocating strategic resources to another area, indicating at least a short-term abandonment of the market).

Thinking applied to the business to generate the options comprises the guts of strategic planning; deciding between the options comprises the heart. These decisions must be based as much as possible on facts, and research can be costly. But without research, how can it be known if a proposed restaurant can saturate or has saturated one city and also if its major strength is in its product (which would lead to geographical expansion) or in its operating skill (which, for example, would dictate new menu concepts for a different meal occasion or an entirely new restaurant prototype appealing to a new market segment)? Armed with these options and willing to make a decision, management can easily undertake the ensuing planning steps:

Formulating objectives. At this point in the planning process, we have a well-thought-out picture of the threats and opportunities that confront the business. We know how well we are equipped to deal with each of these both from a resources point of view and relative to the major competition. It is now time to begin to formulate the company's objectives, which will capitalize on the opportunities and minimize the threats.

Setting the objectives is a process that must involve the top management of the business if it is to be successful, for it is here that decisions involving the future direction of the company are made. Without the involvement and agreement of top management, the requisite resources are not likely to be committed for their achievement. In addition, without top management support, it is not likely that middle management will give each objective the necessary attention. This is one common pitfall to successful planning.

There are several different ways in which objectives can be formulated:

○ In the *top-down planning* approach, normally associated with highly centralized companies, the president states the objectives and requests plans for management to achieve the objectives. These plans are then reviewed and accepted or revised by the president. The classic problems with this approach are getting management and employee commitment to the objectives as well as getting all of the necessary input and research necessary to set well-designed objectives. In spite of these drawbacks, the top-down approach is frequently used successfully.

○ In the *bottom-up planning* approach, guidelines and objectives are not articulated by the senior executive. Rather, management does its own planning, by department or division, and then submits the plans (objectives) to the president for review. There are three specific problems with this approach:

— Without the involvement from the top, which has the only true "big picture" of the business, conflicting objectives from departments are often submitted. In this case, the most persuasive managers are generally the most successful in getting plans approved. This can be detrimental, particularly when departments or divisions are competing for scarce resources.

— Without the involvement and coordination from top management, tunnel vision often sets in. This results in maintenance of the status-quo–type objectives rather than truly creative and aggressive objectives.

— Without top management involved in and listening to the discussions and the alternatives evaluated based upon the research, it is more difficult to get a total commitment to the objectives from the top. This can be disastrous.

○ A third approach to planning and objective-setting and planning is to involve the president in the setting of the broad first-level objectives and then let management suggest subobjectives and plans.

○ Finally, in smaller companies, the senior executive can use his or her top managers to help in developing objectives. This has many advantages in small companies because of the typical lack of a research staff.

As we discussed earlier in this chapter, objectives should be set in every area that is important to the growth and survival of the firm. In larger companies, Drucker's eight key result areas (see page 285) demand attention. In smaller companies or in departments or divisions of middle-sized companies, there may be other areas that demand attention.

For example, assume that a large restaurant and nightclub has found that during its vital period it was serving mostly 18-to-25-year-olds with an average income of $8,000 per year. A study of existing trends reveals that the state legislature is attempting to raise the legal drinking age to 21; this is an unfavorable trend. In addition, research shows that during the coming five-year period, the economy is likely to fluctuate dramatically owing to the energy situation and international interdependence. The result of this would be periods of relatively high unemployement, particularly in the 18-to-25-year-old age category. This scenerio can be identified as a threat to the restaurant. One objective of the business, given the above scenerio, might read as follows:

> To increase our market penetration into the 26-to-35-year-old age category with an average income of $15,000 per year. This increase will be a minimum of 10 percent per year for the next five years.

Notice that this objective has the following characteristics:

○ It addresses the "what," not the "how"

○ It is quantified; a 10 percent increase per year in an identified specific market segment

○ It has a date; annually for five years

○ It is based upon a systematic approach which matches an internal weakness to an unfavorable existing trend that is in turn linked to an unfavorable future trend

Strategy selection. As a wise old man once said, "There may be many ways to skin a cat." Actually, much of the strategy selection is done when the various options are evaluated. However, it is worthwhile to consider each specific objective and rethink new means to accomplish each one. For example, an objective to improve employee turnover (concerning employee performance and attitude) could be accomplished with a paternal stance on the part of the company (additional benefits, profit sharing, and stock options) or with a competitive stance (high wages); or a profit objective may be accomplished with increased sales, or cost reduction.

Strategies are always broad courses of action. They operate on specific objectives and one strategy may have ramifications that affect several objectives. This is as it should be. The more simply the direction of the company/operation can be stated, the better the communication and implementation will be. To illustrate this, consider a strategy of a private club which wants to increase sales by installing a quality, price/value (but limited) wine list. This offering would satisfy various objectives: improved menu selection (innovation); limited inventory (reduce financial resources); increased profitability (greater sales); development of new revenue sources (market position); and increased productivity (more sales per employee if they are well trained in the product and are "sold" the tip incentives). A proven way to develop strategies is to write them down on a grid on which the eight classical objectives form the columns and alternative strategies form the rows. The more important strategies are those that address either the highest number of objectives or a single objective that is ignored by other strategies. Again, decisions must be made. Based on these decisions, the next planning step, documentation, is begun.

Task 5: Documentation

Determining the "how" in the planning process consists of putting an operations-oriented "road map" together which addresses each of the major objectives and strategies of the business. Each program should be written in such a manner that it addresses the following questions:

○ Why is this action program necessary? What objective is it designed to achieve? By which strategy?

○ What is the program? What are its measurable results and what are the performance measures that can be used to serve as control points?

○ Who has the primary responsibility for the program? Are there any support areas?

○ When will the program be implemented? When will it begin to show results? When is it expected to achieve the objective for which it is being designed? When are the review dates for checking whether or not it is on target?

○ How much will this program cost and what is the expected payoff? (The payoff should be quantified.) What is the downside risk in cost—i.e., what is the anticipated maximum amount this program could cost.

By requiring that each action program answer each of the above issues, management will be able to rank-order the programs. In addition, there will be no question as to which objective the program is addressing, who is accountable for its results, how it will be executed, and the costs and expected payoff of the plan. Only in this manner can management put together a well-directed road map which directly confronts the opportunities and threats the business faces. There will be no "pet projects," no wandering off in unguided directions, no unproductive conflict between departments or divisions with competing objectives. Every planned move will be directed toward the achievement of one goal—*gaining the competitive advantage.*

Often strategies, programs, and tactics will have supporting subprograms. This is not a problem. In the current and future environment of change, risk is best handled in bite-sized pieces. Therefore, it is not unusual for the results of this portion of the planning process to be a "cluster" of supporting programs.

Once this plan to get from today to tomorrow has been determined and agreed to by operating management, it must be communicated to those involved with its successful execution. They must agree to the plan and promise their efforts to bring about its achievement. These people not only include those directly responsible for implementation but also those who perform support and tracking functions. It is at this point that contingency plans and budgets are also set and agreed upon. The reporting system must be tightly in place so that if the need to move to a contingency plan arises, all involved will be immediately informed and it will be quickly implemented.

The final phase of documentation of the plan involves preparation of the budgets; necessarily, budgets involve detailed line-item forecasts that will provide the first flag of danger. Usually, budgets are prepared for a year in advance, but it is becoming more and more common to revise budgets on a quarterly basis. Such revisions can be used to direct management attention to specific operating concerns without holding it accountable for "numbers" forecast nine months ago. Items normally included in the budget are:

Marketing plan

○ Level of demand to be generated (customer counts, occupancy, etc.)

○ Pricing policy (discounts and increases)

○ Product changes (new menus, entertainment, upgrading, physical plant changes, etc.)

○ Advertising (timing and amount of expenditures, copy thrust, promotions, media plans)

○ Research needs

Income budget

○ Sales forecast (price × demand)

○ Operating expenses (variable costs associated with the sales forecast, identified as both an expected dollar amount and on a per-unit demand basis—i.e., per occupied room, per customer, or per sales dollar)

○ Overhead expenses (fixed costs)

○ Cash flow per period

Capital budget

○ Refurbishing estimates

○ Expansion plans

○ Changes/upgrading of the existing operation

○ Legal or safety requirements

Nonfinancial objectives

○ What will be done for each of Drucker's seven other key result areas? See p. 285.

Cost-reduction analysis

  ○ What can be done away with?

  ○ What can be automated or changed?

  ○ Where can costs be shared (in most companies, a dollar saved is worth at least $2 to $3 in new sales)?

Contingency plans

  ○ Short-term threats (gasoline supply shortages, recession pressures, union strikes, purveyor goes bankrupt, etc.)

  ○ Long-term threats (new competition, gasoline rationing, new highways being built, local crime and violence increases, legal drinking age raised, etc.)

Even armed with all the plans, books, and spreadsheets that will be used for the documentation process, success is not guaranteed. The plans must be monitored continually.

Task 6: Monitoring

Monitoring is the means of supervising the actions taken to attain the stated goals. It has two parts—*performance* and *assumptions.* Supervising performance is usually done by comparing actual results against the budget each month. Variances are analyzed and appropriate actions are taken. For multi-unit operations, this becomes a large task, because each level in the organization must be evaluated. Performance must also be compared against the assumptions on which the plan was built. It is not always enough to accomplish the objectives; the objectives themselves must be evaluated for reasonableness.

Monitoring systems are not complex, but must be completely thought out. Particularly perplexing is the fact that most control systems are myopic. They focus attention on short-term profit improvement and can jeopardize the long-term success of a business. Consider the restaurant that has achieved spectacular earnings growth mainly by raising prices. It is forced to continue to raise prices to show more growth on an ever-increasing base, until finally it finds a new competitor next door who has a price-value strategy. What happens? Our restaurant goes bankrupt!

The Other Half of Planning

Once a business has put together a plan for survival and growth, it is halfway there. The other part of this business partnership is *expert execution of the program and strategies.* Without proper implementation, the full benefit of proper planning cannot be realized. It is much more rewarding to manage when the company has well-thought-out goals that have been quantified and communicated to the implementers, and when the system by which management is keeping score of performance is open, fair, and tracked so that all key employees always know how they are doing.

Summary   American business history is full of examples of how proper planning, linked with effective execution, has paid off time and again for companies large and small. It is also full of examples of one-time giants such as W. T. Grant and Penn Central Railroads which, partly because of the lack of a good planning process, have had to file bankruptcy.

Strategic planning does not guarantee that a business will grow and prosper. However, it does significantly increase the odds of success. Most industry executives will argue that for the best-run companies, planning must be an integral part of the management process.

Notes   1. Benjamin B. Tregoe and John W. Zimmerman, "Strategic Thinking: Key to Corporate Survival," *Management Review,* Februry 1979, p. 9.

2. Peter F. Drucker, *Management: Tasks, Responsibilities, Practices* (New York: Harper & Row, 1974), p. 100.

3. Murray L. Weidenbaum, *The Future of Business Regulation, Private Action and Public Demand* (New York: AMACOM, 1979), p. 33.

4. Maurice J. Mascarenhas, "Strategic Planning, the Imperative for Survival," *The New Agriculture,* Winter, 1976, p. 35.

5. James K. Brown, *This Business of Issues: Coping With the Company's Environments* (New York: The Conference Board, Inc., 1979), p. 11.

General References

Planning Executives Institute, "Managerial Planning," Vol. 28, November/December 1979, Oxford, Ohio.

Nicolas S. Majluf, "Towards the Formalization of Strategic Planning: A Conceptual Framework," Sloan School of Management Technical Report 7, Boston, December 1978.

Appendix A:
An Exercise in Collective
Bargaining Simulation for the
Hospitality Industry

This exercise is designed to help you learn about union–management relations by giving you an opportunity to be a participant in a simulated renegotiation of an actual contract between a large hotel and the union representing its employees.

Knowledge about unions and skill in dealing with them is essential, since the impact of organized labor upon the wages and working conditions of the hotel and restaurant industry is both substantial and complex.

Where employees are *not* unionized, a variety of management practices may affect the potential attraction a union may have for employees. Where employees *are* unionized, many management decisions are subject to the terms specified in the labor contract. This means that if you work in a hotel or restaurant where employees belong to a union, management cannot act unilaterally insofar as wages and working conditions are concerned. It must consult the contract and perhaps the union first.

In essence, collective bargaining—the process of negotiation, administering, and interpreting an agreement between the parties—means that management and union representatives sit down at a table and discuss, deliberate, argue, persuade, bargain, haggle, and try to influence each other regarding the items they wish to include in a contract. By law, they must bargain in good faith. That is to say, they must meet, continue to meet, offer proposals and counterproposals, and try to reach agreement. Their eventual agreement is then written up as a contract to which all parties affix their signatures.

Generally speaking, most collective bargaining contracts are negotiated by a single company and a single union. However, in the larger cities of the United States, multi-employer bargaining is common in the hotel and restaurant business. For the employers, this has the advantage of reducing competition from other establishments by limiting the advantages they might achieve in separate negotiations with the union—for example, lower wages for banquet personnel enabling competitors to offer lower food and beverage prices to convention groups. For the unions, it is more efficient to bargain with several large employers at once, since it helps to create stability in the labor-market area and to set a pattern for smaller establishments to follow.

In this exercise, the instructor will assign each student to either a union team or a management team, and will designate a chairperson for each team. The chairperson in turn will assign to each team member the duties and/or role to be performed during negotiations. Management and union teams will negotiate an agreement.

To facilitate this process, research will be conducted by both sides to gain information about other industry agreements—both inside and outside the hotel and restaurant industry; current industry trends as reflected in the annual reports of Pannell, Kerr Forster & Co., and Laventhol & Horwath; cost-of-living data as reflected in the Consumer Price Index of the U.S. Department of Labor; and such other background data as may be deemed desirable.

At your initial bargaining session, management and union proposals are exchanged. Each side may ask the other to explain or clarify its proposals in order to determine how important they might be to the proposing side or how well thought out or defensible they might be.

Neither team wants the other to know how far it will ultimately go to reach an agreement or how important each item of its proposal may really be. Thus, some proposals may be viewed as desirable but not critical; some may be merely for trading purposes; while still others are absolute "musts."

As negotiations proceed, proposals are accepted, amended, or withdrawn. Counterproposals are made, and ultimately compromises are reached. Generally, the easiest-to-bargain issues are disposed of in the beginning, whereas the more important issues usually are taken up last. If, as sometimes happens, one party makes a demand that is so far "out of the ballpark" that the other party cannot even come close to finding an acceptable compromise, an impasse or deadlock may result. If this should occur during classroom bargaining, the instructor will act as mediator and endeavor to assist the parties by offering alternative suggestions or proposals. In rare and unusual instances, the teacher may function as an arbitrator by actually deciding the dispute after hearing both sides.

In the end, the parties reach agreement on the terms of the new contract and present their jointly signed statements of their respective agreements to the instructor for analysis and subsequent feedback to the class.

Although this classroom exercise may at times—just as in real life—be bewildering, confusing, frustrating, or irritating, it nonetheless yields a vivid appreciation, understanding, and grasp of all the basic steps involved in the collective bargaining process. Within the brief time span of three class periods of approximately two hours each, each participant will have gone through the same "close encounters" that exist in "real-world" negotiations.

Thus, the following pages describe the mechanics of collective bargaining simulation so that all participants will have an equal opportunity to learn how to negotiate the renewal and revision of an existing contract with the Hotel Employees & Restaurant Employees International Union, AFL-CIO.

As outlined in the pages immediately following, it is important to follow a certain sequence of steps in preparation for this exercise:

Steps to be Followed in the Classroom Simulation

1. In the initial class session, the instructor will distribute team lists showing organization of the entire class divided into management teams and union teams, each with a chairperson designated by the instructor (see *Exhibit 1*). As a general rule, this simulation functions best if there are no more than four members of each team seated across the table from one another.

2. Before the opening bargaining session (i.e., the *second* class session of the exercise), it is important that every member of the class become familiar with this material. To this end, a checklist of steps as shown in *Exhibit 2* has been included to help you sharpen the focus on what you must do in order to be successful in this undertaking. Do not underestimate the value of *early* preparation. There is no substitute for conscientious *advance* planning of your bargaining proposals, the arguments and counterarguments likely to be most effective, and the strategy that you will follow in presenting or defending your case.

3. The *second class meeting* is the opening session of actual negotiations. As the checklist of items in *Exhibit 2* indicates, this is the first encounter with your opponents. It is preceded by your having prepared and handed to the instructor at the beginning of this session your team's demands, ranked in their order of importance. As shown in *Exhibits 3A and 3B,* this document also indicates to your instructor what your team realistically expects to settle for at the conclusion of negotiations.

Depending on whether yours is a management team or a union team, you have also prepared in advance your list of demands, as shown in *Exhibit 4,* for presentation to the other side. The question as to which team gets to present its demands first is always settled by negotiation at the beginning of this session.

The presentation of your team's demands affords an ideal opportunity to explain, clarify, and advocate persuasively all of your proposals. Some find it advantageous at this beginning stage to introduce evidence in support of their side, without necessarily disclosing all of their "fire power" until the opponents have been heard.

When each team has completed its opening presentation, it will then need to hold a caucus in order to react to its opponent's proposals. Meeting separately to assess one another's strengths and weaknesses, all teams attempt to rank the relative importance of opponents' demands and to identify the principal differences in positions, noting points of narrow difference or overlap as well as those of wide divergence.

4. Actual negotiations begin only *after* your team has had ample opportunity to "get its ducks in line." Your plan of attack encompasses all the arguments, trading points, and potential compromises your team visualizes as being worthwhile.

In the process of planning the course of your negotiations it is necessary to observe certain *ground rules*. These are set forth in the next section.

5. Generally, negotiations are already underway by the end of the second class session. In any event, the opening of the *third class session* calls for heavy reliance upon all of your bargaining techniques and strategy, since this is the session at which the parties are expected to reach agreement on the terms of a new contract.

In considering the *strategies* that are to be employed in these negotiations, it is always useful to bear in mind at least two of the typical approaches in which negotiators frequently become involved. One is the so-called *piecemeal approach*. With this approach, negotiators try to settle the issues one by one, such as the easiest ones first; or the list of union demands in chronological order; or the list of management demands in chronological order. Each item is dealt with as a separate issue, argued out, disposed of, and filed away while attention is turned to the next item.

The second strategy is the reverse of the *piecemeal* approach. This is the *total approach*. It regards nothing as settled until everything is settled. Trading points are offered and discussed, and then laid aside as others are brought forward. Every issue remains open until the right psychological moment when the whole picture comes into focus and the parties are ready to accept a total agreement. This latter strategy is frequently the one pursued by management people because they are accustomed to thinking in terms of total costs of the whole package, and

therefore they do not wish to get "trapped" into agreeing to any one proposal until the costs of all the other proposals have been carefully weighed.

Obviously, neither strategy by itself is a sure-fire formula for success. Most negotiators employ something of each in their search for a compromise of the issues. Not infrequently, after each side has felt out the other and found out just which demands have been included for trading purposes and which are really vital to a final settlement, forward movement is initiated with the "easy-to-hard" items approach until a residue of just a few unresolved issues remains. In the end, these are shuffled, reshuffled, and reworked until just the right mix is achieved.

When this occurs, usually near the end of the *third class session,* a fair amount of spirited trading takes place, leading to a final resolution of all outstanding issues and ultimately to a contract, the principal terms of which are jointly signed by the chairperson of each team (see *Exhibit 5* for information to be reflected in this document).

6. The fourth and *final class session* entails an evaluation of the entire simulation exercise, first by the instructor and then by the participants.

Customarily the instructor leads off with feedback from all of the participants based upon his or her analysis of each team's demands, expectations, and the terms of each final settlement. This is the opportunity to make observations about bargaining strategy, tradeoffs and compromises, and the relative successes or failures of the collective bargaining process.

For their part, student participants will feed back their reactions concerning the realism—or lack thereof—of this exercise as an experiential, skill-building approach to collective bargaining. In addition, students will have the opportunity to discuss their individual bargaining strategies and to venture opinions as to why some teams may have taken a beating while others were phenomenally successful in accomplishing their objectives.

1. No team is to consult with ANY other team, either union or management, during the course of this exercise. **Ground Rules for**

2. All demands must evolve from within the framework of the Hotel **Collective** Scenario (including the individual profiles of the participants). Within **Bargaining** this general framework, however, members of the teams are urged to use **Simulation** their imagination in composing their demands.

3. For the purpose of these negotiations, the number of demands each team may make shall be limited to *not more than six.* (Wages, for example, may be regarded as *one* demand.)

4. The parties are not at liberty to extend the contract. The contract deadline for these negotiations will be the close of the third class session. At that time, there will either be agreement between the parties on the

terms of a new contract or there will be a deadlock which neither the parties' nor the instructor's mediation efforts have been able to resolve. (The latter situation seldom occurs.)

The Hotel
Scenario

The Caledonian Hotel is a 1200-room property in the Detroit area. It is one of the best-known older hotels, and is favored by many of its commercial guests both because of its accessible location and its exceptionally well-liked and able general manager. As the operating figures suggest, occupancy has been declining for the past several years, while the average room rate paid by the guests has been creeping up.

The owners have authorized the expenditures of several million dollars in recent years to upgrade the physical appearance of this aging hotel and they now find it difficult to understand why their investment is not yielding better financial results. Up until now, the company has always gone along with its local management on union contract settlements, even though some of those settlements have been quite costly. Now, however, the situation is one of "belt-tightning" as far as the company is concerned, because all of the current economic indicators generally suggest a period of declining business, and this in turn will have an adverse impact on hotels.

The union senses that the hotel management is now being forced to operate with a sharper pencil than ever before, and so it is becoming more sensitive to its rights under the contract by filing grievances more often than in the past. The hotel's attempt to lay off senior employees and to hire less expensive part-time employees in such categories as maids, waiters and waitresses, and dishwashers is being firmly resisted.

On economic issues of wages, holidays, vacations, and other fringe benefits, the union is firm in its assertion that the hotel industry generally, and specifically in Detroit, lags behind other American industries, and it is determined in these upcoming negotiations to narrow the gap substantially, if not to close it. Hotel workers live in the same neighborhoods as workers from other industries, and comparison of their respective straight-time hourly earnings confirms the union's claim of economic lag in the hotel industry.

On the other hand, this hotel argues—as do competitor hotels—that hotel wages and working conditions have never been and, in all probability, can never be equal to those of manufacturing industries. There is, therefore, a clear mandate from the owners of the hotel to the local management to resist any such comparisons during the upcoming negotiations and to heed a stringent reminder that "this year we simply cannot afford to increase our wage costs any more." Whether or not the owners mean to say that they will take a strike rather than submit to any kind of a union wage increase, however modest, remains to be seen. But to paraphrase the local manager, the owners have said, in substance, "Don't give them anything, and make it retroactive!"

Management Team

1. *Vice president of human resources*—In this role, you are concerned with *people*. You are normally responsible for the needs of employees, their selection, placement, training, development, rewards, and protection. You bargain with them collectively about wages and working conditions, wherever such matters are covered by union contract. Even though you are a member of management, and therefore must keep your eye on the "bottom line," your position is nonetheless a difficult one because of your sensitivity to both sides wherever labor relations are concerned.

2. *General manager of the hotel*—As this person, you are responsible for the entire operation of the 1200-room Caledonian Hotel. You have been the manager for the past five years and are increasingly concerned about costs and profits. On the one hand, you have had to spend huge sums to refurbish the guest rooms and public spaces at a time when competition has been very keen and occupancy declining. On the other hand, the company owners believe that you should be producing a greater profit because of capital outlays, and that now is not the time to spend a lot of money in raising wages and increasing the cost of fringe benefits for employees.

No matter what happens, you are in a difficult position. If the union goes on strike, your sales and profits are in jeopardy. If you settle for an increased payroll cost which the union demands will necessitate, then your profits will decline unless either sales or employee productivity is sharply increased. And you are not optimistic about either of the latter events coming to pass.

Furthermore, your own job may be at stake if your company gets the impression that you are unable to cope with the myriad problems, including labor problems, that are associated with the job of being general manager of a hotel.

3. *Comptroller of the hotel*—If you play this role, you will be the person who deals with the figures. Cost is usually a major factor in almost all issues of negotiation—so your analysis of the cost of any proposed increases in wages and/or benefits is crucial, as are your recommendations for any management counterproposals that might be attractive to the union and yet be less costly for the hotel company. You were originally hired as the hotel auditor, being responsible for the daily, monthly, and annual financial statements, as well as for the system of internal controls governing hotel revenue and expenses, as required by the Uniform System of Accounts.

As the hotel grew, your staff gradually enlarged to the point where the company promoted you to be comptroller and you in turn promoted your assistant auditor to take your job as hotel auditor. As union demands are received and company counterproposals are debated, your services are much in demand. The general manager wants to know how much the union demand package costs, as well as the cost of alternative counterproposals. Also, he or she may want to know the answer to such questions as:

a. How much per year does each cent-per-hour increase cost the company?
b. How much per year will it cost the company if its payroll is increased by 1 percent, 2 percent, etc.? Since costs are an obvious concern to you as comptroller, you will want to be prepared to investigate and recommend the best cost approach to any wage and/or fringe benefit package to be offered by the company.

4. *Personnel director*—You are responsible for recruitment, training, wage and salary administration, labor contract administration, grievance handling, and other miscellaneous employee-relations duties. Your day-to-day contacts with union representatives are generally productive, and thus far you've always been able to settle grievances before they reached the arbitration stage. Whenever preparations for negotiation of new contract are undertaken you are expected to advise the management team about such matters as:

a. The Consumer Price Index
b. Current and prospective labor market conditions
c. Wages currently being paid by other hotels in your area for key union occupations (for example: maids, bartenders, bellmen, cooks, waiters and waitresses, etc.)
d. The pattern of recent HRE union contract settlements in your city, state, or region
e. Special problems related to health and welfare programs and pension programs—their costs and their benefits

Union Team

1. *President of the local union*—You are the one who unionized Detroit Hotels some years ago, following union organization of the auto industry. You are regarded as a respected veteran of the labor movement, and as an indefatigable fighter for the members of the HRE union. Some of the younger members of your union feel that because of your advancing age you tend to side with the interests of the older members (seniority, pensions, resistance to mandatory retirement, etc.), where they would prefer to see you fighting a bit harder for more cash in the pay envelope and bigger hospital and medical insurance benefits to help them pay for the family medical expenses. No one, however, doubts your sincerity and devotion to the union cause, nor is anyone a more eloquent spokesperson for it than you are.

2. *Vice president of the local union*—You were an active union member and hotel bartender before going into the military service. Upon completion of that service, you returned and shortly thereafter were

elected to the office of union vice president. Under the terms of the G. I. Bill you have been enabled to take all the union–management relations courses offered in the evening division of the local community college, thus raising the level of your contract negotiation skills somewhat above that of your fellow union members.

Because of your relative youth, the younger members of the local look to you for support in their concerns for higher wages, better medical benefits, and mandatory retirements so as to open up promotional opportunities for those whose advancement would otherwise be stymied until the senior employees die or become incapacitated by old age.

3. *Secretary-treasurer of the local union*—You are one of the original organizers of the union. You have been a union leader ever since, serving for some years as business agent and more recently as secretary-treasurer, a position into which you were promoted following a mild heart attack. You are aware of the growing dissension. You know that the union president is on the side of the older workers who fear loss of their jobs to younger, more promotable, and more easily trained younger workers. Also, you know of the union vice president's sympathy for the younger workers' concern for higher wages and faster promotion. In spite of the pressure from both sides and the inevitable tensions which your heart specialist says you must avoid, you are trying to remain as objective as possible. You are mature and are experienced in negotiations. When it comes to analyzing the financial advantages and disadvantages of various package proposals, you have a keen eye for what will sell and what will not sell. Also, you are a careful guardian of union funds, having in mind that there must be enough money in the treasury to support a strike, should one ever become necessary. Your relationships with cooperating unions are friendly enough so that their financial support can be counted upon if your local should ever get involved in a long, drawn-out strike.

4. *International union representative*—You are the person who provides the link between the International Union, whose headquarters are at Cincinnati, and the local. You will present information showing what your International union has successfully negotiated with hotel companies in other cities, and in the event of a serious deadlock in negotiations, will recommend to the general president of the International whether or not the International should support the local by sanctioning strike action and making strike funds available. In addition, your leadership qualities may be put to the test whenever local union officers find it difficult, if not impossible, to control some of the more militant union members whose behavior threatens to jeopardize the outcome of what otherwise promises to be successful contract negotiations.

In a word, you are looked upon by both sides as a statesman of the labor movement, with the heavy responsibility for championing a point of view that ultimately will benefit hotel employers as well as hotel employees.

Hotel financial statement for five years immediately preceding these negotiations

	1978	1979	1980	1981	1982
Room revenue	2,900.0	3,100.0	2,850.0	2,625.0	2,490.0
Food revenue	2,000.0	2,140.0	2,000.0	1,900.0	1,800.0
Beverage revenue	950.0	990.0	750.0	700.0	685.0
Other revenue	---	---	---	---	---
Total Revenues	5,850.0	6,230.0	5,600.0	5,225.0	4,975.0
Hotel cash payroll	2,600.0	2,750.0	2,600.0	2,530.0	2,225.0
% cash payroll to rev.	44.4	44.1	46.4	48.4	44.7
Employee benefits	570.0	655.0	600.0	590.0	590.0
% benefits to rev.	9.7	10.5	10.7	11.2	11.8
Room occupancy %	48.0	51.0	46.0	41.0	40.0
Av. rate per occ. room	16.25	17.00	18.00	18.15	18.25
Net profit before fed. tax	590.0	570.0	400.0	225.0	205.0

Note: All revenue figures shown above are expressed in thousands of dollars. Thus, for example, total revenues for the last column above should be read as $4,975,000.
Number of hotel employees: 750
Food cost was 38% for the year shown in the last column above

Exhibits

Exhibit 1

Roster of Management Teams	Roster of Union Teams
Team 1	Team 1
Name of student, chairperson	Name of student, chairperson
Name of student	Name of student
Name of student	Name of student
Name of student	Name of student
Team 2	Team 2
(Continue as shown above)	(Continue as shown above)

Note: Each team should have no more than four members, so that when they are seated at the bargaining table it will be comfortable for teams to face each other from opposite sides of the table.

Exhibit 2 Collective Bargaining Checklist

1. *Distribution in class of team assignment lists with designations of chairpersons*
    A. Instructor will review entire simulation process; distribute a *timetable* showing dates, time, and location of future negotiating sessions; and generally make sure that the procedure for this exercise is clear to all participants

2. *Preparation for negotiations*
    A. Teams to read this entire section for collective bargaining simulation

B. Team members to familiarize themselves with the scenario— and to sharpen the focus on issues and problems which they wish to negotiate about

C. In addition, all teams must

Develop bargaining proposals and positions

Do library research on average hourly earnings of hotel workers compared to other industries

Develop arguments and counterarguments

Develop strategy

Meet separately both in class and outside of class; number of meetings will depend upon the number of issues team wishes to negotiate and upon the diligence of the team members

3. *Opening bargaining session*
   A. Teams to present ranked demands to instructor (Exhibit 3)
   B. Teams to present initial demands to opponents (Exhibit 4) with brief verbal arguments for support
   C. The chairperson will

   Introduce team members

   See that ground rules are adhered to

   Serve as moderator for the team (call on members of committee to present demands in their area of responsibility)

4. *Strategy meeting*
   A. Teams meet separately—*outside of class*—to react to opponents initial presentations and

   Discuss weaknesses in own position or preparation

   Discuss opponents positions

   Attempt to discover opponent's weaknesses

   Attempt to rank importance of opponent's demands

   Attempt to predict major sources of differences, minor sources, overlap of positions
   B. Use information to plan strategy (arguments, compromises, tradeoffs, etc.)

5. *Bargaining sessions*
   A. Negotiate demands
   B. Caucus when team is split on an issue or not sure what decision to make
   C. Negotiations to be concluded at time set by instructor

6. *Evaluation session*
   A. Summarize changes that are to be included in the new contract
   B. If impasse occurred, parties to discuss why they think settlement was not reached
   C. Discuss strategy employed and problems encountered
   D. Discuss value of collective bargaining simulation and ways in which it can be improved the next time

Exhibit 3A   Initial demands made by the management team*

Team number _____

Rank order of importance to team	Initial demands	Expectations as to what team will finally settle for at the conclusion of negotiations

*Note: To be presented *only* to instructor at the beginning of the first bargaining session.

Exhibit 3B   Initial demands made by the union team*

Team number _____

Rank order of importance to team	Initial demands	Expectations as to what team will finally settle for at the conclusion of negotiations

*Note: To be presented *only* to instructor at the beginning of the first bargaining session.

Exhibit 4   Initial demands as presented to opponents*

(List changes desired in present contract and any *new* demands additional to contract changes)

Team number _____   Check one:
                                      Management _____
                                      Union   _____

Article # and section # of present contract	Contract changes desired, and any new items to be included

*Note: To be presented to opponents at the first bargaining session.

Exhibit 5 Summary of New Contract Terms*

Team number _____   Signatures:

_____

Management team chairperson

_____

Union team chairperson

Previous contract clause (Identify by article number and section number)	New contract clause corresponding to that shown in left-hand column. If there was no prior contract provision for the item or items shown below, write the word "None" in the appropriate space in the left-hand column.

*Note: To be presented to instructor at conclusion of negotiations.

Appendix B: Contract Between the Detroit Hotel Association and Local #24, Hotel, Motel, Restaurant Employees, Cooks and Bartenders Union, AFL–CIO

AGREEMENT

This Agreement is made and entered into by and between the following Hotels:

Hotel St. Regis
Hyatt Regency-Dearborn
Northfield Hilton
Somerset Inn

(hereinafter referred to as the EMPLOYERS and HOTELS) acting by and through the HOTEL ASSOCIATION OF GREATER DETROIT (hereinafter referred to as the ASSOCIATION) and the HOTEL, MOTEL, RESTAURANT EMPLOYEES, COOKS AND BARTENDERS UNION, LOCAL 24, OF THE HOTEL EMPLOYEES AND RESTAURANT EMPLOYEES INTERNATIONAL UNION, AFL-CIO (hereinafter referred to as the UNION).

WITNESSETH

In consideration of the mutual promises and covenants expressly stated herein, the parties agree as follows:

ARTICLE 1
Recognition — Union Membership
Employee Hiring — Check-Off

Section 1. Union Recognition

The EMPLOYERS recognize the UNION as the sole and exclusive bargaining representatives of employees in a unit composed of the classifications referred to in the schedules of this Agreement.

The term "employee" shall cover all employees in the classifications listed on and covered by Schedules A, B, C, D, E, and F attached. Managerial, supervisors,

confidential employees, guards and all security personnel as defined by the Federal Labor Laws are excluded from this Agreement.

Section 2. Union Membership

(a) The EMPLOYER agrees that it is a condition of employment that all employees of EMPLOYERS covered by this Agreement who are members of the UNION in good standing on the date of the execution hereof, shall remain members in good standing, and that all employees of the EMPLOYERS covered by this Agreement who are not members of the UNION on the date of the execution hereof shall, on the 31st day following the effective date of this Agreement, become and remain members in good standing of the UNION.

(b) All new employees covered by this Agreement shall become and remain members in good standing of the UNION on the 31st day following the date of their employment.

(c) In the event any employee fails to tender his/her membership dues, initiation or reinstatement fees in accordance with the foregoing subsections, the EMPLOYER agrees, upon written notification by the UNION, to discharge said employee, within five (5) calendar days from the date of the receipt of such notification. The UNION shall send said notice to the EMPLOYER by certified mail.

Section 3. Employee Hiring

In order to facilitate the employment of necessary employees, to assure qualified personnel of an efficient system of locating employment and to insure the EMPLOYERS of a regular source of available employees, the UNION agrees to operate a job referral system in a non-discriminatory manner for employees within its jurisdiction. All persons who are referred to EMPLOYERS by the UNION shall be identified by job referral slips issued by the UNION and delivered to the EMPLOYERS by the individual being referred, except as hereinafter provided.

It is understood and agreed by the UNION that the operation of this job referral system shall be on a non-discriminatory basis and according to the following terms, conditions and standards:

(a) It is agreed that the EMPLOYERS shall have the right to reject any job applicant referred by the UNION. In the event any applicant is rejected, the EMPLOYER shall request that additional applicants be furnished by the UNION from its job referral system.

(b) When this job referral system fails to supply qualified workers to an EMPLOYER within forty-eight (48) hours after a request is made or on demand for employees, the EMPLOYER may hire new employees from any other source. The EMPLOYER shall notify the UNION of the name, address, social security number and date of employment of such new employees within five (5) days after date of hiring.

(c) The UNION shall establish and maintain appropriate registrations for qualified applicants available for employment in the established job classifications, and the conduct of this activity by the UNION shall be in accordance with the application of the above terms, conditions and provisions.

(d) The UNION agrees to permit newly hired non-UNION employees to become members of the UNION upon making application for membership and the payment of the customary initiation fees and regular dues.

(e) The EMPLOYERS and the UNION agree that all employees shall be hired based upon their job related qualifications and without discrimination as to any of the protected groups or categories established by local, Michigan or Federal Equal

Employment Opportunity Laws, as well as Employee Relations and Immigration Laws.

(f) This non-discriminatory policy shall apply to all employment policies, practices and procedures, including, but not specifically limited to, hiring, upgrading, demotion, transfer, recruitment, rates of pay and selection for training.

Section 4. Check-Off

The EMPLOYER shall deduct from the pay of each employee dues, initiation and/or reinstatement fees established by the UNION in accordance with its Constitution and By-Laws. No such sums shall be deducted from employee's wages until the employee has voluntarily signed a card authorizing such deductions. Such assignment shall be irrevocable for a period of one (1) year, or the termination of this Agreement, whichever first occurs. If notice of revocation is not given prior to the end of such period, the authorization shall be automatically renewed for successive periods of one year thereafter, with the same privilege of revocation at the end of each such period. Deductions shall be made from the first payroll period of each month and transmitted to the UNION within fourteen (14) days thereafter, with forms, supplied by the UNION, showing the name, social security number, job classification and amount of deductions of each employee. The Employer agrees to add to such check-off the names, addresses, social security numbers, job classifications and dates of hire of all newly hired employees who have completed thirty (30) days of employment.

ARTICLE 2
Union Rights

Section 5. Union Representatives

Authorized representatives of the UNION shall be permitted to visit the premises of the EMPLOYERS at all reasonable hours for the purpose of transacting UNION business. They shall, upon entry of the premises, notify the Manager or his/her designee of their presence. Representatives of the UNION shall not interfere with the operations of the EMPLOYERS while transacting such UNION business.

Section 6. Union Stewards

Regular shop or department stewards shall be allowed reasonable time off from work, without loss of pay, in handling and adjusting grievances on the premises of the EMPLOYERS which arise in their own departments. Grievances of an emergency nature may be handled during working time and any steward leaving his work to handle such a grievance shall first obtain permission from his supervisor. The EMPLOYER agrees that there will be no discrimination against an employee because he is carrying out the duties of Shop Steward. Shop Stewards may handle grievances in departments other than their own if the grievance is of an emergency nature and the department steward is not available.

Section 7. Union Meeting

UNION officers and stewards shall be excused to attend UNION meetings, without pay, upon reasonable notice to the EMPLOYER.

Section 8. Union Conventions

Duly elected delegates to UNION conventions or assemblies shall be excused from work, without pay, for the purpose of attending such conventions or assemblies without any loss of rights or privileges upon reasonable notification to the EMPLOYER. Time off for local conventions shall not exceed seven (7) calendar days, and time off for international conventions shall not exceed fifteen (15) calendar days.

Section 9. Payroll Books and Records

Payroll books and records of the EMPLOYER shall be made available to the UNION on written request to enable the UNION to administer this Agreement. When the purpose of the demand is stated in writing, the records shall be provided within a reasonable period of time after receipt of the written demand.

Section 10. Employer Notification

The UNION shall notify each EMPLOYER in writing of their current authorized UNION representative and UNION stewards; provided, however, that the UNION shall notify the EMPLOYER of any changes in such personnel within five (5) calendar days of said change. Said notification shall be sent by certified mail.

ARTICLE 3

Management Rights

Section 11.

The EMPLOYERS shall remain vested with full and exclusive control and direction of the management and operation of the Hotel and its employees. By way of illustration, each EMPLOYER retains the sole right:

(a) to direct the work force and to determine the policies and methods of operating its business, except as expressly limited by the specific provisions of this Agreement;

(b) to decide the number and type of machines, equipment, material, products and supplies to be used or operated;

(c) to determine the extent to which the Hotel and/or its equipment, and the various departments/rooms, and sub-departments/rooms thereof, shall be operated, expanded, reduced, shut down, discontinued, merged, liquidated, or relocated;

herein. This Agreement embodies all the restrictions on management rights.

ARTICLE 4

Work Week – Hours of Work – Designation of 6th and 7th Days – Reporting for Work – Definitions of Steady Employees and Extra Employees

Section 16. Supervisory and Excluded Personnel

Supervisory or excluded employees as defined by Federal Labor Law shall not perform the work of bargaining unit employees, except during relief periods, absenteeism, sickness, rush periods and emergency situations.

Section 17. Work Day – Work Week

Eight (8) hours of work shall constitute a work day and five (5) days of work in the established payroll week of an EMPLOYER shall constitute a work week, except as it applies to banquet servers.

Section 18. Overtime

Time and one-half shall be paid for all hours worked in excess of eight (8) hours in any one day and for all hours worked in excess of forty (40) hours in an EMPLOYER'S work week. There shall be no pyramiding of overtime, and overtime hours paid on a daily basis shall not be included in paying overtime on a weekly basis. The provisions of this section shall not apply to banquet servers.

Section 19. Designated Sixth-Seventh Day.

An EMPLOYER shall designate one day in its payroll week as the designated 6th day, and one day as the designated 7th day of each steady employee. An EMPLOYER shall have the right to designate any day in its payroll week as the designated 6th day and any

(d) to decide the amount of supervision and direction of the working force;

(e) to be the sole and final judge of the qualifications of all applicants, with the absolute right to select and determine the employees it will hire;

(f) to determine staffing levels for a department/room;

(g) to establish or revise work schedules;

(h) to introduce new, different, or improved methods and procedures in its operations, and to otherwise generally manage the business.

Section 12.

Each EMPLOYER further retains the right to suspend, promote, demote, transfer, discipline, release, layoff, and discharge employees, provided the exercise of this right will not discipline unjustly or discharge employees subject to other applicable provisions of this Agreement.

Section 13.

It is agreed that each EMPLOYER has the right to make such rules and regulations, not in conflict with this Agreement, as it may from time to time deem best for the purpose of maintaining order, safety, and/or effective and efficient operation of the Hotel, and/or the individual departments thereof.

Section 14.

An EMPLOYER not exercising any function hereby reserved to it, or exercising any such function in a particular way, shall not be deemed a waiver of the right to exercise such function or preclude it from exercising the same in some other way not in conflict with the express provisions of this Agreement.

Section 15.

All economic and non-economic items that have been considered have been resolved and are contained

319

day as the designated 7th day of each steady employee. An EMPLOYER shall be required to designate two (2) consecutive days as the designated 6th and 7th day of a steady employee. An EMPLOYER shall not change the work schedules of employees, except as permitted in Section 15, to circumvent the payment of overtime, or to interfere with the rights of seniority station assignments and days off. When a change is made which has this effect, overtime shall be paid. If an employee shall be requested to work either the 6th or 7th day, which will result in the employee's working six (6) days in the work week, he shall be paid time and one-half for said day, whether said 6th day of work occurs on the designated 6th or 7th day of the employee's work week.

Section 20. Non-Consecutive Days

Notwithstanding the above provisions of this Article, and only at the request of an employee, the EMPLOYER may make the 6th and 7th days of the employee's scheduled work week non-consecutive.

Section 21. Change of Sixth and Seventh Day

An EMPLOYER shall have the right, once every thirty (30) days, upon giving seven (7) days notice, to change the work schedules and/or the designation of the designated 6th or 7th days of an employee, and designate any other days in its payroll week as the designated 6th and 7th days of an employee. Schedule changes can be made on less than seven (7) days notice and/or more often than every thirty (30) days only when necessary for unforeseen circumstances, with prior notice to the Union.

Section 22. Overtime Pay

All work performed on the employee's 6th consecutive day shall be paid for at the rate of one and one-half times his regular hourly rate of pay. All work performed on the employee's 7th consecutive day shall be paid at the double rate of hourly pay. If an

employee is absent from work during his regular schedule of hours, the employee must make up such lost time at his straight time hourly rate of pay before receiving premium pay for either the 6th or 7th consecutive day of work. Steady and steady-extra banquet servers shall be compensated only at the rates of pay specified in Schedule E.

Section 23. Work Schedules

All work schedules for steady employees shall be posted one (1) week in advance. Whenever reasonably possible, an EMPLOYER shall establish work schedules so as to afford employees a choice of work schedules in the same job classification on a seniority basis, subject to the provisions of Section 70.

Section 24. Report-In Pay

(a) Steady employees, steady-extra employees, and extra employees reporting for work on any day shall be paid for four (4) hours work, even if no work is performed. Said employees shall be paid in full for that day if they perform any work, but are sent home early due to shortage of work. This provision shall not apply in any case of extreme emergency in any department of any Hotel, extreme emergency being defined as fire, tornado, flood, hurricane, riot, civil commotion, or Acts of God. Employees shall, however, when reporting during any such emergency, be paid for all hours actually worked and in no case less than one-half of their regular rate of pay for said day.

(b) If the EMPLOYER schedules a mandatory meeting, employees shall be required to attend. Those employees who are attending on their day off shall be paid four (4) hours pay, at their straight time hourly rate, or the established minimum wage, whichever is greater. In the event the meeting exceeds four (4) hours, the employees will be paid as above for the duration of the meeting. Those employees who are either required to report earlier or remain later than their normally scheduled shift shall be paid for that portion of time not within their normally scheduled shift at their straight time hourly rate, or the established minimum wage, whichever is greater. Attendance at non-mandatory meetings on the employee's day off shall be on a voluntary basis only, and without pay.

Section 25. Overtime Work

Employees shall work overtime only when requested to do so by their supervisors, and not otherwise; provided, however, steady employees shall not be required to work their respective designated 6th or 7th days of work, nor more than eight (8) hours in any one (1) day, unless a sufficient number of employees do not volunteer for the overtime and/or premium pay time required. In the event sufficient employees do not volunteer for the overtime and/or premium pay time required, the least senior employee working the job shall be required to work the overtime and/or premium pay time. This section shall not apply to or cover extra employees, or those exempt pursuant to Federal Law.

Section 26. Rotation of Overtime

When overtime is required within a specific job classification in a department, it shall be rotated, whenever reasonably possible, among the employees in such specific job classification within the department so that the overtime, so far as possible, may be shared among such employees.

Section 27. Steady Employee – Extra Employee – Steady-Extra Employee

A steady employee is defined as an employee who is hired as such and is normally scheduled to work four (4) days or more per week, or any other employee who works four (4) days or more per week for a period of sixteen (16) consecutive weeks and then requests to be designated a steady employee, provided, however, that this provision shall not be used to circumvent the hiring of steady employees where the work force would normally be composed of steady employees.

(a) An extra employee is defined as an employee who is hired as such and is normally scheduled to work less than four (4) days per week. Extra employees shall be paid at the extra scale of wages as listed on the wage schedules or $1.00 per day above the steady rate unless otherwise listed.

(b) A steady-extra employee is defined as an extra employee who is hired as such, has completed his/her probationary period, is on a list maintained by the EMPLOYER and whose first obligation is to work for the EMPLOYER in its operation in the Hotel. There shall be no specified weekly hours or set schedules for steady-extra employees. The EMPLOYER shall endeavor to notify steady-extras of their work schedules for the week by Thursday of the preceding week.

Section 28. Meal and Break Periods

All steady and extra employees working an 8-hour shift shall receive one meal, not to exceed one-half hour, and two 15-minute breaks within their scheduled eight (8) hours. Any steady and extra employees working a 4-hour or 6-hour shift shall receive one meal, not to exceed one-half hour. These meals and breaks will be scheduled by the EMPLOYER as business permits and at such times as not to interfere with the efficient operation of the Hotel. The station of any employee during his/her meal/break period will be covered by another employee whenever possible. If, during the meal/break period, it becomes necessary that the employee return to the work station, the employee shall return to take care of any service that is required or necessary.

ARTICLE 5
Wage Rates and Specific Working Conditions of Local 24

Section 29. Minimum Rates

The minimum rates of pay for the job classifications covered by this Agreement are set forth in the Schedules in the Appendix.

Section 30. Payment of Wages

Wages of steady employees shall be paid weekly. Steady banquet servers shall receive their checks from the payroll department of the EMPLOYER. All banquet servers (steady or extra) shall receive a voucher setting forth the amount of wages due them, together with the service charge due, and the date and name of the party or function for which they are being paid. The wages of all banquet extras shall be sent to the office of the Union and shall be paid by the EMPLOYER on its regular weekly payroll date covering the wages for the preceding week.

Section 31. Higher Rates

The wage rates set forth on the attached wage schedules shall be considered as minimum rates only and this Agreement shall not interfere with the right of employees to receive higher wages for superior knowledge, ability, merit or any other reason. The non-listing of a job classification on the wage schedules shall not preclude the UNION from representing any employees properly coming within the jurisdiction of the UNION. Any employee now receiving wages higher than the contract minimum rate for his job classification shall have such differential maintained during the life of this Agreement, as long as he occupies the same job classification.

Section 32. Job Classifications

The listing of job classifications in the wage schedules

in the Appendix shall not be construed to mean that EMPLOYERS must hire employees in all such job classifications. Provided, furthermore, if such classifications are filled, EMPLOYERS are under no obligation to insure they are always thereafter filled. However, when employees are hired by EMPLOYERS in any of these job classifications, such employees shall be paid at the rate scheduled for the specific job classification.

Section 33. Benefits and Privileges

The purpose of this Agreement shall be to achieve mutual understanding, harmony and cooperation between the UNION and the EMPLOYER and its employees; to provide sound working conditions for the employees; to secure a prompt and fair disposition of grievances; to eliminate all interruptions of work and interference with the efficient operation of the EMPLOYERS' Hotels; to obtain maximum efficiency in the Hotels; and to set forth the Agreement covering rates of pay, hours of work and conditions of employment to be observed by the parties during the life of this Agreement.

(a) No provision of this Agreement shall be used to deprive any employee presently employed by an EMPLOYER of any benefits or privileges authorized by the EMPLOYER which such employee enjoys upon the date of the execution of this Agreement or to reduce the wage rate of any employee presently employed by an EMPLOYER on the date of the execution of this Agreement if the wage rate paid to the employee is higher than the contract minimum wage rate for his job classification, provided, however, that if any new employees are employed by the EMPLOYER hereafter, the EMPLOYER shall have the right to employ them in accordance with the job classification rates set forth in the attached Schedules.

(b) No provision of this Agreement shall be used to deprive any employee of any benefit or privilege

322

ARTICLE 6
Vacations

Section 37. Amount of Vacation

Steady employees, upon completion of continuous employment as set forth below, with an EMPLOYER, or within the establishment in which they are employed, shall receive vacations with pay as follows:

(a) Employees who have completed one (1) year of continuous service, but less than two (2) years of service with the EMPLOYER – one (1) week's vacation;

(b) Employees who have completed two (2) years of continuous service, but less than twelve (12) years of continuous service with the EMPLOYER – two (2) weeks' vacation, subject to the provisions of subparagraph (d) below;

(c) Employees who have completed twelve (12) years of continuous service with the EMPLOYER – three (3) weeks' vacation;

(d) Effective January 1, 1983, employees who have completed ten (10) years of continuous service with the EMPLOYER – three (3) weeks' vacation; and

(e) Effective January 1, 1984, employees who have completed twenty (20) years of continuous service with the EMPLOYER – four (4) weeks' vacation.

Section 38. Computation of Vacation

(a) Vacation pay shall be computed on the basis of forty (40) hours at the employee's straight time hourly rate for each week of vacation to which the employee is entitled. Employees in the Banquet Department of the EMPLOYER who are on steady payroll, punch time clocks and receive their wages and service charges direct from the Hotel shall be considered as steady employees for the purpose of

which is granted by an EMPLOYER during the term of this Agreement that exceeds the terms and provisions of this Agreement, provided that such benefit or privilege is granted by the EMPLOYER to the employee in writing. If any benefit or privilege is granted by an EMPLOYER to an employee in writing during the term of this Agreement, a copy of the same shall be mailed to the UNION. No benefit or privilege granted by an EMPLOYER during the term of this Agreement which exceeds the terms and provisions of this Agreement shall be effective unless granted by the EMPLOYER in writing.

Section 34. Discrimination

The wage scales and conditions shall apply to male and female employees. Whenever in this Agreement the masculine gender is used, it shall be deemed to include the feminine gender. The UNION and the EMPLOYERS agree there shall be no discrimination by either party which violates applicable local, Michigan or Federal Equal Employment Opportunity Laws.

Section 35. Midnight Shift

All employees employed on the midnight shift shall be paid a shift differential of fifteen cents (15¢) per hour. The midnight shift shall be considered as any shift commencing between 11:00 p.m. and 4:00 a.m.

Section 36. Employee Scheduling

No employee shall be scheduled to work less than sixteen (16) hours from the beginning of his/her last scheduled shift unless the employee agrees. This shall not apply to banquet servers.

vacation payments. At the discretion of the EM-PLOYER, the EMPLOYER may decide to give a separate check for each week of vacation pay to which an employee may be entitled.

(b) All steady banquet servers employed under Schedule E shall receive payment for their vacation, calculated on, and equal to, one and one-quarter times the employee's average weekly pay (wages, not including gratuities and/or service charges).

Section 39. Extra Employees

Extra employees shall not be eligible for vacation payments unless specified in the attached Wage Schedules.

Section 40. Pro Rata Vacation Pay

Steady employees having continuous employment in accordance with the provisions of Section 37 above but working less than five (5) days of eight (8) hours each per week shall be paid on a pro rata basis based upon the number of hours worked each week, with full cash payment thereof to be made in advance.

Section 41. Layoffs and Vacation Pay

If a steady employee is laid off or discharged by the EMPLOYER, except for reasons specified in Section 43 below, he shall receive his earned vacation pay computed on a pro rata basis of one-twelfth (1/12th) of his earned vacation for each month worked, or major fraction thereof, since the last hiring date of the employee.

Section 42. Pro Rata Vacation Pay and Resignation

If an employee quits after having worked three (3) months or more of his current vacation year, he shall receive his earned vacation pay, provided two (2) weeks' notice is given by the employee to the EMPLOYER of his intention to quit, the earned vacation to be computed on a pro rata basis of one-twelfth (1/12th) for each month worked, or major fraction thereof, since the last hiring date of the employee.

Section 43. Quitting Without Notice or Discharge

If an employee quits without giving notice as provided in the preceding Section or is discharged for proven dishonesty, such employee shall not be eligible for the payment of any current vacation benefits.

Section 44. Scheduling of Vacations

The vacation period of employees shall be scheduled by the EMPLOYER in accordance with his requirements. The choice of time off during such vacation periods shall be selected on a seniority basis whenever possible. If the scheduled vacation period of an employee is cancelled by an EMPLOYER and no other vacation time is available, the employee shall receive pay in lieu of such vacation, in addition to his/her regular pay.

Section 45. Sale of Hotel and Vacations

In the event an EMPLOYER sells its Hotel or establishment, or by any other means ceases to operate such establishment, the EMPLOYER shall pay each of its employees whose periods of employment shall have or will entitle them to a vacation, the cash equivalent of any vacation which said employees shall have earned to the date of the cessation of operations. In the event of the sale of the Hotel or establishment, this clause may be waived if the new owner or operator agrees in writing, and the UNION is supplied with a copy of such written agreement, to schedule and pay vacations on the basis of employment with the former EMPLOYER bridged to his own period of operations.

Section 46. Posting Vacation Schedules

Schedules for vacations are to be posted in advance so that seniority employees can have their choice of days off.

ARTICLE 7
Holidays

Section 47. Holidays – Steady Employees

Steady employees shall be paid their straight time hourly rate for the following holidays if not worked and double their straight time hourly rate if said holidays are worked, to-wit: Memorial Day, Independence Day, Labor Day, Thanksgiving Day, Christmas Day, New Year's Day and employee's birthday. In addition thereto, steady employees will be paid time and one-half their regular straight hourly rate of pay for all hours worked commencing at 6:00 p.m. December 31 to 2:00 a.m. January 1.

Effective January 1, 1984, steady employees shall receive their anniversary date as an additional paid holiday. Should an employee's anniversary date fall on the day immediately preceding, the day of, or the day immediately following any of the other above holidays, the employee shall, with the prior approval of the EMPLOYER, select and take an alternate day off as a paid holiday.

Section 48. Computation of Holiday Pay

If an employee works one of the above designated paid holidays, and it falls either on his designated 6th day or his designated 7th day, the employee shall receive premium pay as follows: On the employee's designated 6th day, or 7th day if the 6th day is not worked, two and one-half (2½) times his straight time hourly rate shall be paid; on the employee's designated 7th day if the 6th day was worked – three (3) times his regular straight time hourly rate shall be paid.

Section 49. Steady-Extra and Extra Employees

All steady-extra and extra employees, working on a paid holiday, shall receive double their straight time hourly rate for all hours worked, except as provided in Schedule E for banquet employees.

Section 50. Eligibility for Holiday Pay

In order to become eligible for holiday pay in accordance with the foregoing Sections, an employee must work his/her last scheduled workday preceding and his/her first scheduled workday following said holidays, unless excused by the EMPLOYER on account of sickness, physical disability or other reason, or unless the employee is on approved vacation, or unless the day before or the day after the holiday is a regularly scheduled day off for the employee. An employee shall be eligible for holiday pay in accordance with the provisions of Section 52.

Section 51. Personal Leaves and Holiday Pay

An employee on personal leave of absence, or an employee who has been on sick leave for more than five (5) days immediately preceding such holiday, shall not be entitled to holiday pay.

Section 52. Probationary Employee and Holiday Pay

An employee shall not be eligible for holiday pay for a holiday not worked until he has been in the employ of an EMPLOYER for more than thirty (30) days.

Section 53. Layoff and Holiday Pay

An employee who has been laid off because of lack of work shall be paid for a designated holiday if said holiday occurs within seven (7) calendar days of his layoff.

Section 54. Vacations and Holiday Pay.

If one of the aforesaid holidays falls during a period when an employee is on approved vacation, said employee shall receive an extra day's pay or a substitute day, at the employee's discretion.

Section 55. Failure to Work on Holiday

If an employee fails to report for work on a holiday that he/she is scheduled to work, such employee shall forfeit all pay for that holiday unless such employee is excused by the EMPLOYER on account of sickness or physical disability.

Section 56. Not Applicable to Extra Employees

The provisions of Article 7 shall not apply to or cover extra employees except as provided in Section 49 above.

ARTICLE 8
Health – Welfare – Pension Program

Section 57. Welfare – Culinary Plan

Effective January 1, 1982, the EMPLOYER shall contribute to the Hotel Employees and Restaurant Employees International Union Welfare Fund, (hereinafter referred to as the HEREIU Fund) the sum of sixty cents (60¢) per day from the first day of employment for each day worked by a steady employee, with a minimum of $3.00 per week for each week worked by steady employees, except those covered by the HEREIU Welfare Fund Hotel Plan as provided in Section 58 of this Article. (A steady employee is defined as an employee who is regularly scheduled to work four days or more per week for his participating EMPLOYER.) The EMPLOYER shall contribute to the HEREIU Welfare Fund the sum of sixty cents (60¢) per day for each day worked by all other employees covered by this Agreement. Effective January 1, 1984, the per day contribution shall be increased to sixty-five cents (65¢) per employee, with a minimum contribution of $3.25 per week for each week worked by steady employees. Such contributions shall be used for insurance coverage for employees eligible for benefits under the Washington National Insurance Company Culinary Plan or a successor carrier as may be designated by the Trustees from time to time.

Section 58. Welfare – Hotel Plan

All steady employees as defined in Article 4, Section 27, who are not covered as an individual or dependent on a comparable group plan fully paid for by another EMPLOYER, and who are eligible for individual coverage under the HEREIU Welfare Fund Hotel Plan, shall have contributed by the EMPLOYER an amount not to exceed fifty-five dollars ($55.00) per month commencing January 1, 1982; and fifty-six dollars ($56.00) per month commencing January 1, 1984, to the HEREIU Welfare Fund in lieu of the contributions set forth in Section 57 of this Article. Such contributions shall be used for insurance coverage for employees eligible for benefits under the Washington National Insurance Company Hotel Plan or a successor carrier as may be designated by the Trustees from time to time. Should any employee desire to cover his or her spouse and/or family under the program, said employee shall be permitted to do so at the employee's own expense in accordance with the regulations established by the Trustees.

Section 59. Pension Program

For the term of this Agreement, the EMPLOYER shall contribute, in addition to the contributions provided for in the preceding Sections, the sum of eighty-five cents (85¢) per day commencing January 1, 1982 for each day worked by an employee covered by this Agreement to the Hotel Employees and Restaurant Employees International Union Pension Fund, (hereinafter referred to as HEREIU Pension Fund) for the purpose of establishing and paying pensions to eligible employees as provided in an Indenture of Trust establishing the HEREIU Pension Plan.

Section 60. Contributions

Contributions as provided in this Article are payable for any period while an employee is on a paid vacation or a paid holiday.

Section 61. Employee Data

The contributions provided in the preceding Sections shall be paid monthly, together with a report of employee data on a format prescribed by the Trust Funds no later than the 15th day of the month following the month for which they are to be made. Said employee data required shall include name, address, social security number, sex, date of birth, date of hire, days or weeks of employment, length of employment and such other information as the Trustees may determine necessary in order to comply with the record keeping requirements of E.R.I.S.A. and/or to properly provide welfare and pension benefits to participants.

Section 62. Binding Agreement

The EMPLOYER and the UNION agree to be bound by the Agreement and Declaration of Trust of said HEREIU Welfare Fund as may from time to time be amended, and they do hereby irrevocably designate as their respective representatives on the Board of Trustees, such Trustees as are named in said Agreement and Declaration of Trust as EMPLOYER and UNION Trustees, together with their successors selected as provided herein, and agree to be bound by all actions taken by the Trustees pursuant to said Trust Agreement.

Section 63. Records

In order to properly pay benefits, keep a record of employees' rights to benefits, and to comply with federal law, the EMPLOYER and UNION agree to make available for inspection and audit by the Fund such records of bargaining unit employees as the Fund may require, including, but not limited to, names of employees and dependents, ages, dates of hire, classification, sex, social security number, wages and hours, days or weeks of employment.

Section 64. Arrearage

In the event the EMPLOYER is in arrears in the payment of contributions, it shall be liable to any employee, spouse and/or dependents for loss of benefits resulting therefrom, and the EMPLOYER shall be required to pay to the Fund interest on all unpaid contributions at the rate of eight percent (8%) per annum computed as of the date such contributions are due and payable, and to pay reasonable legal and other expenses incurred in the collection of said delinquent contributions, or in the obtaining of said information.

Section 65. Binding Arbitration

Notwithstanding any other provision of this Agreement concerning the settlement of disputes or grievances, all disputes or grievances involving the provisions of this Article, including any controversies with respect to contributions owed to the Fund, shall be resolved by arbitration in the following manner:

(a) The UNION, the EMPLOYER, or the Trust Fund, or their respective representatives or attorneys, shall serve upon the party against whom claim is made a notice of intent to arbitrate. Said initiating party shall thereafter request the American Arbitration Association to designate an arbitrator, who may be a permanent arbitrator, to hear and resolve the claim or dispute. The American Arbitration Association shall set the time, date and place of arbitration and shall give written notice thereof to all parties, which notice shall be sent not less than twenty (20) days prior to the date of the hearing. The arbitrator shall thereafter mail, or cause to be mailed, a copy of the award to the parties.

(b) In the interest of avoiding additional costs and delay of arbitration, except as otherwise provided hereunder, the Expedited Labor Arbitration Rules of the American Arbitration Association shall govern all arbitrations conducted hereunder.

(c) The decision of the arbitrator shall be final and binding on the EMPLOYER, the UNION and the Fund and may be enforced in any court of competent jurisdiction. The arbitrator shall have no authority to alter, amend, or modify this Agreement.

Section 66. Employment Eligibility

An employee shall be eligible for HEREIU Welfare Fund Hotel Plan benefits as provided in Section 58 above on the first day of the month following ninety (90) days of employment.

Section 67. Layoff, Leave, Resign and Discharge

(a) In the event of a layoff, the EMPLOYER shall continue to contribute the monthly amount of HEREIU Welfare Fund Hotel Plan cost for an eligible employee for the month following said layoff.

(b) If an eligible employee is on an approved leave for reasons of bona fide illness or proven temporary disability in accordance with the terms and conditions of this Agreement, the EMPLOYER will continue the monthly contribution to the HEREIU Welfare Fund Hotel Plan for the first three (3) months of said approved leave.

(c) Those employees eligible for the HEREIU Welfare Fund Hotel Plan who shall take or will be on a "leave of absence", including, but not limited to, UNION business, exclusive of the first three (3) months of an approved leave of absence for reasons of bona fide illness or proven temporary disability, or on temporary layoff, shall be permitted to continue said coverage at their own option and their own expense, for a period not to exceed one (1) year.

(d) An eligible employee who quits or is discharged shall not be entitled to any additional monthly contribution to the HEREIU Welfare Fund Hotel Plan.

(e) The EMPLOYER shall pay into the Fund the monthly contribution for any employee returning from a temporary layoff, for the month of the employee's return, provided that the employee returns to work by the 15th of that month. In no event shall an EMPLOYER make more than one monthly contribution for any employee in any month.

ARTICLE 9
Seniority

Section 68. Definition

(a) An employee's "seniority" shall be the period of his/her most recent, continuous service with the EMPLOYER within the bargaining unit job classification per department/room covered by this Agreement expressed in terms of years, months and days. If two (2) or more employees began working on the same day, their seniority shall be determined by lot. The principle of seniority shall be applied to the extent and in the circumstances and manner set forth in this Agreement.

(b) The EMPLOYERS agree to recognize the seniority of an employee in specific job classifications within each department/room, with steady and steady-extra employees carrying separate seniority; there shall be no bumping of days off or shifts. If a vacancy occurs within a department/room, employees may bid the vacancy for the then existing work schedule, in the following manner and order only:

1) steady employees, according to seniority, in the specific job classification in the subject department/room;

2) steady-extra employees, according to seniority in the specific job classification, in the subject department/room.

Section 69. Layoffs and Recalls

(a) During layoffs or reductions in the working force, the employee with the least seniority in the job classification affected shall be laid off first. When the working force is again increased, employees on layoff shall be recalled in the order of their job classification seniority.

(b) When an employee is notified, in writing, at the time of layoff when he/she is to report back to work, he/she shall report back at such time without further notice. When an employee is not notified at the layoff time when he/she is to report back to work, he/she shall be given reasonable advance notice of when to report back to work. This notice will be given by certified mail to the last address furnished the EMPLOYER by the employee with a copy to be sent immediately to the UNION.

(c) No extra employees in job classifications shall be used where seniority employees within the same job classification are on layoff, except in cases of emergency or where the EMPLOYER cannot contact laid off employees in the same job classification.

(d) In the event a layoff becomes necessary, an affected employee shall be allowed to return to his/her original job classification in any department/room from which he/she had previously been transferred, provided as follows:

1) The employee had completed their probationary period in that classification in any department/room;

2) The employee is then qualified to perform the required work without training, in the opinion of the EMPLOYER;

3) The returning employee must take the work schedule, including shift and days off, of the least senior employee for the period of time needed by the EMPLOYER to comply with the provisions of Article 4, Section 21, after which they may exercise their seniority rights as provided in Article 9, Section 70.

The seniority of an employee exercising bumping rights under this Section shall be subject to and governed by the provisions of Section 75 (a) regarding accumulated and frozen seniority.

The employee must exercise his/her bumping rights at the time of layoff.

Section 70. Shifts, Days Off, Vacation and Assignment

Senior employees shall have preference of shifts, days off and vacation periods. In dining rooms where stations are not rotated, senior employees shall have their choice of stations and dining room assignments, provided that the employee is qualified for the specific job requirement within the department/room. Choices for station assignments and shifts shall be made as openings occur.

Section 71. Probationary Period.

The first forty-five (45) days of employment worked by each newly hired employee shall be considered his/her probationary period.

(a) A probationary employee shall not have seniority rights until completion of his/her probationary period.

(b) A probationary employee may be discharged, without recourse by the UNION or the employee, to the grievance and arbitration procedure.

Section 72. Loss of Seniority

Seniority and job rights shall terminate for the following reasons:

(a) Voluntary quitting or retirement;

329

(b) Discharge for just cause;

(c) Failure to return to work after recall as provided;

(d) Failure to return to work promptly at the end of an authorized leave of absence, unless due to Act of God;

(e) Being on layoff for a period equal to his/her seniority or one (1) year, whichever is less.

(f) Is absent for three (3) consecutive days without notice to the EMPLOYER, in which event notice shall be given as soon as possible, but not more than ten (10) days from date absence first occurred, except in any event where an employee is unable to give such notice to the EMPLOYER due to circumstances beyond his/her control.

Section 73. Notice of Layoff

If a steady employee is laid off for lack of work for a period of five (5) or more working days, the EMPLOYER shall notify the employee affected at least three (3) days prior to the effective date of the layoff, provided, however, in the absence of such notice, the EMPLOYER shall pay the employee three (3) days pay.

Section 74. Extra Employees – Layoff

No extra employees in job classifications shall be used where seniority employees within the same job classifications are on layoff, except in cases of emergency, or where the EMPLOYER cannot contact laid off employees in the same job classification.

Section 75. Transfers and Promotions

(a) An employee transferred or promoted to a new job classification shall retain and continue to accumulate seniority in his original job classification, and shall accumulate seniority in the new classification as of the date of transfer. If the employee returns to his former job classification, he shall have accumulated seniority from his first date of hire in that classification, and shall have frozen seniority in the classification from which the employee is returning. Should the employee subsequently move to said position, he shall have the seniority earned in that classification to his credit.

(b) A transferred employee shall have probationary status in the new job classification for the first forty-five (45) days worked. At any time during this probationary period, the EMPLOYER may return the employee to his/her former job classification, or the employee may elect to return.

(c) During this probationary period only, if the EMPLOYER returns an employee to his/her old job classification, or if an employee decides to return to his/her old job classification, he/she shall have, and be subject to, the same bumping rights and limitations as provided above in Section 69 (d) for laid off employees.

Section 76. Employees Promoted to Supervisory Positions

An employee transferred to a supervisory position shall, for forty-five (45) days after such transfer, have the right to return to his/her former bargaining unit position without loss of seniority.

ARTICLE 10

Grievance and Arbitration Procedure

Section 77. Grievance Procedure for Employees

Should differences arise between the EMPLOYERS, the UNION and/or the employee as to the application and meaning of this Agreement, the following procedures shall be followed:

Step 1. The employee shall take up the matter with his/her supervisor on an informal basis, in order to settle the matter promptly. An aggrieved employee may have the Union steward assist him/her with Step 1, if he/she so desires.

Step 2. If the grievance is not satisfactorily settled in Step 1, the aggrieved employee or the UNION shall, within fourteen (14) days from the date on which the incident giving rise to the grievance occurred, or within fourteen (14) days after the incident giving rise to the grievance first became known, file a written grievance with the General Manager or the Personnel Director; provided, however, the fourteen (14) day time requirement may be waived by mutual agreement in writing, and provided further, that discharge grievances may be filed at Step 2.

(a) The written grievance shall set forth the facts giving rise to the grievance, including the date and persons involved, and designate the provisions of the Agreement which allegedly have been violated. Failure to file such written grievance within fourteen (14) days shall result in such grievance being presumed to be without merit and it shall be barred from further consideration.

(b) The representatives of the EMPLOYERS and the UNION will confer within ten (10) days after receipt of such written grievance in an effort to settle the grievance, unless the time limit is extended by mutual agreement of the parties in writing. If not settled at this conference, the EMPLOYER shall issue a decision in writing on any such written grievance within seven (7) days from the time such grievance meeting is adjourned.

Section 78. Grievance Procedure for Employers
Should differences arise between the EMPLOYERS and the UNION as to meaning and application of this Agreement, the following procedure shall be followed:

Step 1. The EMPLOYER and/or the Association may take the matter up with the authorized UNION representative on an informal basis, in order to settle the matter promptly.

Step 2. If the grievance is not satisfactorily settled in Step 1, the aggrieved EMPLOYER and/or the Association shall, within fourteen (14) days from the date on which the incident which gave rise to the grievance occurred, or within fourteen (14) days after the incident giving rise to the grievance first became known, file a written grievance with the UNION; provided, however, the fourteen (14) day requirement may be waived by mutual agreement in writing.

(a) The written grievance shall set forth the facts giving rise to the grievance, including the date and persons involved, and designate the provisions of the Agreement which allegedly have been violated. Failure to file such written grievance within fourteen (14) days shall result in such grievance being presumed to be without merit and it shall be barred from further consideration.

(b) The representatives of the EMPLOYER and the UNION will confer within ten (10) days after receipt of such written grievance in an effort to settle the grievance, unless the time limit is extended by mutual agreement in writing of the parties. If not settled at this conference, the UNION shall issue a decision in writing on any such written grievance within seven (7) days from the time such grievance meeting is adjourned.

Section 79. Arbitration Procedure
If the grievance cannot be satisfactorily settled by the above steps of the grievance procedure, either of the parties may request arbitration by giving the other

party written notice of its desire to arbitrate within seven (7) days after the EMPLOYER or the UNION has made its final written answer as provided in Step 2 (unless the EMPLOYER and the UNION mutually agree to extend the time limit in writing), in which event the grievance shall be arbitrated according to the following procedure:

(a) The parties shall attempt to mutually agree upon an arbitrator. If they are unable to mutually agree, the party desiring to arbitrate shall request the Federal Mediation and Conciliation Service (with a copy of such request to the opposite party) to furnish the parties with a panel of ten (10) names of impartial arbitrators. If the parties are unable to agree upon the arbitrator from this list, a second list shall be furnished with ten (10) names of impartial arbitrators. The parties shall strike the names alternately until a final arbitrator is determined. The party desiring arbitration shall first strike the name from the second list.

(b) The expenses of the arbitrator shall be borne equally by the UNION and the EMPLOYER; each party bearing the expense of its own representative, witnesses and other preparation and presentation expenses.

Section 80. Final and Binding

Any decision reached at any stage of these grievance proceedings or by the arbitration procedure shall be final and binding upon the parties as to the matter in dispute. The EMPLOYERS, the UNION and the aggrieved employee shall thereafter comply in all respects with the result of such decision reached.

Section 81. Arbitrator Limited to Terms of Agreement

The arbitrator shall not have any right or authority to add to, to modify or subtract from any of the terms, conditions or sections of this Agreement.

ARTICLE 11
Leaves of Absence

Section 82. Requests for Leaves

Leaves of absence without pay for reasonable periods of time, not to exceed four months, shall be granted by an EMPLOYER to employees for reasons of bona fide illness, including maternity. Such leaves of absence for bona fide illness shall not affect employees' vacation or seniority rights.

(a) Requests for medical leaves of absence shall, on the request of the EMPLOYER, be accompanied by a doctor's certificate showing the nature of the illness and the estimated length of time the employee will be unable to perform his/her job, except in cases of extreme emergency when a certificate shall be provided within a reasonable period of time. Upon the expiration of said leave, the employee shall furnish the EMPLOYER with a statement signed by a physician establishing the fitness of the employee to return to his/her job. The EMPLOYER reserves the right to have said employee examined by the EMPLOYER'S designated physician at no cost to the employee. If the physicians do not agree, then the EMPLOYER may designate a third physician to further examine the employee to resolve any disagreement that might exist.

Section 83. Mutual Agreement Extensions

Leaves of absence without pay, not to exceed two months, may be granted by mutual agreement between the EMPLOYER and the employee for other reasons, but under such conditions the EMPLOYER shall determine, in advance, the extent, if any, to which vacation rights shall be affected.

Section 84. Additional Extensions

Any leave of absence that may be granted may be

extended, with the approval of the EMPLOYER, beyond the time allowed therefore as set forth above. Approved sick and maternity leaves not exceeding one (1) year shall be considered as time worked in the computation of seniority, provided, however, that vacation benefits shall not accrue after the first four (4) months of any such leave.

Section 85. Approved Leave and Accrued Vacation Time

An employee who has a vacation accrued at the time of being granted an approved leave of absence, or who is absent because of illness, may elect to include such accrued vacation in his time off.

Section 86. Leaves and Extension in Writing

All leaves of absence and extensions of leaves of absence must be in writing, signed by the EMPLOYER, and a copy sent to the UNION and a copy to the employee.

ARTICLE 12
Rights of Employees

Section 87. Discrimination

The EMPLOYER agrees not to discriminate against, or discharge, any UNION member because of his or her proper UNION activity.

Section 88. Posting of Schedule

The EMPLOYER shall post in a conspicuous place in the employees' service area, a schedule indicating the days off of employees, the starting and quitting times, and the vacation period allowable.

Section 89. Bulletin Board

A bulletin board shall be provided by the EMPLOYER for the sole use of the UNION for posting notices of UNION meetings and other proper UNION activities.

Section 90. Printing Cost

The cost of printing this Agreement shall be borne equally by the Hotels and the UNION.

ARTICLE 13
Concessionaire

Section 91. Concessionaire Clause

In the event an EMPLOYER turns over to any person or persons the operation of any department of its Hotel, the EMPLOYER shall notify the tenant of the terms and provisions of this Agreement before the execution of any lease. In addition, the EMPLOYER shall give ten (10) days notice to the UNION in advance of the execution of any lease, so that the UNION may contact and negotiate with the lessee for the execution of an agreement by the lessee to be bound by the terms and provisions of this Agreement. Failure of the lessee to meet this obligation shall give the UNION the right to strike the lessee.

ARTICLE 14
Locker Room

Section 92. Locker Rooms

The EMPLOYER shall provide sanitary dressing rooms for all of its employees and lockers with lock and key free of charge for steady and steady-extra employees. An EMPLOYER shall be responsible for any losses sustained by its employees for its failure to comply with this provision. Should the EMPLOYER wish to inspect the lockers, the EMPLOYER'S representative shall be accompanied by a UNION steward or his/her designee.

ARTICLE 15
Uniforms

Section 93. Required by Employer

The EMPLOYER shall furnish, clean and maintain all uniforms that are required to be worn by employees except regulation uniforms of waitresses, waiters, bartenders, bar and bus persons.

The regulation uniform is:

(a) Waitresses:

Black dress, white collar, white cuffs, apron and black shoes, or white dress, white apron and white shoes.

(b) Waiters:

Black pants, black coat, white shirt, black tie and black shoes.

(c) Bartenders, bar persons, bus persons (male):

Black pants, white shirt, black tie, black shoes.

(d) Bartenders, bar persons, bus persons (female):

Black skirt, white blouse, black shoes.

Section 94. Shirt – Blouse

Other employees who are required to wear plain white shirts (male) or blouse (female) shall provide, clean and maintain said garment.

Section 95. Standard Work Shoes

All employees, except those excused by the EMPLOYER, shall wear standard work shoes provided by the employee. The EMPLOYER shall provide other than standard work shoes it may require. Standard work shoes shall be defined as black, white or brown shoes, with the color of same to be determined by the EMPLOYER.

Section 96. Uniforms Laundered by Employee

If the EMPLOYER requires that the employee launder uniforms, then the EMPLOYER will reimburse the employee three dollars and fifty cents (3.50) per week, or such amount that may be provided by law, whichever sum is greater.

ARTICLE 16
Combination Jobs

Section 97. Rate of Pay

When an employee occupies a position which combines two or more job classifications of work, then (except as otherwise provided) such employee shall be paid at the rate of the highest job classification. Hotels may not, by virtue of this provision, evade the hiring of an employee in a higher job classification where such employee in a higher classification would normally be hired, according to the usage of the trade.

ARTICLE 17
Standard Training Program

Section 98. Program

All training programs shall be instituted by agreement between the individual Hotels and the UNION.

ARTICLE 18
Strikes and Lockouts

Section 99. No Strikes or Lockouts

Both the UNION and the EMPLOYERS recognize the service nature of the hotel business and the duty of the Hotels to render continuous and hospitable service to the public in the way of lodging, food and other necessary hotel accommodations. There shall be no lockouts, strikes or work stoppages of any kind prior to the termination date of this Agreement as set forth in Section 106. If neither party gives notice of its desire to negotiate any change in this Agreement not less than sixty (60) days prior to the termination date as set forth in Section 106, then there shall be no lockouts, strikes or work stoppages until either party gives notice, as provided in Section 106, of its desire to negotiate changes in the terms and provisions of this Agreement.

Section 100. Exception

The foregoing provisions of this Article shall not apply in the event an EMPLOYER or the UNION refuses to comply with the arbitration provisions of this Agreement.

ARTICLE 19
Successorship

Section 101. Sale or Transfer

This Agreement shall be binding upon the successors, assigns, purchasers, lessees or transferees of an EMPLOYER, whether such succession, assignment or transfer be effected voluntarily or by operation of law, or by merger or consolidation with another company, provided the establishment remains in the same line of business.

ARTICLE 20
Bereavement

Section 102. Bereavement Leave

If death occurs in the immediate family (father, mother, sister, brother, son, daughter, current spouse, grandparent) of an employee, a bereavement leave of four (4) days with pay will be granted to steady full-time employees for the purpose of attending the funeral.

ARTICLE 21
Personal Leave Days

Section 103. Employees Covered

All steady employees, upon the completion of three (3) years continuous service, shall be allowed three (3) personal leave days per anniversary year, four (4) personal leave days after four (4) years of continuous service, and five (5) personal leave days after five (5) years of continuous service. These days may be taken upon forty-eight (48) hours advance written notice to the EMPLOYER, except in cases of emergency or sickness where such notice cannot be given. Such personal days must be taken during the employee's anniversary year, and at such times as to not interfere with the normal operation of the EMPLOYER'S business. A request for a personal leave day will not be unreasonably withheld by an EMPLOYER. All personal days must be taken by the employee. No employee will be entitled to pay in lieu of taking a personal leave day, nor will any employee be allowed to accumulate personal leave days.

ARTICLE 22
Jury Duty

Section 104. Jury Pay

Any steady employee who is called to, and reports for, jury duty shall be paid by the EMPLOYER for each day spent in performing jury duty, if the employee otherwise would have been scheduled to work for the EMPLOYER and does not work, an amount equal to the difference between:

(a) The employee's regular straight time hourly rate for the number of hours, up to eight (8), that he otherwise would have been scheduled to work, and

(b) The daily jury duty fee paid by the Court (not including travel allowance or reimbursement of expenses). If an employee is dismissed from jury duty, he shall report for work to the Hotel during the balance of his regular work shift.

Section 105. Employee Notification

In order to receive payment under this section, an employee must give the EMPLOYER prior notice that he has been summoned for jury duty, and must furnish satisfactory evidence that jury duty was performed on the days for which payment is claimed.

ARTICLE 23
Term of Agreement

Section 106. Duration

This Agreement and all schedules attached hereto shall continue and remain in full force and effect until the conclusion of the last scheduled work shift on December 31, 1984, and neither party shall demand any change in this Agreement and the schedules attached hereto during the term hereof. This Agreement shall continue in full force and effect from year to year thereafter, unless either party desires to negotiate changes in this Agreement and the schedules attached hereto, and serves written notice on the other party by certified mail not less than sixty (60) days prior to December 31, 1984.

IN WITNESS WHEREOF, the parties have executed this Agreement as of the 1st day of January, 1982.

HOTEL ASSOCIATION OF GREATER DETROIT

Hartmut Stauss, *General Manager*
Hyatt Regency

John Ribon III, *General Manager*
Somerset Inn

Barry Gregory, *General Manager*
Hotel St. Regis

Arthur Gimson, *General Manager*
Northfield Hilton

Thomas H. Finnerty, *Attorney* for
Hotel Association of Greater Detroit

HOTEL, MOTEL, RESTAURANT EMPLOYEES, COOKS & BARTENDERS UNION, LOCAL 24

Herbert Triplett, *Secretary-Treasurer*

Vaden Hairston, *President*

SCHEDULE A
Kitchen Employees

Minimum rates are hereby established for the job classifications in the following grades; said rates to become effective on the date above each column:

Daily Rate Effective for the Period From:

GRADE I
Pastry Chef, Sous Chef, Night Chef, Head Butcher, Banquet Chef, Chief Kitchen Steward, Gardemanger.

1-1-82	1-1-83	1-1-84
$45.86	$48.66	$51.86

GRADE II
Broiler and Roast Cook, Saute Cook, Swing Cook, Butcher, Assistant Gardemanger, Saucier.

1-1-82	1-1-83	1-1-84
$43.86	$46.66	$49.86

GRADE III
Fry Cook, Head Baker, Head Pastry Cook.

1-1-82	1-1-83	1-1-84
$41.86	$44.66	$47.86

GRADE IV
All Other Cooks, Baker, Pastry Cook, Assistant Kitchen Steward.

1-1-82	1-1-83	1-1-84
$40.86	$43.66	$46.86

GRADE V
Head Pantry and Salad Maker, Head Sandwich Maker.

1-1-82	1-1-83	1-1-84
$35.86	$33.66	$41.86

GRADE VI
All Other Pantry, Salad and Sandwich Persons, Vegetable Preparers.

1-1-82	1-1-83	1-1-84
$35.36	$38.16	$41.36

GRADE VII
Utility Workers. Stewards

1-1-82	1-1-83	1-1-84
$35.36	$38.16	$41.36

Receiving Clerks

1-1-82	1-1-83	1-1-84
$35.36	$38.16	$41.36

Storeroom Employees

1-1-82	1-1-83	1-1-84
$35.36	$38.16	$41.36

EXTRA RATES
Cooks

1-1-82	1-1-83	1-1-84
$46.86	$49.66	$52.86

Pantry Person

1-1-82	1-1-83	1-1-84
$36.86	$39.66	$42.86

Utility Workers

1-1-82	1-1-83	1-1-84
$36.36	$39.16	$42.36

OTHER SPECIFIC WORKING CONDITIONS

1. If, during the meal or break periods, it is necessary or required for the kitchen employees to assist in the preparation or delivery of meals, the kitchen employee shall return to his station to take care of any service that is required or necessary.

2. The listing of any job classifications in any of the above designated grades shall not be construed to mean that an EMPLOYER shall be required to hire employees in such classification or in any designated grade.

An EMPLOYER shall have the right to designate the grade to be filled when employing new employees.

3. There shall be no stations in any of the above designated grades. An employee occupying a classification in any grade shall be required to perform the work of any other classification in the same grade (and in a lower kitchen grade when necessary).

4. There shall be no split shifts for kitchen employees.

5. All kitchen employees hired on or before December 31, 1977 shall receive six (6) personal leave days per anniversary year after six (6) years of continuous employment. All kitchen employees hired on January 1, 1978 or after shall receive the same benefits as all other employees covered by this Agreement.

SCHEDULE B
BAR EMPLOYEES

Wages

Rates — The following rates are hereby established as the minimum hiring or replacement rates for the following job classifications, said rates to become effective on the date above each column:

Daily Rate Effective for the Period From:

	1-1-82	1-1-83	1-1-84
Bartenders	$41.86	$44.66	$47.86
Extra Bartenders	43.36	46.16	49.36
Extra Bartenders —			
4 hours	21.68	23.08	24.68
Bar Porters	35.36	38.16	41.36
Extra Bar Porters	35.36	38.16	41.36

Steady bartender employees presently employed for full shifts will not be replaced by 4-hour extra bartenders.

OTHER SPECIFIC WORKING CONDITIONS

1. Bartenders shall not be allowed to work split shifts, nor shall they work as servers.

2. Where there is a bar set up for serving drinks and where cocktails are mixed in any department, bartenders shall be employed. Where a bar is set up for serving drinks, a server shall not have the right to stand back of the bar to mix and pour drinks to serve to guests at the bar or to hand to the other servers for serving to guests. No server shall tend bar.

3. Steady bartenders may be requested but shall not be required to work overtime in the Banquet Department of the EMPLOYER.

4. Bartenders shall be paid at only one of the above rates for each shift.

5. Whenever possible, bartenders shall be scheduled by seniority on a rotation basis in the Banquet Department, except where a special customer requests, in which case the bartender will forfeit his next turn.

6. Extra bartenders may be required to work an 8-hour shift at one or more parties in the Banquet Department. In case of an emergency covering overload periods, extra bartenders may be assigned to work on front or service bars.

SCHEDULE C
HOUSEKEEPING, SERVICE, VALET PARKING, LAUNDRY, VALET DEPARTMENTS, HEALTH CLUB

Daily Rate Effective for the Period From:

	1-1-82	1-1-83	1-1-84
HOUSEKEEPING			
Housekeeping Attendant	$35.36	$38.16	$41.36
Steady-Extra & Extra Housekeeping Attendant	36.36	39.16	42.36
Lead Housekeeping Attendant	36.36	39.16	42.36
Houseperson	35.36	38.16	41.36
Tailor	39.61	42.41	45.61
Sewing Room/Linen Room Attendant	35.61	38.41	41.61

Daily Rate Effective for the Period From:

	1-1-82	1-1-83	1-1-84
SERVICE DEPT.:			
Guest Service Attendant/Door Attendant	$24.48	$25.68	$26.88
Guest Service Host/Hostess	37.86	40.66	43.86
Lead Guest Service Attendant	26.26	27.46	28.66
Dead Work (Guest Service Attendant-non-tipped work – per hour)	4.37	4.72	5.12
VALET PARKING:			
Valet Parking Attendants	24.48	25.68	26.88
Lead Valet Parking Attendants	30.40	31.60	32.80
Valet Parking Cashier	36.36	39.16	42.36
LAUNDRY/VALET:			
GRADE I Wash Attendant, Shirt and Garment Presser, Cleaner-Spotter, Valet Presser, Tumbler Attendant.	$41.36	$44.16	$47.36
GRADE II Sorter, Flat Work Attendant, Marker.	36.36	39.16	42.36
HEALTH CLUB: Health Club Attendant	37.06	39.86	43.06

OTHER SPECIFIC WORKING CONDITIONS

1. Housekeeping Attendants shall not be required to do more than sixteen (16) rooms or their equivalent within the work day.

2. When Attendants are required to general house-clean rooms, the work load will be reduced by one room for each room that is general house-cleaned.

3. The EMPLOYER will endeavor to assign senior Attendants to specific sections. From time to time, depending upon occupancy and other factors, the EMPLOYER may change the sections to be cleaned. Less senior employees shall work swings in the Housekeeping Department.

4. Attendants shall be required to remove room service trays and equipment only to the hallway adjacent to the room.

5. There shall be no split shift for housekeeping employees.

OTHER SPECIFIC WORKING CONDITIONS

1. Employees employed under Schedule C shall not be required to work a split shift.

SCHEDULE D
DINING ROOM EMPLOYEES

Daily Rate Effective for the Period From:

	1-1-82	1-1-83	1-1-84
DINING ROOM SERVICE:			
Steady – 8 hours	$23.84	$25.04	$26.24
Steady – 6 hours	18.82	19.72	20.62
STEADY ONE MEAL SERVERS:			
3 hours or less	10.66	11.11	11.56
4 hours or less	12.87	13.47	14.07
DINING ROOM – OTHERS:			
Captain	38.36	41.16	44.36
Bus Attendants	33.36	36.16	39.36
Host/Hostess	36.36	39.16	42.36
Cashiers and Order Takers	36.36	39.16	42.36
Cafeteria Servers	32.86	35.66	38.86
ROOM SERVICE SERVERS:			
Steady – 8 hours	23.84	25.04	26.24
Steady – 4 hours or less	13.20	13.80	14.40
(Shift to begin between 6:00 a.m. and 10:00 a.m. only)			
Cashiers and Order Takers	36.36	39.16	42.36

OTHER SPECIFIC WORKING CONDITIONS

1. Steady one meal servers who work on the basis of the above 3 or 4 hour rates shall be entitled to vacation benefits and holiday benefits on a pro rata basis based upon the number of hours worked by them and all other benefits of the contract on a proportionate basis.

2. Steady one meal servers who work more than their scheduled hours on a shift shall be paid at their hourly rate for such hours.

3. Dining room employees shall be permitted to work split shifts. The maximum work day in case of a split shift for 8-hour employees shall be 8 hours within 11 hours, provided, however, that employees working split shifts shall not work more than two consecutive meals. The maximum work day in case of a split shift for 6-hour employees shall be 6 hours within 9 hours.

4. Where split shifts are worked, only one split shift shall be permitted per day.

5. All dining room employees who work split shifts shall receive $1.50 per day additional.

6. Steady servers or dining room employees shall not be permitted to do banquet service except when the UNION cannot furnish extra employees. Laying off to do banquet service or other extra work is prohibited.

7. Captains shall be defined as persons who greet guests, escort them to tables, make the station and shift assignments of other dining room employees and prepare and perform tableside service.

8. Hosts and Hostesses shall be defined as persons who greet guests and escort them to tables and may perform other dining room functions not performed by captains.

340

SCHEDULE E
BANQUET EMPLOYEES

WAGES:

1. Breakfast, Lunches and Miscellaneous Parties: (6:00 a.m. to 2:00 p.m.)

(a) Servers – 3 hours or less (includes set-up and clear off)

1-1-82	1-1-83	1-1-84
$10.91	$11.51	$12.11

(b) Servers shall serve 20 guests.

(c) When the Hotel and the Union are unable to supply sufficient number of servers, all servers may be assigned more guests than normal maximum and shall receive overs on all set-ups over the maximum.

(d) Additional guests will be $.50 each.

2. Coffee Breaks:

(a) Coffee breaks, meetings and continental breakfast shall be paid the service charge plus the following hourly rate:

1-1-82	1-1-83	1-1-84
$3.20	$3.35	$3.50

(b) Servers shall set-up and service 50 guests for continental breakfasts and 100 guests for coffee breaks.

(c) If servers serve an increment of 100 additional guests at the same coffee break function, they shall receive, in addition to the rate listed above, the following hourly rate:

1-1-82	1-1-83	1-1-84
$3.55	$3.70	$3.85

3. Receptions:

(a) A reception is a function where only bite sized hors d'oeuvres are served.

(b) A banquet server shall be required to set-up and clear their own station in addition to hors d'oeuvres service and passing hors d'oeuvres.

(c) There shall be one server for every 50 guests; for each increment of 50 guests served, the server will receive one additional function rate.

4. Dinner: (2:00 p.m. to 10:00 p.m.)

(a) Servers – 4 hours or less (includes set-up and clear-off)

1-1-82	1-1-83	1-1-84
$14.03	$14.63	$15.23

(b) Servers shall serve 15 guests unless as noted in 1 (c), then:

(c) Additional guests will be $.65 each.

5. Functions after 10:00 p.m.:

(a) Servers – 4 hours or less (includes set-up and clear-off)

1-1-82	1-1-83	1-1-84
$15.43	$16.03	$16.63

(b) Servers shall serve 15 guests unless as noted in 1 (c), then:

(c) Additional guests will be $.65 each.

341

6. **Buffets:**

   (a) Servers before 2:00 p.m. – 3 hours or less (includes set-up and clear-off)

1-1-82	1-1-83	1-1-84
$11.76	$12.21	$12.66

   Servers after 2:00 p.m. – 4 hours or less

15.03	15.63	16.23

   (b) Servers shall serve 35 guests unless as noted in 1 (c), then:

   (c) Additional guests before 2:00 p.m. – $.50 each.

   Additional guests after 2:00 p.m. – $.65 each.

7. **Follow-up Service:**

   Follow-up service is a function when the main entree is served from the floor and servers are required to service all areas with the main entree in follow-up order.

8. **French Service:**

   French Service shall be when any portion of the main course is French served, or when any three or more courses are French served, excluding beverage, rolls, butter, sauces, etc.

   Servers shall only be required to serve 10 guests per server on French service; if additional guests are served, it shall be $.95 per additional guest.

9. **Dead Work:**

   Dead work or work done in excess of the above listed shifts shall be compensated for at a premium rate to the 1/2 hour in excess of the above listed function rates. This rate shall be:

1-1-82	1-1-83	1-1-84
$3.55	$3.70	$3.85

10. Banquet servers serving drinks to guests at bar parties with tickets with no service charge included shall be paid the following for 4 hours or less:

1-1-82	1-1-83	1-1-84
$18.80	$19.80	$20.80

    When the service charge is added to the price of tickets, servers shall receive the function rate plus the service charge. One server shall be employed for every 50 guests when serving drinks at such parties. 25% of the 12½% service charge is to be divided between servers.

11. Banquet servers, after completion of their party work, may be transferred to the dining room to work with a check book at the following hourly rate:

1-1-82	1-1-83	1-1-84
$2.95	$3.10	$3.25

    Banquet servers shall not be transferred when a steady server is on lay-off in a dining room.

12. When banquet servers are called upon to serve more than one function, they shall be paid, in addition to their guaranteed function rate, one-half additional rate for each additional function served, providing the functions are served within the same meal period.

13. Banquet servers assigned to work a private party in a suite shall be paid the following hourly rate:

1-1-82	1-1-83	1-1-84
$4.20	$4.35	$4.50

    Plus the 15% service charge on all food and beverages served, unless a captain is assigned to work the party, in which case the server shall receive 12½% and the captain 2½%.

14. Banquet servers shall receive vouchers setting forth the amount of wages due them. Such wages shall be sent to the office of the Union, together with the service charge due, with a voucher setting forth the amount of the service charge and the date and name of the party or function for which it is being paid, provided, however, that banquet servers who are regularly employed may pick up their check from the payroll department of the Employer. The wages of banquet servers to be sent to the office of the Union shall be paid by the Employer on its regular weekly payroll date covering the wages for the preceding week.

SERVICE CHARGE:

1. A service charge of fifteen percent (15%) shall be added to all food and beverage banquet checks. This service charge should be divided as follows:

   (a) Food Service: $12\frac{1}{2}\%$ to the servers
   $2\frac{1}{2}\%$ to captains and headservers

   (b) Liquor Service: 75% of $12\frac{1}{2}\%$ to the banquet bartenders
   25% of $12\frac{1}{2}\%$ to servers
   $2\frac{1}{2}\%$ to captains and headservers

2. When a bartender is not employed, the $12\frac{1}{2}\%$ liquor service charge shall go to the server.

3. When servers are not employed, the $12\frac{1}{2}\%$ liquor service charge shall go to the bartender.

4. When a bartender or server is not employed in liquor service, the $12\frac{1}{2}\%$ liquor service charge shall go to the bar porter or bus attendant setting up the function.

5. If no servers are employed at liquor functions and bar porters or bus attendants are used to set-up and clear, 75% of the $12\frac{1}{2}\%$ liquor service charge goes to banquet bartenders and 25% of the $12\frac{1}{2}\%$ liquor service charge goes to bar porters or bus attendants.

6. The $12\frac{1}{2}\%$ liquor service charge on wine and champagne (by the bottle or carafe) or punch, served by servers, shall be shared equally by the servers.

7. Hors d'oeuvres Service: The servers working hors d'oeuvres shall share the $12\frac{1}{2}\%$ service charge equally, with $2\frac{1}{2}\%$ to captains and headservers.

OTHER SPECIFIC WORKING CONDITIONS:

1. Servers shall perform set-up, service and clear-off for their assigned station for the function rate of pay.

2. Set-up shall be defined as when tables are in place with tablecloths on them and all set-up equipment is in the room or immediately adjacent to the room.

3. Clear-off shall be defined as when all set-up and service equipment is removed down to the tablecloths.

4. Dead work is defined as when banquet servers are called upon to set-up and clear-off for more than the number of guests assigned to them or to perform any service not on their own station within the said meal period.

5. During their regular periods of work as specified in the wage section above, employees may be assigned side work (related in any way to the

343

function being worked) for periods when they are not serving or on their meal break.

6. Banquet servers may be required to set up and clear their own assigned stations. Servers may be requested but not required to either set up or clear other than their assigned station. Servers who set up or clear other than their assigned station within the function period shall receive, in addition to the function rate, the dead work rate to the nearest half hour.

7. Banquet bus attendants, when used, shall assist the servers but receive their assigned banquet duties from supervisors only.

8. Banquet servers may mix and serve highballs and may serve cocktails previously mixed by Union bartenders.

9. No cash collections or plate passing of any kind by banquet servers shall be permitted.

10. Banquet employees shall be entitled to one meal for each meal worked, meals to be eaten on the Employer's time but when employees are not busy, and at such times as not to interfere with the efficient operations of the Hotel. Time allowed for meals shall not exceed one-half hour for each meal worked. The station of any employee during his eating period shall be covered by another employee whenever necessary or required.

11. If any extra service charge or extra remuneration is left by the party holding or sponsoring the banquet for the employees who are employed at the banquet, the full amount thereof shall be made known to those in charge of the banquet. The amount of such service charge or extra remuneration shall be distributed to the employees working the banquet, with any captains, headservers who supervised or were in charge of the banquet to participate on the same basis as provided in the agreed contract distribution.

12. The Union reserves the right to see that the distribution of the fixed service charge and extra service or remuneration is in accordance with the terms of the collective bargaining agreement. The Union reserves the right to see each check. The Employer shall maintain records of service charges received or distributed and the actual banquet checks. Such records shall be kept for at least one year.

13. Banquet servers shall not be required to sweep floors, wash glasses or silverware, move pianos, tables, chairs or do other housepersons or porters work.

14. All steady and steady-extra banquet servers shall be paid holiday pay for the holidays set forth in Article 7. Holiday pay shall be the dinner function rate. All banquet servers shall be paid double the function rate for work performed.

15. Extra banquet servers' New Year's Eve rate after 6:00 p.m. shall be $33.50 for 6 hours or less, and an additional $8.00 for breakfast.

16. Stewarding Department employees shall not be required to work split shifts. Stewarding Department employees may, in addition to their other duties, be assigned to assist in dishing up individual portions for banquets.

17. Banquet functions in public function rooms shall be handled by banquet department personnel.

18. All steady and steady-extra banquet employees shall receive vacation pay on a pro-rated basis for time worked.

Banquet Housepersons

1-1-82	1-1-83	1-1-84
$36.36	$39.16	$42.36

OTHER SPECIFIC WORKING CONDITIONS

1. Banquet housepersons shall not work split shifts.

SCHEDULE F
CLERICAL EMPLOYEES

Wage Rates: The following wage rates are hereby agreed upon as the minimum hiring or replacement rates for the following specific job classifications, said rates to become effective on the date above each column:

Daily Rate Effective for the Period From:

	1-1-82	1-1-83	1-1-84
FRONT OFFICE:			
Room Clerk, Trainee	$37.36	$40.16	$43.36
Room Clerk	39.36	42.16	45.36

Trainee Room Clerk to be promoted to Room Clerk at the end of ninety (90) days.

	1-1-82	1-1-83	1-1-84
FRONT OFFICE CLERKS	35.51	38.31	41.51

To cover the following classifications:
Reservation Clerks, Mail and Information Clerks, File Clerks, Key Clerks, Typists.

	1-1-82	1-1-83	1-1-84
FRONT OFFICE AUDIT:			
Cashiers	38.86	41.66	44.86
Telephone Operators	36.36	39.16	42.36
ACCOUNTING:			
Bookkeeper	38.36	41.16	44.36
Clerks	36.01	38.81	42.01
Typists	35.51	38.31	41.51
Secretary	37.36	40.16	43.36
MISCELLANEOUS:			
Timekeeper	35.36	38.16	41.36
Checkroom Attendant – 8 hours	35.36	38.16	41.36
Checkroom Attendant – 4 hours or less	20.58	21.98	23.58

OTHER SPECIFIC WORKING CONDITIONS

1. Employees covered by Schedule F shall not work split shifts.

2. Employees covered by Schedule F who work as extras shall be paid $1.25 per day above the steady rate.

Appendix C: Typical Narrative Description of Pre-Opening Activities for an Overseas Hotel Managed by a U.S. Company

Arrival of the resident general manager

Six to nine months prior to opening

The resident general manager and his or her family arrive in the city in which the hotel is located. He proceeds to select a suitable temporary residence that he will occupy until he can move into the hotel. He then selects an office, which should be away from the site and accessible to prospective employees. It would be very helpful if, prior to his arrival, the resident director or the construction project manager could do some exploratory work on both available office and housing accommodations.

Selection of temporary city office

In selecting the office, the resident general manager must keep in mind that, before moving into the hotel, this office will house him and his secretary and will also serve the needs of the personnel manager. Therefore, the office should have room enough for interviewing as many as 2,500 to 3,000 employees in a period of about three months. The sales manager and his or her representatives and secretary will also need space in this office.

Early activities of the resident general manager

During the period immediately after his arrival, the resident general manager spends the first months or so learning the city, meeting important people, visiting the competition, and becoming intimately familiar with the plans of the hotel. He goes to the site from time to time to familiarize himself with the status of the construction and FF & E (Furniture, Fixtures and Equipment) installation work, but until the month prior to opening, most of his time is required elsewhere. He also begins to consider the renting of the stores and the selection of a lawyer to furnish legal advice on matters concerned with operation of the hotel.

An important part of his early activities will consist of formulating an overall sales and advertising policy. In connection with this he will begin immediately to interview candidates for the job of sales manager and will make specific recommendations both in sales and advertising for the final plan of pre-opening activities. For example, it will probably be very advantageous to have a sales specialist assist the local sales manager in contacting wholesale tour operators and prominent travel agents and in developing group leads. This person will probably be a specialist in the area; he or she might be borrowed from the home office or might be on a consultant fee.

Six to eight months prior to opening   The sales manager normally will be hired at this time. He or she will need a secretary and within a month will hire one sales representative; possibly two months before the hotel opens, another will be hired. The sales manager will spend his time working on the local promotional pieces; visiting travel agents and wholesale tour operators in the whole area; setting up files on conventions and group movements; traveling to the cities that are big producers; meeting and entertaining local businesspeople, probably in conjunction with the resident general manager; and, in general, concentrating on activities that will assure the hotel of a high occupancy and a maximum amount of local business.

Three to six months prior to the opening   The home office personnel coordinator arrives. In Europe, three months prior to opening should be sufficient, but in undeveloped areas six months or even longer may be required. For a time it might be possible for this person to use the resident general manager's or the sales manager's secretary while he or she is doing his preliminary research. He must study the laws of the principal cities and the country; set up the internal regulations for the hotel; review the prospective staff with the resident general manager, search the market in the city for available trained personnel, consider the method of obtaining department heads and assistants from other cities if necessary, consult with the resident general manager on foreign personnel desired, check with the Department of Labor to find the best methods to advertise. He will then hire the personnel manager for the hotel and several clerks and typists. Finally, he begins interviewing employees. In a hotel with 600 employees, it is entirely possible that as many as 3,000 people will have to be screened.

The construction project manager may be asked to assist in the selection of the engineer for the hotel, two to three months prior to opening.

The home office manager of hotel accounting arrives, bringing with him the cost accounting supervisor. The hotel chief accountant should also arrive at this time, after having completed his or her training in another one of the company's overseas hotels. They will also require some space in the temporary office. The manager of hotel accounting and the chief accountant will work with the personnel department to screen and to hire their own staff, and the cost accounting supervisor will begin preparations to move food and beverage and operating supplies into the hotel, making out the Kardex files, etc.

The home office food and beverage director and the food and beverage manager of the hotel will arrive. They will begin their preliminary work in reviewing the entire food and beverage operation based on menus already developed, working with the personnel office to screen the assistant maitre d's, captains, bartenders, etc. and prepare to open the kitchen and begin serving food. The chef, the steward, and the purchasing agent will begin their work this week also, so that everything will be in readiness to open the kitchen on time. The home office assistant to the cost accounting supervisor will also arrive and that person and the cost accounting supervisor and several storeroom helpers will begin putting the food and beverage and operating supplies into the storerooms of the hotel starting one month prior to opening. The housekeeper will arrive and with an assistant housekeeper and several workers begin putting laundry and linen supplies in the linen room. Therefore, the linen room should be completed as well as the housekeeper's office at this time. The storerooms and linen rooms should have all shelving completely installed.

Facilities Required

○ Food and beverage storage facilities (including refrigeration) for 50 persons

○ Linen room complete with shelving

○ Housekeeper's office

The resident general manager moves his residence and office into the hotel. The hotel sales office, personnel office, and accounting office are also occupied. Hiring of hotel employees will continue to be done in the city office until the hotel opens. Home office training consultants move into the hotel. The housekeeper moves into the hotel.

Very possibly, two or three members of staff who have not yet located accommodations also move into the hotel. The kitchen opens and begins serving meals. The food is prepared by the chef and a couple of cooks. The maitre d', assistant maitre d', and a couple of captains are on hand to serve. Kitchen space should be entirely clear, including all the food preparation area. There should be an area in the dining room closest to the kitchen where food can be served. By this time the storerooms have supplies in them, and more supplies are being put in daily. The accounting office has a number of people working in it, and they are beginning to store forms. The hotel personnel office is setting up employees' record files. The linen room and housekeeper's office are beginning to stock their linen and supplies. They have already prepared the thirty rooms on the first bedroom floor for the home office consultants and will service these rooms each day. The home office director of maintenance arrives and begins checking on all the operating equipment. The home office laundry consultant arrives to participate in the shakedown of equipment and to open the laundry if no defects are found in the shakedown operations. All of the executives and department heads described above are preparing material for their training program.

Facilities required

○ All remaining food and beverage storage facilities that do not require refrigeration

○ Apartment for resident general manager and family

○ Office for:
  Resident general manager (with telephone)
  Sales manager and assistants
  Personnel manager (with telephone)
  Chief accountant and staff

○ Thirty rooms on first guest floor suitable for occupancy by key personnel with lights and water and temporary heating if required

○ Kitchen facilities for family-style meals for 50 persons

○ Laundry equipment ready for final shakedown

○ End of main dining room near kitchen

○ Locked storage facilities for china, glass, silver, linen, and other operating supplies

Three weeks prior to the opening

Both the director of maintenance and the laundry manager consult with the personnel manager relative to employees in their respective departments. At this time there should be telephones in all of the offices mentioned above, and it would be most helpful to have two telephones on each of the three public floors, since the elevators are all being used for the installation of FF & E at this time. The laundry goes into operation during the third week prior to opening.

Facilities required

○ Two telephones on each of the three public floors

○ Laundry in full operation

- Front office with telephone

- Thirty rooms on first guest-room floor (occupied by key personnel) complete except for telephones

- Remainder of rooms on first guest-room floor furnished for use in training maids

- Remainder of kitchen equipment

- All boiler-room equipment

- All electrical except standby generators

- All other utility equipment except air conditioning and refrigeration (refrigeration should be adequate to handle food storage for 100 persons by third week)

This is the beginning of the intensive training period. In some of the undeveloped countries, training may have to begin before this, but for at least two weeks, on-the-job training must be conducted on the site and in the hotel. This means that the front office should be completely finished, including the telephone installation; the dining-room construction work, including painting, should be completed and decorating at least three-quarters complete, in order not to interfere with training of waiters. By this time the rooms installation should be far enough along so that the housekeeper can begin making up the rooms and so that the assistant housekeeper will have an area large enough for training the maids. The coffee-shop area should be clear enough to be used for training. The rooms service area should be complete, because food will be served in the employee dining room at the beginning of the second week prior to opening. The bars themselves should be complete, even though the table area may not be finished, to permit ample time for stocking the bar and training.

Two weeks prior to the opening

Although limitations of space preclude inclusion of the trainers' lesson plans for each supervisory and nonsupervisory group, it should be emphasized that all training follows a four-stage pattern:

- Classroom instruction (lectures, discussions, role playing, and simulation with use of videotapes).

- Extensive use of imitation/simulation sessions. For example, in training waiters and waitresses for the restaurants, the front-desk staff may be used as guinea-pig customers and may be instructed to act with enthusiasm, indifference, or disgust and anger . . . so as to test waiter and waitress reaction.

- A critique session in which errors are identified, explained, and corrected.

- On-the-job dry runs with more than ordinary supervision, in order to raise the level of individual employees' performance and self-confidence. The company does not want employee mistakes, following the hotel opening, to be justified by the excuse of their being new to the job. If errors are made, they are to be frankly admitted, not excused.

Facilities required

○ Kitchen complete in every detail

○ Main dining room nearing completion and available for training service personnel

○ Electrical system complete including standby generators

○ Public bars complete except for table areas

○ All refrigeration equipment in operating condition

○ Air-conditioning equipment ready for final shakedown

○ Telephone switchboard in operation, with telephones in all offices and all rooms on first bedroom floor

○ First and second guest-room floors completely furnished

○ Coffee shop in suitable condition for training personnel

○ Employee dining room in usable condition

One week prior to the opening   The hotel is now in operation 24 hours a day, and every service that will be available to guests on opening day should now be available. There will be a full staff, and interference from construction people in most areas of the hotel would deter the employee training program. The areas in which this would interfere the least, however, would be the lobby, guest-room furniture installation, the dining room, during its final phase of decoration, the seating area in the bars, and the coffee-shop furniture installation.

Facilities required

○ Main dining room complete in every detail

○ Coffee shop complete in every detail

○ Employee dining room complete in every detail

○ Half of total number of guest rooms complete in every detail

○ Furnishing of remaining guest rooms, lobby, bars, and other public rooms in condition that will allow completion in five working days

○ At least two telephones in operation on each uncompleted floor

○ All maintenance equipment and tools on hand

○ Spare parts for maintenance of equipment on hand

ALL CONSTRUCTION AND FF & E INSTALLATION WORK WILL BE COMPLETED ONE DAY BEFORE OPENING.

The grand-opening party should be planned for 30 to 60 days after opening when the normal "shakedown" period is completed.

Invitations to such a party (or series of parties) should be sent to people who can send business in some way (recommended invitation list of home office executives will be forwarded to the general manager): The press, of course, is most important; press kits will be supplied by the home office. (It is suggested that these be presented along with an invitation to the editors of the newspapers and managers of local radio and TV stations. Also, one or two rooms should be set aside for press use (and marked accordingly) the evening of the party. One person should be delegated to meet members of the press and assist them in setting up photographs, answer their questions, and see that they meet owners, guests of honor, etc.)

○ Local businesspeople

○ Local government officials with whom the hotel should be on a friendly basis

○ Other hotel/inn and restaurant owners/managers in the community

○ Officials of nearby military installations (including the housing officer)

○ The manager and touring directors of auto clubs and officials of nearby cities; airline and auto-rental desk personnel

○ Clergy from all local churches and synagogues

○ All realtors

○ Executive secretaries and representatives of secretary clubs and associations, etc.

○ It is a smart move to invite all the airport limousine and taxi drivers to some similar party a day or two after the grand opening party

Invitations should be mailed about two weeks or ten days prior to the party. It is best to invite "Mr. and Mrs." and invitations should be professional and well printed, with the exact time stated—e.g. from "7:00 to 9:00 P.M." Primarily for press photographs, etc., there should be a brief ceremony in which there is a "ribbon cutting" by some well-known person (governer, mayor) along with the owner and the manager. Speeches should be short—since this is merely the prelude for the party.

Exhibit the various types of guest rooms, suites, and public rooms. Also, it's a good idea to station well-trained employees, designated by large name tags as "hosts" and "hostesses," to explain all facilities and rates; they should also have brochures to pass out.

It may be best not to provide giveaways. They can be costly. A few simple touches, such as a huge bucket of roses—to be given guests as boutonnieres or corsages as they enter—will add a lot. Name tags may also be provided. In any event, the owners and managers should wear name (and title) badges and should be on a receiving line.

Make provision for parking cars and handling traffic. The services of regular police officers in uniform may be needed. In cold weather, provide for coat and hat checking.

The party—usually a good simple standup cocktail party (with hors d'oeuvres, entertainment, a short ceremony, etc.)—is best. If the weather permits, take advantage of patio, garden, swimming-pool areas for such a party. The opening ceremony should be short (20 minutes or less); in it, the Master of Ceremonies should introduce:

○ Guests of honor, entertainment personalities, dignitaries, etc.

○ Home office executives—who will present the company flag along with the national flag of the country in which the inn is located.

○ The owners and manager. The owner's speech should stress the fact that this marks the inn's actual entry into the life of the community, which it hopes to serve with distinction.

Appendix D: Feasibility Study—Proposed Hilton Inn, Austin, Texas

The purpose of this study* was to conduct sufficient analysis to enable us to determine the economic feasibility of a proposed Hilton Inn to be located adjacent to the Highland Mall Shopping Center in Austin, Texas. Upon the completion of our research, we were to determine:

- The size of facilities and type of operation which would meet the demands of the area
- The timing as to when the hotel should open
- Estimates of income and expenses for the proposed hotel at various occupancy levels.

Scope of Study

Based on these objectives, the scope of our study included, but was not limited to the following:

- Examination of the site including desirability as to visibility, access and other factors
- Review of economic and demographic factors affecting the present and future market potential for the Hilton Inn
- Examination and analysis of competitive and planned hotel facilities
- Identification of the probable room demand arising from each major market segment

---

*Laventhol & Horwath, 1972.

○ Estimates of attainable occupancy levels and average room rates

○ Preparation of pro forma financial statements.

Summary and Conclusions

The following is a brief summary of the findings and conclusions of this report:

General Market Characteristics

Economic and demographic barometers including population, income, employment, industrial and business activity indicate Austin is strong and expanding. Austin's good economic health is reflected by the key barometers summarized below:

Barometer	Historic growth rate (percent)
Population	3– 4
Retail sales	7– 8
Building permit values	25–28
Business activity	20–22
Airline passengers	20–22
Convention delegates	10

Area attractions include the State Capitol, the LBJ Library, the University of Texas and the Hill Country.

Supply and Demand Analysis

The market segments comprising room demand are:

Market segment	Percent of market	Projected growth rate (percent)
Individual commercial	70%	15
Convention and group commercial	18	15
Transient/tourist	12	10

There are 1,725 competitive first-class rooms in Austin. By 1973, 2,060 rooms should be available. Present estimated minimum occupancy for all competitive properties is 81 percent.

It appears that the proposed 248-room Hilton Inn can enter the market in 1974 without significantly affecting the competitive properties' annual occupancy rate. A 10.8 percent market penetration, the proposed facility's proportionate share will result in a 78 percent annual occupancy. We believe an 80 percent annual occupancy is possible by the second full year of operation with a concentrated sales effort.

Site Analysis

The site is contiguous with Highland Mall just south of Highland Mall Boulevard on Middle Fiskville Road. The visibility of the site is excellent from Interstate Highway 35. A major interchange is being planned at Interstate 35 and State Highway 290. When completed in 1976, accessibility to the site will be more difficult.

Proposed Facilities

Preliminary plans indicate the proposed Hilton will have a nine-story tower of 200 rooms with 48 rooms poolside. The appearance is impressive and modern.

The hotel market mix is anticipated to be commercial—50 percent; convention-group—45 percent; and tourist—5.

The room mix and rates are:

Number of Rooms	Type of room	Rate Single	Double
60	Single kings	$17.50	$21.50
122	Double double	21.50	25.53
16	Executive singles	23.00	27.00
48	Poolside	23.00	27.00
2	Master suites	40.00	45.00

Financial Analysis

The average room rate based on the stated rates, room mix and projected occupancies is calculated to be $19.95. Projected occupancy levels are 75 percent as our pessimistic estimate, 80 percent as our realistic estimate, and 85 percent as our optimistic estimate.

House profit, before interest expense, depreciation, local taxes, fire insurance, income taxes and other capital expenses is 75 percent occupancy—$894,900; 80 percent occupancy—$979,800; and 85 percent occupancy—$1,060,100.

The objectives of this section are:

General Market Characteristics

1. To determine Austin's general economic health

2. To provide growth projections which can be associated with particular market segments and thus develop a separate growth factor for each segment

3. To characterize Austin's population, its spending abilities, its stability and its vulnerability to economic fluctuation

4. To provide a background for considering the relative market for hotels and motels.

Economic Overview

All economic barometers indicate that the economy of Austin is well balanced and enjoying an influx of new industry and population that should continue to increase in the future. Exhibit 1 (see p. 369) highlights the key barometers we believe to have the most significance with respect to your project.

Population Population growth is a good indicator of the development of a community. Austin's population has grown steadily since its inception in 1839. During 1960-1970, Austin's 35 percent growth rate led all Texas cities over 100,000 in population. Forecasts for 1970-1980 made by the National Planning Association predict a 34 percent population increase for Austin, which is the third-highest projected growth rate in the nation for cities over 250,000 population.

Enrollment, University of Texas Many students at the University of Texas make Austin their second home during the school year. Enrollment during the 1971-1972 school year was 39,503. Over 83 percent of the student body was from outside Travis County. Enrollment has increased 91 percent since 1960.

Employment Austin has attracted new industry, expanding its labor force as shown below:

Year	Total employment	Total new employees added	Percent increase
1965	99,205		
1966	105,440	6,235	6.3
1967	113,025	7,585	6.7
1968	120,020	6,995	6.2
1969	127,200	7,180	5.0
1970	133,700	6,500	5.0
1971	140,400	6,700	5.0
Average yearly increase			5.6

Meanwhile, unemployment has remained below national averages. The unemployment rate has been one of the lowest in Texas.

Industry is well diversified as shown in this employment distribution for 1972:

Category	Number employed	Percent of total employed
Manufacturing	13,060	8.9
Construction	10,710	7.3
Trade	29,370	20.1
Government	52,500	35.9
Other	40,600	27.8
Total employed	146,240	
Total unemployed	2,860	1.9% of
Total civilian labor force	149,100	labor force

Source: Texas Employment Commission.

Building permit activity The table below shows dwelling units and building permit activity since 1960:

Year	Dwelling units authorized		Building permits issued	
	Number	Value	Number	Value
1960	4,477	$ 27,809,138	3,341	$ 46,239,657
1965	6,187	44,355,865	4,002	71,491,537
1967	8,704	68,236,600	4,455	131,640,835
1969	9,922	90,792,000	4,613	150,972,872
1970	8,760	71,869,000	4,914	134,229,838
1971	12,532	107,426,600	5,983	202,463,278

Source: Building Inspection Division, City of Austin

Industrial and Business Activity Although the Texas state government is the largest employer in the city, there are over 380 other manufacturers and businesses in Austin. The University of Texas has a faculty of over 3,000. Bergstrom Air Force Base is the 12th Air Force headquarters, with 6,080 military and civilian personnel. Other major employers include: International Business Machines, Tractor, Inc., Texas Instruments, Glastron Boat Company, and Westinghouse Electric.

Retail sales in the metropolitan area have increased 36 percent during the 1966-1970 period, as shown below. The slight decline in 1970 was due to the national economic recession.

Year	Austin ($ millions)	Percent increase/ decrease
1966	$344.16	
1967	381.44	10.8
1968	425.06	11.4
1969	479.68	12.8
1970	470.02	(2.1)
Average yearly increase 6.9		

Source: Austin Chamber of Commerce.

Dun and Bradstreet, in a 1971 survey of building permits, ranked Austin sixteenth among cities with the highest value of building permits. For its size, Austin's position was noteworthy: it ranked ahead of Boston, Atlanta, Washington, D. C., Cincinnati, and Detroit.

Other factors

○ *Income:* Living costs, as surveyed for the 1971 report by the Bureau of Labor Statistics, indicated Austin had one of the lowest living costs in the nation. The "minimum," as set for a family of four living in Austin, required $6,362 per year in living costs, while $9,408 was required for moderate comfort. The effective income of Austin in 1970 was $3,207 per capita and $10,529 per household.

○ *Housing:* Census data indicates 54,580 families were buying homes and 45,025 lived in apartments or rental units in 1970. The value of homes and apartment rent levels are shown on the facing page. At the time of the census, 10.9 percent of the available apartments and 2.1 percent of the homes were vacant. Development of new homes and apartments is taking place north and south of the center city. The northern side of the city seems to have the predominant development and growth at this time. The Colorado River acts as a natural barrier to expansion and appears to be slowing development to the south.

○ *Transportation:* Transportation is an extremely important factor in the success of a motor hotel venture. The location of a property in relation to the destination and routes of the traveler has been recognized for many years.

Austin is accessible by highway, air, and rail. Four major airlines connect Austin with the rest of the nation through Robert Mueller Municipal Airport. This airport also offers two private aircraft terminals. The commercial passenger terminal was completed in 1961, when the main runway was extended to 7,300 feet in length. The Missouri Pacific, Southern Pacific, and M.K.T. railroads serve the region.

The Austin area is served by U.S. Interstate Highway 35, U.S. Highways 79, 81, 183, 290 and State Highway 71. Austin's central location places it within 350 miles of 19 other Standard Metropolitan Statistical areas of Texas. Only Amarillo, El Paso, and Lubbock are beyond that distance. The site for the proposed motor hotel on Interstate 35 and State Highway 290 provides good accessibility from the highway system and airport.

○ *Area attractions:* Aside from the commercial activity, Austin offers several area attractions which generate a significant demand for motor hotel facilities. The most important attractions in relation to the proposed project are the State Capitol; the LBJ Library; Texas Hill Country; the University of Texas; and the Highland Mall Shopping Center.

○ *Convention facilities:* Austin has only modest convention facilities, just south of the Colorado River at Congress Avenue. Meeting space for 6,000, plus additional space for smaller groups, is available in the Municipal Auditorium.

There are plans for the remodeling of the present convention facilities and construction of additional facilities. These plans will be presented to the voters during the Spring of 1973. The present factor discouraging increased convention business is the lack of hotel-motel rooms. Few rooms are available for convention groups because of high demand generated by other market segments.

Conclusions

Austin is enjoying remarkable growth and is in excellent economic health. Based on our research and analysis, we believe the following growth projections to be realistic and significant to the markets for the proposed motor hotel.

Economic barometer	Historical growth percent	Projected future growth percent
Population	3– 4	3– 4
Employment	7– 8	5– 7
Retail sales	7– 8	6– 8
Building permits	25–28	20–23
Business activity	20–22	18–20
Bank deposits	18–22	15–18
Airline passengers	20–22	15–18
Convention delegates	10	15–18

The objectives of this section are:

Supply and Demand Analysis

1. To identify the dominant categories of people who use overnight accommodations in the Austin area, and estimate their relative proportion, volume, and growth rates

2. To estimate the demand for rooms

3. To inventory the total number of competitive first-class rooms in the market area

4. To project operating results for the competitive properties

5. To determine the relationships between the projected supply and demand

6. To estimate the occupancy which could be achieved by the proposed property.

Market Demand

A summary of market segments and their projected growth rates as shown below:

Market segment	Percent of demand	Projected annual growth rate
Individual commercial	70	15
Convention-group commercial	18	15
Tourist/transient	12	10

With an overall growth rate of over 14 percent room demand will double in 7 years.

Supply

Exhibit 2 (see p. 370) lists the major properties and rooms available in Austin. Also listed are estimated occupancies and market mix.

Various surveys indicate that 78 hotels and motels provide 4,343 rooms in Austin. Not all of these rooms would be considered acceptable by the discriminating traveler. Many poor-quality rooms remain available because of the shortage of better accommodations.

Several properties, due mainly to age, have dropped out of the hotel market. The Commodore Perry Hotel in downtown Austin has been rented as office space. The Terrace Motel has group facilities but is now renting its rooms as apartments. The Driskill Hotel, a downtown landmark, is being remodeled and restored. The restaurant/grill has reopened and the hotel will probably reopen in early 1973 with 114 rooms.

Announced properties The following other properties are announced or under construction:

Location	Name	Number of rooms	Comments
South IH 35	Quality Motel	173	Under construction
South IH 35	Motel 6		Under construction
South IH 35	Colonial Inn		Acquiring property

Rumored properties Within the last six months, Marriott Corporation surveyed Austin for a possible motor inn site. Although nothing was announced, it was believed the possible site would be in North Austin, probably at IH 35 and Highway 290 on the northeast corner of the intersection. High land prices might have been the reason nothing was announced.

A continuing rumor, concerning the Villa Capri, states that the University of Texas wants the land for expansion of the campus. La Quinta is rumored to be considering expansion.

Projected supply The competitive properties surveyed have a minimum estimated average occupancy of 81 percent and a probable average occupancy as a group of 85 percent or more. The 81 percent occupancy level will be assumed to be the room demand for 1972.

The 1972 rooms supply is 1,725. The Quality Motel under construction will be finished in 1973 and will add 173 rooms. We believe that the Motel 6 will be more oriented to the transient and tourist market and will not be directly competitive. Instead, the Motel 6 will hurt the "mom and pop" motels. Including the 48 rooms that Howard Johnson's will add, and the Driskill's 114 rooms, there should be 2,060 available first-class rooms in Austin by mid-1973.

Supply and Demand

The chart below estimates the area occupancy for competitive first-class rooms based on the growth of market demand and the projected lodging supply.

Year	Projected room demand	Projected room supply	Rooms added	Anticipated area Occupancy percent
1972	1,400*	1,725		81
1973	1,596	2,060	335	77
1974	1,792	2,310	250	78
1975	1,988	2,485	175	80
1976	2,184	2,730	245	80

* Demand base—14 percent growth rate is 196 rooms annually.

Based on the supply and demand assumptions, and facts known at this time, it appears that the proposed property could enter the market in 1974 without significantly affecting the average competitive properties' annual occupancy rates.

If the proposed property had a market penetration of 10.8 percent, its proportionate share, a 78 percent occupancy would be achieved. With a concentrated sales effort and competent management, we believe that the proposed property would experience an 80 percent occupancy by the second full year of operation. Our pessimistic estimate is 75 percent, while our optimistic projection is 85 percent.

Conclusions

The following conclusions can be drawn from material presented in this section:

○ Market segments in Austin hotel-motels are:

Market segment	Percent of market	Projected annual growth rate
Individual commercial	70	15
Convention/commercial	18	15
Transient/tourist	12	10

○ These market segments will double the room demand in Austin in 7 years.

○ Of the 4,343 rooms available in Austin, only 1,725 are competitive.

○ An additional 335 rooms will be added to the room supply by 1973.

○ Based on known facts, and supply and demand assumptions, it appears that the property can enter the market in 1974 without adversely affecting the area's average room occupancy.

○ We believe that the proposed property should achieve an 80 percent occupancy during the second full year of operations.

Site Analysis   The objectives of the site analysis are to evaluate

○ Location of the property, including such factors as visibility, egress and ingress

○ Accessibility to market sources, area attractions and market generators

○ Factors that could add or detract from the planned use of the site

Location

The site faces Interstate Highway 35 near the intersection of State Highway 290, adjacent to the Highland Mall Shopping Center. Interstate Highway 35 extends north towards Dallas-Fort Worth and south to San Antonio and Laredo. State Highway 290 connects Austin to Houston.

The hotel site is on Middle Fiskville Road, just south of Highland Mall Boulevard. The Mall and site have good visibility from the Interstate and should have good visibility after the proposed interchange at IH 35 and 290 is completed in 1976.

Accessibility to the site, however, will be more difficult with the new interchange. The major off ramp will be Airport Boulevard which will be the first off ramp west of the interchange on Highway 290.

Proximity to Area Attractions and Market Generators

Austin is moving north. When the IH 35-290 Interchange is completed, Austin will have expanded northward making the intersection of IH 35 and 290 the geographic center of Austin.

The University of Texas, with its conferences and other activities, will provide a steady clientele for the proposed property. Other motels are closer to the university but the superior facilities and the newness of the proposed motor hotel will make it competitive.

Although other properties are closer to the convention center/municipal auditorium, with an aggressive sales effort the proposed motor hotel will be competitive with the Sheraton Crest for small convention and group commercial business. The site is well located to the commercial and industrial areas of Austin. Tourists will find the motor hotel's location convenient to the LBJ Library, the University of Texas Football Stadium, and the State Capitol. Both tourists and convention guests will enjoy shopping at the nearby Highland Mall with its diversity of stores.

Proposed   According to preliminary plans, the proposed Hilton Inn will have 248
Facilities   rooms. A nine-story tower will contain 200 rooms, while 48 rooms will be located poolside. Restaurant facilities include a dinner house/lounge seating 192 and a coffee shop seating 86. Meeting space of 12,688 square feet will accommodate 510 to 913 people, depending on seating arrangements. There will be 301 parking spaces.

The architectural design of the hotel is smart and elegant, but at the same time casual. The combination of wood, glass, and other materials combine to form an impressive facility. There isn't a competitive property in Austin that will be as impressive. The property's newness will accentuate the oldness of properties such as the Chariot Inn and Villa Capri.

Expected Hotel utilization

We believe that the proposed motor hotel will experience the following market mix: commercial—50 percent; convention group—45 percent; and tourist—5.

Based on current LKH&H Motor Hotel surveys and operating results of competitive properties in the Austin Metropolitan Area, a 40 percent double-occupancy rate can be anticipated.

Room Mix

Because of the discriminating commercial market and competitive environment, rooms should be smartly furnished. King size beds would be advantageous in rooms suited to executives. Some rooms might contain a work table and couch that could convert into a double bed. Rooms in the two-story wing might have a furnished patio and extra floor space. Based on our analysis of the market, we believe the following room mix and rate structure to be appropriate:

Number of rooms	Type room	Rate	
		Single	Double
60	Single Kings	$17.50	$21.50
122	Double Double	21.50	25.50
16	Executive Singles	23.00	27.00
48	Poolside Rooms	23.00	27.00
2	Master Suites	40.00	45.00
248			

Management Trends

New management trends often influence the physical hotel facility. The following trends are those that we are aware of which should be considered by the architect:

○ *Data processing:* on-line computer systems handling reservations, registration, guest charges, night audit, back-office accounting plus other management reporting functions are now becoming feasible.

○ *Advanced kitchen equipment:* microwave, quartz-infrared, convection ovens and other new equipment have changed food production times and methods.

○ *Convenience foods:* convenience foods, commonly used today, require less production space and equipment but more freezing and storage area.

○ *Electronic bar control:* Electronic bar control systems are another new management technique. They could require special wiring but would reduce liquor storage space, since liquor would be purchased in gallons and half-gallons and stored within the immediate bar area. The liquor would be dispensed and accounted for automatically.

○ *No-iron linen:* No-iron linen would eliminate ironing and make an in-house laundry more practical. Many hotels now use no-iron linen.

○ *Disposable ware:* being used more and more for room service, disposable ware reduces the amount of space required for the storage of china and glassware and requires less dishwashing capacity and space.

○ *Conventions:* the trend in conventions is towards half work and half play. The amount of shopping, recreation and nightlife, therefore, become extremely important in attracting conventions to the hotel.

○ *Waste disposal:* new, air conditioned compactors are now available. Aside from the cleanliness factor, less space would be required if a compacting system were used.

○ *Telephone equipment:* while most hotels today still lease telephone equipment, many have purchased their own. Although purchasing the equipment requires a larger capital investment, it allows the hotel telephone department to operate at a profit, versus the traditional loss.

○ *Buffet-style food service:* to help reduce payroll cost, the trend toward buffet-style food service is spreading widely. Breakfast buffets in particular are very popular.

○ *Guest room services:* in an effort to provide extra services to their guests and at the same time reduce room service payroll cost, new in-room service equipment has become popular. Guest room ice makers, refrigerators, food and beverage dispensers are currently found in some first-class hotels.

Financial Analysis
The feasibility of a venture is dependent upon the earnings power of the project and the investment that will be required. Accordingly, we have projected income and expenses based on our analysis, experience and assumptions. A summary of our projections is included at the end of this report as Exhibits 3-5.

Rooms Department (Exhibit 6)

Room sales were determined using a rate structure similar to the existing competition and the aforementioned room mix. The resulting average rate was calculated to be $19.95.

The annual occupancy levels used were 75 percent as our pessimistic estimate, 80 percent as our realistic estimate, and 85 percent as our optimistic estimate. In the calculation of the room revenue for these occupancies (detailed in Exhibit 11), we assumed that the commercial market segment would be primarily single and the other markets would require double occupancy, yielding an average double occupancy rate of 40 percent.

In projecting the departmental expenses for the rooms department, payroll taxes and employee benefits were projected on the basis of 10 percent of cash payroll. This amount includes provisions for uniforms, employees' meals and other fringe benefits. It was also assumed that the property would use an outside laundry. The other operating expenses shown on this schedule are based on our recent studies and experience with comparable properties.

The resulting annual profit for the rooms department is: 75 percent occupancy—$1,035,800; 80 percent occupancy—$1,115,500; and 85 percent occupancy—$1,186,700.

Food and Beverage (Exhibit 7)

Food sales were computed based on estimates of restaurant utilization contained in Exhibit 12. Utilization was determined from our experience with similar facilities and statistics contained in *The Commercial Lodging Market* (Michigan State University). The average check estimates were based on the present performance of comparable facilities.

Beverage sales were calculated on the basis of 40 percent of food sales. Food and beverage costs were estimated to be 38 percent and 28 percent of their respective sales categories.

The projected profit generated by the food and beverage department is: 75 percent occupancy—$266,500; 80 percent occupancy—$284,700; and 85 percent occupancy—$307,200.

Telephone Department (Exhibit 8)

In motor hotels, it is typical for the telephone department to generate a net loss due to the cost of equipment rental. The loss anticipated for the subject property ranges from $3,400 at 75 percent to only $1,400 at 85 percent occupancy. The losses are predicated on the assumption that the latest in local, long distance and inter-house direct-dialing equipment will be installed in order to minimize the payroll cost in this department.

Developments have made it possible to purchase, rather than rent, telephone equipment. If this course were pursued, it would be possible to operate this department at break-even or possibly at a nominal profit.

Other Income (Exhibit 9)

This schedule illustrates the type of other income the motor hotel could generate at the various occupancy levels. Included in other income are commissions from vending machines, guest laundry, newsstand sales, etc.

Undistributed Operating Expenses (Exhibit 10)

Undistributed operating expenses include administrative and general, advertising and promotion, heat, light and power and repairs and maintenance.

Administrative and general This group of expenses, as projected, ranges from $213,200 at the 75 percent occupancy level to $231,500 at the 85 percent level. Since the Hilton Inn will be a national franchise, we have included a 4.0 percent franchise fee in our projections. This fee, which is a function of room sales, ranges from $53,800 to $61,400 per year. One percent is applied to national advertising.

Advertising and promotion   Expenses in this category include agency fees, outdoor signs, magazines and newspaper ads and other advertising costs. Payroll and related costs are also included for a sales department.

Heat, light and power   Expenses for heat, light and power total $54,000 at 75% annual occupancy, increasing to $57,000 at 85%.

Repairs and maintenance   We project an annual repairs and maintenance cost ranging from $67,300 to $74,900. The estimated cost does not include any provision for replacement of furniture, fixtures and equipment, or future alterations or improvements to the property.

House Profit

House profit is defined as the profit available before provision for interest, depreciation, local taxes, fire insurance, income taxes and other capital expenses.

Based on our estimates of income and expenses previously discussed, the resulting house profit is: 75 percent occupancy—$894,900; 80 percent occupancy—$979,800; and 85 percent occupancy—$1,060,100.

Exhibit 1 Economic barometers

	1960	1965	1967	1969	1970	1971	1960–1971 difference	Percentage	Yearly percentage
Population	216,200	244,900	261,500	275,100	305,300	N/A	+ 89,100	+41.2%	+ 3. %
Enrollment, University of Texas	20,461	24,001	27,345	32,155	35,678	39,089	+ 18,628	+91.0	+ 7.6
Employment		99,205	113,025	127,200	133,700	140,400	+ 56,940	+68.2	+ 6.2
Retail sales ($ millions)	$239	$316	$381	$480	$470	N/A	+ $231	+96.7	+ 8.8
Building permit value ($ millions)	$46.24	$65.18	$131.64	$150.92	$134.23	$202.46	+ $156.22	+33.8	+28.1
Business activity index (based on bank debits)	115.3	174.4	209.5	353.7	342.1	411.4	+ 296.1	+25.7	+21.4
Bank deposits ($ millions)	$276	$419	$523	$677	$786	$966	+ $690	+25.0	+20.8
Motor vehicle registration	86,399	113,380	127,609	139,823	158,355	198,368	+ 111,969	+13.0	+10.8
Airline passengers (total)	155,950	276,843	380,884	536,087	592,486	555,973	+ 400,023	+25.7	+21.4
Utility connections									
Water	51,733	61,550	64,819	72,695	72,695	79,603	+ 27,870	+53.9	+ 4.5
Electric	61,110	75,901	81,228	92,239	97,867	104,558	+ 43,448	+71.1	+ 5.9
Gas	50,096	62,819	66,049	71,064	72,582	75,489	+ 25,393	+50.7	+ 4.2
Telephone	90,218	127,187	151,907	190,234	206,477	226,778	+ 136,560	+15.1	+12.6

Source: Austin Chamber of Commerce.

Exhibit 2 Competitive properties analysis

	Location	Number of rooms	Room rates Single	Room rates Double	Group facilities maximum seating	Number of restaurant seats	Average annual occupancy (percent)	Market mix Commercial	Market mix Tourist	Market mix Convention
South Austin										
Ramada Gondolier	IH 35	123	$12.00–$13.00	$15.00–$16.00	Yes–150	148 R-72 Bar	83%	70%	10%	15%
Holiday Inn South	IH 35	173	14.00	20.00	No	90	83	65	15	20
Sheraton Crest	Downtown	300	15.50– 20.50	21.50– 24.50	Yes–600	150 R-200 Bar	73 +	45	5	50
Downtowner	Downtown	150	14.00– 21.00	18.00– 25.00	Yes–250	120	75 +	65		35
North Austin										
Villa Capri	IH 35	275	13.00– 15.00	18.00– 22.00	Yes–1,200		75 +	30	5	65
Rodeway-University	IH 35	50	10.00– 10.50	13.00– 15.00	No	No	80 +	60	10	30
Rodeway Inn	IH 35	59	10.00– 10.50	13.00– 15.00	No	No	80 +	60	35	5
Ramada North	IH 35	80	10.00– 11.00	13.00– 14.00	No	43	80 +	90	5	5
La Quinta	IH 35	115	12.00	15.00	Yes– 50	No	85 +	75	5	20
Holiday Inn North	IH 35	99	12.00	17.00– 18.00	No	90 R-30 Bar	78-80	75	20	5
Chariot Inn	IH 35	161	11.75– 13.75	17.75– 19.75	Yes–300	120	78-80	70	5	25
Howard Johnson's	IH 35	140	14.00	18.00– 22.00	Yes–350		80 +	80	15	5
Total		1,725					81%			

Exhibit 3 Proposed Hilton Inn—Austin, Texas: Statement of estimated income at 75 percent occupancy

	Net sales	Cost of sales	Payroll and related expenses	Expenses	Income (loss)
Operated departments					
Rooms	$1,345,200		$184,300	$125,100	$1,035,800
Food and beverage	1,098,800	$393,900	342,700	95,700	266,400
Telephone	50,200	53,100		500	(3,400)
	2,494,200	447,000	527,000	221,300	1,298,900
Other income	9,400				9,400
Gross operating income					1,308,300
Undistributed expenses:					
Administrative and general			61,000	152,200	
Advertising and promotion			28,600	50,300	
Heat, light and power				54,000	
Repairs and maintenance			23,100	44,200	
			112,700	300,700	413,400
House profit	$2,503,600	$447,000	$639,700	$522,000	$ 894,900
Ratio to total sales	100%	17.9%	25.6%	20.8%	35.7%

Exhibit 4 Proposed Hilton Inn—Austin, Texas: Statement of estimated income at 80 percent occupancy

	Net sales	Cost of sales	Payroll and related expenses	Expenses	Income (loss)
Operated departments					
Rooms	$1,444,300		$194,500	$134,300	$1,115,500
Food and beverage	1,153,300	$413,500	355,200	99,900	284,700
Telephone	53,600	55,500		500	(2,400)
	2,651,200	469,000	549,700	234,700	1,397,800
Other income	10,100				10,100
Gross operating income					1,407,900
Undistributed expenses:					
Administrative and general			61,000	161,700	
Advertising and promotion			28,600	50,700	
Heat, light and power				55,500	
Repairs and maintenance			23,100	47,500	
			112,700	315,400	428,100
House profit	$2,661,300	$469,000	$662,400	$550,100	$ 979,800
Ratio to total sales	100%	17.6%	24.9%	20.7%	36.8%

Exhibit 5 Proposed Hilton Inn—Austin, Texas: Statement of estimated income at 85 percent occupancy

	Net sales	Cost of sales	Payroll and related expenses	Expenses	Income (loss)
Operated departments					
Rooms	$1,534,800		$205,200	$142,900	$1,186,700
Food and beverage	1,209,600	$428,400	369,900	104,100	307,200
Telephone	57,000	57,900		500	(1,400)
	2,801,400	486,300	575,100	247,500	1,492,500
Other income	10,700				10,700
Gross operating income					1,503,200
Undistributed expenses:					
Administrative and general			61,000	170,500	
Advertising and promotion			28,600	51,100	
Heat, light and power				57,000	
Repairs and maintenance			23,100	51,800	
			112,700	330,400	443,100
House profit	$2,812,100	$486,300	$687,800	$577,900	$1,060,100
Ratio to total sales	100%	17.3%	24.5%	20.5%	37.7%

Exhibit 6   Proposed Hilton Inn—Austin, Texas: Rooms Department

	At annual occupancy of		
	75 percent	80 percent	85 percent
Net Sales	$1,345,200	$1,444,300	$1,534,800
Departmental expenses			
Payroll	167,500	176,800	186,500
Payroll taxes and employee benefits	16,800	17,700	18,700
Laundry	47,100	50,600	53,700
Linen and glassware	13,500	14,400	15,400
Cleaning supplies	6,700	7,200	7,700
Contract cleaning	2,700	2,900	3,100
Guest supplies	12,100	13,000	13,800
Reservations and referral system	18,800	20,200	21,500
Miscellaneous	24,200	26,000	27,700
Total departmental expense	309,400	328,800	348,100
Departmental income	$1,035,800	$1,115,500	$1,186,700
Statistics			
Average room rate	$19.95	$19.95	$19.95
Ratio to room sales			
Payroll and related benefits	13.7%	13.5%	13.4%
Total departmental expenses	23.0	22.8	22.7
Departmental income	77.0	77.2	77.3

	At annual occupancy of		
	75 percent	80 percent	85 percent
Net Sales			
Food	$ 862,700	$ 905,400	$ 949,300
Beverage	236,100	247,900	260,300
	1,098,800	1,153,300	1,209,600
Cost of sales			
Food	327,800	344,100	360,700
Beverage	66,100	69,400	67,700
	393,900	413,500	428,400
Gross profit on sales	704,900	739,800	781,200
Departmental expenses			
Payroll	311,500	322,900	336,300
Payroll taxes and employee benefits	31,200	32,300	33,600
Music and entertainment	11,000	11,000	11,000
Laundry	17,600	18,500	19,400
China, glassware, silver and linen	14,300	15,000	15,700
Cleaning supplies	12,100	12,700	13,300
Paper supplies	7,700	8,100	8,500
Menus, printing and stationery	5,500	5,800	6,000
Kitchen fuel	4,400	4,600	4,800
Miscellaneous	23,100	24,200	25,400
	438,400	455,100	474,000
Departmental income	$ 266,500	$ 284,700	$ 307,200
Statistics			
Ratio to departmental sales:			
Food cost	38%	38%	38%
Beverage cost	28	28	28
Payroll and related	31	31	31
Departmental income	24	25	25

Exhibit 8 Proposed Hilton Inn—Austin, Texas: Telephone Department

	At annual occupancy of		
	75 percent	80 percent	85 percent
Net Sales	$50,200	$53,600	$57,000
Cost of service			
Net cost of calls	35,100	37,500	39,900
Rental of equipment	18,000	18,000	18,000
	53,100	55,500	57,900
Gross loss	(2,900)	(1,900)	(900)
Departmental expenses	500	500	500
Departmental loss	$ (3,400)	$ (2,400)	$ (1,400)
Ratio to room sales	(.3%)	(.2%)	(.1%)

Exhibit 9 Proposed Hilton Inn—Austin, Texas: Other Income

	At annual occupancy of		
	75 percent	80 percent	85 percent
Commissions, guest laundry and vending machines	$6,000	$ 6,300	$ 6,600
Cigars, newsstand and curios	3,400	3,800	4,100
Departmental income	$9,400	$10,100	$10,700
Ratio to room sales	.7%	.7%	.7%

Exhibit 10 Proposed Hilton Inn—Austin, Texas:
Undistributed operating expenses

	At annual occupancy of		
	75 percent	80 percent	85 percent
Administrative and general			
Payroll	$ 55,500	$ 55,500	$ 55,500
Payroll taxes and employee benefits	5,500	5,500	5,500
Franchise fee	53,800	57,800	61,400
Office expense	7,900	8,400	9,000
License and dues	3,700	3,700	3,700
Travel and entertainment	2,400	2,800	3,200
General insurance	11,000	11,000	11,000
Credit card commissions	26,500	28,400	30,200
Accounting and legal fees	7,000	7,000	7,000
Provision for bad debts	14,700	15,700	16,600
Miscellaneous	25,200	26,900	28,400
Total departmental expense	$213,200	$222,700	$231,500
Ratio to room sales			
Payroll and related	4.5%	4.2%	4.0%
Total departmental expense	15.8	15.4	15.1
Advertising and promotion			
Payroll	$ 26,000	$ 26,000	$ 26,000
Payroll taxes and employee benefits	2,600	2,600	2,600
Brochures	2,000	2,400	2,800
Newspapers and magazines	11,000	11,000	11,000
Radio and television	1,500	1,500	1,500
Outdoor	17,900	17,900	17,900
Miscellaneous	17,900	17,900	17,900
Total departmental expense	$ 78,900	$ 79,300	$ 79,700
Ratio to room sales			
Total departmental expense	5.9%	5.5%	5.2%

Exhibit 10 Proposed Hilton Inn—Austin, Texas:
Undistributed operating expenses (continued)

	At annual occupancy of		
	75 percent	80 percent	85 percent
Heat, light and power			
Utilities	$ 46,000	$ 47,000	$ 48,000
Miscellaneous	8,000	8,500	9,000
Total departmental expense	$ 54,000	$ 55,500	$ 57,000
Ratio to room sales	4.0%	3.8%	3.7%
Repairs and maintenance			
Payroll	$ 21,000	$ 21,000	$ 21,000
Payroll taxes and employee benefits	2,100	2,100	2,100
Building repairs	6,000	6,000	7,000
Equipment and furnishings	17,000	18,000	19,000
Painting and decorating	9,500	10,500	11,500
Miscellaneous	11,700	13,000	14,300
Total departmental expense	$ 67,300	$70,600	$ 74,900
Ratio to room sales			
Payroll and related	1.7%	1.6%	1.5%
Total departmental expenses	5.0	4.9	4.9

Exhibit 11 Proposed Hilton Inn—Austin, Texas: Calculation of average room revenue and average room rate

Type of room	Number of rooms	Rate structure		Expected revenue at 100% occupancy	
		Single	Double	Single	Double
Single Kings	60	$17.50	$21.50	$1,050	$1,290
Doubles	122	17.50	21.50	2,135	2,623
Executive Singles	16	19.50	23.50	312	376
Poolside Doubles	48	19.50	23.50	936	1,128
Master Suites	2	50.00	75.00	100	150
	248				5,567
				$4,533	$4,533
100% double differential					$1,034

Calculation of average revenue

Single revenue		Double differential	Double occupancy*	Occupancy		Daily rooms revenue	Average room rate
[$4,533	+	($1,034	.40)]	75%	=	$3,710	$19.95
[$4,533	+	(1,034	.40)]	80	=	3,957	19.95
[$4,533	+	(1,034	.40)]	85	=	4,205	19.95

* Estimated double occupancy percentage.

Exhibit 12 Proposed Hilton Inn—Austin, Texas: Projected food and beverage sales

	Average check	75 percent occupancy		80 percent occupancy		85 percent occupancy	
		Covers	Sales	Covers	Sales	Covers	Sales
Coffee shop—86 seats							
Breakfast	$1.50	186	$ 279	195	$ 293	205	$ 308
Lunch	1.75	90	157	95	166	99	173
Dinner	2.25	48	108	50	113	52	117
Total coffee shop	1.70		$ 544		$ 572		$ 598
Annual coffee shop sales			$ 198,700		$ 208,800		$ 218,300
Dining room/ lounge— 192 seats							
Lunch	$2.75	150	413	157	432	165	454
Dinner	5.50	120	660	126	693	132	726
Total dining room			$ 1,073		$ 1,125		$ 1,180
Annual dining room			$ 391,600		$ 410,600		$ 430,700
Beverage sales—annual			236,100		247,900		260,300
Banquet sales—annual			272,400		286,000		300,300
Total annual food and beverage sales			$1,098,800		$1,153,300		$1,209,600

Index